YOUNG OFFENDERS AND THE STATE

A CANADIAN PERSPECTIVE ON DELINQUENCY

W. Gordon West

■□ BUTTERWORTHS
□□ TORONTO

Young Offenders and the State: A Canadian Perspective on Delinquency
© 1984 by Butterworth & Co. (Canada) Ltd.

Printed and bound in Canada.

Canadian Cataloguing in Publication Data

West, W. Gordon, 1945 –
Young offenders and the state: a Canadian perspective on delinquency

Bibliography: p.
Includes index.
ISBN 0-409-87583-X

1. Juvenile delinquency. 2. Juvenile delinquency –
Canada. I. Title.

HV9069.W48 1984   364.3'6   C84-098939-3

Sponsoring Editor: Janet Turner
Editing/Design: Robert Goodfellow
Cover Design/Figure Art: Julian Cleva
Production: Jim Shepherd

The Butterworth Group of Companies

Canada
Butterworth & Co. (Canada) Ltd., Toronto and Vancouver

United Kingdom
Butterworth & Co. (Publishers) Ltd., London

Australia
Butterworths Pty. Ltd., Sydney, Melbourne, Brisbane, Adelaide, and Perth

New Zealand
Butterworths (New Zealand) Ltd., Wellington and Auckland

Singapore
Butterworth & Co. (Asia) Pte. Ltd., Singapore

South Africa
Butterworth Publishers (SA) (Pty) Ltd., Durban and Pretoria

United States
Butterworth Legal Publishers, Boston, Seattle, Austin, and St. Paul
D & S Publishers, Clearwater

To
CHERYL,
CAREY,
and
KYLE

Contents

PREFACE xi

ACKNOWLEDGEMENTS xv

1 Images of Delinquency: Young Thugs or Homeless Waifs 1

Popular Knowledge of Delinquency 2
  Personal Knowledge 2
  Public and Media Knowledge 3
  Official State Knowledge 6
Sociological Knowledge of Delinquency 8
  Sociological Data 8
  Definitions and Conceptions 8
    Statistical 9
    Moral 9
    Normative 10
    Legal 10
    Labeling/Interactionist 12
    Conflict 13
  Theoretic Sociological Explanations 14
    Social Overviews 15
      Order/Consensus/Functional/
        Liberal Theories of Society 15
      Conflict/Dialectical/Marxist
        Theories of Society 17
      Canadian Social Formation 18
    Criminology in Canada 20

2 Historical Perspective on State Justice for Juveniles 23

Historical Status of Children and Youth 24
Canadian Juvenile Delinquents Act, 1908 29
Understanding Legal Regulation:
  Conflict Theory 35

Conflict Theory   36
Some Criticisms   40
Conflict Explanations of Juvenile Justice   43
Conflict Theory Elaborated:
    The State and the Law   46
State Theories   47
Law and the Legal System   51
Conclusion   52

3   **Official Statistics and Anomie Theory:**
    Social Class as the Explanation   55

Official Statistics   56
    Age   57
    Trends   57
    Types of Offences   61
    Sex   66
    Race and Ethnicity   66
    Social Class   68
    Urban-Rural Differences
        and Neighborhood   68
    Family   70
    School Failure   70
    Peer Group Relations   71
Summary   71
Anomie and Strain Theories   71
    Anomie Theories   72
    Leyton's Triple Delinquency   74
Criticisms   75
    Theoretic and Definitional   73
    Methodological Criticisms: Problems with
        Official Statistics   77
    Empirical Refutation   79
    A Criticism of Leyton's Theory   81
Conclusion   82

4   **Self-Report Delinquency, Control Theory,**
    and Gender   85

Self-Report Delinquency   85
    Age   86
    Trends   87
    Types of Offences   87
    Sex   87

Race and Ethnicity 88
Social Class 88
Urban-Rural Differences
  and Neighborhood 89
Family 89
School Failure 89
Peer Group Relations 90
Volume 90
Control Theory 92
Criticisms of Self-Report Data and Control Theory 96
Problems in Self-Report Data 96
Criticisms of Control Theory 97
Gender 99
Traditional Malestream Theoretic Blindness:
    Official Data and Genitalia 100
The Data 103
New Theories: Role Socialization and Structure 104
Towards a Feminist Theory of Female Delinquency
    and Patriarchal Justice 108

**5 Peers and Subcultural Ethnography:
Interaction Theory and Age** 113

Need for Observational Field Research 113
*Adolescent Subculture: Straights,
    Greasers, and Freaks* 115
The Subcultures 115
  Straights 118
  Greasers 121
  Freaks 124
Affiliation Patterns 127
Symbolic Interactionist Theories of Delinquency 128
Symbolic Interactionism 128
Some Classic Symbolic Interactionist Theories
    of Delinquency 129
  Differential Association 129
  Matza's Drift/Neutralization Theory 130
  Labeling or Social Reaction Theory 131
  Symbolic Interactionist Theory 133
Substantive Example of Interaction Theory:
    Age Status and Autonomy 134
Some Criticisms 138
  Ethnographic Research 138
  Differential Association 139

Drift Theory   139
Labeling Theory   139
Symbolic Interactionist Theory   140
Adolescent Autonomy Theory   141
Age Structure: Adolescent Subculture,
   Affiliation, and Autonomy   142

6   Schooling: Discipline and Surveillance
in Inculcating Legal Subjectivity   145

Schooling and Delinquency   147
   Failure, Delinquency, and
      Control Theory Factors   147
   Schooling and Jobs   149
   The Social Organization of Schools   151
   Classroom Organization: The Social
      Construction of Order and Deviance   153
Criticisms of the School Failure and
   Classroom Dynamics Analyses   163
Schooling: Discipline, Surveillance,
   and Subjectivity   165
Conclusion   169

7   Juveniles in Justice   171

Juvenile Justice System   172
   Self-Report Delinquency   172
   The Victims   174
   The Police   176
   The Court   179
   Dispositions: Community   186
   Dispositions: Incarceration in
      Training Schools and Group Homes   187
   The Effects   190
Theoretic Conceptualizations   193
   Careers Through Liberal Bureaucratic
      Institutions   193
      Delinquent Careers and Statuses   193
      Organization Theory   195
   Some Critical Alternatives   196
      Legal Subjectivity   196
      Justice in the Capitalist State   197

**8   Juvenile Justice Policies and Politics:
Reformism in the Canadian State**   201

Social Policy Experiments   202
Some Reforms   203
   Policy to Eliminate the
         Causes of Delinquency   203
   Law Reforms   207
   Reforms in Responses   209
   Understanding Policy Research   213
*Towards a Political Economy of
         Canadian Delinquency*   215
   The Young in the Contemporary
         Canadian Social Formation   215
   Extending State Theory   219
      State and Class   219
      Ideology   220
      Law   221
Conclusion   223

9   Summing Up   225

   Needed Research   227
   Theoretic Integration   229
   Some Key Theoretic Problems   232

BIBLIOGRAPHY   237

INDEX   261

Preface

The bizarre, the exotic, the unusual, the different, and perhaps the off-color, or even lurid all have some intrinsic interest for most of us because of their shock value. By surprising us and showing us how some people do things differently or unexpectedly, they pique our curiosity and force us to think. Studying delinquency might also provide us with insights into personal problems of our own past or present (for example, our sexuality), those of family members or relatives (for example, regarding a teenage cousin involved in drugs), or those of friends or acquaintances (for example, about the delinquency of a camper counseled during summer employment).

Delinquency is also a topic about which everyone feels that he or she knows something. Like the weather, "what the kids are doing" is a guaranteed conversation opener in any pub or at any cocktail party. Indeed, many public issues of concern or debate are addressed in studying delinquency. Teenage sexuality and abortion, marijuana laws, school vandalism, youth riots, court overcrowding – all these publicly debated topics are addressed in the sociology of delinquency.

Delinquency is an important aspect of "the law and order debate" (Taylor 1981). It is used in our discourse to help define what kind of society we are, and where we are going. As will be revealed in the course of this book, there are many distorting myths about delinquency that hinder rational discussion or response. On a more explicitly political level there is much government expenditure in social service programs, welfare, and corrections attempts to deal with delinquent behavior. Some knowledge of delinquency seems crucial to participating publicly as an informed citizen in contemporary Canadian society.

This book is intended to appeal to a number of student interests commonly found in undergraduate sociology courses. Many students (perhaps in more specialized programs in law, social work, or education) are curious about delinquency because they anticipate such knowledge might be useful to them in future careers. School teachers, police officers, social workers, probation officers, counselors, and parents all need some understanding of juvenile misbehavior. In offering the best available sociological research and theories, it is to be hoped that some sound basis will be established to enhance such training and provide a ground for reasoned responses.

In addition to these personal or popular interests, however, delinquency has had a central relevance in sociology as a discipline, having been sociology's favorite deviance. Many sociologists (especially more conservative ones) define sociology as being centrally concerned with the establishment, continuation, and change of social order (for example, Parsons 1951). Threats to that order, or aberrations from it, its genesis from or collapse into disorder, are theoretically interesting for the light they shed on the general problem of order, disorder, and change. More recently, radical sociologists have also become interested in the topic. Most of the research conducted by sociologists in the general topic of deviance has actually focussed specifically on delinquency to such an extent that one might claim whatever we know is about delinquency, and very little about deviance in more general terms. For our present task of understanding delinquency this is an asset rather than a problem.

Sociology approaches the study of delinquency somewhat differently from other disciplines. And while conceding that there may be some effect from physiological or biological factors, sociology insists that these are always culturally and socially mediated.

These other disciplines can quite possibly better address certain specific delinquent acts or some types of delinquency. In this book, however, these will be largely ignored, leaving for other criminologists any attempt at a grand, interdisciplinary synthesis. While it is popular to conceive of delinquency as abnormal or unusually aberrant behavior (even if not specifically sick or evil), this book will argue that it is better understood as being socially constructed, regulated, and produced.

This is certainly not to claim, however, that delinquency is *the* most important topic for either research or policy considerations. Indeed, a major theme in this text is that most delinquency consists of "chicken feed" or "garbage" offences that are not worth the public expense or reaction that they have generated in contemporary society. While the young have always occasionally misbehaved, and we now know almost all youngsters commit some delinquency or other, most of these are minor offences, and most of the young more often than not grow up to be as "straight" and law-abiding as the rest of us. Although juveniles seem to commit almost half the "serious" criminal incidents occupying policy dossiers, very few of these involve personal violence, and the actual property value lost is low compared with that in adult offences.

We should keep in mind, then, that the nature and causes of juvenile misbehavior may be quite different from those of adults. This is especially so as juveniles have been subject to special regulations known as status offences, as we shall see further on (especially in chapter 2).

In trying to examine the deeper structural conditions of delinquency, I have relied, of necessity, on many central illustrations drawn from my own various work and research projects over the past two decades. While attending university, I earned money by working three summers in camps for inner-city (often delinquent) youngsters, and running weekly boys' club meetings in Toronto and Chicago settlement houses and YMCAs. Between seeking degrees, I was a full-time, detached youth worker (street gang outreach worker). This experience took me through the gamut of Toronto delinquencies and social agencies for a couple of years. For better or worse, my own sociological experience has traversed structural functionalist (anomie) theory, interactionism, control theory, Canadian political economy, and neo-Marxist-conflict theory. Not coincidentally, over the past fifteen years, this has involved me in various participant observation projects (with young "predelinquents" in Toronto, adolescent gangs in Chicago, thieves and classroom deviants in Toronto, and justice system personnel in Kingston), official record analyses (of Canadian, Ontarian, Torontonian, and Kingstonian data), a self-report survey (in Kingston area schools), and a diversion experiment (again in Kingston).

This analysis of the social and legal status of children and youth in Canada accurately depicts their situation through most of the present century. The major part of the research results reported in this book derive from data collected under these legal conditions, as does most of our traditional and theoretic understanding of delinquency.

Nonetheless, it is true that over the last decade there have been numerous changes in the legislation governing delinquency. Quebec, for instance, has considerably revamped its entire youth legislation; Ontario has taken less dramatic steps in eliminating section 8 (the "neglected children" clause) from its Training Schools Act; most widely known are the federal government initiatives to replace the Juvenile Delinquents Act, finally resulting in the passage of the Young Offenders Act in 1982, and its proclamation in April 1984. The reader should be aware, then, that the legal situation is presently in considerable flux, and that the present changes may alter the nature of delinquency considerably. Only time will tell, but my belief is that these legislative changes will again turn out to be more cosmetic than behavioral.

It should be immediately noted that in this book we are dealing with controlling the youth in one historically specific social situation; Canada in the late twentieth century is one of the more economically developed countries of the world, and is firmly within the Western European cultural heritage. In contrast to Latin American or African countries, for instance, its "youth problem" is regularized and sufficiently contained that it can be addressed as one involving "delinquency," rather than being seen as part of entire communities and populations that are "marginal" (Sumner 1981). References will be made regularly throughout this text to British and American research as well as Canadian. Because these countries have had and continue to have great influence on Canada, such findings usefully complement the often scarce Canadian materials, and theoretical developments in Britain and the United States have stimulated much work in Canada. Nonetheless, it is important to remember that such references also augment the difficulties of applying the claims in this book beyond the narrow orbit of northern North America and Western Europe.

Although there are various edited readers, some deviance texts, and justice system texts, there is no other extant sociological text on delinquency in Canada. In bringing together research and theory, I have sought to provide a more general compilation of information on the topic, drawing on the growing literature produced by Canadian criminologists. This will inevitably raise as many questions as it answers, and reveal a number of serious gaps in our knowledge. It is hoped that it will stimulate further research by others.

Such an exercise necessarily involves integrating the available information, synthesizing the various sociological theories. In assessing the strengths and weaknesses of diverse explanations, I have sought to examine their utility in understanding Canadian phenomena and issues. Like many other Canadian sociologists of my generation, I have found the indigenous political economy tradition of Innis (1950) and others (for example, Grayson 1983) consistent with international conflict theorizing that has increasingly focussed on the capitalist state. The following can then be seen as contributing to this more general literature by examining the construction of juvenile misbehavior by the Canadian state. The utility of such a theory will only be demonstrated if others proceed to elaborate on it far beyond the tentative exploratory effort attempted here.

Acknowledgements

As everyone who has ever written knows, the attribution of individual authorship is always misleading, as so many others contribute in so many ways. Although some influences are general, they are nonetheless profound: my parents instilled in me a curiosity and concern for issues of social justice; legal professionals like George Thomson and youth workers like Grant Lowery have incessantly badgered me to become a less irrelevant academic. Undergraduate professors like Thelma Mc-Cormick and Ernest Lillienstein prodded me towards methodological rigor; and others like John O'Neill and Ken Reshaur persisted in inculcating in me the humanistic tradition of social inquiry. Graduate faculty like Howard S. Becker and John I. Kitsuse helped me formulate issues in order to bring together abstract theories and social concerns in the disciplinary areas of deviance and education. I hope I have remained true to their precepts.

Numerous references in the text make it obvious how much my work on delinquency has been carried out jointly with colleagues. Eldon Bennett, Heather Berkeley, Chad Gaffield, Mary Morton, Laureen Snider, and Ian Gomme have all coauthored initial drafts of papers and reports drawn upon extensively in this text. Others such as Shelly Gavigan, Dorothy Chunn, Livy Visano, Frank Pearce, Phil Scraton, John Fitz, Paul Willis, Roger Dale, Nigel South, John Lea, Jock Young, Ian Taylor, Jim Hackler, Marc Leblanc, Stan Divorski, Chuck Reasons, John McMullan, Bob Ratner, and John Clarke have taught me much through patient hours of debate and exchange.

Jock Young, Ian Gomme, Eoin Murphy, and Marg Reitsma-Street have all reviewed large parts of the manuscript and offered helpful comments and advice. And without the unfailing patience of Butterworths editors David Hogg, Janet Turner, Robert Goodfellow, and Linda Kee, the book would never have been completed. The cheerful, swift typing of Vivian Crossman turned my scrawl into legible script. The support of colleagues and the patience of students at the Ontario Institute for Studies in Education and the Centre of Criminology, University of Toronto have sustained me.

And as always, those closest have borne the worst burdens of tolerating a cantankerous writer in the same household. I thank them most, and promise Cheryl, Carey, and Kyle I will desist from working on (at least some!) weekends in the future.

W. G. W

□   □   □   □   □   □   □

Dr. West and Butterworths gratefully acknowledge permission of authors and publishers to reprint portions of the previously published material listed below.

Every effort has been made to contact authors and publishers to obtain permissions.

Allyn and Bacon	Sarason, S. B. *The Culture of the School and the Problem of Change*, 1971.
Cambridge University Press	Johnson, R. E. *Juvenile Delinquency and Its Origins*, 1979.
The Canadian Review of Sociology and Anthropology	West, W. G. Book review of E. Leyton, *The Myth of Delinquency*, Vol. 18:1 (1981).
Centre for Contemporary Cultural Studies	Clarke, J. "Learning the Three R's; Repression, Rescue and Rehabilitation," stenciled paper, 1975.
Collier-Macmillan	Esland, G. "Teaching and Learning as the Organization of Knowledge," in M. F. D. Young (ed.), *Knowledge and Control*, 1971.
	Keddie, N. "Classroom Knowledge," in M. F. D. Young (ed.), *Knowledge and Control*, 1971.
Free Press	Becker, H. S. *Outsiders*, 1963.
Heinemann	Sumner, C. (ed.)., *Crime, Justice and Underdevelopment*, 1981.
Holt, Rinehart and Winston	Box, S. *Deviance, Reality and Society* (2nd ed.), 1981.
Hutchinson	Fine, B. "Law and Class," in B. Fine et al. (eds.), *Capitalism and the Rule of Law: From Deviancy Theory to Marxism*, 1979.

Lippincott

Sutherland, E., and Cressey, D. *Principles of Criminology*, 1955.

Little, Brown

Quinney, R. *Critique of Legal Order*, 1974

McClelland and Stewart

Houston, S. "The Waifs and Strays of a Late Victorian City: Juvenile Delinquents in Toronto," in J. Parr (ed.), *Childhood and Family in Canadian History*, 1982.

Prentice, A. *The School Promoters*, 1977.

Merlin

Thompson, E.P. *The Poverty of Theory*, 1978.

Methuen

McLaren, P. *Cries from the Corridor*, 1980.

Ontario Ministry of Community and Social Services

The Ontario Training Schools Act, Sections 2, 8, 9.

Ontario Ministry of Education, Interim Research Project on Unreached Youth

Byles, J. *Alienation, Deviance and Social Control*, 1969.

Open University Press

Fitz, J. "The Child as a Legal Subject," R. Dale et al. (eds), *Education and the State*, Vol. II, *Politics, Patriarchy and Practice*, 1981.

Prentice-Hall

Schur, E. *Radical Non-intervention: Rethinking the Delinquency Problem*, 1973.

Routledge and Kegan Paul

Werthman, C. "Delinquents and School," in B. Cosin et al. (eds.), *School and Society*, 1971. Originally appeared in *The Berkeley Journal of Sociology*.

Ryerson

Rogers, K. *Streetgangs of Toronto*, 1945.

This Magazine is About Schools

Macdougal, C. "You Need Imagination in the Hole," 1969.

University of Chicago

Platt, A. *The Child-Savers*, 1969, rev. 1974.

University of Montreal

Fréchette, M. et al. "A Continuum of Social Adaptability," Social Sciences and Humanities Research Council of Canada, *Report*, School of Criminology, Le Groupe de Recherche sur l'Inadaptation Juvénile, 1981.

Wiley

Chambliss, W. J. "Functional and Conflict Theories of Crime," in W. Chambliss and N. Mankoff (eds.), *Whose Law? What Order?*, 1976.

Front Cover Photograph: Miller Services Limited

1

Images of Delinquency:
Young Thugs or Homeless Waifs

To prevent break-ins the variety store was covered by a protective wire mesh. One kid was trying to scale it like a human fly, but his feet were too big to gain a secure footing and he soon gave up. Outside the store several boys stood spitting into rain puddles which filled the holes in the sidewalk. Two teenagers in overalls slumped against the wall, uncorked a bottle of cheap wine and took several quick swallows. The empty bottle was tossed down a mud slope to the street below, where it smashed into pieces and woke up a toddler sleeping nearby, who started to cry. Children sat on the slope, watching the street, and drawing figures in the dirt with their bare toes, while two laughing kids somersaulted down, somehow managing to stop themselves before they tumbled into the traffic. I saw two girls from my class sitting on the curb across the street, smoking. One waved her hand while the other frowned and flicked her cigarette in my direction.

McLaren 1980, 135

Delinquency may initially seem a straightforward topic of investigation. One might hope to gather the facts, analyze them, construct adequate theoretical explanations as to how they come about, and take appropriate applied social action.

Further reflection, however, will indicate that matters are not quite so straightforward. For delinquency is not simply a behavior, or even a collection of diverse behaviors. But like all social actions (Weber 1947) it is *meaningful* behavior. Killing someone is murder in some circumstances, a soldier's duty in others; taking goods from someone's house is sometimes theft, sometimes it is a neighborly privilege. Since meaning is not intrinsic to objects or behaviors, but rather attributed to them, we must examine the bases of our own interpretations. How do we come to know about delinquency, and how do we understand it?

We know about delinquency in very different ways, perhaps even so different that it seems we are considering different topics or phenomena. Nor surprisingly different sociological interpretations, analyses, and theoretical explanations have resulted. One major theme of this book will be the attempt by sociologists to reconcile such knowledge and explanations.

POPULAR KNOWLEDGE OF DELINQUENCY
Personal Knowledge

Almost all of us, looking back, can remember some incidents of at least minor misbehavior on our own part, ranging from lying and cheating, surreptitious fouls in sport, playing hooky, through pinching pennies from Mom's pocketbook, childhood squabbles, minor thefts of candy and comic books from neighborhood stores, to getting drunk, and petting heavily at teenage parties. Most of us do not consider such actions to have been very serious.

Many of us have gone a bit further – terrorizing the schoolyard by running in a juvenile "street gang," scribbling graffiti on walls and fences, smoking marijuana and sharing it with friends, extorting a bit of cash from younger children, joyriding in a car, gambling at cards, breaking into unoccupied buildings or cottages, or smashing the odd streetlight or school window. Although somewhat foolish, we often look back on such pranks as due to overexuberant youthfulness, though acknowledging our good fortune at not being caught.

And most of us have known (and a few of us were) "real delinquents," youngsters who fought with teachers, ran away from home, stole cars or bicycles for parts, got pregnant, and were not only arrested but sent to court, and perhaps even to training school. We often find it difficult to understand how such delinquents come from "good homes," or "turn bad" in high school after being "such nice kids" in elementary school. Many people have also experienced delinquency by being victims of such acts.

All such direct personal knowledge is a valuable resource in understanding delinquency. It is true, of course, that our personal experiences are only that, and may not be typical, and hence may not be generalizable. The vividness of such existential knowledge, however, is undeniable in that we *know the incidents did happen*, and must be accounted for in some way by various theories. Additionally, existential knowledge usually includes a strong belief that some considerable part of human behavior is *willed*, or voluntary in some intrinsic sense. We *could* have refrained from those delinquencies, our assailants did not *have* to commit their bad deeds (ignoring the rare incidents of extreme mental illness). The legal concern with demonstrating criminal intent addresses this, but how can such notions of free will be reconciled with social science's search for causes? Our own experiences thus provide each of us with a part of the puzzle of knowing about delinquency.

Most of us, looking back at our direct experiences of delinquency, either as perpetrator, victim, or witness, are likely to contemplate these personal incidents in some wonderment. Did our selling illicit drugs to younger friends at school really constitute us as "traffickers in narcotics"? Did those cottage break-ins make us "young thugs and vandals"? Were our teenage acquaintances, even though they did make us go too far too fast, "vicious rapists"? Were our working-class neighbors really criminals?

These personal experiences of either committing a delinquency, or being the victim of a delinquency, thus provide opposite images of delinquency. We make distinctions between "real" delinquency and pranks, between "rough" and "respectable" youngsters. The former are more likely to resemble the depictions quoted at the beginning of this chapter, involving youngsters who live in depressing, inadequate, slum housing, in cities or neighborhoods that decent people avoid. We picture the individual delinquent as certainly deprived if not also truly depraved, perhaps of low intelligence, emotionally dwarfed, vicious, and lacking in morality. Part of the interest in studying delinquency perhaps derives from attempting to reconcile the discordant nature of our direct experience with these much stronger popular stereotypes.

Public and Media Knowledge

These scattered personal experiences of delinquency are augmented on a daily basis by the mass media. It is rare indeed that newspaper front pages do not include incidents of spectacular delinquencies in their efforts to sell papers. Prime-time North American television is more than half filled with police dramas, which producers have found draw large audiences and steady sponsorship. Although rare, spectacular events are favored; murders and youth riots make much more exciting television than the far more frequent but mundane incidents of petty theft or traffic violations. The CBC's crime series "Sidestreet" sealed its own fate to some considerable extent by depicting real-life Canadian incidents, which audiences failed to find "thrilling" enough in comparison with more fictional American extravaganzas. The domination of Canadian television by American (especially New York) programming gives a very one-sided depiction that tends to ignore our own national and local experiences.

Even ostensibly objective news reportage of delinquency is highly selective, shaped by professional journalistic imperatives of "getting the story," meeting deadlines, and emphasizing graphic detail and photos (Muncie 1981). Individuals are highlighted rather than abstract social arrangements. Because the news media usually do not have direct access to crime or delinquency, they tend to rely upon authoritative sources such as politicians, police spokespersons, or welfare workers. Their reports thus overwhelmingly favor the "official" version (rather than the delinquent's or even the victim's story). Furthermore, in terms of structure, the reportage of delinquency consistently isolates "real delinquents" from the conforming majority, to which minor sinners are then assimilated (Hall 1971, 21).

Such fantasies and distortions in continuous crime news reporting might not matter much, except that to some extent seeing seems to become believing. Public opinion polls consistently rank crime and delinquency as second or third among social problems offered to respondents for consideration (just after inflation and unemployment): 69 percent and 72 percent considered them very important in 1978 and 1977. That only 1 to 17 percent spontaneously mentioned them as concerns would indicate that very few people worry about being victimized; and those who have been burglarized in Toronto are *more* tolerant than those who have not been burglarized, which strongly suggests the ephemeral nature of such beliefs, and further suggests that they rest on somewhat flimsy knowledge bases (Bertrand 1982). Livingstone and Hart (1980; Livingstone 1978) found that the Ontario public was more concerned about student discipline than any other educational matter (51 percent dissatisfied with student discipline, compared with 41 percent dissatisfied with value obtained for taxpayers' money, and 29 percent dissatisfied with the school system in general). Those furthest from direct knowledge of schools and children (namely, the childless) were the most concerned. This is quite consistent with other research (see for example, Mann 1970), indicating that such surveys of mass opinion tend to tap ideological "code words" at a level abstracted from direct personal experience. People seem to be responding, then, to "delinquency" and "indiscipline" with a kind of automatic, knee-jerk reaction, without much consideration.

Furthermore, Bertrand argues (1982, 17) "There is indication from in-depth studies of attitudes that words like 'crime' and 'criminals' are used restrictively by people to cover the most extreme, serious and depersonalized occurrences." If such is the case, then an interesting transformation of knowledge occurs: When the code word "delinquency" is presented on public opinion questionnaires, respondents tend to equate the serious and spectacular depictions of delinquency from the (mainly American) mass media with official statements that delinquency in general is increasing (even though most official delinquency is minor). The more specific and less "coded" the questions, the more respondents rely upon their personal (Canadian) experiences, which in most cases they classify as being minor offences. American imperial media knowledge and more superficial public opinion poll knowledge, then, usually sharply contrast with local experiential knowledge.

But the discussion of delinquency as a public issue in features, editorials, political news stories, and parliamentary debate, relies heavily on media information and opinion polls. Perhaps relying on police television drama images, certainly utilizing news stories, such debate on delinquency reciprocally feeds into and feeds from public opinion in such ways as to obliterate the possibility of seeing that most of the (apparently increasing) total delinquency rate consists of those minor delinquencies typically experienced. The large numbers are mistakenly assumed to be typically serious (as in the American police television dramas).

A number of research studies have indicated how popular moral panics about delinquency seem to rely more upon newspaper created crime and delinquency waves than upon actual behavior (Hall et al. 1978).

Perhaps one of the most spectacular incidents of this kind revolved around the infamous July 1977 "shoeshine boy murder" of twelve year old Torontonian Emmanuel Jaques (Ng 1981). Jaques was homosexually assaulted and raped, forced to take illicit drugs, then murdered; three men were found guilty of the crimes in February 1978. While the events of the murder itself are undeniably horrendous, the surrounding media and political response are of more direct interest here. No mention was made of the criminologically highly atypical nature of the case: about 90 percent of officially reported sexual child molestation is heterosexual, not homosexual, and very few such incidents involve physical coercion (Mohr 1975). There is good reason to believe that most of it occurs with family members, neighbors, or friends of the child, although there certainly are also willing juvenile prostitutes, and victims. Murder in such cases is extremely rare.

Moreover, such rape-murders of children occur very infrequently, though recurringly. In 1973, ten year old Kirk Deasely was killed in similar circumstances (homosexually raped, then murdered, with over a hundred human bites over his body), but with almost no public outcry. The Jaques murder, by contrast, resulted in extensive news coverage, statements and reports from public officials, a special campaign to "clean up Yonge Street" (especially in regard to juveniles involved in running away, sex, and drugs), and a consequent series of police harassments, and public campaigns against homosexuals.

Why, then, was there such a public furor in one case, but not in the other very similar one (Ng 1981)? Since the murders were so similar, the answer must be sought elsewhere than in the "facts of the case." Instead, one must consider the central role of the news media, particularly the three Toronto newspapers, and the more general political context. Since 1973, Mayor Crombie had tried on a number of occasions to "clean up" the sex industry on Yonge Street. Initially, his efforts were solidly opposed by civil libertarians. By 1977, however, police expressions of concern that "organized crime" was involved, the desire of "legitimate" merchants (especially those in the expensive new Eaton Centre) to give the street a different image, and the increasingly strident newspaper campaigns had swung public opinion around somewhat. The Jaques murder occurred within days of yet another merchant, police, and media supported city report on the need for a cleanup, and provided the perfect organizing issue. Official spokespersons and interested parties can thus be seen to have exploited the murder for their own political ends. While the Jaques case is perhaps the most spectacular recent episode of such media portrayal and use of delinquency, one can find many others (Bell 1960; Hall et al. 1978; Sutherland 1950; Taylor 1980).

Nonetheless, media knowledge of delinquency has some undeniable advantages compared with simply personal knowledge. The media provide more extensive information than most people ever directly experience, and often provide different types of knowledge than a person would likely encounter directly (for example, regarding Glasgow street gangs or New York rackets.) The media, being public, enable the exchange and sharing of personal knowledge. This at least offers the hope of articulating various individual beliefs and opinions into a "general will" of consensual public opinion, about which collective action might be taken. Media and public knowledge thus hold out the promise of generalizing beyond our own, provincial experiences. Furthermore, since media and public knowledge is so central in policy debates, it becomes important in its own right, whether or not accurately reflecting people's experience.

Official State Knowledge

Confronted with the above problems in personal and media knowledge, many people consider the official statistics on delinquency produced by the police and the courts to be more reliable and valid than their own inferences. For well over a century these statistics have provided much of what we know about delinquency, and have been a key resource for social researchers. Indeed, the relationship between government needs for official social bookkeeping and the development of the social sciences has been so close that some argue it has seriously distorted social research (Therborn 1976). Nonetheless, it must be acknowledged that such official statistical offices conscientiously attempt to standardize reporting procedures (hence avoiding media sensationalism and distortion), try to cover the field as thoroughly as possible (hence avoiding the parochialism of personal experience), have been maintained far beyond any individual researcher's lifetime (although not infrequently changing procedurally), and (not unimportantly) generally provide free data to any investigator. Some patterns hold with remarkable consistency across jurisdictions, and within smaller units such as provinces and towns. One cannot ignore such an important source of data, which, in many ways, constitutes delinquency.

Official statistics do offer considerable information about delinquency, and indeed, much more information could be mined from official records. But most contemporary criminologists (Taylor 1978; Giffen 1979; McDonald 1976) argue that such statistics are not as useful as they first appear, and that they actually tell us more about police and justice personnel behavior than about delinquents. As will be discussed in chapter 3, there are serious omissions. Surveys show that most offences are not reported to the police, so there is far more delinquency than the statistics indicate (Scanlon 1982); indeed most high school students report some delinquent act during the previous year (Gomme, Morton, and West 1984). There are also serious biases. Some types of crime (corporate fraud or co-operative delinquencies without victims – drinking alcohol, for instance) are more seriously underreported than publicly noticeable crimes with victims (such as mugging). Furthermore, some rather astonishing variations in rates across jurisdictions of charged juveniles underline the extent to which police force size and discretion determine the official rates (Hackler and Paranjape 1983). Police statistics are collected not for research purposes, but to serve the administrative needs of state agencies, justifying programs, budgets, personnel complement, and the like. This not only suggests that some of the statistics may be self-serving, but that many research questions are not directly addressed (such as how delinquency develops).

Governments also provide important knowledge about specific types of crime by establishing special commissions to report on crucial topics (LeDain et al. 1970). These commissions usually go beyond simply gathering official statistics collected by police and courts, but instead commission special research studies, listen to expert witnesses and so forth. Nonetheless, there obviously remains heavy reliance on government definitions of the appropriate topics, issues and concerns, as well as continued reliance on the official statistics and justice system spokespersons.

SOCIOLOGICAL KNOWLEDGE OF DELINQUENCY
Sociological Data

Because of these kinds of difficulties with personal knowledge, media reports, and official statistics, sociologists have increasingly sought their own data collection methods in searching for the truth about delinquency. Sociologists have attempted to use scientific methods to collect and analyze data as objectively as possible, free from personal biases, and according to procedures that others could check. Testing their own ideas against the facts, theories might be proven or disproven, and knowledge secured. Accordingly, experiments, social surveys, and participant observation techniques have been used in research on delinquency. This text will focus on that type of knowledge and we will examine the pros and cons of such methods extensively in chapters 4, 5, and 8.

It is interesting that some of these social science findings closely replicate those from other areas of knowledge. Self-report surveys, for instance, verify official statistics in revealing that males are more likely to commit serious delinquencies than females, and that property crimes predominate. On the other hand, some findings are radically different: almost all youngsters report some delinquent behavior, and there are very few class differences.

At this point enough has been made of self-report data to raise some general questions appropriate for this introductory chapter. Even with the best utilization of such social research data collection techniques, how much does such data alone tell us? In a very real sense, the collection of "facts" alone still leaves us quite unsatisfied that we know much about delinquency, for the facts alone do not explain anything, and at best only suggest that delinquency is related to some social characteristic or another. Furthermore, if different knowledge reveals different related characteristics, which is correct? Or can this different knowledge be reconciled somehow? Simply collecting more data will not solve these questions. Rather, to more fully understand delinquency, we need concepts and theories as well as facts. It is to these we now turn.

Definitions and Conceptions

The astute reader will have already noticed one possible answer to our problems in reconciling diversified knowledge of delinquency. The above discussed kinds of knowledge do not all use consistent definitions of delinquency. If official statistics and self-report research in some sense talk about somewhat different phenomena, it should not be surprising that they find different amounts of delinquency. Indeed, some readers may have become frustrated by the avoidance of any definition of delinquency to this point. This avoidance has been quite intentional, however, for in discussing delinquency we regularly switch between different definitions.

Although we generally assume we know what delinquency is, and can distinguish "serious" from "petty" misdemeanors, upon further examination, definition is not quite so easy as first thought to be. A number of definitions have been offered by sociologists for studying delinquency, each of which has some strengths, but each of which has some drawbacks. The following lists the most commonly used ones.

STATISTICAL

Definitions of DQ

Some statisticians claim that deviance in general and delinquency in particular consists of any behavior that is atypical or unusual juvenile behavior. This suggests measuring delinquency objectively, without reference to anyone's personally biased beliefs. We could possibly separate "real delinquents" from "foolish kids" by doing head counts, and finding, for example, that very few youngsters murder, a few more commit armed robbery, many more steal, and even more have violated liquor laws. But in self-report questionnaires, over ninety percent of high school boys report committing some delinquent acts; hence, it is the nondelinquent, "goody-goody" youngster who is unusual, who is statistically deviant. We must recognize "delinquency" thus has an inescapably moral aspect beyond head counting; it refers to what youngsters should *not* do, even if almost everybody is doing it.

MORAL

A second definition claims that delinquency is immorality; it is behavior that is wrong. Some sociologists (and many other people) have argued (usually on religious or natural-law grounds) that certain behavior, real delinquencies such as murder, incest, treachery, and the like, are *mala in se*, "evil in themselves," and universally condemned in all societies as wicked and immoral. Other acts, such as traffic violations, are only *mala prohibita*, regarded as fundamentally culture-bound, and varying from society to society (Hagan 1977). But if one attempts to define "real delinquency" without reference to a cultural context, to specify a behavior is not sufficient; taking the life of another is not delinquent if it is in self-defence, or the aborting of an embryo in a hospital clinic. Indeed taking the life of another may even be demanded by society in warfare. When one includes such culturally specified niceties, the definition of an act of killing as deviant is no longer universal. This makes crosscultural comparisons highly suspect; the same behavior may be understood quite differently in different places, times, and societies.

NORMATIVE

A third definition states that delinquency is the violation of the norms and values of a particular society and culture. Proposed by structural-functionalists or anomie/strain theorists (see chapter 3), this view sees society being co-ordinated by everybody sharing common values or norms (that is, children should be obedient, violence towards others should be avoided, and so forth). Delinquents would thus violate these norms that even they share. Such values are specified for particular statuses (for instance, sexual intercourse is permitted within marriage, but suspect without, especially for the young); roles (that is, policemen may use violence forbidden to the rest of us); or subcultural groups (for example, children partaking of a glass of wine with the family meal is permitted among Italian Canadians); or situations (for instance, skinny-dipping is permitted on an isolated, single-sex, boy scout, canoe trip). Hagan (1977) has proposed that one can thus recognize the degree of deviance according to (a) severity of the reaction, (b) the degree of consensus, and (c) the social evaluation of harm.

Most modern nation-state societies, however, are quite complicated and diverse, combining members of different ethnic, religious, and language groups, and it is difficult to specify common norms and values. What, for instance, do a teenage Ojibwa trapper in Northern Ontario, a high school Quebecois separatist, an aspiring Bay Street corporate lawyer, a Hutterite farmer's daughter, a Newfoundland parochial school student, a teenage mother, and a Vancouver working-class street urchin have in common (other than a Canadian passport)? They probably all advocate respect for human life, oppose homicide and rape, but are clearly divided on the issues of abortion for teenage pregnancies, marijuana use, or corporal punishment in schools. Where is the central consensus?

LEGAL

Lawyers suggest that delinquency may be defined as behavior that any society authoritatively defines as such; in modern societies it is behavior illegal for minors. Even though norms and values may not be shared, and interpreting them may always remain fundamentally a problem, modern societies do in fact authoritatively resolve such disputes through law. Chiefs, priests, and wise men have sat as arbitrators; and in modern societies, legal systems are established to hand down definitive judgments. Some sociologists argue that legal systems embody societies' central values and important norms; since they consist in part of written statutes and case law, one can refer to these to gain precise definitions of deviance.

Nettler (1974) suggests that (a) there is no crime without law and a state to punish it; (b) there is no crime if the act is justified by an excusing condition (for instance, self-defence); (c) there is no crime without intention; and (d) there is no crime where the offender is deemed incompetent or without mental capacity to decide right from wrong.

The legal definition does offer some hope of precision while incorporating specific cultural values into our definitions of deviance, yet ambiguities remain. Disputed legal cases indicate a serious lack of easily interpreted agreement as to what laws and acts mean; overturned decisions and appeals indicate the law is not as clear as one might naïvely assume. At what point in the legal process can one take the definition to be authoritative?

But there is also a serious substantive problem with the legal definition. Are the traffic violations, petty thefts, and liquor offences that make up the bulk of court cases the events we think of when discussing the "delinquency problem"? Using a legal definition may include many such morally minor peccadilloes. On the other hand, it may leave out some activities that many or even most people consider deviant, even though they are usually legal. For instance, teenage necking on public buses, or defiant posturing towards parents and teachers is usually legal, but most Canadians would regard them as morally deviant.

In sum, even if we could agree upon where in the legal process to draw the line, the legal definition includes some behavior that most people do not regard as really delinquent, and excludes other behavior many people do regard as deviant.

In addition, juvenile delinquency is a particularly gray area of law. Delinquency is centrally concerned with criminal law, not including civil law which embraces property, contract, and torts. Delinquency is a violation of the Juvenile Delinquents Act (now replaced by the Young Offenders Act) of Canada, committed without excuse and penalized by the state (Tappan 1947).

The Canadian Juvenile Delinquents Act which has been in force since 1908 states that delinquency includes not only any child who violates the Criminal Code, any other federal or provincial statute, or any municipal bylaw, but also goes on to include any child "guilty of sexual immorality or any similar vice," and any child "liable by reason of any other act to be committed to an industrial school or juvenile reformatory under the provisions of any dominion or provincial statute." The terms (such as "any other vice") are nowhere defined; some judges have included glue-sniffing, while others have deemed juvenile consensual sex to not be "sexual immorality." Furthermore, as Weiler (1978) and others have made clear, somewhere between a quarter and a half of training school inmates have been confined under "child neglect" or welfare clauses of provincial Training Schools Acts. Strictly interpreted, such "needy" youngsters, who may have committed no crime, are also delinquents. The vagueness and interconnectedness of the relevant statutes provide a far from clear series of definitions (see chapter 2 for more on this). It is thus often very much a "judgment call" as to whether the Juvenile Delinquents Act was broken, or a person is a "real" delinquent.

LABELING/INTERACTIONIST

"Labeling theorists" (phenomenologists, ethnomethodologists, or symbolic interactionists) have suggested yet another definition. In the words of Howard S. Becker, "Deviant behaviour is behaviour that people so label." (1963, 9) Delinquency is thus seen as a social construct. This definition recognizes the cultural and normative variability of applications of the deviant label to behavior and persons; the law is seen as only one way in which "delinquency" is attributed to acts and actors. Being socially typed as sexually promiscuous, for instance, might be far more socially consequential for a high school girl than being found delinquent in a juvenile court. The attribution of deviance is more socially important than the simple commission of an act. In some cases (for instance, those that result in being sent to a training school), being judged guilty of a delinquency has social consequences of deeper import than the activity itself. The development of this labeling approach during the 1960s coincided with the findings of self-report studies to force researchers to make a clear distinction between official delinquents, labeled as such, and delinquent behavior, which is often not officially recognized. Studies of training school populations, for instance, cannot be taken as representative of that population that commits even legal delinquency, but only of those caught and incarcerated. Such official statistics may well tell us more about the behavior of the officials (that is, the police and judges) producing the statistics than those deviants about whom they are ostensibly produced. The fundamental claim of labeling theorists is that the behavior of both deviant and official are perhaps hopelessly intertwined; "delinquency" is constituted from the interaction of youngsters and officials.

Interactionist definitions of delinquency, however, may still leave us frustrated, for they insist on leaving for empirical resolution the question of what will be labeled delinquent in any particular context. One can never claim to know in advance, in the abstract, what is delinquent, but can only know *post hoc*. Comparative research becomes difficult if not impossible. Who is required to do the labeling is also left unresolved. Can one effectively label oneself? Or is definitive labeling dependent upon an official, thus returning us to the problem discussed above under the legalistic definition. Which official is required – the policeman, the judge, or someone else?

CONFLICT

While recognizing the cultural variability of delinquency, its intertwining with the law, and the ambiguities of labeling, conflict theorists have emphasized that juvenile delinquency is essentially political and economic. They argue that the behavior that is labeled delinquent is that which is deemed by officials to be contrary to the interests of the powerful, especially the dominant economic class (Liazos 1974).

Laws, of course, are not simply neutral, the expressed wishes of some imaginary social consensus. Laws are made through a political process. While we frequently brag about our parliamentary democracy representing the will of the people, it is noteworthy that the Canadian Senate, our Upper House, was instituted precisely to protect the interests of the propertied, who supposedly have a greater interest in the social well-being. Royal assent (based on the arbitrary biology of race and breeding) is still technically required. Political campaign contributions are overwhelmingly from vested interests (that is, corporations, rather than street urchins), and clearly have an impact on the outcome of elections. And even this marginally democratic system has only been in existence for the past century; most of our criminal legislation predates democracy and the extension of the franchise, being founded upon law established in monarchical Britain by a Whig aristocracy/plutocracy.

Issues of contention also remain in this definition. Prohibition of some types of delinquency (for example, murder) is more appropriately described as being in everybody's interest, not just the upper class's. And some behavior which would seem to be in the interest of capitalists (for example, forming monopolies or combines in restraint of trade) is legally prohibited. If strong support for law and order, and school discipline campaigns come from working-class populations, and the latter are the most frequent users of police services, can one really maintain that the law and its agents lack support from among the least powerful, the most exploited? Perhaps this conflict definition is not so much a *definition* of delinquency, as an orienting *hypothesis*, which focusses attention on a most important social characteristic of delinquency; it is nonetheless a hypothesis needing careful evaluation.

There is also a rather reductionist tone in such formulations. Rape, and many other sexual offences, theoretically challenge the general analysis we have been developing here by suggesting that crude economistic explanations are not adequate for understanding *all* kinds of delinquency. Their existence suggests that our notions of political economy must be considerably widened to take account of at least one other structural factor of perhaps equal magnitude to class: gender. We will develop these considerations throughout.

Stepping back somewhat from the above formulation, Colin Sumner (1981, 3) has offered a more powerful yet flexible neo-Marxist definition.

> [delinquency is] social censures, rooted in dominant ideological forma-
> tions, which in general can only be said to have a variable proximity to
> their supposed empirical referents . . . [Delinquency] is not best defined
> as a set of distinguishable behaviours offending collective norms, but as
> a series of flexible ideological terms of abuse or disapproval which are
> used with varying regularity and precision in the practical networks of
> domination.

Such a definition not only highlights the necessity of actively connecting laws to any particular behaviors, but also reasserts issues of the ideological constitution of delinquency at cultural and political levels.

In this book we will basically use this last definition of delinquency, while remaining sensitive to issues raised in other definitions (especially the legal interactionist ones). Centering one's definition on illegal behavior is heuristic in that most research in deviance has been done with this definition in mind. This narrower legal definition will also allow us to illustrate the advantages of the political economy perspective of this text by assessing the conflict hypothesis just mentioned. Our assessment will demand that we theorize more precisely the relationship of the legal apparatus to control the young in capitalist states, returning us to considering the law. Nonetheless, where appropriate in particular substantive discussions, research using other definitions will be dealt with. The reader should thus continually remain alert to the possibility that apparently discrepant research results occur because of the ambiguity of the term.

Definitions and conceptions are necessary to understand delinquency because they allow us to sort through and classify the "facts" or data about it in more comprehensible ways. They are not, however, sufficient to explain delinquency. For that, we would want to understand not just that delinquent acts occur, or that they are of certain kinds, and committed by certain types of people in certain circumstances. We would also want to understand such definitionally organized data in their interrelatedness. This requires some knowledge of causes or determinations. Theory attempts to provide such explanatory knowledge.

Theoretic Sociological Explanations

> The Causes which fill our streets with children who either manifest the
> keen and sometimes roguish propensity of a precocious trader, the daring
> and adroitness of the thief, or the loutish indifference of the mere dull
> vagabond, content if he can only eat and sleep, I consider to be these:
>
> 1. The conduct of parents, masters, and mistresses.
> 2. The companionship and association formed in tender years.

3. The employment of children . . . and the training . . . to a street life.
4. Orphanhood, friendlessness, and utter destitution.
Vagrant dispositions and tastes on the part of children which cause them to be runaways . . . (Mayhew 1861, 468; 1981, 189).

The problems with definitions, data collection methods (which often produce different "facts"), and the nature of a wide variety of substantive types of delinquency (ranging from precocious sex, to minor theft, to murder) combine to make good explanations of delinquency difficult.

Most of this book will examine in detail sociological attempts to develop a number of major theories specific to delinquency: conflict theories in chapter 2, anomie theories in chapter 3, control theories in chapter 4, and interactionist theories in chapter 5. A substantive integration of these will be attempted in chapter 6, and an elaboration especially drawing upon conflict theories in chapters 7 and 8.

SOCIAL OVERVIEWS

Theories specific to delinquency, however, make crucial, often unexamined assumptions about the nature of the wider society. Such middle-range theories about delinquency (Merton 1968) need to be articulated to more general views of society to gain a more comprehensive understanding, and to link research knowledge on delinquency to analyses of our society as a whole.

Many social scientists suggest that there are two main theories in understanding contemporary societies: order/functionist/liberal ones, and conflict/dialectical/Marxist ones (see Horton 1966; Hagan 1977; Marchak 1975; McDaniel and Agger 1982). Each will be briefly outlined in turn.

Order/Consensus/Functionist/Liberal Theories of Society

In general, order theories derive from such sociologists as Comte (1912), Durkheim ([1893] 1933), and Parsons (1951). They argue that social existence requires orderly relationships, which derive from common values that co-ordinate citizens' activities towards consensual ends, in a society functioning like a <u>social organism</u>. Modern Western societies are seen as having evolved from European feudalism through the growth of individual liberties and the rule of law, the freeing of economic competition through the free market, and the extension of economic benefits and political participation through the democratic franchise.

Any resultant existing social problems such as delinquency are regarded as either unfortunate, inevitable concomitants of the system, or inadvertent but technically solvable problems. Power elites or unequal incomes, for instance, are seen as necessary to attract and reward the most talented individuals to the most socially necessary positions. Some inequalities, such as Canadian native children's educational failure, which is connected to their delinquency, are seen as needing correction through better welfare payments or more appropriate curriculum. Such systemic inefficiencies are capable of correction on a piecemeal, "fine-tuning" basis, leaving the essential outlines of the system intact. The free circulation of elites is seen as guaranteed by free market competition and by democratic elections, which allow a pluralist interplay of social interests in determining legislative outcomes. Centralization of authority and decision making, however, is seen as demanded in order to ensure co-ordination of a complex society. Laws and bureaucracies are rationally organized in modern societies to achieve maximum efficiency and fairness. Professional expertise is needed to deal with social problems, and this can only be developed and used efficiently through unequal systems of reward and authoritatively co-ordinated organizations.

Although many of its ideal claims are attractive (for example, political freedoms and liberties being guaranteed), and its empirical claims hold some considerable weight (for example, that there actually is some substantive success in guaranteeing civil liberties in Western liberal democracies), closer examination reveals a number of problems in the liberal view of society that has just been outlined. The notion that occupations are located in a hierarchy of skills according to supply and demand, with access provided to individuals through merit and training needs to be seriously qualified. The supply and demand is often manipulated and controlled (for example, by professional entrance standards), birth and wealth are more influential than individual merits such as intelligence, a class structure persists, and so forth. There is actually little individual mobility between social classes, and discrimination on the basis of gender and ethnicity is also restrictive (Porter 1965). Although the economy centers on a formally free market, wealth generally is transferred by heredity and the accident of birth rather than being acquired through meritorious behavior. Centralization of ownership into a few large concentrations of corporations distorts the market severely, and these corporations are governed as private entities, not democratically. Modern advertising attempts to create a mass market of needs that are artificially stimulated as much as genuine, yet companies rely on publicly funded infrastructures of roads, communications, and the like. The world-wide concentration of capital in a few centers turns other areas into dependent peripheral economies. Even in the formally free and democratic political sector, economic wealth has a strong influence on election outcomes; behind the alternation of governing parties lies a huge and stabilizing civil service focussed on maintaining "the system." (For a more detailed discussion, see Marchak 1975.)

As a result of these problems with a liberal overview, an alternative has been articulated that fits these facts much more closely.

Conflict/Dialectical/Marxist Theories of Society

Conflict theories of society derive from such sociologists as Karl Marx ([1867] 1967), C. W. Mills (1959), and W. Clement (1975). They argue that societies are maintained by force or coercion, judiciously combined with ideological mystification, rather than just genuine value consensus around common goals, with continuous conflict between groups with opposing goals and values. Marxists emphasize that in capitalism, the fundamental conflict occurs between labor and capital, grounded in their contradictory relations of production. Each society must be understood in terms of its historical specificity. There is a need for a critical analysis of social order, a refusal to regard taken-for-granted understandings as accepted. No social research can be value free, and good social research must seek to assist progressive social change.

Modern Western societies are seen as having evolved from European feudalism through forceful bourgeois revolutions, whereby particular (bourgeois) classes asserted their domination over other (aristocratic and proletarian) ones. Although some civil liberties have resulted in increased individual freedoms, the liberal notion of the rule of law ignores substantive inequities, and is only concerned about equality of opportunity, not equality of condition. Although enormous increases in material productivity have undeniably accrued over the past couple of centuries, enormous and increasing inequalities of wealth have also resulted, not simply on a random basis, but systematically biased by race, class, age, and gender. The extension of the democratic franchise has resulted in some popular control over autocratic rule, but remains systematically distorted through governmental/bureaucratic setting of agendas, inequitable campaign financing, and ideological dominance of the bourgeoisie. Resulting social problems and delinquency are regarded as not necessary for any functioning social order, nor as mere aberrations in the system, but as systematic contradictions necessarily generated by capitalism. The extraction of surplus value, whereby employers derive more value (profit) for products sold than they pay in materials or labor, systematically tends to generate inequalities, crises of consumption, centralization of ownership, and resultant social problems. Class conflict, then, is the basis of social problems and deviance (including delinquency), but also positive in bringing about progressive social change. Thoroughgoing revolutionary change, however, depends on the adequate development of class consciousness among the exploited, the working class.

There is no real circulation of elites, but rather the perpetuation of a closed-class system maintained through economic inequities and privilege, intergenerational inheritance, and the law. The appearance of genuine articulation of different interests within the political system is regarded as a sham, with the outcomes systematically biased in favor of the ruling class. Class relations now extend beyond the boundaries of single countries, in an articulated world system of imperialism and underdevelopment.

CANADIAN SOCIAL FORMATION

Such social overviews must be evaluated not only for their theoretical coherence and elegance, but also for the closeness of fit with available data. Although there are many disputes regarding detail, I believe that the predominant empirical analyses of Canadian society tend to support the second or conflict view much more than the first or consensus view. This text will thus rely upon understanding that the most accurate analysis of Canadian society is provided by a rich tradition of studies loosely called "Canadian Political Economy" (see Grayson 1983, for an excellent introduction).

Within this scholarly tradition, Canada is seen as best analyzed in terms of a metropolis-hinterland dialectic (Davis 1971; Frank 1972; Glenday et al. 1978). This land has fundamentally served, since the time of early explorations by Europeans, as a natural resource base for succeeding empires: first French, then British, and now American. Harold Innis (1950) is credited with formulating Canadian history in terms of an economy based upon the export of staples – raw materials that are transported to and then processed in the metropolis elsewhere (typically overseas in the imperial center) before being resold to hinterland areas at a profit. Fish and furs have been succeeded by wheat, minerals, water, and energy resources, but the fundamental pattern persists. The prime beneficiaries of this policy have also remained the colonialist powers: first of France, then of Britain, and now the corporate elites of the United States, while those members of the upper strata of Canadian society have been consistently rewarded for facilitating such activity by skimming enough off the top to build strong mercantile, banking and, for a time, manufacturing sectors. Moreover, the metropolis-hinterland tension is also seen to exist in the relationships between the various regions of Canada, with the mercantile and financial centers of Ontario and Quebec dominating the economies of the North, East, and West.

For instance, prior to Confederation, the Hudson's Bay Company enjoyed monopoly privileges granted and protected by the British Crown that extended over half of what is now Canada, land that "belonged," by virtue of residence, to many Indian tribes.

Recently, Gaucher (1982) has completed some groundbreaking work on the uniqueness of the Canadian political configuration. He points out that the failure of the local incipient aristocracy (the Family Compact in Ontario and the Chateau Clique in Montreal) to avert and themselves suppress the 1837 rebellions necessitated the intervention of British imperial forces. In quelling the rebellions and exiling their leaders and activists, any incipient political expression by either yeomen, commodity-producing farmers or the fledgling working class was also suppressed. In trying to assure peaceful rule and continued staples supply to England, the British established through Durham's report a "quintessentially bourgeois state": power was structured to facilitate the operations of the capitalist merchants and manufacturers of Montreal and Toronto. Both Grits and Tories fundamentally represented this single, though fractionated, rising class, with neither being an aristocratic holdover party, nor a contesting working-class radical one. To this day, Canadian political party support is better understood as an expression of racial and religious groupings than in class terms (which better explain party support in other Western countries).

Politics in Canada have always been shaped by the relations of production. The evolution "from colony to nation" (Lower 1946) has often been depicted by liberal and conservative historians as an upward trend directed by benevolent leaders; however, the original powers and privileges of the colonial governors have been reluctantly and grudgingly transformed into our contemporary liberal democracy. The radical farmers movements following the First World War and the incipient labor movements were effectively co-opted by the Mackenzie King Liberals. Increasing free trade with the United States followed, orchestrated by a welfare management state seeking to quell industrial conflict. Political democratic rights have been contained and accommodated, leaving the economic organization basically intact. Ensuring the maintenance of "peace, order, and good government" has often meant ensuring a fertile ground for profit-reaping (*cf.* Clark 1976).

The economic elite have consistently dominated the political process, to their own economic advantage (Goff and Reasons 1978; Snider 1977, 1978; Bliss 1974; Levitt 1970; Stanbury 1977). McKie (1976:9–10) has pointed out that members of the economic elite enjoy direct personal access to cabinet ministers, a privilege not granted to leaders of any other group, and that they regularly are invited to exercise even more influence by becoming members of boards and commissions that recommend new policy directions. They thus exert direct influence through their political contacts and law-making roles, and indirect influence through their ideological dominance (Porter 1965; Clement 1975; Marchak, 1975). The political elites in Canada have consistently acted as though they saw their role as being "to regulate social relations in the interests of capital accumulation" (Teeple 1972, x). The government has come to identify policies that benefit the economic elite as synonymous with the national interest. As Miliband put it, ". . . the governments of advanced capitalist countries have never been neutral, they have . . . used the state power on the conservative as against the anti-conservative side" (1969, 76). Lately, the importance of foreign capital to the Canadian state has become the focus of attention and concern as theorists have pointed out how the needs of world capital have shaped the policies of the Canadian government (Godfrey and Watkins 1970; Laxer 1970; Levitt 1970; Task Force on the Structure of Canadian Industry, 1968).

CRIMINOLOGY IN CANADA

Much excellent work has recently been done towards developing an understanding of the overall Canadian social formation, and in particular how the Canadian state and its political elite relate to the class structure. There has, however, been almost no examination of the Canadian legal system from the viewpoint of political economy. The legitimating and coercive functions of the state (Panitch 1977) have been almost ignored. General theories of society such as those of consensus and conflict need to be extrapolated to address questions of crime and delinquency.

Criminological research in Canada has been weak institutionally, with just a few centers developed over the last two decades. Only in the last ten years have many sociological studies become available. What research has been done has been highly correctionalist in its orientation, often in order to obtain government funding. Not surprisingly this has resulted in most of the research being positivistic and empiricist, with few attempts at systematic theoretical analysis or integration (see Snider and West 1980). Often trained abroad, Canadian sociologists studying delinquency have seldom attempted to integrate the specific middle-range theories of this phenomenon with any overviews of Canadian society. Consequently, we are left with a major problem in that the empirical studies of delinquency in Canada have tended to rely upon anomie, control, and interactionist theories, which tend to assume the consensual model of society. Very few studies have been done using conflict theory, which I believe is more consistent with the best overall analysis of Canada. If a revived political economy tradition joined with recent neo-Marxist state theory (Panitch 1977) has become the most intellectually exciting and viable analysis of our society (Clement 1975; Grayson 1983), it must be considered in understanding delinquency in Canada.

To elaborate such understanding, a theory is required that has a historical perspective derived from the Canadian political economy tradition, a recognition of the central role and conflicting functions of the contemporary state, and the inclusion of the best and most relevant recent criminological thinking about delinquency. Given this description of Canadian society, we need to ask what is the meaning of delinquency within it.

In a very real sense, then, rather than simply recounting everything that is known about delinquency in Canada, this book will attempt to outline an integrated theory of delinquency, including a number of research issues to be addressed. In so doing, we will be as vexed with posing questions about Canadian delinquency correctly, as with answering them. The rest of this book will try to suggest that one must consider how delinquency is constituted or determined historically, in legal and popular discourse, economically, socially through the family, education, and popular subcultures, as well as interactionally and within specific political justice system agencies.

2

Historical Perspective on State Justice for Juveniles

We also saw some of the young Arabs [street urchins] bareheaded and barefooted, with their little hands in their pockets, or squatted on the street, having the usual restless, artful look peculiar to their tribe . . . The girls were all prostitutes or thieves, but had no appearance of shame. They were apparently very merry . . . As we entered Queen Street, we saw three thieves, lads of about fourteen years of age, standing in the middle of the street as if on the outlook for booty. . . . Bands of boys and girls were gamboling in the street in wild frolic, tumbling on their head [sic] with their heels in the air, and shouting in merriment, while the policeman was quietly looking on in good humour.

Mayhew 1861, 174–6; 1981, 152–4

In Mayhew's description of the London criminal rookery of St. Giles, juvenile behavior had become a public concern to members of Western societies. What had been regarded as peccadilloes of human nature came to be defined as correctable social problems worthy of legal attention. Within the general concern about public disorder in the burgeoning nineteenth-century cities, the young often seemed the most threatening, but also the most amenable to reform (Lee 1982). Only in this century, however, has *juvenile delinquency* existed in the legal sense of the term. Before the passage of the Juvenile Delinquents Act (JDA) in 1908, legally there was no such thing as juvenile delinquency, but only crime by young persons, generally responded to in the same legislation as crime by adults.

Social control of juveniles has enduringly remained an issue in Canada as in other Western industrial societies. Juveniles figure prominently not only in official police statistics, but also in self-report surveys, popular images of deviance, and moral panic. Adolescence thus competes with male sex and school failure as the strongest correlates of deviant behavior (West 1975). Although teenagers are relatively unorganized and inexperienced (especially as they do move out of this age status), and their delinquencies rarely constitute the serious threat of organized or corporate crime, their problematic moral situation seems to indicate a "break" in the hegemony of the legal order (and, behind that, the state).

Fundamental to understanding delinquency, then, is some consideration of the legislation governing the behavior and situation of the young. What are the origins of the legal category of delinquency, and what links do these origins have to other events in Canadian society? Before examining the legislation directly, we must try to put it into historical perspective in order to understand its advent. This will require some prior examination of the historical position of children and the family in the specific nature of the Canadian social formation. By the end of the chapter, we will be in a position to begin to formulate some theoretical understanding of delinquency, providing a context for the causal analyses of delinquent acts to follow in chapters 3, 4, and 5.

HISTORICAL STATUS OF CHILDREN AND YOUTH

> *"The importation of children taken from the reformatories, refuges and workhouses of the old world" the commissioners concluded, was "fraught with much danger and . . . calculated, unless conducted with care and prudence, to swell the ranks of the criminal classes in this country." They strongly recommended that if the practice were to continue "such precautions be taken" as would "effectually prevent the bringing into this country of children of parents known to be criminal," or of children who had "spent their whole lives in an atmosphere of vice and crime" and were "so saturated with evil" and knew "so little of good." In 1892 the federal inspector of penitentiaries argued that "these street Arabs" speedily returned "to their old habits, on arriving in Canada, and, as a consequence, became a burden and an expense upon the taxpayers of the Dominion in our reformatories, gaols, and penitentiaries."*
> Sutherland 1976, 30 (Quoting from *Report*, 1891, 215, 432–51, 738–42, 540, 729; Canada 1893, vii)

> *In 1889, Kelso estimated that Toronto had "between six and seven hundred boys and about one hundred girls" who were sent out on the streets "by drunken and avaricious parents to earn money by the pre-*

carious selling of newspapers, pencils, etc.," but who more frequently
used their work "as a cloak for begging and pilfering."

Sutherland 1976, 103

Before the great agricultural advances, modern medicine and health care, hygienic sewage disposal, and the like, life near the end of the middle ages in Western Europe was often short and nasty. Infanticide was not uncommon (de Mause 1974, 25), especially of female babies; abandonment was frequent. Child-care practices were often, by contemporary standards, neglectful or brutal: children were wet-nursed if parents could afford it, often swaddled tightly, left uncleaned, or "toughened" in punitive ways (Empey 1978, 26–32). Nor surprisingly, death rates were high, with perhaps a quarter or third dying in their first year, only half surviving to age twenty-one, the average life expectancy being thirty (Gillis 1974, 10–11). Given the mortality rates, children would not have been emotional investments for many parents. They were often trained by example (role model) or through brutal battering.

Medieval French children, Ariès argues (1962), were treated much more as small adults, as indicated by their dress, games, ages of religious confirmation, and legal status. Most children entered fully into adult activities, participating with adults in sex, games and social events, adding to economic endeavors in the fields and shops, living in large, extended households of servants and apprentices, as well as relatives. They often worked from the age of seven side by side with older members of the community, or were apprenticed to neighboring craftsmen. Education occurred "naturally" in such settings, or in non-age-graded schools (Ariès, 1962). There were movements in the 1700s, however, that sought to redefine childhood as innocent, in need of special protection and special training regarding discipline.

English research (Musgrove 1964) strongly supports the argument that this change from medieval status coincided quite directly with the industrial revolution, and the accompanying urbanization. Musgrove (1964) argues that the burgeoning middle-class professionals, unable to easily pass on their trades directly to their offspring, transformed the public school to this purpose. In addition to securing intergenerational continuity, the English public school created a new age-status: adolescence. Working-class children joined their parents in the great immigration from country farms to city factories, sharing in their new monetary independence and industrial drudgery. Concern over child labor, training for a widening democracy, and union fear of job competition resulted in Factory Acts in 1833 and 1847 restricting child labor. Universal compulsory education acts followed in 1870, 1876, and 1880 (Musgrove 1964,

76–7) as much to control "street arabs" and forestall working-class-run schools, as to educate, and meeting stiff resistance from working-class families dependent on their children's income. Johnston (1976) has indicated how school curricula were carefully designed to rigorously maintain the existing class order as well as secure minimal skills of reading and writing to allow "proper" participation in the expanded franchise (through deference to authority).

Only recently (Parr 1982; Sutherland 1976; Houston 1972; Prentice 1977) has there been any available material on the social conditions experienced by most Canadian children before the turn of the century. It is reasonable to see these as developing from the imperial centers in France and Britain, although the young here continued to play a more central economic and social role in the rural agricultural areas where most early Canadians lived. The family was central in French Canadian habitant society (Moogk 1982), as it had been among natives (Amerindians). Increasing population density on the best land, however, meant a steady exodus of the young for open territory to the West, or incipient industry in the new urban centers (Brookes 1982).

By the middle and late 1800s, the larger Canadian cities experienced many of the same problems as did French, British, and American ones (Sutherland 1976). The very real economic growth experienced in Canada in the late nineteenth century was reflected in increasing urbanization, a changed occupational structure, and the achievement of a unified and rapidly expanding federal state. Poverty that in rural areas had been bearably supplemented by neighbors and relatives, and different, potentially deviant behavior that had been relatively hidden, became much more apparent in the cities that sprung from the wilderness. The urban-rural time lag experienced in these changes by Western European countries was shortened in Canada, where cities on the European model almost instantly developed in a primeval wilderness.

As the century progressed, youth and their behavior were more clearly seen as a major social problem. The belief that there was a growing "youth problem" clearly coincided with the above changes in the broader social order. Whereas during early industrialization, children were grossly exploited for low wages, their partial humanitarian exclusion from the labor market had by the end of the nineteenth century made them an expendable surplus population, a nuisance about which something had to be done. Burgeoning slum areas, the enforced idleness resulting from the passage of anti-child-labor legislation, "foreign" immigration, and fears of impending social disorder through epidemics and street crime focussed attention on the working-class young (although there were other problems, such as alcoholism, poverty, urban boredom, and the like). Egerton Ryerson, the "father of the Ontario public school system," in 1848 expressed the opinion that the immigrants from the Irish famine "accompanied by disease and death," were possible "harbingers of a worse pestilence of social insubordination and disorder" (Prentice 1977, 56).

Control over immigration was seen as a potential for averting difficulties before they arose; and banishment was also regarded as a cheap disciplinary response to troublemakers that was employed (for instance during the 1837 rebellions in Upper and Lower Canada; see Gaucher 1982). But the major institutional solution proposed to deal with crime and delinquency was the establishment of a universal compulsory public school system.

Some schools, of course, existed in Canada from the first settlements. In 1807, Ontario voted funds for district grammar schools for the aspiring middle classes; common schools were governmentally aided by 1816. Still, it was the upper and middle class few who went to such schools, training as apprentice clergy, clerks, or rulers. Universal, compulsory, public education became a major political issue throughout the rest of the nineteenth century and constituted the major social effort to deal with youth. For instance, in 1871 Ontario made school attendance compulsory for seven- to twelve-year-olds for four months a year, but mass public education was not provided until 1880, or enforced in Ontario until 1891.

Questions of organization and discipline preoccupied the early educators, especially as concerns about a perceived growth in crime became widespread (Houston 1972). Bishop Strachan argued in 1844 that, "The effective instruction of Upper Canadian children in schools . . . would result in the comparative emptying of jails in this province, and relieve the courts of a good portion of their business." (Prentice 1977, 80). The school promotors thus described their organizations as "a branch of the national police," the "cheapest form of moral police." (Prentice 1977, 132).

The schools were planned architecturally to be as inexpensive as possible, to allow maximum control and surveillance and promote order. Classes were large, often numbering some 60 pupils per teacher. Although attendance was spotty during the early years (Sutherland gives a figure of 75 percent in 1889; 1976, 158), enrollment doubled over the next three decades, especially growing in the secondary sector. Prentice notes (1977, 17) how reformers like Ryerson changed schooling from voluntary to compulsory, organized it as a system, centralizing control in the provincial ministry through an inspectorate, and established normal (teacher-training) schools and curriculum regulations. The schools (and later correctional institutions) were publicly financed, relieving industry of the burden of training and disciplining future workers.

Arguing that education must be a universally recognized good, the school promoters sought to keep it above the "pettiness" of party politics

(Prentice 1977, 120); they disqualified any articulation of opposition; yet they clearly sided with and addressed bourgeois (mercantile and industrial) interests. This could only be expected, given Gaucher's (1982) argument regarding the two major Canadian parties being quintessentially bourgeois. Potential class conflict between the respectable (educated) and poor (uneducated) could be eliminated, the school promoters believed, through universal compulsory schooling. Proper English indicated proper breeding and Christian morality, and appropriate respect for property and the authority of its possessors.

The school thus offered an institution whereby the state could control and exercise surveillance over not just all children, but almost all families in addition (Fitz 1981b; Shaw 1981). The state could thus take an active part in helping to construct or promote those adult-child and family relations it deemed appropriate, while undermining others; it could shape the next generation's homes (Sutherland 1976, 173; Fitz 1981b). Although during Ryerson's time there had been some debate over the state's right to so intervene (Prentice 1977, 176), by the turn of the century such intervention was so widely accepted that it was not again seriously challenged until the 1950s.

Domestic and gender relations, of course, had birth rate and population size implications that were of increasing interest, especially to European states, for the previous century (Davin 1978). European wars had made governments aware of the need for a large population to staff an army. This became translated into the moral duty of women to bear children and rear them properly in order that the values of civilization represented by the British Empire could be defended.

Feminist scholars in particular have recently elaborated upon these issues (Barrett and McIntosh 1982). Concern with a proper family upbringing fundamentally meant that children should be reared in morally conforming, two-parent homes: a child without a resident patriarch was especially likely to be poor, and in moral danger. Women were exhorted to self-sacrifice for the good of their offspring, and also for the pleasure of their husbands, without whom all their efforts vis-à-vis the children were likely to come to naught (Prentice 1977, 110–115). Ryerson had women excluded from university (Prentice 1977, 113). The state, then, was clearly articulating its preferences in the field of supposedly "private" domestic relations (Donzelot 1979). Sutherland (1976, 12) and Leon (1978, 40–44) document that notions about the "good family" had become so clearly articulated by the end of the nineteenth century that Children's Aid Societies felt morally justified in breaking up families that did not conform (Sutherland 1976, 18).

Organized youth clubs and groups particularly sought to prepare the young of the working class for duties in the running of the Empire (Blanch 1979). The ideologies of the YMCA, Boys' Brigade, and Boy Scouts, for example, all had distinctly jingoistic and morally uplifting tones. Many of these organizations were led by ex-military officers, encouraged the wearing of modified military uniforms, formulated activities around military drills, and organized themselves along quasi-military lines.

The Canadian urban youth problem was greatly exacerbated during the late 1800s by the arrival of some seventy-five thousand homeless British waifs and street urchins; this transport of surplus metropolitan labor to labor-short farms in imperial hinterlands had been propounded on humanitarian grounds, but soon again raised a prolonged and serious debate within Canadian elite circles as to the proper nature of childhood (Prentice 1977; Leon 1978; Sutherland 1976; Clarke 1975), and the proper social institutions for the young. Sutherland's quote, " 'doption, sir, is when folks gets a girl to work without wages," (1976, 10) indicates the mixing of humanitarian and economic motives and concerns. Furthermore, there was consternation about bringing in Britain's "worst stock"; they were "morally unfit to become companions of other children," and because of their "bad heredity" they "must have a bad effect on the race as a whole" (Sutherland 1976, 32).

Despite the rather negative aspects of social control that are being emphasized in this discussion, it must also be acknowledged that the school promoters did succeed in achieving many of their more worthwhile humanitarian goals. By the end of the century they established the needs of children as being part of the educational and socialization agendas, attempted to provide practical employment skills, offered something of a common cultural experience to allow people living in this part of the world to communicate, and – perhaps most valuable of all – established better standards of public health.

THE CANADIAN JUVENILE DELINQUENTS ACT, 1908

It is against this background series of specific, nineteenth-century, Canadian concerns about children that one must view changes in their legal status. Increasing urban slums, unruly foreign immigrants (not accompanied by parents), rampant school truancy (often supported by "ignorant" parents), overtaxed social agencies – all these problems suggested that stronger state intervention was required if social reform was to be truly realized. The origins of the juvenile justice system, then, lie in the same movement as the educational changes (Houston 1972; Platt 1969). For those children who did not conform in the regular schools, additional measures were needed that extended the scope of prohibitions specified in adult criminal legislation and school acts. The poor were identified as being particularly crime-prone by clergy and other professional social "pathologists," who attempted to emulate the success of positivistic natural science in predicting social disease. "Predelinquent" children of unfit parents thus became as eligible for state intervention as those who had already committed crimes. "The distinction between *neglected* and *criminal* in effect translated as *potentially* vs. *actually* criminal" (Houston 1972, 263).

It must be understood, then, that from the beginning, the childsavers' interests went far beyond punishing, correcting, or even preventing criminal actions by the young. The most energetic leaders of the movement were intent on building something approaching a new Utopia,

> . . . aimed at imposing sanctions on conduct unbecoming youth . . . more concerned with restriction that liberation . . . Their central interest was in the normative behavior of youth – their recreation, leisure, education, outlook on life, attitudes to authority, family relationships and personal morality . . . It was not by accident that the behavior selected for penalizing by the child-savers – drinking, begging, roaming the streets, frequenting dance-halls and movies, fighting, sexuality, staying out late at night, and incorrigibility – was primarily attributable to the children of lower-class migrant and immigrant families (Platt 1969, 99, 139).

Juvenile crime and misbehavior were seen, then, as evils linked to drunkenness, sexual immorality, sloth, and poverty.

In preindustrial Canada, the Church had recognized children as responsible adults at age seven, and British law held them as potentially accountable for their actions as adults. They were often treated with the characteristic severity of preindustrial society, but in a political world where few had many rights, they were not noticeably inferior. The ancient common law necessity of demonstrating mental capacity regarding knowledge of right and wrong by those between seven and fourteen gradually became more enshrined as courts and juries were increasingly reluctant to impose harsh penalties on young malefactors.

As the nineteenth century progressed, the previously dominant puritan religious explanations of crime began to be modified by utilitarian, progressive, positivist views. Crime was not simply evil, but socially costly; and affairs should be arranged to make it as harmless as possible and less draining upon the body politic. This could be done by arranging a system of punishments tailored to make each particular crime too costly to the potential offender. Furthermore, if this were done correctly, crime could possibly be eliminated; evil need not always be with us, as economic and political progress had revealed how humankind might progress ever upward. Finally, careful study of criminals was needed so that social scientists could determine the environmental and psychological causes of crime, and instruct politicians on how to eliminate it. Early examination of criminal populations using official statistics seemed to reveal what the reformers feared: that most offenders came from urban areas, were poor, had been reared in inadequate, neglectful, often single-parent households, and were often of immigrant stock. Furthermore, many of the offenders seemed to have atavistic or immature physical and mental characteristics.

Besides establishing a legal system of punishments of escalating severity to deter, it was essential to reform those who nonetheless offended. And because it was thought that confinement in institutions was the best means of intervention, during the nineteenth century a program was undertaken to build such institutions as schools, hospitals, and reformatories (Rothman 1971; Foucault 1977; Ignatieff 1978; Prentice 1977).

Although universal public education had become the main state response to the "problem of youth," publicly financed correctional facilities were developed quite early to assist the schools (truancy and indiscipline being major problems), remove offenders from the streets, provide for the neglected, and resocialize potential young criminals. The experiment with schools for social control had not been a total success. One official reported in 1857 that the Toronto common schools had "failed altogether to bring that particular class of children, in any way at all, within the restraining influence of our schools." The problem of "unschooled vagrant children" in fact, was to remain virtually unsolved throughout the Ryerson era (Prentice 1977, 156–7).

Although many such Canadian leaders in the nineteenth century were equally obsessed with the fear of social chaos, they also, like Ryerson, believed devoutly in the potential perfectibility of people. Impressed by the new penitentiary systems of Pennsylvania and New York, the early Canadians decided to erect one of their own, and built Kingston Penitentiary in 1835 (Beattie 1977). The regime was initially organized around the New York model of separate cells for sleeping and congregate work areas, although overcrowding almost immediately led to shared accommodation. Discipline was strict and harsh; from the first years there were recorded incidents of youngsters in their teens being whipped for laughing or communicating by signaling (all talk between inmates being forbidden). There was no segregation by age or sex in the early years. And almost from the beginning there were repeated scandals revolving around charges of corruption and cruelty to the inmates; and despite their considerable power to resist full investigation, early governors were dismissed on substantial findings that the charges were well-founded.

Despite the establishment of Kingston, and the advent of municipal police forces in the 1830s in the major Canadian cities, formal law enforcement and penal institutions were not regarded as the only solutions to the problem of order and delinquency.

Periods favoring reformatory institutionalization, industrial school rehabilitation, and probationing of young offenders preceded by decades the formal passage of the Juvenile Delinquents Act (Leon 1978). An Act for Establishing Prisons for Young Offenders and an Act for the More

Speedy Trial and Punishment of Young Offenders were passed in 1857. In the succeeding decades, other institution-providing legislation followed, but by the end of the century, the leading childsavers challenged the institutions by viewing the family, either natural or foster, and with or without professional probation worker support, as the best milieu for rearing law-abiding citizens (Sutherland 1976, 108–23). The traditional role of women as nurturers was thus reinforced, while at the same time being transformed; the ideal employment for middle-class women outside the home continued to be caring for the young, as teachers, social workers, probation officers, and reformatory matrons and cottage mothers (Platt 1969, 75–100).

Elsewhere in the Western world as well as in Canada, childsavers' efforts took similar patterns, and they stepped up their crusades, increasingly focussing on the need for special ways and means of handling young criminals. In 1889 in Chicago and 1908 in England, they succeeded in establishing juvenile courts (Platt 1969; Muncie 1981) with broad undefined powers to intervene in the lives not only of those who committed crimes, but also those who apparently might do so, as indicated by their condition of neglect. The courts formalized the evolving subordinate position of children as needing separation from adults and adult activities, made previously informal practices legal, and provided wide scope for enforcement (Empey 1978).

Houston (1982) presents some interesting material that strongly suggests that the late nineteenth-century childsavers were acting as classic moral entrepreneurs (Becker 1963) by identifying a problem, defining and describing its parameters, offering solutions, and mobilizing political support for them. Her data offer little evidence of any increase in real delinquent activity, but suggest rather a stepped-up propaganda campaign that utilized overplayed images of urban waifs, exaggerating their number and needs, slandering working-class family life and parent behavior.

> The very traits that came to single out certain youngsters as delinquent (precocity and independence of adult authority) precisely opposed the institutionalized dependency that was becoming characteristic of middle-class youth. By the end of the nineteenth century, a life style – a *street culture* – had become the most common definition of juvenile delinquency (Houston 1982, 131).

Interestingly, various charities that established children's homes were voluntarily resorted to by children and parents during domestic economic crises. Also, many youngsters who had to work enrolled voluntarily in night-school courses to improve their career chances.

The passing of the Canadian Juvenile Delinquents Act in 1908 redefined the legal status of the young, established a formal legal category of delinquency, and allowed for setting up organized systems of probation and juvenile courts. The Act, as revised in 1929, defined as a "juvenile delinquent,"

> any child who violates any provision of the Criminal Code or of any Dominion or provincial statute, or of any by-law or ordinance of any municipality, or who is guilty of sexual immorality or any similar form of vice, or who is liable by reason of any other act to be committed to an industrial school or juvenile reformatory under the provisions of any Dominion or provincial statute.

It should be noted immediately that the common law understanding that age seven was a minimum for knowledge of right from wrong was retained; the upper age limit has varied (sometimes by sex) from province to province, ranging from sixteen (Ontario, Alberta, New Brunswick, Nova Scotia, PEI, the Yukon, Saskatchewan, and the Northwest Territories), through seventeen (British Columbia and Newfoundland), to eighteen (Manitoba and Quebec). Secondly, key terms such as "sexual immorality" or "any other vice" are nowhere explicitly defined. The therapeutic or reformist tone of the Act is clear.

> where a child is adjudged to have committed a delinquency, he shall be dealt with not as an offender, but as one in a *condition of delinquency*, and therefore requiring help and guidance and proper supervision.

With such undefined, sweeping powers, juvenile court trials were to be conducted by special judges, in separate courts, and in private. Judges and probation officers were given special investigatory powers, including access to hearsay evidence and no necessity to reveal confidential information to defendants; procedural rules were minimal. No automatic right to appeal was present, and dispositions ranged from warning and release to indeterminate sentences with the guilty remaining under the courts' jurisdiction until age twenty-one. Dispositions were not linked to the gravity of the offence, but were tailored to the child's needs. The vagueness of this legislation, its lack of due process, the inclusion of a wide range of juvenile status offences (for example, truancy), and wide dispositional powers left the treatment of juveniles open to administrative arbitrariness, and subsequently allowed much of its humanitarian potential to be undermined in its implementation.

Training school placement has been the ultimate sanction of the juvenile law. Ideally, the juvenile justice system is "to secure for each child within its jurisdiction such care, custody, and treatment as should have been provided by the child's natural parents" (Cohen and Short 1966, 85). The Ontario Training Schools Act, 1931, as amended and now R.S.O. 1980, c. 508, offered the following provisions:

2. The purpose of a training school is to provide the children therein

with training and treatment and with moral, physical, academic, and vocational education.

8. [repealed in 1975 by the Ontario Legislature]
   (1) Upon the application of any person, a judge may order in writing that a child under 16 years of age at the time the order is made be sent to a training school where the judge is satisfied that:
      (a) the parent or guardian of the child is unable to control the child or to provide for his social, emotional, or educational needs;
      (b) the care of the child by any other agency of child welfare would be insufficient or impracticable, and
      (c) the child needs the training and treatment available at a training school . . .

9. A judge may order that a child be sent to a training school where:
   (a) the child is at least 12 years of age and under 16 years of age at the time the order is made; and
   (b) the child has contravened any statute in force in Ontario, which contravention would be punishable by imprisonment if committed by an adult.

By the provisions of the Training School Act, in conjunction with the Juvenile Delinquents Act, youngsters who were neglected by parents, had no community facility able to take them, and were sent to training school, were also legally delinquent. The same institution provided for "good" youngsters who were victims, and for "bad" youngsters who were victimizers, on the grounds that the former were delinquents in the making. More will be said of the actual operations in chapter 7, and of the very recent legislative revisions in chapter 8. Almost all of the research reported in this book, however, was carried out under the old legislation quoted here.

The circle of special provision for rearing of the young is completed by noting the activities of the Family Courts (Chunn 1983). The Magistrates' Jurisdiction Act, 1929 (S.O. 1929, c. 36) gave designated juvenile court judges jurisdiction over a range of provincial social legislation (for example, the Children's Protection Act, R.S.O. 1927, c. 279; Adoption Act, R.S.O. 1927, c. 189, and the like). The 1934 Juvenile and Family Courts Act of Ontario was challenged, but reaffirmed by the 1938 decision of the Supreme Court of Canada, allowing eventual designation of all Ontario Juvenile Courts as Juvenile and Family Courts in 1954. A central concern, of course, was not only the regularization of domestic relations, but the enforcement of support payment orders by husbands/lovers/fathers.

As with similar efforts in Britain (in 1908) and the United States (in 1899, in Chicago), there can be little doubt that many of the reformers meant well. The initial concerns regarding provision of shelter, medical attention, and food, coupled with their concerns to eliminate child abuse and exploitation of child labor in factories clearly were in "the best interests of the child" (Sutherland 1976). Yet they simultaneously showed very little concern for the wishes of individual children or parents, and felt fully justified in imposing their own moral standards based on an increasingly hegemonic view of childhood. British reformers had no compunction about farming thousands of children out to Canadian families who clearly wanted them most as cheap labor (Bagnell 1980). On both sides of the Atlantic, reformers were equally concerned with social control and humanitarian treatment. Their focus was clearly upon moral training, character development, and good work habits. Beyond provisions for probation supervision, free lunches at schools, and public health measures, they carefully eschewed concern with the causes of the poor economic conditions of the lower classes. The factory labor system that fundamentally underlay the miseries of the families that concerned the childsavers was assumed, and hence was beyond their interest. Indeed, it is remarkable how almost everything else but these conditions of production was singled out for correction!

The only real dispute concerning the 1908 Juvenile Delinquents Act was between the traditional controllers, the police, and the aspiring controllers, the social workers. Leon (1978) discusses how some police magistrates saw the Juvenile Delinquents Act as too lenient, but he also notes that almost nobody expressed concern about the increasing deprivations of civil liberties. The battle between the social workers and the police was clearly a battle for jobs and jurisdiction. In winning this competition, the childsavers partly separated juvenile justice from the adversarial legal system and made it part of an administrative welfare program. We are left to guess how the affected, mainly working-class parents and children felt about this. They had no representation in Parliament from either bourgeois party.

UNDERSTANDING LEGAL REGULATION: CONFLICT THEORY

Having outlined the social status of children and youth within the Canadian social formation, and sketched the advent of the Juvenile Delinquents Act, it is now time to try to place these events and situations into theoretic perspective. What determined the historically evolving status of Canadian young people, why and how did social and political forces combine to change it? How are we to understand the legal regulation of the young? How do politics affect it?

In chapter 1 we indicated that these questions are best addressed by conflict theory, and it is to it that we will now turn. The development of the delinquency and childsaving legislation would seem to provide a clear example of certain subordinate, class-related styles of behavior (for example, regarding youthful precocious autonomy) being declared illegal by a dominant group that perceived them as conflicting with their own interests. Furthermore, the analysis of the Canadian social formation offered in chapter 1 suggests the particular appropriateness of using a conflict theory of delinquency. After introducing some general tenets of conflict theory, we will offer abstract criticisms, then attempt to apply it specifically to understanding delinquency, and further criticize this application.

Conflict Theory

A number of versions of conflict theory have been developed over the past couple of decades, ranging from the early suggestions of culture conflict from Thorstein Sellin (1938), through Walter Miller's (1958) arguments that lower-class, male gang members merely acted out their own indigenous cultural values (rather than feeling strain, as in anomie theories), on through some labeling theorists who recognized conflict between labelers and labelees.

Especially in North America, these strands have been woven into a Weberian-based conflict theory concerned with subordination and superordination (Turk 1969; Quinney 1969). Conflict is seen as arising from systematic social inequality. Interest groups in conflict exert varying degrees of influence upon legislation and upon enforcement in a pluralist model of democratic politics. Turk (1976) points out that conflict theorists use basic terms and concepts in a way different from conservative or order theorists: conflict theorists define law as power, see conflict as being ubiquitous, and see social order as being a more or less temporary balance of power.

Turk (1969), McDonald (1976), and other North American conflict theorists, however, are rather positivistic. Because of the Weberian origins of their theories, they do not explicitly link crime and criminalization to conditions of production, as is done in the materialist analysis attempted here. There is thus a lack of explanation as to the basis of dominant groups' power over subordinate ones. Nor do they pay explicit attention to the evolution of criminal law and activities through history, relating them to changing dominant modes of production within specific historical formations.

The first significant contemporary attempt to move conflict criminology beyond positivism came from three British criminologists, Ian Taylor, Paul Walton, and Jock Young (1973, 1975). In a masterful and erudite criticism of other theories, they argued that the material basis of society shaped legal norms and crime. More specifically, they suggested that excess profits from the extraction of surplus value created serious material injustice and inequality, encouraged property crime, and shaped the utilization of the criminal justice system for social control by the bourgeoisie. While retaining labeling theory's interest in a conscious human actor, they argued that a different constitutency other than the state officials who usually fund research, or simply other academics, must be addressed by progressive criminologists; the key justification for criminology is to ally itself with the oppressed to bring about social change. The test of a progressive social theory was not its simple verification by facts collected from an oppressive present reality, but its efficacy in bringing about social change.

Thio (1978) moves towards specifying these considerations in arguing that power is the key element in understanding deviance. He suggests that the powerful in society engage in low-consensus deviance, which is regarded as less serious, is more profitable, and has a low probability of being labeled. Furthermore, he suggests the powerful are more deviant: since there is less chance of them being labeled, there is less control over them; since they have more access to resources, they have greater opportunity for deviance; since they are likely to have unusually high aspirations, they are more likely to experience greater subjective deprivation.

Quinney (1977) follows a similar argument with a specifically Marxist orientation in suggesting that capitalism generates crimes of exploitation, repression, and oppression by the powerful, and crimes of resistance and accommodation by the proletariat. The former refers to such activities as corporate crime (both of property and violence), the latter to ordinary street crime or employee theft. In an earlier book Quinney (1974, 16–17) outlined the following radical propositions:

1. American society is based on an advanced capitalist economy.
2. The state is organized to serve the interests of the dominant economic class, the capitalist ruling class.
3. Criminal law is an instrument of the state and ruling class to maintain and perpetuate the existing social and economic order.
4. Crime control in capitalist society is accomplished through a variety of institutions and agencies established and administered by a governmental elite, representing ruling-class interests, for the purpose of establishing domestic order.
5. The contradictions of advanced capitalism – the disjunction between existence and essence – require that the subordinate classes remain oppressed by whatever means necessary, especially through the coercion and violence of the legal system.

6. Only with the collapse of capitalist society and the creation of a new society, based on socialist principles, will there be a solution to the crime problems.

Chambliss (1976) also elaborated the following list of conflict propositions, offsetting them against functionalist (mainly anomie) ones, here adapted to address delinquency. They may be seen as a criminological version of the consensus-conflict debate over the basic nature of contemporary societies outlined in chapter 1.

ON THE CONTENT AND OPERATION OF THE [DELINQUENCY] LAW

Functionalist Hypotheses	*Conflict Hypotheses*
1. Acts are defined as [delinquent] because they offend the moral beliefs of the members of the society.	Acts are defined as [delinquent] because it is in the interests of the ruling class to so define them.
2. Those who violate the [delinquency] law will be punished according to the prevailing customs of the society.	[Children] of the ruling class will be able to violate the laws with impunity while those of the subject classes will be punished.
3. Persons are labeled [delinquent] because their behavior goes beyond the tolerance limits of the community.	[Children] are labeled [delinquent] because it is in the interests of the ruling class to so label them, whether or not the behavior would be tolerated by "the society" at large.
4. The lower classes are more likely to be arrested for and convicted of [delinquency] because they commit more [delinquency].	The lower classes are more likely to be labeled [delinquent] because the bourgeoisie's control of the state protects [the latter] themselves from such stigmatization.
5. As societies become more specialized in the division of labor, more and more laws will become restitutive rather than repressive (penal).	As capitalist societies industrialize and the gap between the bourgeoisie and the proletariat widens, penal law will expand in an effort to coerce the proletariat into submission.

ON THE CONSEQUENCES OF [DELINQUENCY] FOR SOCIETY

Functionalist Hypotheses	*Conflict Hypotheses*
1. [Delinquency] establishes the limits of the community's tolerance of deviant behavior and increases moral solidarity among the members of the community.	[Delinquency] enables the ruling class to create false consciousness among the ruled by making them think their own interests and those of the ruling class are identical.

2. [Delinquency] necessitates the expenditure of energy and resources to eradicate it and is thus an economic drain on the society.

[Delinquency] reduces surplus labor by creating employment not only for the [delinquents] but for law enforcers, locksmiths, welfare workers, professors of criminology, and other people who benefit from the existence of crime.

3. [Delinquency] offends the conscience of everyone in the community, thus creating a tighter bond among them.

[Delinquency] diverts the lower classes' attention from the exploitation they experience toward other members of their own class, rather than toward the capitalist or economic system.

4. [Delinquency] makes people aware of the interests they have in common.

Defining people as [delinquents] permits greater control of the proletariat.

5. [Delinquency] is a real problem which all communities must cope with in order to survive.

[Delinquency] is a reality which exists only as it is created by those in the society whose interests are served by its presence.

ON THE ETIOLOGY OF [DELINQUENT] BEHAVIOR

Functionalist Hypotheses

1. Every society has a set of agreed-upon customs (rules, norms, values) which most members internalize. [Delinquent] behavior results from the fact that some members get socialized into [delinquent] behavior.

2. [Delinquencies] are more frequent among lower classes because the agencies of socialization (especially the family, but also the neighbourhood, schools, other adults and peer groups) are less likely to work effectively, that is, in ways that lead to the internalization of non-[delinquent] norms and behaviors.

3. The lower classes are more likely to be arrested because they commit more [delinquencies].

4. [Delinquency] is a constant in societies. All societies need and produce [delinquency].

Conflict Hypotheses

[Delinquent] and non-[delinquent] behavior stem from people acting in ways that are compatible with their class position. [Delinquency] is a reaction to the life conditions of a person's social class.

[Delinquent] acts are concentrated in lower classes because the ruling class can see that only acts which grow out of lower-class life are defined as [delinquent].

The lower classes are more likely to be arrested and will then be labelled [delinquents] because the bourgeoisie controls those who manage the law enforcement agencies.

[Delinquency] varies from society to society depending on the political and economic structures of society.

5. Socialist and capitalist societies should have the same amounts of crime if they have comparable rates of industrialization and bureaucratization.	Socialist societies should have much lower rates of crime because the less intense class struggle should reduce the forces leading to and the functions of [delinquency].

We will examine these hypotheses throughout this text.

Yet another version of conflict theory from a Marxist perspective is offered by Steven Spitzer (1975). He argues that the ways in which problem populations are defined and reacted to depends upon the specific problems they provide and the costs of social control to capitalist society. The state has the option of normalization, conversion, containment, or support. He argues that there is a need to understand why capitalism produces both particular deviant behaviors and particular social reactions. In a fairly classical Marxist way, Spitzer holds that attention to the mode of production is crucial; one needs to do historically specific analyses. A capitalist social structure will develop deviant populations if people call into question the social order or its preconditions, the distribution of goods, the ways of socialization, or dominant ideology.

Spitzer's ideas are further developed specifically in regard to youth by the Schwendingers (1976). They see capitalism needing ever higher profits; these can be made by using more machines to produce goods, thus releasing workers. If markets could constantly expand, such labor could be absorbed, but they cannot expand limitlessly. Relegation of part of the work force to nonproductive status provides another short-term solution. Humanitarian sentiments reacting to the former gross exploitation of the young, the perceived need to train the young as workers and as citizens, and the need to acculturate "foreign" children have led to the particular marginalization of youth.

Some Criticisms

There is certainly considerable ambiguity within conflict theories as to whether an etiological or causal theory of criminal behavior is being proposed, or whether conflict theory centrally addresses only macrolevel determinants of law and enforcement, leaving the explanation of delinquent behavior for other theories (for example, control theory). Does capitalist society, in other words, engender more working-class delinquency (because of oppressive conditions), or does it simply give rise to a higher official working-class delinquency *rate* (because of the biases of official processing of offending behavior). It is possible, of course, that both factors are operating, but their relative weight remains obscure. In this book, since so little neo-Marxist work has been done on the immediate causes of delinquent behavior, we will utilize anomie, control, and labeling theories (chapters 3, 4, and 5). Conflict theory, however, can help us understand how the factors relevant to these other theories are themselves determined.

However, much more specification is needed regarding *how* class structure is linked to both crime and crime control, for not all of Chambliss' propositions cited above are equally well established. For instance, his claims regarding the invulnerability of ruling-class violators and the expansion of penal law are subject, if not to dispute, to some reinterpretation and refinement in the light of some current evidence from the Canadian context. Some types of crime, such as domestic homicides, may not fit well with his contention that crime is a rational response to class position, but would seem to invoke gender relations at least as much. Many of Chambliss' statements would more appropriately be stated in probabilistic terms, especially in view of the necessity for the state to juggle the functions of legitimation and coercion (see pages 47 to 51.)

Some earlier criticisms of conflict theories have resulted in more careful reformulations. Hagan (1977) has charged that conflict theory does not well account for those crimes, such as murder, about which there is almost complete consensus. However, while almost everyone in this society (as in other societies) would agree that taking another's life without "adequate cause" should be proscribed, the apparent consensus often breaks down when applied to specific cases such as abortion and capital punishment. Furthermore, there is nothing in conflict theory that denies that some beliefs held by working-class persons are enshrined in the law, provided that these are beliefs that do not conflict with the interests of the elites. Indeed, Turk (1976) admits the possibility of class differences in criminal behavior, but at the same time draws attention to the class basis of the processes of legislating these behaviors as criminal. Those crimes that Hagan lists as being consensually prohibited (such as rape and murder) constitute only a tiny proportion of the violations detailed in the Criminal Code of Canada, in contrast with the multiplicity of offences against property (such as break and entry, and theft), which much more clearly relate to economic interests. McDonald's data (1976) also show that if criminal law really reflected community consensus, it would prescribe and assign priority to very different offences in many cases than it does.

Quinney, Chambliss, and others have ignored the debate within Marxism itself, whereby some theorists deny that there can be a specifically Marxist theory of delinquency, arguing that Marxism is only directly concerned with analyzing the mode and relations of production (Hirst 1975; Bankowski, Mungham, and Young 1977). Marx, himself, of course, paid very little attention to criminals, referring to them in the most derogatory terms as "lumpenproletariat," a "dangerous class," a "social scum," a "passively rotting mass thrown off the lower layers of society"

(Marx and Engels [1848] 1950, 41). He thus attempted to draw a clear distinction between productive, solid, working-class people and those involved in illegalities, a practice often followed by orthodox Marxists today (Livingstone 1983) – but a practice with little regard for extant data indicating the widespread nature of criminal and delinquent behavior throughout society. A more subtle analysis is Engels' *The Condition of the Working Class in England in 1844* ([1892] 1958).

Most contemporary neo-Marxists reject the rather narrow economism implied in such definitions, but the integration of analyses of deviance with general Marxist theory must be explicated much more specifically. To be more explicit, traditional Marxist theory has been accurately accused of being monocausal in suggesting that all human behavior can be explained by reference to the economy. Contemporary neo-Marxists accept this criticism, instead arguing that Marx sought explanation of the social relations of production (West 1984) – production including the production of art, language, and culture in general, not just economic activities narrowly defined. Furthermore, feminists in particular have challenged Marxists by arguing that gender is as fundamental a concept in understanding the organization of human society as is class, that gender cannot simply be reduced to class (Barrett and McIntosh 1982). This will be further discussed in the next two chapters.

Furthermore, we may extend the arguments put forward by feminists and ask whether age is not also an equally fundamental concept (Fitz 1981b; Gaffield and West 1978). This is especially relevant given the strong relationship between age and delinquent or criminal behavior (see chapter 3).

There are also some ethical and moral ambiguities as to whether some deviance is being celebrated (for example, street gangs opposing the police) or condemned (for example, if gangs are raping or assaulting ethnic minority groups) (Cohen 1979). If it is accepted that some control is necessary in any society, what reforms can be regarded as progressive and what repressive, and what would the nature of social control in a truly just socialist society be like? The introduction of value commitments and attempts to change society make some people nervous, and threatens to obviate the need for further research. Most neo-Marxists, however, regard practice without theory a serious error. Mungham (1980) further notes that conflict theory has been noticeably inadequate in providing many concrete short-term or midrange directions for reform. If all evils are included in the definition of crime (for example, the Schwendingers include imperialism and sexism, 1975), what is specific to criminological analysis?

The Marxist theories of Quinney and Chambliss suffer from a lack of sophistication. They assume an instrumentalist rather than structuralist theory of the state: they rather naïvely assume the state is simply the executive committee of the capitalist class, acting in its interests (see section on the state and the law, pages 46 to 52). While these conceptions have considerable structural similarities with the Canadian political economy tradition and analyses of the state, if the inappropriateness of earlier transplanted theories is to be avoided, they need to be rooted in and modified by reference to the specific history and structure of Canadian society.

There are additional empirical problems. Perhaps because this theory is that most recently elaborated in criminology, there is a dearth of material addressing its propositions and claims, let alone evidence supporting them. A number of conflict criminologists have not worked out any coherent and considered view on the use of data from the various methodologies, frequently falling back on easy-to-hand, official statistics, while decrying the bias they find in this official material. And further, there are places where the available data challenge conflict claims. For example, the police are most frequently called by working-class persons, who thus obviously do not regard them as simply oppressors. Many repressive law-and-order campaigns are supported by working-class persons (Thomas, Gage, and Foster 1976). And the police themselves are recruited largely from working-class populations. If the law is an instrument of capitalist oppression, how is it that there are laws ostensibly against capitalist interest (such as anticombines legislation)?

CONFLICT EXPLANATIONS OF JUVENILE JUSTICE

The legislative regulation of juveniles may be regarded as a test of conflict theory. Does it explain the status of children and the young in Canadian society, the advent of the 1908 Act, and the present state (especially legal) situation of young people?

Tony Platt, in a landmark study of American legislation (1969, 1974), argues such a conflict perspective, claiming that the 1899 Illinois delinquents act exemplified the legal domination of one group over another, the control of working-class children by middle-class childsavers. The background of rapid industrial growth, large-scale foreign immigration, urbanization, and the prevalence of natural science solutions to social problems provided a similar background to the advent of juvenile justice legislation in Canada. Moral entrepreneurs (drawn from correctional workers; leisured, newly emancipated middle-class women; supporting conservative groups; and educators) secured legislative support in gaining official recognition of a social problem: the independence of working-class youth (including those "predelinquents" committing only "precocious" acts, not crimes).

Platt (1969) argues that the American childsavers wanted *increased* sentences to enable further control of delinquents, threatened the coherence of the working-class families they sought to supervise, and sought to establish the dependency of youth. The resulting welfare-administrative solution consisted of the establishment of juvenile courts without guarantees of due process, depoliticization of the status of (especially, working-class) youth, and the failure to provide better "treatment" facilities. Platt thus opts for a conflict interpretation of the social regulation of the young.

In contrast, Hagan and Leon (1977, 589) argue that Platt holds "a perspective that is (1) prone to logical errors, (2) largely unconfirmed, (3) often unconfirmable, and (4) possibly quite frequently false," and attempt to marshal Canadian data to prove their case. They argue that, contrary to Platt's claim, there is no evidence that the number of incarcerated juveniles increased, as they found that 123 Toronto youngsters were imprisoned in 1911 (the year before the Canadian court opened), and only 85 were institutionalized in 1912. But even in their own data, there are 387 other cases classified as "Suspended Sentence and Adjournments (including commitments to industrial schools, Working Boys Home, Orillia Hospital, Ontario Hospital and Training Schools)," and 191 "Others (including wards of the Children's Aid Society, home placements and transfers to higher courts)." These unknown numbers of children removed from their homes doubtlessly experienced "being sent up" no matter the formal title of the placement. Sutherland presents evidence that the number of youngsters incarcerated in various types of institutions kept pace with the population growth (1976, 146–9), contrary to the claim of Hagan and Leon (1977), based on ambiguous Toronto data. So Hagan and Leon's claim for decreased incarcerations would seem unsupported by Canadian data.

Hagan and Leon would seem correct in arguing that the major effect of the 1908 Act was to allow probation sentences to be used, and even more dramatically, to allow "informal" probation officer "counselling/interviews." Hence the overall effect was to "increasingly intervene in informal systems of social control, particularly the family" (Hagan and Leon, 1977, 597), but surely such socially coercive (though technically legal) intervention must be understood as the real exercise of increasing state control over the young.

Secondly, Hagan and Leon (1977) further claim that the involvement of the ruling class was peripheral, as most reformers were themselves middle-class professionals. Yet Leon's other work (1978) and Sutherland's (1976, 14–15, 112, 120) clearly establishes connections between the leading moral entrepreneurs such as Kelso and Scott, and judges, ministers, cabinet members, and senators, as well as newspaper editors, doctors, clergy, and other solid and respectable community members. Scott himself was Master of the Supreme Court of Ontario, and his father was able to introduce the bill in the Parliament of Canada as he was a

senator. The overwhelmingly substantiated analyses of the relations between government and business in Canada indicate that the bourgeoisie
exercises at least a strong veto option (Porter 1965; Clement 1975). Nonetheless, we must try to understand more precisely the nature of this
relationship.

Hagan and Leon claim that no extension of jurisdiction was involved,
yet the clauses labeling those youngsters liable to industrial school incarceration as delinquents, and those guilty of "sexual immorality or
any similar form of vice" likewise (though the latter came into force as
amendments in 1924) clearly *do* extend the jurisdiction. The two-thirds
to three-quarters of incarcerated juvenile females sent to training school
under section 8 of the unrevised Ontario Training Schools Act have been
living proof of such extended jurisdiction, as have been the 25 to 35
percent of the incarcerated boys.

Finally, Hagan and Leon (1977) state that "whether the eventual success of the advocates of probation served the basic interest of the ruling
elite is unknown, and probably unknowable." This is perhaps the most
difficult question to address, as it would necessitate a sustained systemic
analysis that would be very difficult, especially within a positivist framework. One must begin to move beyond an instrumentalist theory of the
state and address structural questions; that is, one must have regard for
state functions other than simple capital accumulation (such as maintaining order and legitimacy – see the next section, page 47). As Fitz
(1981b, 30) put it more generally:

> Those who wish to argue for a concomitance between the rise of capitalism
> and the creation or invention of the concept of childhood must not only
> demonstrate the rise of "new" classes, but, more fundamentally, dem-
> onstrate the connection between the capitalist mode of production, par-
> ticularly at the level of the class appropriation of surplus value produced
> by wage labour and at the level of the organization of productive enter-
> prises; they must also demonstrate how these are necessary to the con-
> ditions for the social construction of childhood. In other words, at the
> theoretical level one must demonstrate the connection between the or-
> ganization of production on capitalist lines and the expulsion of children
> from the labour force.

Although some of Hagan's and Leon's criticisms of Platt's analysis seem
accurate, basically these criticisms have cogency *within* his overall approach, namely, within a conflict interpretation of the social use of law.
For instance, it seems hardly credible to assert that all Canadians at the
turn of the century held common values: natives, Quebecois, Irish immigrants, and older Anglo elites were hardly grouped around common
values regarding childrearing. There was indeed resistance by working-
class populations (Houston 1972, 1982; Sutherland 1976), and the new
children's legislation regarding schooling and justice would seem to have

been the imposition of standards of childrearing upon various ethnic and working-class groups by a dominant Protestant Anglo-Saxon elite.

Clarke, in discussing the English situation (1975), moves towards addressing some of the issues raised by Hagan and Leon regarding the class relations of the origins of juvenile justice. Drawing upon some of the theoretical modifications of conflict theory mentioned above, he phrases the question as an issue not of narrow legalistic support of capitalist profit, but of a broader one of dominant ideologies and a more general apparatus of social control. This

> opens . . . a consideration of the role of law in the "disciplining" of subordinate classes to the logic of a bourgeois social order; and secondly it asks the question of why youth and the question of youthful (mis)behaviour would be accorded a privileged position in discussions about the direction and nature of the Social Order (Clarke 1975, 1).

Clarke thus argues that a range of nineteenth-century state interventions into working-class lives and life-style must be examined in conjunction; that the law in its formality and ostensible equity is an ideal forum for the expression of apparently cross-sectional interests, while enabling the use of coercive force against particular populations.

> I have already argued that the central locus of discipline in capitalism is the workplace. I now want to add two other institutions which are concerned with socialization and discipline – the family and school – to which are given the functions of preparing the future labour force. My suggestion is that the contemporary concern with adolescence (and the political and social instability which attracts the attention) derives directly from the position of the adolescent in relation to this nexus of institutions – adolescents are *marginal* to all three (Clarke 1975, 5).

The removal of youth from the factories left them free of that discipline; the burden of the English social surveys and childsavers was to define traditional working-class families as inadequate and neglectful in their childrearing; even the advent of legislation compelling school attendance had left about a quarter of the juvenile population "unserved" (Sutherland 1976, part IV; Musgrove 1964, 69–76). Juvenile justice, then, was developed as a "backstop" for moral disciplining: if probation officers were not able to get legally "voluntary" compliance through threatened or implied court action, the might of the state stood ready to coerce physically. As in Canada, reformatories became the dominant form of imprisonment for the young in England throughout the nineteenth century, followed by the passage in 1908 of the English Juvenile Court Act to deal with not only young criminals, but the neglected.

CONFLICT THEORY ELABORATED: THE STATE AND THE LAW

Criticisms of earlier versions of conflict theory pushed it in a Marxist direction in searching for plausible explanations of the origins of social conflict. Further criticisms by scholars such as Hagan and Leon of empirical attempts to apply it in explaining juvenile delinquency as well as the more abstract logical criticisms outlined above, have forced conflict theorists to extend and specify their claims. The most important developments have been the incorporation and development of theories of the state and the law, to which we will now turn.

State Theories

One might ask why the state theories that have developed rapidly in the last decade are important to criminology. Besides the obvious answer that it is state apparatuses that comprise the criminal justice system and indeed create the field of criminology ("no crime without a law"), little attention has been directed to how criminology is shaped through its major funding source lying in state resources. Beyond these pragmatic concerns, however, the rise of conflict and critical and Marxist criminology has explicitly identified state policy as centrally intertwined with crime, especially as the instrument of continued bourgeois rule (Quinney 1977). Although theoretically conceded as a particularly important site of coercion and legitimacy, little concrete research has been done in Canada in which any implications for state theory are developed from criminological findings. Central issues revolve around the questions of why in modern society political power takes the form of the state apparatus. By what mechanisms is state power exercised?

The conditions of production seen as underlying delinquency neither exist naturally, nor are they maintained without considerable effort. Power does not simply reside in the economic elite alone, but in other institutional sectors, including the political. State theories hypothesize that contemporary states must play a mediational role. Management of the conditions of production and the delinquency they engender, falls to the state in capitalist society.

It is first necessary to outline the wider traditions these state theories draw upon, for there is not one but a number of state theories available.

Miliband (1969), Poulantzas (1973), and others have attempted to overcome the rather inadequate picture of the state as simply the executive committee of the ruling class or bourgeoisie. They have extended the definition of the state beyond the government and administrative bureaucracies to include the military and police, the judiciary and courts, the publicly owned media and education, and the subcentral governments (provinces and municipalities). They have attempted to trace the relationships between state elites and social classes, generally finding that the capitalist class has inordinate influence on, for instance, senior justice personnel. They have suggested that the state functions in crucial ways to maintain and reproduce the existing social order: first, by guaranteeing continued accumulation of profit; secondly, by securing and defending coercively the existing social order; and thirdly, by maintaining its legitimacy (Panitch 1977). That is, those who have political control try to create a climate in which the business sector prospers and builds up capital, while simultaneously placating the lower, working classes who create the wealth, and the middle classes who administer it. Thus the state acts, in the long term, in the interests of the upper class. These three general functions of the state are seen as fulfilled in various concrete institutions throughout the state system, although particular organizations may emphasize a particular function.

There are many debates and theoretical refinements within the broad outlines of this state tradition. Miliband's (1969) "instrumentalist" argument that the elite control an essentially neutral state instrument through its members' occupation of key offices has been severely criticized by Poulantzas' (1973) "structuralism." The latter has convincingly argued that even when anticapitalist parties of the social democratic left (for example, the Canadian New Democratic Party) have captured governments, their actions are structured and limited by the preconditions of capitalism: they must please business, balance the budget, and the like. Further, the state must remain separate from any *particular* capitalist powers if it is to act to preserve capital in *general*. Fundamentally, the state is still seen as closely allied with the dominant economic classes. But even with such evidence as Porter's (1965) and Clement's (1975) suggesting an *instrumentalist* position (that the state is the instrument of the ruling class), a *structuralist* argument has considerable weight in that the state often acts with relative autonomy in ways apparently opposed to immediate or particular capitalist interests. For instance, the passage of legislation regulating corporate criminal activities might be favored by few corporations, though insuring the continuation of the existing order; it thus suggests a more independent role for the state elite.

Therefore, the state is fundamentally seen as co-ordinator of the economic and other sectors of society, various state institutions playing a mediating role. The state thus mitigates conflicts and eases tensions in the potentially explosive contradictions inherent in contemporary capitalist society that are grounded in the imperatively co-ordinated, corporately elitist economy. The relentless search for profits, for instance, perpetuates a continual cycle of boom and bust, inflation and unemployment; and education systems, increasingly attempting to remove the training of the labor force from the private sector, have simultaneously functioned to absorb excess labor force members by extending the length of time spent in compulsory, "basic" education (Lockheart 1975). Various transfer payments have regulated consumer demands despite little change in the relative distribution of income (Johnson 1972; Hamilton and Pinard 1977), while labor law has succeeded in regulating the relations of employment largely in favor of the employers rather than the employees. This involves skilled manipulation as various organs of the state act to sustain business confidence and increase investment, while others attempt to pacify the less fortunate with ideology, and all the accoutrements of the welfare system. In times of social unrest and dissension, attempts at legitimation by the state tend to increase, and much "progressive" legislation is generated. However, coercion typically accompanies legitimation, the balance of the two being determined by the unique history of that particular state.

Poulantzas' earlier work (1973) depicts state activity in a particularly passive mode of guaranteed success, however, implying that the state acts automatically and always successfully. The German capital logic or state derivation theorists (Holloway and Picciotto 1978) have taken up this argument of general preconditions, but criticized both instrumentalist and structuralist views for their "superfunctionalism" (or assumption of automatically successful action) and for their ambiguity in claiming that the state is "relatively autonomous" or independent of capital. They see these problems originating in the unquestioning use of the base-superstructure metaphor, the economistic idea that the economy determines all social life, providing a "base" from which the state and other institutions arise. Instead, they insist on seeing both the economy and the state as equally derivative from capitalist social relations (for example, the extraction of surplus value). They thus advocate analyses of the forms or general types of the historical and logical development of capitalism, developing comparisons across specific contents. For example, just as commodities are all reduced to a common denominator of monetary value, so are delinquencies reduced to common legal penalties.

Despite the increasing sophistication, these formulations are not beyond some theoretical difficulties. Poulantzas' work especially has been criticized for its striking similarities to Talcott Parsons' structural functionalism (1951); that is, accumulation, coercion/order, and legitimacy functions closely resemble adaptive goal attainment and pattern maintenance integrative requisites; without emphasizing inherent conflict there is a tendency towards superfunctionalist, passively guaranteed reproduction of the system; actions and struggles by actors and collectivities seem doomed to systematic irrelevance; the distinction between concrete activity and analytic functions remains problematic (Clarke 1977). We will discuss these problems of functionalism in chapter 3. Offe and Ronge (1975) have argued against such superfunctionalist positions by claiming that the state depends on capital accumulation for its own revenue, effects accumulation indirectly, assumes responsibility for management, and works to secure popular consent. Offe emphasizes that these tasks inherently contradict each other, providing the site of class struggle and the dynamic for social change. In concealing the class nature of the capitalist state, he suggests that the state has selective mechanisms that exclude anticapitalist interests, include procapitalist interests, and yet maintain a class-neutral appearance. One might consider the delinquency legislation in such terms.

Some of the passive, glossing concepts relatively unexamined in the state debate are hotly contested in other circles. "Mode of production" can no longer easily be taken to refer to the economic (Williams 1976). "Determination" of the state by the mode of production "in the last instance" is not straightforward causality: Wright (1977) has suggested that it variously means "limits," "mediation," "selection/exclusive/inclusion," "reproduction of contradictions," "reproduction and nonreproduction," and "transformation." Willis' (1977) study of how working-class children get working-class jobs through their delinquent subcultural resistance will be examined in chapter 5. It brings out these complexities in its excellent ethnographic detail, graphically indicating Althusser's (1971) overly simplistic notion of reproduction.

Epistemologically, the relation of theory to the real world remains ambiguous in many conflict formulations, as it is somewhat unclear how and why particular concrete social institutions fulfill certain functions, and whether or not a reform of a particular institution means it is no longer meeting the same functional requisite. Exactly what events are required to meet a particular functional need (for example, capital accumulation) are not specified, so the theory is most useful in *post hoc* interpretations. Analytic distinctions between ideological and repressive functions of the law and justice system are often vague or absent.

Roger Dale (1982) has suggested a number of important modifications that move these analyses of the state clearly to a mode that gives more attention to human activity. The functions of the state can be reconceived as "core problems" that must be addressed, with various possible outcomes (including the failure to resolve them). These core problems need not be seen as exhaustive of the contemporary state's activities, and they cannot all be specified in advance since they are historically determined. Similarly, solutions cannot be specified in advance, being in part the outcome of active class struggle and human action. In any class state, contradiction and resistance are inevitable, and need to be examined. The state must be recognized as not being monolithic or completely united; it has its own interests, and subunits are often in conflict, doing contradictory things. State policy-makers are not omniscient or infallible, and are capable of making mistakes; in addition, there are usually problems in implementing even "perfect solutions." Since the core problems or needs of the state are contradictory, their solutions continue to be likewise, generating further struggle and change in a dialectical manner. Unlike structural functionalism's "value differentiation" providing a source of social change, capital accumulation is recognizably a material driving force, retaining Marx's emphasis on nonidealist causes.

The coercive and ideological securing of capitalist order is increasingly seen as the state's key task, one that also should be of central interest to criminology (since Althusser's [1971] essay, "Ideology and Ideological State Apparatuses," education has also been deeply interested in such matters). Gross material inequalities, injustice, and the like, are seen as provoking a recurring series of legitimation crises (Habermas 1975). Although the present crises of the state may well be seen as determined in the last instance by capitalist crises of accumulation, most recent theories argue that the proferred resolutions are hammered out on the ideological level, a ground of particular relevance to moral issues and with a considerable latitude available to activistic setting of agendas and terms of debate. This implies that nothing so immutable as economic or demographic necessity decides policy, just as nothing so rational as criminological research does, but rather that resolution is equally determined by popular democratic discourse (Laclau 1977). The political economy emphasis, then, must be complemented at the more activist and cultural levels to understand particular outcomes at any historical conjuncture, as Hall, et al. (1978), and Taylor (1980) so cogently argue. Ideology functions to protect the overall system by hiding and distorting, revealing partial truths, and reconstituting the context of events.

Law and the Legal System

While such analysis of the uses of ideological discourse in popular political debates about moral panics is important, if such theories are to avoid being idealist, more attention must be paid to the concrete operation of the legal system itself. Within a critical perspective it is evident that the justice system in all its branches performs a key mediating function. The police (and also the military, especially in their role as aids to the civil power), though typically from a low-profile, backup position, remain ready and alert to exercise coercive force when predominant interests are threatened. Though liberal democratic ideology regards law as impartial, given the hegemony of the economic elites in other institutional sectors of our society, it surely strains credulity to hold that these same forces refrain from exercising their sway in the legal system.

Most of the best lawyers work in larger firms, serving not justice, but the interests of their corporate clients. The "best" careers run from the proper background through prestigious law schools, to partnership in major downtown law firms, to corporate boards of directors, to legislatures. Overwhelmingly, judges' appointments are contingent on their affiliation with the political party in power. It is fairly clear that the judiciary strongly tend to be members of the economic upper class, and overwhelmingly tend to be conservative in the sense of making judgments that reflect what they deem to be in the best interests of the existing society. They have traditionally been concerned to protect "property" (Miliband 1969, 124–30).

The legitimation of the institutions of justice has been easily accomplished. Their ideals are manifestly those of equality and fairness, legal interpretations seem to be open to jurisprudential debate, and access to the legal system is "guaranteed" by state-sponsored programs of legal assistance, so that all classes can attain impartial "justice." We would argue that this view of liberal democratic fairness is an oversimplification that has been challenged far too seldom, given the predominantly conservative bias of Canadian criminologists. We will follow up on some of the implications of this theory in later chapters.

These notions of law and power are most appropriate for our analysis here. From the beginning of this chapter, we have been examining the legal definition of delinquency, since the criminal law would seem to provide a clear definition as well as harsh sanctions. It has allowed us to argue that a neo-Marxist conflict theory is most useful in helping to understand the origins of the legal notion of delinquency (especially given the centrality of property offences by delinquents) and its linkage with capitalist conditions of production. At this point we must begin to move beyond the exclusive concern we have had with delinquency legislation and examine how control and discipline would seem to be equally structured by the dull daily compulsion of labor as much as by police sanctions.

We will remain committed to examining delinquency in the Canadian historical formation throughout this text, returning especially to Canadian political relations in chapters 6, 7, and 8.

CONCLUSION

We have examined the historical origins of children's situation, and of the concept "juvenile delinquency," and the institutions that were created to deal with troublesome youth. Compulsory schooling, juvenile reform schools, and the Juvenile Delinquents Act (1908) have been analysed as crucial innovations in reducing youth to second-class citizens (Leon 1978, Prentice 1977). The vagueness of the legislation, lack of due process, status offences (applied mainly to working-class youngsters), and the like, have all outweighed the humanitarian potential of the legislation. Juvenile delinquency was thus analysed as the creation of an emergent dominating Canadian capitalist class intent on maintaining control of working-class youth in burgeoning industrial cities.

Returning to Hagan and Leon's criticism of conflict theory, it is not necessary to assume a severely reductionist position of regarding the state as directly responsive to the needs of capital. Juvenile justice policy, and wider legislation regarding the rearing of the young, have been as concerned with the constitution and reproduction of gender and age relations as with reproducing capital relations (Land 1980; Gavigan, 1981; Donzelot, 1979; Fitz 1981a). Thus, though the economic system might best be seen as the creator of youth as a problem population, the intervention of the state to create institutions (schools and reformatories) to deal with it provides a primary example of government attempts to ameliorate contradictions, simultaneously assisting in the accumulation of profit, the engendering of legitimacy, and the exercise of coercion.

It is apparent that such abstract formulations of conflict theory as we have presented are in accord with the most persuasive interpretation of Canadian society in general. Our use of the Canadian political economy tradition casts the study of juvenile delinquency in a new light. Questions have been raised regarding the origins of the legal category, and links suggested to wider and more profound events taking place in Canadian society. Obviously, more historical and legal work is needed for further clarification. Available empirical research materials have nonetheless been set in a wider context of class relations and production modes. The position of young people in advanced capitalist society becomes a salient theoretical and empirical issue. When we turn to control theory and labeling theory explanations of deviant behavior in chapters 3, 4, and 5, they must be incorporated into this wider framework. Finally, the political economy perspective suggests how contemporary contradictions regarding the status of the young have fomented discontent with the existing legislation, and led to reform bills, a topic to which we will turn in chapter 8.

The activistic mode of state theorizing does introduce a whole new set of problems and raises a series of important issues to be addressed in concrete analyses of delinquency.

3

Official Statistics and Anomie Theory: Social Class as the Explanation

. . . warrens of refuge for activities which shun the light of day. The eastern half of the area is a congested area teeming with Anglo-Saxon children.

The people of this area make a very interesting study. It abounds with "people of the shadows." In an area of this kind the comedy and tragedy of life rub elbows every day: all the excesses and weaknesses of the flesh are exhibited. Bay rum and rubbing alcohol addicts make the park their meeting place, and, from time to time, the patrol wagon may be seen loading up. Into this atmosphere at times wanders [sic] the simple emotional people of the Lord, singing hymns, praying and preaching fervently, in the hope of turning a few from their sins. In the eastern half of the area the people are mainly English, Irish and Scotch. These people are sturdy working class people, inclined to be suspicious, many of them decent and clean, others, physically dirty and morally corrupt. Children growing up in an area of this kind are exposed to influences which exaggerate the evils of life. Bad language, gambling, drunkenness, prostitution, are all too familiar. In the limited time at my disposal I discovered seven gangs. Five of these gangs I worked with during the summer . . .

This distict was roughly bounded on the north by Carlton Street, on the east by the River Don, and on the west by Jarvis Street, on the south by the lakefront.

Our worker was in this area during the summer of 1943.

The causes of high delinquency in the Moss Park–Riverdale district were given to me as follows:

1. *Bad housing is a basic fault. Many houses have no bath-tub, and they are dirty and neglected.*
2. *The parents use foul and abusive language in directing the children.*
3. *A tradition has been established in the district for certain forms of delinquency, and a boy has not "graduated" until he has had certain experiences with the police.*
4. *Parents are working and children are locked out of their homes with no place to go. These children hang around stores, etc., and get into trouble . . .*

We were impressed with the fact that it was possible to take groups of boys on extended hikes without the knowledge or consent of their parents. This situation is alarming because it shows a lack of interest on the part of the parents in the activities of their children.

Rogers 1945, 48, 42, 80

OFFICIAL STATISTICS

As was obviously the case in Rogers' research, many people believe that delinquents come from the "wrong side of town." We see them as poor kids from deprived families. Many feel delinquency is caused by a lack of parental care for their offspring, perhaps a lack of discipline, and too much irresponsibility, easy divorce, and poverty. Though we fear it is rapidly increasing, we also tend to see delinquency as an unusual, antisocial event.

In most cases, these beliefs rely on official statistics. Chapter 1 introduced the fact that one of the major sources for our ideas about delinquency consists of official statistics collected by state agencies. Since the early 1800s, police, courts, and correctional institutions have generated annual reports of their activities in dealing with crime and delinquency. These have been demanded by legislatures to justify budget expenditures and to offer some general bureaucratic accountability for the activities of criminal justice agencies. Though there is considerable attempt to standardize reporting across jurisdictions, we must keep in mind that these statistics are products of capitalist state agencies, not "objective facts" beyond particular interests. We will examine these difficulties in more detail at the end of this chapter. Initially, however, we need to examine how state agencies see delinquency; what acts do they object to, what populations do they single out for attention, and the like. What is the nature of official delinquency in the capitalist state? Who were the 35,491 youngsters charged in 1980 in Canada, excluding British Columbia, and what were their 97,264 offences, including British Columbia? (See table 3.1.)

Age

As in Britain (Muncie 1981, 6) and the United States (Greenberg 1977; Empey 1978) most offences are committed by teenagers and young adults between the ages of twelve and twenty-five. Fully one-third to one-half of the "index" or serious criminal code violations (which include murder, rape, wounding, robbery, break and entry, theft, and auto theft) are committed by juveniles, though persons aged seven to sixteen comprise only about 20 percent of the total population, and those in the delinquency-prone age range of twelve to fifteen constitute far less than one-tenth of Canadians (see table 3.2).

Violent offences peak in the early twenties, and property offences in the mid to late teens (Empey 1978, 122 for United States data). In the most frequently occurring type of "real crime" (property offences), juveniles constitute a major portion of "the problem." This is particularly true of thirteen to fifteen year olds who comprise about 80 percent of all juveniles charged.

Trends

Providing more cause for alarm, most official reports suggest crime and delinquency have been getting worse since World War II. Giffen (1979, 47) shows that the official rates for juvenile delinquency have risen dramatically from 273 per 100,000 in 1951–55 to 481 per 100,000, in 1961–65. But he also notes that the 1951–55 rates were very low, having fallen from a high of 532 per 100,000 in 1941–45, which in turn was well above the rate in 1900. Whereas a short-term perspective indicates an increase, long-term ones suggest a cyclical rise and fall.

It can be said that over the past three decades, the justice system has been dealing with greater numbers of juveniles, as well as higher rates (as measured against the general population). As shown in American studies (Empey 1978, 127), as young males have increased as a proportion of the population, crime and delinquency rates have risen (Tepperman 1977, 216). It is noteworthy, however, that since the late 1970s, the number of juvenile delinquents in many jurisdictions has actually dropped, while the adult rate has continued slowly upwards (see figure 3.1). At least in part, this may be attributed to the fact that those who were born during the post–World War II "baby boom" have now passed juvenile age.

TABLE 3.1
Nature of Delinquency Charges by Age and Sex of Child, 1980
(Number of Delinquencies)

Delinquencies	Grand Total	AGE 7	8	9	10	11	12	13	14	15	16	17	Other[1]	SEX[3] Male	Female
Grand Total	97,264	22	85	223	692	1,413	3,786	8,359	17,773	29,651	21,029	11,727	2,504	86,124	11,140
Criminal code violations	72,961	20	85	206	673	1,348	3,500	7,468	15,001	23,182	12,054	8,382	1,042	65,767	7,194
Offensive weapons	919	–	–	1	1	11	33	72	168	302	186	139	6	856	63
Sexual offences	473	–	–	–	2	12	41	56	92	164	63	41	2	445	28
Disorderly conduct	604	–	–	1	–	5	4	27	104	230	135	85	13	514	90
Murder	17	–	–	–	–	–	–	–	6	4	1	6	–	13	4
Murder, attempted	21	–	–	–	–	–	1	–	1	5	6	8	–	18	3
Manslaughter	7	–	–	–	–	–	–	–	3	3	1	–	–	5	2
Automobiles	1,936	–	–	–	–	1	4	16	111	314	709	743	38	1,802	134
Assaults	2,186	–	1	4	14	28	104	178	471	721	352	264	49	1,732	454
Theft over $200	6,116	–	8	5	28	101	220	600	1,260	2,089	1,053	674	80	5,756	362
Theft under $200	13,217	3	20	45	169	375	1,013	1,914	3,170	4,199	1,392	722	195	10,610	2,607
Take motor vehicle	1,452	–	1	1	4	10	43	160	386	596	176	58	17	1,310	142
Theft, other & unspecified	1,212	–	–	2	–	1	20	44	180	341	288	331	5	1,100	112
Robbery	1,418	–	–	1	5	11	23	82	203	332	344	406	11	1,329	89
Break and enter	25,376	12	24	79	262	456	1,158	2,462	5,215	8,230	4,252	2,889	337	24,224	1,152
Possession of stolen goods	5,435	–	5	11	70	87	262	676	1,265	1,950	759	274	76	4,748	687
Forgery & similar crimes	1,365	–	–	–	3	2	23	84	241	403	382	213	14	1,118	247
Fraud	363	–	–	–	–	2	15	55	42	117	52	76	4	306	57
Mischief	6,641	4	18	42	96	194	399	747	1,277	1,878	1,057	801	128	6,195	446
Arson & other fires	437	1	6	10	12	23	36	52	113	98	47	32	7	395	42
Attempts & accessories	1,312	–	–	2	3	13	48	101	297	426	228	176	18	1,251	61
Breach of probation	295	–	–	–	–	4	8	21	72	107	52	22	9	254	41

Other criminal code offences	2,157	–	2	2	4	12	45	121	324	673	519	422	33	1,786	371
Federal statute violations	4,657	–	3	–	1	6	68	193	617	1,471	756	426	1,116	3,932	725
Narcotic control Act	2,221	–	–	–	–	2	13	86	345	918	492	336	29	1,977	244
Possession of narcotics	1,820	–	–	–	–	2	10	75	300	801	367	238	27	1,632	188
Other, unspecified N.C.A.	401	–	–	–	–	–	3	11	45	117	125	98	2	345	56
Food & Drugs Act	133	–	–	–	–	–	1	2	8	52	30	39	1	112	21
Juvenile Delinquents Act	2,182	–	–	2	1	4	50	96	244	459	217	27	1,082	1,751	431
Immorality, vice	168	–	–	–	–	1	29	24	37	35	23	18	1	70	98
Return to court	1,154	–	–	2	1	3	19	71	199	405	192	4	258	900	254
Contribute to delinquency	860	–	–	–	–	–	2	1	8	19	2	5	823	781	79
Other federal statute violations	121	–	–	1	–	–	4	9	20	42	17	24	4	92	29
Provincial statute violations	19,202	2	–	14	17	57	209	683	2,116	4,933	8,128	2,700	343	16,004	3,198
Traffic related offences[2]	10,429	–	–	2	7	18	79	296	913	2,296	5,709	919	190	9,430	999
Liquor related offences	6,890	–	–	1	2	3	43	163	676	1,992	2,240	1,668	102	5,198	1,692
Education related offences	811	2	–	4	6	28	54	127	298	265	5	–	22	445	366
Trespassing	322	–	–	5	2	5	14	31	63	131	33	28	10	269	53
Other provincial statute violations	750	–	–	2	–	3	19	66	166	249	141	85	19	662	88
Municipal by-law violations	444	–	–	–	1	2	9	15	39	65	91	219	3	421	23
Unknown	–	–	–	–	–	–	–	–	–	–	–	–	–	–	–

1. Other includes adults and unknown ages.
2. The offences under the Highway Traffic Act in Manitoba here under-reported for 1980.
3. Included with males are companies charged in Quebec with contributing to delinquency. Companies comprise approximately 0.05% of the number of males indicated in this table.

SOURCE: Canadian Centre for Justice Statistics (1980), *Juvenile Delinquents* (Ottawa: Canadian Centre for Justice Statistics, 1980). Reproduced by permission of the Minister of Supply and Services Canada.

FIGURE 3.1
Number of Adults and Juveniles Charged for
Selected Offences, Canada, 1969–1979ᴾ

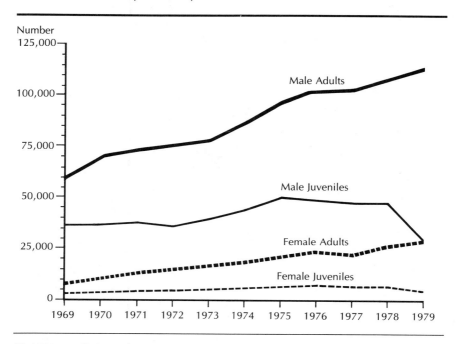

(P) 1969 – preliminary data.

N.B.   – The offences selected for inclusion in this group are murder, manslaughter, attempted murder, rape, wounding, robbery, breaking and entering, theft over/under $200., and motor vehicle theft.
     – This graph depicts absolute numbers, not rates.

■ The number of adult males charged more than doubled between 1969 and 1979.
■ The number of female adults charged more than tripled over the same period.
■ The number of juvenile males charged for these offences increased by 31% between 1969 and 1978, then decreased significantly. At the same time juvenile females exhibited an increase of 128% between 1969 and 1978, then a significant decrease in 1979.
■ The decrease in the number of juveniles charged in 1979 was mainly due to the introduction of the Youth Protection Act in Quebec and to the lowering of the juvenile age limit for females in Alberta.

SOURCE: Solicitor General, *Selected Trends in Canadian Criminal Justice* (Ottawa: Ministry of the Solicitor General, 1979).

Types of Offences

Although the large absolute volume of offences for which juveniles are charged, and their predominance in serious property offences are cause for alarm, closer examination of the types of offences will allay some of this concern, as they are of considerably less seriousness than they would at first appear (see table 3.2).

Juveniles have higher rates than adults for a number of property crimes (for example, break and entry, theft: Statistics Canada 1969). Indeed, some three-quarters of their offences are property crimes. The most frequent incidents consist of ordinary theft (both petty and over $200 – 21 percent of the juvenile charges), break and entry (26 percent), and motor vehicle theft; in these legal categories are such activities as shoplifting, house burglary, and the like (Leblanc, Biron, Fréchette 1981, 11). But the offences committed are usually relatively minor and show little sophistication. These are not the offences of professional thieves. Nor are they usually "serious" or even of a semiprofessional nature (*cf.* West 1979, 1980, 1979-80, 1983). Consequently the actual dollar loss they cause is low.

In general, street property crime that comprises the bulk of officially handled juvenile incidents is far less costly than property crime by either blue- or white-collar (adult) employees. And this employee crime, though more easily prosecuted, is in turn far less costly than organized crime, which in turn seems to be less profitable and more easily countered than corporate crime. Both of these latter types of crime enjoy wide public support when attempts are made to control them, because they provide desired services (for example, gambling), or are unnoticed (for example, monopolies).

The United States governmental President's Commission on Crime (1967) estimated that although some $600 million were lost in ordinary theft of the kind juveniles favor, half that much (some $282 million) was lost in embezzlement and forgery alone (which are almost exclusively adult white-collar crimes, the former usually perpetrated by the individual on his employer). Twice as much ($1.350 billion) was lost in (adult) fraud, and a further $1.4 billion was lost in unreported (usually adult) commercial theft (either shoplifting or employee theft). In short, more money is lost through the betrayal of trust either between adult workers and entrepreneurs, or between adult entrepreneurs, or adult entrepreneurs and customers than is lost in ordinary "predatory" theft (which of course involves adults as well as juveniles).

Besides such lucrative blue- and white-collar crimes, which are restricted to employed or employable adults, American research suggests that far more money is lost illegally in organized crime such as gambling, prostitution, drug dealing, bootlegging of alcohol, loan sharking and

TABLE 3.2
Crime by Offence, 1980

Offences	Adults Charged	Juveniles Charged
■ Homicide – total	487	29
Murder, first degree	186	13
Murder, second degree	248	14
Manslaughter	49	2
Infanticide	4	0
■ Attempted murder – total	657	49
■ Sexual offences – total	4,211	1,374
Rape	1,064	242
Indecent assault – female	1,785	842
Indecent assault – male	441	117
Other sexual offences	921	173
■ Assaults (not indecent) total	40,039	7,792
Wounding	1,185	178
Bodily harm	13,816	1,701
Police	4,928	170
Other peace – public officers	467	40
Other assaults	19,643	5,703
■ Robbery – total	7,375	2,641
Firearms	2,257	710
Other offensive weapons	1,822	658
Other robbery	3,296	1,273
■ Crimes of violence – total	52,769	11,885
■ Breaking & entering – total	46,588	42,175
Business premises	19,738	12,509
Residence	21,177	22,416
Other break & enter	5,673	7,250
■ Theft – motor vehicle – total	18,886	10,064
Automobiles	8,572	6,371
Trucks	1,828	1,751
Motorcycles	703	1,076
Other motor vehicles	773	866
■ Theft – over $200 – total	15,689	6,120
Bicycles	169	271
From motor vehicles	3,491	1,541
Shoplifting	1,942	448
Other thefts over $200	10,087	3,860
■ Theft – $200 & under – total	74,532	48,755
Bicycles	1,172	3,770
From motor vehicles	7,515	4,350
Shoplifting	48,460	26,940
Other thefts $200 & under	17,305	13,695
■ Have stolen goods	14,702	3,894
■ Frauds – total	30,681	3,285
Cheques	18,420	1,796
Credit cards	2,252	215

TABLE 3.2 — *continued*

Offences	Adults Charged	Juveniles Charged
Other frauds	10,009	1,274
■ Property crimes – total	195,078	114,293
■ Prostitution – total	1,529	21
Bawdy House	668	6
Procuring	78	8
Other prostitution	783	7
■ Gaming and betting – total	3,184	16
Betting house	117	0
Gaming house	2,529	8
Other gaming & betting offences	538	8
■ Offensive weapons – total	9,567	1,601
Explosives	113	40
Prohibited weapons	1,490	206
Restricted weapons	1,240	101
Other offensive weapons	6,724	1,254
■ Other Criminal Code – total[1]	113,140	33,612
Arson	1,463	1,443
Bail violations	26,004	111
Counterfeiting currency	112	30
Disturb the peace	16,681	3,160
Escape custody	1,711	331
Indecent acts	2,096	708
Kidnapping	369	67
Public morals	213	23
Obstruct public peace officer	5,725	139
Prisoner unlawfully at large	1,658	691
Trespass at night	1,553	991
Wilful damage – private	20,280	16,582
Wilful damage – public	5,160	4,353
Other Criminal Code offences	30,115	4,883
■ Other crimes – total	127,420	35,250
■ Criminal code – total	375,267	161,428
■ Heroin – total	541	12
Possession	276	9
Trafficking	244	3
Importation	21	0
■ Cocaine – total	1,192	22
Possession	599	17
Trafficking	557	5
Importation	36	0
■ Other drugs – total	1,258	113
Possession	853	98
Trafficking	397	15
Importation	8	0
■ Cannabis – total	52,599	4,137

(Continued on next page)

TABLE 3.2 — *continued*

Offences	Adults Charged	Juveniles Charged
Possession	44,464	3,683
Trafficking	7,719	441
Importation	152	1
Cultivation	264	12
■ Controlled drugs – total	548	12
■ Restricted drugs – total	3,093	196
Possession	1,561	131
Trafficking	1,532	65
■ Other federal statutes – total[1]	16,975	2,457
Bankruptcy Act	107	0
Canada Shipping Act	2,151	28
Customs Act	287	2
Excise Act	84	1
Immigration Act	1,908	19
Juvenile Delinquent Act	803	1,645
Other federal statutes offences	11,635	762
■ Provincial statutes – total[1]	342,641	21,666
Liquor Act	299,391	13,682
Securities Act	108	18
Other provincial statutes	43,142	7,966
■ Municipal by-laws – total[1]	27,756	2,420
■ All offences – total	821,870	192,463

1. Excluding traffic offences.

SOURCE: Revised from Statistics Canada (1980), *Crime and Traffic Enforcement Statistics* (Ottawa: Statistics Canada). Reproduced by permission of the Minister of Supply and Service Canada.

protection racketeering. It is rare for juveniles to be directly involved in any of these activities, though occasionally the mere presence of juveniles in such underworld vice causes great public reaction out of all proportion to the circumstances (see Ng [1981], the Jaques case in chapter 1). Furthermore, it would seem that the most lucrative type of property offences consist of corporate crimes such as fraud, illegal monopolies, misrepresentative advertising, price-fixing, fee-splitting, and kickbacks, failure to maintain safety regulations, and the like (McCaghy 1976, 205). Goff and Reasons (1978) point out that more than half of the largest Canadian corporations are recidivistically delinquent, with the fifty largest averaging 3.2 convictions each. A similar degree of recidivism by juveniles would certainly bring them severe legal sanctions.

Turning to the other major type of offence, the overall juvenile rate for violence is only about one-fortieth of their property crime rate. Only some 4 percent of all juvenile charges concern violence, well under the 20 percent of the overall population which is of juvenile age. It is noteworthy that despite the myths and fears of juvenile gangs and violence, disproportionately few of the most serious types of violence (murders, aggravated assaults, or rapes) are committed by juveniles. Given the rapidly increasing official rates of physical child abuse, it is possible that children are more often victims than victimizers. The violent crimes teens do commit are comparatively rare (though occasionally undeniably serious) and less likely to occur between strangers than between workers and employers, or between acquaintances, friends, neighbors, relatives, or family members. It, however, fades to insignificance compared with corporate and state violence. In *Assault on the Worker*, Reasons et al. (1981) argue that the death rate from industrial accidents outnumbers murders by three to one, with Canadian work fatalities among the world's highest. They also suggest that work-related injuries outnumber criminal assaults.

In terms of threat to human life, however, it is becoming increasingly clear that certan nations in the nuclear arms race are far more dangerous than all the adjudged murderers combined, let alone all the delinquents. It is estimated a hydrogen bomb explosion over Toronto would kill some 600 thousand people and horribly injure some 800 thousand more (*Toronto Star* May 4, 1982).

In general, many of the incidents of police contact with juveniles would seem to be minor, as some American studies indicate more than half are settled out of court (Empey 1978, 117–41, 409–40; Krisberg and Austin 1978, 81). Leblanc (1975, 113) reports that over half the police arrests in his Montreal research were for "rebellious" delinquency (or status offences), a figure very close to the 43 percent Hogarth (1974) found among North Toronto youth contacted by the police. Hogarth further found that only half of the remaining youngsters were actually charged and brought to court.

The fact that the courts send so few juveniles away from home further suggests that they consider most of their offences not to be a serious threat to society. Of 97,264 juvenile charges, only 73,098 were sustained as delinquency, and of these, only 6,967 resulted in youngsters being incarcerated. Most of these delinquent episodes are, in fact, of a nuisance nature, though encouraging neighborhood gossip and occupying local youth bureau time.

It is noteworthy that the drug use (of marijuana, narcotics, and the like) for which teens are universally pilloried is less officially noted than alcohol.

Finally, status offences for which only juveniles can be charged (for instance, truancy, "sexual immorality or any other vice," and such) comprise some 10 to 15 percent of the total number of charges. A disproportionate number of youngsters who are incarcerated (especially girls) have traditionally been charged with such offences (Geller 1980; Weiler 1978).

Sex

Official statistics show far more males than females coming to police attention; the ratio in various studies ranges from about five to ten to one. This ratio has been gradually decreasing over the last few decades (Gagnon and Biron 1979, 106). Partly because of the comparatively low base rate, the increase in female delinquency has outstripped that in males. Overall, girls are generally involved in the same types of offences as boys; property offences predominate, violence is much more rare, and status offences fall in between. There are nonetheless two areas of difference; girls are charged with violence proportionately less frequently, and proportionately much more frequently charged with sexual offences or status offences ("sexual immorality or any other vice," or the like). As well, juvenile female offenders are differently processed in the juvenile justice system. Any aberrant sexual behavior warrants particular attention and more severe consequences. In contrast, economic offences are dealt with lightly. Gagnon and Biron (1979, 110) have found generally that Quebec girls are dealt with more harshly as they progress through the juvenile justice system; whereas the arrest ratio to males is 5.7:1, it decreases to 4.4:1 judged delinquent, and 4:1 institutionalized. Furthermore, in their research, 86 percent of the females were incarcerated for "their own protection" (a euphemism for sex and status offences) compared with only 30 percent of the boys. Weiler (1978) has found similar results in Ontario; some two-thirds to three-quarters of the girls incarcerated have been imprisoned for sexual or "status" offences. Smart (1976) and Campbell (1981, 7) cite similar figures for both Britain and the United States (see Giffen 1979, 44 for Canada). It would seem, then, that official delinquency among girls is considerably less than among boys, and girls deemed to be seriously misbehaving are overwhelmingly involved in sexual delinquency.

Race and Ethnicity

From some American research (Shaw and McKay 1942), there is also a belief that ethnic minorities cause more crime through being in "culture conflict." Indeed, until the 1930s, Irish immigrants in Canada had the highest adult crime rate of identified ethnic groups (Tepperman 1977, 193; Hardy 1977). Yet since then, native-born Canadians have had the highest; as ethnic immigrants have become assimilated, their patterns more closely approximate Canadians (Ribordy 1975). For 1951 to 1961, in Giffen's (1979) research, "children with Canadian-born fathers have come to have a much higher probability of being officially labeled as delinquent than those with foreign-born parents."

Although Toronto, Montreal, and other cities indicate the beginnings of "black crime" as an issue (Armogan 1976; Calliste 1980), black occupancy of American mythology as being a crime-prone racial/ethnic group, or the similar Irish occupancy of British mythology, has found the equivalent Canadian racial stereotype focussing on native Indians and Metis (Lautt 1979). They are highly concentrated, with 44 percent living in the Prairies, 21 percent in Ontario, and 18 percent in British Columbia; local neighborhood segregation is even more distinct, with natives often found in declining rural areas. These groups have frequently been segregated on poor reservations, very marginalized within the Canadian social formation, and in this century they have begun to expand in population again. In 1974, for instance, 55 percent of Saskatchewan natives were under 16, compared with only 30 percent of non-Indians. Increasingly, many of these young people have left their rural birthplaces and immigrated to the poorer sections of Western Canadian cities, often unprepared for skilled employment, and discriminated against (Nagler 1975). Such economic difficulties strain family relations, often result in abysmal housing, undermine attempts at sustaining native culture, and so on. Traditional informal education of the young has been systematically undermined by compulsory attendance at residential schools.

The Law Reform Commission report on *The Native Offender and the Law* (1974) noted the unusually high contact of adult natives with the justice system. In British Columbia, Alberta, Saskatchewan, and Manitoba, 14 to 21 percent, 23 to 34 percent, 50 to 60 percent and 40 to 50 percent, respectively, of adult inmates in provincial institutions have been native, compared with native populations of 5 percent, 5 percent, $12^1/_2$ percent and $12^1/_2$ percent respectively. In Saskatchewan, 90 percent of women prisoners have been natives. Most of the offences involve minor crimes (especially involving liquor and vehicles legislation, or nonpayment of fines). Using multivariate analysis of Alberta data, Hagan (1974a, b, c) has argued that natives are not discriminated against regarding alteration of the charge, retention of defence counsel, or initial plea, although he has expressed concern for their disproportionate numbers and problems (1974a, 1977). Wynne and Harnagel (1975) have found that natives have less access to plea bargaining, and Cockerill (1975) has found they are more likely to become recidivists after probation.

All of the above data pertains to adult natives; because of the dearth of information on juvenile native offenders, one must largely speculate from it for the young. But some initial analyses suggest the juvenile rate for youngsters before the court is 353 per 100 thousand compared with 128 per 100 thousand for whites (Havemann 1981). Their generally depressed social situation, of course, would drastically increase the likelihood of native families being deemed inadequate for child rearing.

Social Class

Probably no belief about crime and delinquency is more widely held than that delinquents are inordinately from the working class. Among adults, those with the least education and in the least prestigious occupations are more frequently convicted (Bell-Rowbotham and Boydell 1972). It makes some sort of common sense that the poor would be more tempted to steal, or that economically caused frustrations would more frequently result in violence among the working class. Further, the ethnic and racial minorities discussed above are predominately in the lower ranks of society.

In regard to delinquency also, middle-class youngsters are considerably less likely to be formally arrested, charged, found delinquent in court, or removed from home to a training school or similar facility than working-class youngsters. In his study of Toronto teens, Byles (1969) found that police arrest was five times more likely for working-class than middle-class youngsters; he also reported that about 90 percent of Ontario training school inmates were from working-class backgrounds. Official delinquency is, then, largely a working-class phenomenon.

Urban-Rural Differences and Neighborhood

Regarding urbanization, it is popularly believed that rural settings promote health and conformity, but that cities breed crime. For adults, Ontario (n.d. [1981?]) figures reveal robbery, prostitution, and gaming and betting are more likely in large cities, and large thefts and drug usage somewhat more prominent, but the overall crime rate is slightly higher in small towns and villages (14,209.3) compared with small (11,233.6) or large (10,267.0) cities (Ontario Government n.d. [1981?]). Given that there is a disproportionately smaller number of police per population in larger centres, this finding is all the more remarkable.

Giffen's (1979) analysis using earlier data does suggest more urban crime than rural for adults, but the same rates for juveniles.

There are, however, considerable variations in the official rates of charging juveniles between cities, with ranges from 3.5 to 6.0 per 1,000 (Conly 1977; Hackler 1978). Furthermore, in the classic American research of Shaw and McKay (1942) there are sharp differences between city neighborhoods, with some ethnic working-class communities having much higher official crime rates (compared to white, Anglo-Saxon, protestant, middle-class suburbs).

The industrial revolution solidified notions that particular neighborhoods or communities were crime-prone, which condition city planners and urbanologists sought to eradicate by constructing wide thoroughfares, implementing urban renewal projects, establishing settlement house systems, and the like. Such marginal communities not only continue to exist in the contemporary third world, but also in more developed Western nations such as Britain and Canada. Many neighborhoods, especially public housing ones with large welfare and working-class populations, can be seen as contemporary descendants of the London criminal rookeries. The present world recession has resulted in falling incomes, higher unemployment, and reduced social services in such neighborhoods. A tradition of early school leaving, early marriage, unskilled work, and large families successfully produces a marginal "reserve army of labor," with an integral culture of its own (Mann 1968). There is tension between agencies of social control (welfare, schools, police, and the like) and the local value system, which is depicted as supporting petty crime, pub life, and same-sex or age-peer friendship groups, as well as extended kinship. Broken marriages and teenage gangs seem to support precocious adult-like behavior (for example, early sexual activity) and more serious delinquency.

On the other hand, some depictions suggest a disordered, demoralized noncommunity. Peter McLaren's best-selling *Cries From the Corridor* (1980) claims to realistically depict the Jane-Finch corridor in suburban Metro Toronto as a hotbed of delinquency. More relevant to our concerns here, McLaren's delinquents seem to exist in a disorganized wasteland of highrise public housing (West 1982). There are no friendly or even unfriendly neighborhood policemen, local candy-store owners, dour, hardworking, single-parent welfare mothers, gruff senior citizens, baseball-organizing dads, or the like. For McLaren, any potentially romantic (though unsanctioned) parental love affairs are lurid lust, a few pleasant, socially consumed beers between neighbors always indicate incipient if not full-blown alcoholism. McLaren rather unself-consciously adopts a standard pathological view of neighborhood delinquency, adding to the traditional analysis of broken homes and undeserving poor, hints of racism, sexism, immigration, child abuse, inadequate school programs, and urban planning. McLaren sees the working-class neighborhood as not only different, but deficient and pathological.

Hagan, Gillis, and Chan (1980) have empirically investigated some of these issues in a middle-sized eastern Canadian city/suburb. They argue that being subject to organizational work pressures, police respond to the extra citizen requests and complaints from working-class communities (Hogarth 1974) by eventually themselves taking the initiative in such "offensible spaces." They deploy more officers where they expect complaints. These police expectations are formed in part on the basis of perceived socioeconomic status, housing density, and the like. Partly as a result, working-class areas of towns consistently tend to have higher arrest rates than middle-class areas (Chimbos 1973; Nease 1968). Consistent with many American studies, Leblanc (1975) and his associates have reported police arrest rates in Francophone Montreal working-class neighborhoods as double that in middle-class neighborhoods (19.39 percent versus 10.83 percent), though self-report delinquency was almost the same (91.2 percent versus 86.75 percent).

Family

The commonsensical hunch that family troubles might adversely affect children's behavior is transformed in popular mythology into the notion that divorce and broken homes cause delinquency. It is the case that youngsters in training schools are more often than not from broken homes (Byles 1969). Rising divorce rates, working mothers, and the like have coincided with increases in official delinquency rates, and thereby further increased fears. Tightened children's aid and welfare budgets heighten anxiety that society may not be able to bolster the flagging family. In a review of the literature largely based on studies of official Canadian delinquents, Fischer and Martin (1979) conclude that "broken homes [are] associated with high delinquency if family disruption is associated with the separation." They go on to claim that high delinquency is associated with low parental supervision, low family cohesiveness, and high parental conflict; large family size; infrequent family recreation; high family criminality; and low social class. But these negative effects disappeared with higher intelligence levels, family stability, and noncriminal behavior of parents. More ambiguously, just the right amount of discipline, money allowance, freedom, and responsibility seem to be required; too much or too little are equally disastrous.

There is some irony here, however. Regarding adults, marriage is associated with *less* criminality. The lower-class males who figure so predominantly in adult statistics, "settle down" noticeably when they gain a spouse (West 1980a), even though many of these marriages fail, and hence may be expected to produce delinquents.

School Failure

Given the above relationships between oppressed ethnic membership, disadvantaged neighborhood, low social class, family disorganization, and delinquency, it is not surprising that the latter is also related to educational difficulties. School failure correlates with official delinquency in some American research as highly as .70 (Empey and Lubeck 1971, 65, 77, 82; Polk and Schafer 1972, 44, 67, 111, 171). Even when reading scores, IQ, sex, age, parental socioeconomic status, school neighborhood, and mother's aspirations are controlled, the correlation remains quite high in the .30 to .48 range (Rhodes and Reiss 1969, 19). Canadian adults with low educational achievement have higher official crime rates (Bell-Rowbotham and Boydell 1972, 113). It has also long been known that delinquents tend to be about a year behind their non-incarcerated age-mates in school grades (Statistics Canada 1969a).

Peer Group Relations

Shaw and McKay (1942) were among the first to emphasize that most youngsters are arrested while with others. From this fact, many (for example, Cohen 1955) have argued that delinquency has an undeniable group basis, more specifically, that it centers on gang affiliations.

SUMMARY

The official statistics that we have just reviewed give us a particular picture of the nature of crime and delinquency. Juveniles and young adults seem to be highly likely to misbehave; juveniles are particularly prone to property offences, which make up about three-quarters of their total misdemeanors. There have been dramatic increases since World War II, though the fifties seem to be a low point in the cyclical rise and fall when a longer-term perspective is adopted. Male delinquents greatly outnumber females, though the gap is slowly closing. Ethnic minorities, such as Canadian Indians, seem inordinately delinquent. Working-class youngsters living in urban slum neighborhoods or public housing projects, and those from disorganized families, are particularly likely to become delinquent. Finally, those who fail in school tend to be more delinquent. How might these official facts be explained?

ANOMIE AND STRAIN THEORIES

One of the most important theories of the sociological tradition has attempted to explain such facts as derived from official statistics. The American, Robert Merton first gave it a sophisticated elaboration in 1938 (revised in Merton 1968), borrowing the term "anomie" (or "normlessness") from Emile Durkheim's earlier work on suicide (1897). (We will argue in the next chapter, however, that Durkheim's theory is an early version of control theory.)

Anomie theory is one of sociology's most elegant explanations of delinquency, clearly rejecting psychological approaches in favor of considering social factors as causes. It asks what background factors engender deviance. As such, it has been a favorite theory among sociologists for decades. Furthermore it has been elaborated to explain delinquency in

TABLE 3.3
Merton's Paradigm

Type	Goals	Means
Conformist	+	+
Innovator	+	−
Ritualist	−	+
Retreatist	−	−
Rebel	∓	∓

SOURCE: R.K. Merton, *Social Theory and Social Structure* (New York: Free Press/Macmillan, 1968).

particular, and has hence been fundamental to the formulation of innumerable research projects, especially focussing on adolescent boys.

Although I will argue that the mainline anomie tradition derived from Merton's work is fundamentally flawed, it is an important theory to consider. Its widespread popularity has given it much influence in social policy-making and justice practices; as well, it will serve to illustrate some problems and possibilities of testing theories with empirical data.

Anomie Theories

Merton argued that in democratic societies, all citizens were socialized to aspire to common goals (such as economic success), even though different means were available for different class and ethnic groups to reach such goals. For those with favorable means, conformity remained attractive. People in those groups with a structural disadvantage, however, experienced a disjunction of goals and means (were "anomic"). (See table 3.3.) If they retained a commitment to legitimate goals without having adequate means, they might innovate means of attaining success; and while some of these might be legal (for example, inventions), others (such as making gains by fraud) would be illegal. Merton saw this category of the structurally disadvantaged as generating most of the criminals. Others, however, could be equally "deviant" (in an abstract, sociological sense) if they remained normative in their behavior but abandoned the goal of economic success; Merton cites petty bureaucrats as examples of such ritualists. Still others, having abandoned both means and ends, become retreatists, such as alcoholics and drug users. Finally, some not only abandon society's goals and means, but rebel and substitute others – "born-again" religious sects would be examples. In all cases, behavior is explained by one's position in the social structure, regardless of one's personality.

In 1955, in his book *Delinquent Boys*, Albert Cohen adapted Merton's ideas to try to specifically explain delinquent behavior. Conceding that

Merton's theory was useful for explaining adult crime, Cohen regarded it as inadequate to explain the peculiar nature of much juvenile delinquency. Whereas adults generally steal for gain, he argued, much delinquency is economically senseless behavior, consisting of vandalism, theft of petty items that are then abandoned, malicious attacks on persons, or frequent unruliness (such as talking back to teachers or parents). Cohen cites official statistics to argue that such hedonistic, malicious, negativistic, and nonutilitarian delinquency was concentrated in the working-class male adolescent population. Furthermore, such misbehavior seemed centered in urban street gangs.

Basically Cohen took Merton's argument that our society prescribes a general goal of economic success for all males, while structurally reducing the chances of reaching that goal for many. (He gives females little attention, saying they depend on marriage to successful males for their status.) But Cohen then argues that the educational system is the key to acquiring the academic credentials required for success. Working-class homes, however, produce boys unprepared for successful achievement in schools run by and for the middle class; they therefore suffer a loss of status. Some such children resent this injustice and rebel, rejecting the values of the teachers who rejected them. They undergo a psychological reaction, adopting values (for example, hedonism, negativism, maliciousness) that are antithetical to middle-class values (especially those of respecting property), and this leads to law-breaking acts. Grouping together in gangs for support, these youths socialize younger boys into this self-perpetuating delinquent subculture. Initially, this theory seems a plausible account of many of "the facts." Working-class children do experience more difficulty in schools, and are disproportionately arrested and incarcerated for delinquency (Byles 1969, 230; Statistics Canada 1969, 56). Populations with low educational achievement have the highest official crime rates (Bell-Rowbotham and Boydell 1972, 113). Many acts by gangs seem senseless and rebellious.

Basing their work in New York and Boston, Cloward and Ohlin (1960) suggested a further variation, whereby they argued that different types of delinquent subcultures developed in different neighborhood and ethnic contexts, according to the availability of illegal as well as legal opportunities. Older immigrant and ethnic groups (for example, Italians) were seen as more integrated across generations, and able to offer academically unsuccessful youth illegitimate opportunities in rackets and organized crime. Newer, unintegrated groups (for example, blacks and Puerto Ricans) could not offer such illegitimate opportunities, and their nonacademic youth were thus left with only intergang conflict as a means to establish prestige. Finally, some individual youths who were academically unsuccessful also lacked skills to succeed in either of these deviant activities, and hence retreated into drug use and deviant sexuality. Criminality, "bopping" or conflict, and retreatists gangs and sub-cultures originated in these ways.

These different versions of anomie theory have a number of features in common. They all assume a fundamental consensus in society concerning legitimate goals and means. They all see socially structured pressures or strains generating deviant behavior, regardless of individual psychology. They also assume that delinquency or deviance is non-problematically defined and measured; they are both apolitical and ahistorical. Finally, they are all concerned with relating the officially reported rates of delinquency to social structural differences.

Anomie theories have had significant social impact in programs to eliminate delinquency and crime, especially during the 1960s in the United States in the "War on Poverty" (Maris and Rein 1972; Moynihan 1970). But various Canadian programs invoke the same logic to defend preschool headstart programs, remedial educational plans for delinquents, job-creation plans aimed at the young working-class unemployed, use of detached youth workers to deal with street gangs, community organization projects, and the like. Many welfare state programs (for example, unemployment insurance, family allowances, and the like) attempt to maintain a "floor" to help equalize chances. Such efforts attempt to improve the "opportunity structure" by enhancing the chances for working-class youngsters to succeed (at school and employment).

Leyton's Triple Delinquency

Elliott Leyton's *The Myth of Delinquency: An Anatomy of Juvenile Nihilism* (1979) is a popular Canadian study that can be seen as fitting partly within the anomie tradition, though it also invokes notions of psychological strain. It is an exploratory field study, a welcome contribution on a topic still almost barren of any Canadian material. Leyton focuses on those youngsters who are incarcerated for what he terms typical, nihilistic, "senseless" offences: break and entry, theft, malicious damage, assault, mischief, and unmanageability. He wants to explicitly ignore the more threatening, but much less frequent offences such as murder and robbery, and also ignore the more frequent but perhaps more straightforwardly understandable types of rational property crime. He thus follows in the esteemed tradition of Albert Cohen in trying to understand the specifically juvenile aspects of delinquent obstreperousness that so irritate adults: why do kids often do such "damn fool" things?

On the basis of five months of participant observation in a Maritime training school, examination of official dossiers, and extended in-depth interviews with parents and thirty-two youngsters, Leyton provides us with excellent detailed descriptive case studies of eight delinquents. He finds that the vast majority of such youngsters come from marginally employed, low-income, or welfare families. The youngsters had parents who were sometimes forced to marry because of pregnancy, and who rejected them in such ways as partitioning their room from the family home, threatening to send them away, and the like. Most of the youngsters had been on probation; all got into further trouble. Their delinquencies had a random, senseless quality: acts of petty theft and vandalism were followed by drug and alcohol abuse, promiscuity, unmanageability, and running away from custody. The youngsters often "tried" to get caught by leaving a trail of evidence.

Sandwiching the case studies are introductory and concluding chapters that cursorily review and incorporate parts of some of the major theories of delinquency, such as Cohen's. Leyton agrees that society in general is responsible for creating an underclass suffering from poverty and unemployment. Furthermore, he agrees, that society humiliates such people, making them feel worthless and frustrated. But he then elaborates a familial-psychological dimension, arguing that some such parents take out their frustration on one or more of their offspring, neurotically blaming them for their personal and family troubles. He thus sees delinquent acts as evidence of neglect or rejection by parents. Such scapegoat youngsters come to believe their parents' assessment that they are worthless and evil. Their random and bizarre acts of delinquency are symbolic messages expressing their grief and rage at being rejected. Leyton thus develops an interesting theory of "triple delinquency," which he proposes to account for his material. Society is seen as wronging its underclass, underclass parents as rejecting their offspring, and the latter completing the cycle by offending society in delinquently encoded, desperate attempts to reassert their claims to familial position and identity.

Leyton's policy recommendations flow in part from his theory. He does not pursue a strong class analysis, and offers nothing of substance to correct the first delinquency of society towards its underclass. Instead, he suggests compulsory family counseling to assist such families in avoiding mistreatment of their children, and assistance to youngsters in sorting out their futures. He advocates increased resources for such counseling, and the relaxing of legal restrictions for removing children from unsalvageable homes.

CRITICISMS
Theoretic and Definitional
A number of theoretical aspects of anomie theory have been criticized. Anomie theorists have found it difficult if not impossible to specify the

concrete cultural goals and culturally approved means that are shared by all members of contemporary complex societies. Kitchener Mennonites, Bay Street businessmen, Newfoundland nuns, Quebecois separatists, Peace River homesteaders, Déné hunters, and Vancouver social workers can hardly be seen as sharing a common goal of economic success – nor can their children. The amalgamation of different cultural groups in contemporary nation states specifically provides for interaction without consensus; "subterranean" values abound, varying by situation and status/role (Matza 1964a). Some institutions (for instance, schools) may formally demand accountability of all members to common goals (for instance, academic achievement), but such institutionalization of goals does not imply that all members *themselves* aspire to the goals. Competing goals (such as religious ones, family considerations, or personal happiness) are often held as dearly as wealth or academic success. Furthermore, many people are acculturated directly into these alternative value orientations, and thus might never experience any strain if they did not become economically successful. It is unclear that all delinquent youth would have to go through the school-failure experiences mentioned by Cohen (1955) and Cloward and Ohlin (1960); it is equally conceivable that younger boys could be socialized directly into delinquency through simple imitating their previously failed older brothers or peers. The theory also errs in assuming that personal, subcultural values directly account for behavior; it is quite clearly deterministic. The particular boundaries of any subculture are unclear and perhaps unspecifiable.

Other potential questions are ignored: the origins of definitions of deviance, power relations around enforcement, and the situations of girls are all basically ignored. This easily assumes a conservative ideological bent, implying that the system of reward for cultural conformity is fair, if only the means were equally distributed. It ignores questions of the origins of such unequal opportunity.

These ideological issues become particularly acute regarding conceptualization and definition. As discussed in chapter 1, "delinquency" may refer to "official" delinquency, illegal acts reported to the police. Official delinquency is of social concern not only because it is the subject of much lay discussion, but also because it involves "delinquents," those youths apprehended, charged, found guilt in court, and perhaps incarcerated. But such a definition cannot be equated with any and all acts committed that contravene the legal statutes and are grounds for police action, whether or not they are reported to police and become the subject of court trials. For most delinquent acts are not reported, and hence most of those who commit such acts never become official delinquents. Yet actual behavior is obviously of substantial concern to the anomie theorists. Confusing official delinquency with delinquent behavior is a serious flaw in anomie theory. The factors that may be seen as "causing" a person to commit a delinquency are likely to differ from those that "cause" one's apprehension by the police, although the latter include the former (with the exception of "bum rap" cases, where a person is convicted although not having committed a misdemeanor). Collecting information on official delinquency is much easier, as one has only to refer to the police records; indeed these records were all that were available to the early anomie theorists. Even granting this, surely it is questionable to assume that a single unified theory could explain behavior as diverse as vandalism, drug use, and theft just because they are all labeled "delinquency."

Methodological Criticisms: Problems with Official Statistics

Important as the above questions are, the central difficulties encountered by anomie theories concern their relatively naïve use of official statistics. Since official delinquency statistics report on events (and to some extent young persons) after the fact, they are not particularly good at revealing how delinquencies are carried out, or the victim's circumstances. Because the official agencies gathering the facts are usually also prosecuting delinquents, the latter are likely to be hostile towards them; and we can only gain a limited amount of knowledge of what types of youngsters commit delinquencies. Other than for murder, only some 20 percent (for petty theft) to 50 percent of incidents known to the police are cleared by charges being laid; official statistics provide no data on the perpetrators of most crime! Some rather peculiar and unexplained legal definitions are invoked.

Juvenile rates regarding incarcerations cause confusion in delinquency and neglect cases. Giffen (1979, 31) also notes that adults' cases are recorded only if they go to court and are convicted, whereas juveniles are analyzed even if there is no finding of delinquency! (Manitoba statistics have even included nonjudicial and no-police-contact cases for juveniles.) Legislative amendments (such as Quebec's introduction of the Youth Protection Act, 1979) result in radical changes in official rates, clearly representing changed classification of juvenile behavior rather than behavioral change itself. The new Canadian Young Offenders Act will similarly result in a decrease in official delinquency of some 10 to 15 percent as status offences are eliminated from consideration. Accepting the official statistics then, assumes and works within legal definitions extant under the present power structure. Incidents reported and known to the police are focussed upon, rather than social harm or monetary loss.

There are, however, even more serious problems around the issues of nonreporting. Delinquent behavior is intrinsically behavior that perpetrators generally would like to keep hidden. Perhaps more surprisingly, many victims also fail to report delinquencies to the police. In America, Skogan (1975, 60) reports that 60 percent of all robbery, 56 percent of all larceny, and 40 percent of all burglary is not reported to police. Teevan (1978), and Evans and Leger (1978) report similar figures for Canada.

As mentioned above, even when crimes or delinquencies are reported to the police, only about 25 to 50 percent are cleared by charges being laid; the rest remain unsolved. Furthermore, the police often decide not to lay a charge (or even record the incident), especially in juvenile cases. Hackler's (1978) and Conly's (1977b) preliminary comparisons of charge rates in various Canadian cities indicate anywhere from 4 to 82 percent of juveniles are handled informally without charge.

Many persons charged, of course, are not found delinquent in court. Some plead not guilty and defend themselves successfully. Even more importantly in juvenile court, charges are not infrequently dropped when social or treatment provisions are worked out to the satisfaction of police, Crown prosecutors, and judges. Furthermore, especially given the relatively minor nature of many delinquencies, judges often conclude a case with a *sine die* adjournment (literally, an adjournment "without a day" set for renewing the hearing) to avoid giving youngsters official records as delinquents. In Canadian courts in 1980, only about three-quarters of youngsters charged were found delinquent. Furthermore, of course, very few of those found delinquent are sent to training schools or reformatories (usually around 10 percent).

As a result of all this, the criminal justice system can be viewed as a large funnel, with many acts occurring in the wider society, but very few persons getting to the narrow end of the funnel. Very different official "pictures" of crime emerge depending upon where one slices into this funnel. For adults and juveniles, a Solicitor General report (1979) estimates that only 1/5 of all persons committing an offense are contacted by the police; 1/15 of all actual offenders are charged (1/3 of all contacted offenders); 1/20 of all actual offenders are convicted (3/4 of the persons charged); and 1/600 of all actual offenders are sentenced to incarceration (1/30 of persons convicted).

American research (Empey 1978, 150) similarly indicates that nine out of ten illegal acts (especially the more frequent minor ones) either go undetected or unacted upon by anyone in authority. Even more serious incidents are only likely to be detected in 80 percent of the cases. Such data strongly suggest the possibility that any increase in official rates are less likely to represent more actual delinquency and more likely to represent a change in reactive behavior.

At what point in such a legal process can one take the definition to be authoritative: when someone commits an act that would be deemed illegal if he or she were caught (even though they were not)? (Self-report questionnaires asking people to check off illegal or deviant acts they have performed or been subject to are based on this.) When victims or witnesses complain to police, and the latter record an incident? (But only about half of all property offences recognized by victims are so reported.) When police actually charge someone? (But only about one-quarter of offences known to police are so cleared.) When the case comes to court? Only when a guilty finding is made? (Even though some persons "get off" on "technicalities," or even though many of the cases in juvenile court have been adjourned *sine die*, without a day set to resume the hearing of case for a finding and disposition, as a warning was all the judge deemed appropriate?) Or are the "real delinquents" only those who are finally incarcerated, even though they represent only a tiny fraction of all those who commit delinquency?

One must recognize that the youngsters given official attention by the police and courts constitute a rather peculiar subset of all those who commit delinquencies. Other measures of delinquency, such as self-reports, suggest that working-class youngsters, those from broken homes, or from ethnic minority groups, with different childrearing practices, or those youngsters from "defiant" subcultural groups, or who are individually insubordinate, or (if a girl) sexually precocious, may be inordinately singled out for attention. Fully to understand official delinquency, then, one must also examine how the juvenile justice system constructs it as much as youngsters do. Official delinquents do not represent completely and without bias all delinquents.

Empirical Refutation

The most crucial difficulties with anomie theories such as Cohen's have resulted from refuting data about the nature of delinquent behavior. In the next chapter we will discuss in detail some of the self-report studies of delinquency conducted over the last two and a half decades, their findings, and also problems with them. For now, however, we will assume that the self-report data collected on the basis of the criticism of official statistics developed above is more accurate. Returning to Cohen's theory, the central relationship that he claimed between lower social-class origins and delinquent behavior does not hold, or holds only weakly. Only official police statistics indicate a strong ratio between lower- and middle-class delinquency (of approximately 5:1). Self-report surveys indicate that police records are subject to strong biases because of deployment, reporting, discretion, legal procedures, and the like. When self-report data are used, the ratio drops dramatically to about 1.5:1 or lower, a correlation ranging from .20 to 0 in most studies (see Box 1981; Byles 1969, 37; Polk and Schafer 1972; Stinchcombe 1964). A theory focussing primarily on social-class origins explains only a small amount of the variance in delinquent behavior, though it does explain apprehension. The self-report studies have indicated there is enormously more delinquent behavior than official statistics show. This mistake arose from the lack of sophistication regarding definitions.

Though the theory is thus incorrect in predicting a strong relationship between lower socioeconomic origins and delinquent behavior, its basic sequencing of lower-class background, educational failure, and delinquency is borne out empirically. Although school failure is related both to lower socioeconomic origins and to both definitions of delinquency, the latter two variables are strongly related when delinquency is defined officially, but only weakly related when it is defined behaviorally. Restated, anticipated social class (indicated by school performance) correlates with delinquency behavior much more than does social-class origin (Stinchcombe, 1964). Those with middle-class origins but low occupational prospects are as delinquent as those with working-class origins and prospects, and more delinquent than either those with middle-class origins and prospects, or working-class origins but middle-class prospects (Polk and Schafer 1972, 111). School failure can thus be clearly seen as an intervening variable.

As well as this central problem regarding the class distribution of delinquent behavior, Cohen's, and Cloward and Ohlin's theories have other empirical difficulties. The rebellious reaction formation hypothesized by Cohen remains undemonstrated, and Cohen is ambiguous as to whether each delinquent must undergo it or whether new members are directly recruited (Kitsuse and Dietrich 1959). Short and Strodtbeck (1965) failed to demonstrate that delinquents rejected middle-class values, though they did hold additional beliefs excusing delinquencies. They also failed to find differentiated delinquent subcultures of criminal, "bopping," and retreatist gangs. In any case, the simple experience of failure or strain is inadequate to determine the direction of the resulting behavior (Hirschi 1969), and attitudes do not alone determine behavior. Most delinquents are law-abiding most of the time; anomie theory fails to account for the episodic and probabilistic nature of delinquency (Matza 1964a, 1969). The content of the delinquent subculture as described by Cohen (malicious, negativistic, short-run hedonism) seems an inadequate description given the utilitarian "rationality" of many delinquencies (for instance, stealing goods for profit). The centrality of the gang is overemphasized, as most delinquents are not gang members (Lerman 1967). Nor can subcultural values be assumed to be coterminous with group interaction. Most adolescent groupings are loosely knit. No explanation is given for the important phenomenon of "cooling-out," which most delinquents go through in becoming generally law-abiding, working-class citizens (Matza 1964a, 22).

A Criticism of Leyton's Theory

Many of the same issues that raise problems with anomie theories apply to Leyton's theory of "triple delinquency." He gives no attention to "subcultural" or ethnic variations in Canadian society; these might affect goals, aspirations, and childrearing practices. He ignores the origins of definitions of delinquency, or the moral implications of incarcerating youngsters for acts for which adults could not be charged (the status offences of truancy, "sexual immorality or any other vice," and the like). He never carefully defines nihilistic delinquency (for instance, to distinguish it from "rational" theft).

Most crucially, despite over two decades of criticisms of official statistics such as those reviewed above, he naïvely assumes that a training school population somehow adequately represents all those youngsters committing delinquent acts. Such sampling questions recur throughout his book and amount to a serious flaw. Selecting subjects from a small training school in Atlantic Canada, then attempting a "complete explanation" of not only the attainment of the most serious delinquent *status*, but also of delinquent *acts*, Leyton greatly overreaches his data. Accumulated research by labeling theorists (see chapters 5 and 7) and self-report surveyors (see chapter 4) on justice processing has taught us that youngsters are incarcerated not simply for delinquent acts, but quite explicitly because police and courts see their families as inadequate. We can therefore hardly be surprised to find that training school wards have seemingly inadequate families!

While the data presented in Leyton's case studies are excellent, Leyton is not seriously attentive to theoretical debates or explanations contrary to his own. He does not seriously address whether there are underclass families that do not reject their offspring, or rejected children who do not get incarcerated. While Cohen (1955) and Matza (1964a) are given some consideration, Werthman's discussion (1969; 1971) of precocious adolescents is ignored, although it could plausibly account for most of Leyton's cases, as could later work by Paul Willis (1977) and others at the Birmingham Centre for Contemporary Cultural Studies (Hall and Jefferson 1976). More recent considerations such as Foucault's (1977) analyses of the bureaucratic state's minute interventions into parent-child relations would have been useful in understanding the fragmentation of local community culture, control, and self-determination.

With such an unsophisticated analysis of age structure and class domination, Leyton's policy recommendations are in the same spirit as the old conservative attempts to bolster failing families that have pervaded delinquency policies (though not practice) for over a century. Without a strong class analysis, the first delinquency (of society upon its underclass) is ignored in the recommendations, and any pretence of radicalism ends in bankrupt Fabian welfarism at best. In ignoring such possibilities as decriminalizing juvenile status offences, exercising more police discretion and diversion of juveniles from court, separating welfare problems from criminal justice ones through deinstitutionalization, and the like, and instead advocating more coercive family counseling and easier, less legally restricted incarcerations, Leyton actually ends up by advocating policies through which the capitalist state can exercise more intensive, more destructive control of its underclass.

CONCLUSION

Official statistics have supplied us with a lot of information about delinquency, and stimulated the development of some interesting sociological theories. These have in turn generated much research, not all of which has supported such theorizing. Anomie theory's confrontation with empirical evidence is perhaps one of the better examples in sociology of theory-testing forcing reformulation of our ideas. For not all the conceptualizations involved in this tradition need be entirely abandoned, as we shall see in reincarnating them in later chapters (see also Greenberg 1977, for an excellent review). And many sociologists award more credence to official statistics than has been deemed warrantable here. Wolfgang et al. (1972), for instance, believe that truly serious offenders are segregated with relative accuracy by the justice system. And in their longitudinal study of Philadelphia youngsters, they found that over half of all official offences recorded were committed by a core group consisting of 6 percent of the study group. Other recent research (Hirschi et al. 1979; Elliott and Ageton 1980) has claimed self-report results that indicate that blacks and working-class youngsters in the United States are more delinquent than the rest of the juvenile population; we will further address these claims in chapter 4.

But both the characteristics identified as salient in the official statistics, and the theoretical, methodological, and empirical criticisms of official statistics and anomie theories should begin to arouse some suspicions in the light of our earlier discussions in chapter 2 on the origins of juvenile delinquency as a social concern. For if the juvenile justice system were to effectively function (in support of schools) to control and discipline the young of working-class and ethnic minority groups for entry into the capitalist labor market, police and courts would need to direct their attention towards the young; alarm the public with claims of rising rates; downplay the minor nature of most offences; obfuscate gender differences; concentrate on ethnic minorities, certain neighborhoods, and the working class; direct families into proper patriarchal and ageist relationships; and single out school failures. In the guise of beneficence, the childsavers who created the juvenile justice system intended it to focus its activities on just these very groups.

So what if delinquent behavior is not for the greater part from working-class or broken homes? Of what importance is the fact that juvenile delinquency is of relatively minor social impact, being neither as expensive nor as dangerous as adult crime? Why do state agencies focus our attention on the street property crime that comprises most of the officially handled, criminal incidents, although it is far less costly than property crime by blue- or white-collar employees? Why do state agencies more or less ignore organized crime, which is itself less profitable and more easily countered than corporate crime? What effect does the mass media have in focussing on violent delinquency, though it is comparatively rare (but undeniably serious), and is less likely to occur between strangers than between workers and employers, or between acquaintances, friends, neighbors, relatives, or family members? And why would so much attention be directed towards criminal violence, which fades to insignificance compared with state violence?

We will address these questions further on. For now, let us return to the responses to the failure of anomie theory and official statistics that will enable us to understand delinquent behavior.

4

Self-Report Delinquency,
Control Theory, and Gender

*One worker wrote of one of the others: "He seems to be uncovering a
great deal of immorality." Indicative of this, that worker recorded: "I
had a talk with the shop superintendent. He told me unbelievable stories
of activities in adjoining houses where soldiers visit very young girls
as prostitutes every evening." The other worker wrote in one observation: "The girls mature rapidly and the moral problem is real even with
girls of public school age. The language of the girls indicates that they
are worldly-wise, and it is common for one girl to call another a
'whore.' ". . . Extreme illustrations of filthy language, obscenity, relatively open immorality (heterosexual and homosexual), wilful destruc-
tiveness, vandalism, etc., could quite easily be given here. We cannot see
that doing this would serve our purpose any more than the selections
used. . . . These things are, of course, the superficial aspects – the
symptoms, if you like – of the problem. There are obviously certain
social conditions which help to set these evidences of the problem in bold
relief. The first is their own idleness. Idleness is not "doing nothing"
or a lack of anything to do, but rather a lack of direction, or purpose, or
intention in the activity.*

Rogers 1945, 70

SELF-REPORT DELINQUENCY

As indicated above, the primary effort to obtain knowledge about the
distribution of delinquent behavior, while avoiding the pitfalls of official
statistics, has been concentrated on the development of self-report scales
and surveys. If police and court statistics were too hopelessly biased

and omitting of information and incidents, and direct observation too time consuming, erratic, and ethically questionable, could one not try to simply ask youngsters to anonymously report on their behavior? Such techniques have been used to survey the general public regarding their victimization; but since the age of offenders in such research is generally unknown, it is less useful here.

Using the standardized format of survey questionnaires developed so successfully by market researchers, public-opinion pollsters, and voter-choice predictors during the 1940s and 1950s, innumerable large surveys have been conducted by sociologists over the last twenty-five years. Though some are conducted by personal interview, most have been administered through questionnaires, saving money and time, with little apparent loss of sensitivity, and much gain in anonymity. Schools have provided the most accessible bodies of young people to be surveyed, the necessity of literacy in answering the questionnaires favoring the use of subjects age ten and older. Simple, standard questions ask respondents to indicate how many times in the past year they have committed a particular act of delinquency. In addition, questions are asked about youngsters' background characteristics that are suspected or hypothesized as being related to high reports of delinquent behavior. The development of computer technology has made feasible the statistical processing of the large amounts of data obtained.

Various scales and indexes are developed to isolate different types of delinquency (for example, personal violence versus property offences); weights can be assigned to different behaviors according to seriousness, and so forth. These delinquency indexes are then statistically correlated with selected background characteristics to determine if particular social factors are significantly associated with delinquent behavior.

Although some of these techniques have been employed earlier in research using official statistics, and continue to be employed for comparative purposes, self-report survey analysis, and its accompanying control theory, have pushed research in a more purely neopositivist direction. Delinquency and background characteristics are defined as precisely as possible, with specified indicators tested for reliability and validity. Precise and accurate measurement is stressed, with interval- and even ratio-level scales used as often as is feasible. Hypotheses are stated as clearly as possible, logically interlinked, and tested against the data. Publication of research allows for wide dissemination and challenge.

Interestingly, some of the self-report findings closely parallel those of official statistics; many others, however, diverge. We will try to note these similarities and differences as we review the results.

Age

Regarding age, the official data are corroborated by self-report studies over the last couple of decades (Greenberg 1977; West 1975), which indicate almost all youngsters commit delinquencies every year. It would seem that the young really are more deviant than the rest of us, though we have had few (and somewhat questionable) surveys administered to adults asking them to report on their offences. The self-report data indicate a rapid rise in delinquency beginning around ages ten to twelve, seeming to peak around sixteen to eighteen years of age (Byles 1969; Christie 1965; Leblanc et al. 1981). Byles (1969, 236) found a very strong .724 correlation between age and delinquency in his Toronto research. Fréchette and Leblanc (1979) report that a similar increase through the teen years in their Montreal study was due to increasing status offences, serious delinquency declining for most youngsters (though a small group became more delinquent). Violent offences seem to peak later than those of property.

Trends

Unlike the short-term official trends since World War II, (but reinforcing the questions raised by longer-term trends indicating cyclical rises and falls), self-report research has not generally shown a steady rise in delinquency. In contrast to official reports indicating a 10 percent increase in crime being processed, an American victim survey of households actually shows a decline of 2 percent from 1975 (May 1981, *Justice Assistance News*). Figures for juvenile delinquency, specifically over the last two decades, indicate very little change, with the exceptions of drug and alcohol use (both victimless). There is, however, some indication in self-report data of an increase in offences by females (Gomme 1983). Both the general finding of little or no overall increase, and the slight increase in girls' misbehavior coincides with American research (Empey 1978, 151).

Types of Offences

The self-reports confirm the official statistics in showing that property crimes far outnumber other offences such as violence, status offences, drug use, and the like. The rank order of prominence of offences comparing different self-report studies is quite consistent (Morton, West et al. 1980; Byles 1969; Vaz 1967; Linden and Filmore 1980; Fréchette and Leblanc 1979; Clark and Wenninger 1962). It is remarkable that petty theft or alcohol use always scores first, and that petty theft, alcohol use, school truancy, assault, and vandalism come next. The more serious offences consistently rank last (for example, auto theft, break and entry, as in Fréchette and Leblanc 1979).

Sex

Self-report studies (Fréchette and Leblanc 1979) of juveniles continue to indicate somewhat more male offenders than female, but the ratio (about 1.5–3:1) is usually much smaller than in the official statistics (about 5–10:1), dropping away to almost equivalence in some research (Gomme 1982). Girls generally report proportionately the same kinds of offences as males: property crimes predominate, violent offences are rare, and sexual offences comprise a very small proportion of the total. Interestingly, given the court concentration on sexual offences of girls, considerably fewer engage in precocious sex than boys. Some sex-role stereotyping in actual behavior does remain, with males usually being predominent in the most aggressive offences (violence, armed robbery, car theft, and the like). Female offences against property often involve shoplifting, thereby reproducing in delinquency the conventional female role as shopper-consumer (Hoffman-Bustamonte 1973). Contrary to official statistics on training school inmates indicating a concentration in sexual offences, females in the self-reports tend to be less "specialized," spreading their misbehavior over more types of offences than boys (Gomme et al. 1984).

Race and Ethnicity

At least one Canadian study indicates higher rates of juvenile delinquency for native-born Canadian youngsters compared with foreign born: Byles (1969, 236) found a very strong .495 correlation, indicating Canadian-born boys were much more delinquent than immigrant (largely Italian) boys. (The girls showed almost no difference.) The Frontenac-Kingston data analyzed by Gomme (1982) showed no difference, but this may have been due to the small number of immigrants in the sample. Interestingly in the Canadian context, the francophone Montreal youngsters in the Leblanc research seem similar in behavior to those in the anglophone samples.

In American research almost as many white youngsters as black report committing delinquencies (Empey 1978, 158); blacks, however, seem considerably more likely to commit acts of violence, which, of course, make up a tiny proportion of all offences.

Social Class

Most noticeably, as mentioned in chapter 3, the self-report studies consistently report very little if any social class differences in delinquent acts: middle-class youngsters are almost as likely as working-class ones to be delinquent. Byles (1969, 236), for instance, found .235 correlation with socioeconomic status for Toronto boys, but almost none for girls. Fréchette and Leblanc (1979) report no significant interclass differences for Montreal youth, as does Gomme (1982) for Kingston.

Though some crimes that are more reported among working-class youth are likely seen as more reprehensible (for instance, violent assault), other serious acts (such as theft) reveal no class differences large enough to account for their differential handling, and are a much larger proportion of the total volume of crimes. Some other types of crime and delinquency are more predominantly middle class (such as cheque forgery and car theft); anomie theory has no explanation for these.

Urban-Rural Differences and Neighborhood

Urban and rural rates are similar (Gomme 1982). Byles (1969, 236), however, found geographic mobility to correlate at .235 for males (but only at −.041 for females); also, reflecting the height of the "flower generation" of "hippies" when his study was done, he found strong correlations for males between delinquency and both participation in Yorkville (a drug district) (.857) and identification with Yorkville (.462).

Family

Self-report studies repeatedly find no relation between single-parent homes and delinquency. Unhappiness, weak attachment to parents, or family conflict are far better predictors; regarding misbehavior, one parent is as good as two (Hirschi 1969; Nye 1958). Byles (1969, 236), however, found almost no relation in his Toronto study between delinquent behavior and parent-child conflict, as well as none regarding family cohesion; there was a slight relation (differing for boys and girls) regarding the locus of family authority. Delinquent youths are less "attached" to parents and teachers (Hargreaves 1967; Jensen 1969; Werthman 1969). But rather than simply rebelling against conventional authorities they seem to simply find them less powerful role models, less attractive to emulate.

School Failure

As in the official police statistics, self-report delinquency correlates with school failure and having delinquent associates. The causal sequence or structure, however, appears to be quite different for boys and girls, with school failure being significant for the former, but not for the latter (Gomme 1983).

In American studies, self-reported delinquency is also closely related to accumulated measures of school failure (Hirschi 1969, 128–130; see also Hindelang 1973, 477–482; Kelly 1971, 495–499; Polk and Schafer 1972, 111, 123). Lack of success in education, in addition, correlates with misconduct at school, with scores ranging from .47 to .21 (Empey and Lubeck 1971, 65; Rhodes and Reiss 1969, 19). Low-stream (level or track) and failing students tend to participate less in extracurricular events, including athletics (Polk and Schafer 1972, 40, 78, 98, 137; Hindelang 1973; but *cf.* Elliott and Voss 1974). Low commitment also varies with delinquency (Polk and Schafer 1972, 84, 99, 111, 137). The school is less of a restraining agent for such pupils. "Being good" is seen as having fewer immediate rewards and less payoff in terms of future occupations.

Peer Group Relations

Delinquents tend to cluster together with delinquent peers (Hirschi 1969; Frease 1972). Though they are no more group oriented than nondelinquents (Polk and Schafer 1972, 40), out-of-school activities such as drinking and "cruising" (Polk and Schafer 1972, 121, 111), and more adult-like recreations predominate (Hindelang 1973) than among nondelinquents. Such activities become "normatively" accepted and elaborated into a subculture or perspective. Delinquents thus are more accepting of illegal behavior than nondelinquents, though both groups espouse "middle-class" ideals equally (Short and Strodtbeck 1965). Having delinquent friends increases one's chances of delinquent behavior even if one has high marks (Noblit 1976). Byles' (1969) Toronto data shows no relationship between amount of peer group identification and delinquency. Though official statistics exaggerate the gang nature of delinquency, the majority of self-reported delinquent acts are still committed with friends (Box 1981, 137). Gomme (1982), in analyzing the Kingston data, has found having delinquent friends to be the strongest predictor for girls' delinquent behavior.

Volume

Self-report studies do present one other undeniable difference from analyses of official statistics. The sheer volume of reported delinquency is astonishingly high. The majority of high school youngsters have committed some delinquency in the last year, and almost all have committed some over their lifetimes.

Fréchette and Leblanc (1979) state that 92.8 percent of their Montreal youngsters reported misdemeanors. It is admittedly true that many of these are minor peccadilloes. Nine out of ten of Fréchette's and Leblanc's (1979) subjects reported status offences. But the absolute number of more serious offences far outnumber the official figures. Eighty percent of the Fréchette and Leblanc (1979) youngsters reported criminal code offences, although most were comparatively benign (for instance, petty thefts).

Though for many categories in the Kingston survey (see table 4.1), only a small proportion of respondents reported delinquent episodes during 1977, it is nonetheless quite remarkable that a great number of

TABLE 4.1
Delinquent Acts Self-Reported for 1977
Percentaged (*N* in brackets)

Behavior	Never %N	1–2 times %N	Several %N	Very Often %N
Skip School	52 [222]	35 [150]	11 [47]	2 [10]
Stayed out all night without permission	73 [312]	19 [81]	5 [23]	2 [9]
Ran away	91 [389]	8 [35]	1 [4]	0 [1]
Used Alcohol	38 [162]	30 [128]	22 [96]	9 [40]
Used Other Drugs	73 [312]	14 [59]	8 [34]	4 [19]
Theft under $5	43 [186]	44 [190]	11 [45]	1 [6]
Theft $5–50	85 [364]	12 [52]	2 [7]	1 [5]
Theft over $50	93 [400]	4 [15]	2 [9]	0 [1]
Car Theft	90 [384]	9 [37]	2 [7]	0 [1]
Break and Entry	84 [360]	13 [57]	2 [9]	1 [2]
Vandalism	69 [297]	24 [102]	4 [18]	1 [6]
Assault	67 [289]	26 [111]	5 [22]	1 [5]

NOTE: *N* = 429

SOURCE: M. E. Morton, M. G. West, et al., *A Research Evaluation of the Frontenac Juvenile Diversion Project* (Ottawa: Solicitor General, 1980) p. 58.

youngsters (in absolute terms) reported delinquencies: 62 percent alcohol use, 48 percent school truancy, 27 percent staying out all night without parental permission, 27 percent using drugs other than alcohol, 57 percent minor theft, 16 percent break and entry, 15 percent theft between five and fifty dollars, 7 percent theft over fifty dollars, 10 percent car theft, 31 percent vandalism, 33 percent assault. Although some of the first-mentioned items are relatively minor juvenile ("status") offences, the latter categories indicate some serious misbehavior. Our Kingston survey subjects reported a conservatively estimated 2,500 acts of delinquency in one year, and a crude estimate suggests that all youngsters in the Ontario county studied would commit approximately 100,000 such acts (Morton, West et al. 1980).

Any good theory to explain the self-report facts about delinquency must take into account the above findings. It must explain why delinquency increases dramatically through the teenage years, peaking at between the ages of sixteen and eighteen; explain why girls' rates seem to be increasing, but not the boys; recognize the dominant offence pattern as theft, and that boys' and girls' patterns are similar; recognize that girls are only slightly less delinquent than boys; recognize ethnic variation; recognize little or no social class differences or urban-rural differences; explore family relations beyond crude intact-split dichotomies; include school failure as a correlate, at least for boys; recognize the role of delinquent peers, though delinquents are no more peer oriented than nondelinquents; and, finally, accept that there is much more delinquent behavior than that known to the police, and that almost all youngsters commit delinquencies every year, even if most of these are minor.

CONTROL THEORY

Anomie theory had been developed when only official statistics (and some observational studies) were available. By the late 1960s, the increasing use of self-report studies and labeling-theory-inspired criticisms of official statistics (discussed below) led to the rearticulation of control or bond theory. Drawing on Durkheim's early work (1897), and reconsidering the impact of the family psychosociologically, theorists such as Hirschi (1969) and Nye (1958) assumed clear social consensus around legitimate values. They argued that it was sensible, however, to assume people were free to break the law unless restrained by social ties or bonds. This view contrasts sharply with anomie theory's assumption of initial socialization being adequate to insure conformity until some strain, such as school failure, produces frustration, which results in deviance. The bonds consisted of commitments or rational calculations of means-ends considerations; attachments, or emotional connections and sensitivity to others; beliefs, or moral evaluations of right and wrong; and involvements, or time allocated to conventional activities. These bonds were subjectively assessed by people, could vary in strength, and could change over time as they re-evaluated their side bets.

The weakening of these controls leaves the person free to deviate; their strengthening promotes conformity. This explanation avoided the complexity and nondemonstrated aspects (such as reaction formation) of Cohen's theory. It left for empirical resolution a number of questions that Cohen incorrectly assumed (such as the content of the delinquent subculture). It retained a probabilistic quality that corresponds nicely with both the data and more humanistic conceptions of human factors as being partially nondetermined.

Hirschi and Nye were quite positivistic and deterministic in their formulations. A British sociologist, Steven Box (1981), has argued that bond theory could also be nicely integrated with considerations of free will and human subjectivity, as the bonds are subjectively evaluated and require human consciousness for interpretation. Furthermore, Box argued that the explanatory power of the theory could be extended by including facilitating factors that positively encouraged deviance. These consist of secrecy (opportunity to commit deviance without detection), skills (or abilities with technical capacity), supply (or opportunities and materials required), social support (or encouraging others), and symbolic support (or a rationale making the deviant behavior acceptable).

There is considerable empirical support for control theory, especially by American research regarding delinquency. Those who are less committed to conventional institutions, who have the least to gain by conforming, deviate. Thus, those students for whom the school has least to offer, at present or in the future, are more likely to be delinquent. Empey and Lubeck (1971) found that school failure (a measure of commitment) correlated at an astounding .76 and .80 with delinquency, Hindelang (1973) that school grades correlated at − .71 and − .67, and Rhodes and Reiss (1969) that English marks correlated with delinquency at − .61.

Similar results are obtained for those who are least emotionally attached to parents or teachers, who are also more likely to commit delinquent acts (see also Jensen 1969). Those who least believe in the rightness of the moral order prove to be least likely to uphold it. And those without involvements are more likely to commit delinquencies. Generally, empirical tests show that even better predictability can be obtained by extending "pure" control theory to incorporate elements from other traditions, as Box suggests. In terms of research confirmation regarding the relatively minor delinquent acts common to most adolescents, control theory is a clear, hands-down winner in comparison with anomie theory.

Control theory would also seem to explain suggestively the predominance of youth in the self-report data (and, to some extent, their inordinate appearance in official statistics). Ironically, adolescent status places its incumbents in such a position as to directly encourage delinquency. Adolescents often question their subordination in schools while not yet having firm commitments in stable employment, feel fewer harsh consequences from juvenile law, have yet to established attached relations with new families, though having loosened ties with their families of origin, vociferously question stereotyped moral beliefs, and chronically complain of boredom (noninvolvement). It is not surprising then that the admittedly weak evidence comparing age groups regarding delinquent behavior (Christie 1965; Wallerstein and Wyle 1947) suggests that teens commit more individual acts of deviance. Given the weakness of self-report data on different age groups, such an explanation must remain tentative, but it seems quite plausible that even if juveniles were subject only to adult law in adult courts, their dependent social situation would thus likely encourage them to be more criminal than adults. The very marginalization of youth, then, dialectically reinforces their character as a problem population.

Schooling as a social institution would seem often to augment these factors rather than reduce them. In terms of specific educational policies, control theory reinforced anomie theory's arguments that reduced school failure (in conjunction with moral education, attachment to teachers, and heightened involvements) would reduce delinquency (Polk and Schafer 1972).

The predominance of property crime among the young should hardly be surprising. Ross (1973) and others (for instance, Gordon 1971) have established strong correlation between unemployment and property crimes. As private industry in Canada has been unable to absorb those of the post–World War II "baby boom" as they hit labor-market age, almost half of the unemployed in Canada are under twenty-five, and the rates of unemployment for teenagers are two-and-a-half to three times the national average (Committee on Youth 1971; *Toronto Star*, 1975). (Lack of income, of course, also means that the young command less private space, and are more open to police surveillance.)

Over the last decade, a few impressive Canadian tests using path analysis have been made of control theory in its extended form. Basically, Linden and Filmore (1980), using Edmonton data, Leblanc (1981) and his colleagues, using Montreal data, Hagan, Simpson, and Gillis (1979), using Toronto suburban data, and Gomme (1982), using Kingston, Ontario data, have all found strong support for the theory. We will review Gomme's findings as an example.

Gomme (1982) sought to test not only control theory variables, but to compare them with differential association and strain/anomie ones. (His measure for testing differential association theory [discussed in the next chapter] was possession of delinquent friends, which fits precisely Box's extension of control theory to include group or social support.) It can thus be seen as an elaboration of control theory. Gomme found relationships linking age, delinquent associates, belief in the legitimacy of the law, sex, and school failure (for boys) to be associated with self-report delinquency overall. The first three factors affected status offences and drug usage alone for males and females; the first two factors were also strongly associated with criminality in general, and theft in particular. Social class was not associated; only male delinquency was associated with school failure (Gomme's measure of commitment). The social control variables explained more of the variance than did those from the other theories. All these variables combined into an extended control theory model explained 50 percent of the variance in delinquency among boys, and 36 percent among girls (still a highly predictive set of relationships by sociological standards) (see figure 4.1). This is very similar to the 57 percent of the variance explained by a combined model for the Montreal sample (Leblanc 1981) (see also Linden and Filmore 1980).

These results are very similar to those in the most recent British (Rutter

FIGURE 4.1
Causes of Delinquency (Male and Female) for Frontenac County

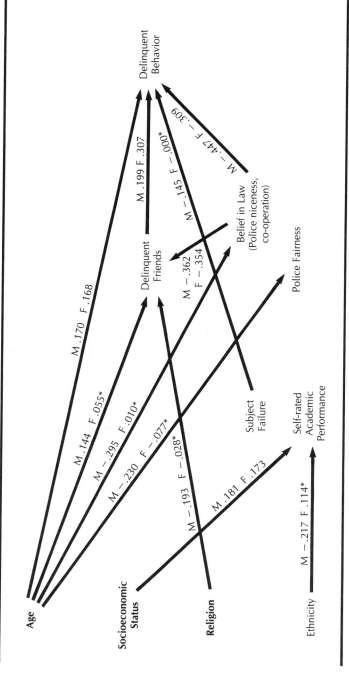

*Not significant at probability < .05.

SOURCE: Constructed from I. M. Gomme, "A Multivariate Analysis of Self-Report Delinquency Among Students." ED.D. dissertation, OISE/University of Toronto, 1982. And "Predictors of Status and Criminal Offences Among Male and Female Adolescents in an Ontario Community." Paper presented at the annual meeting of: American Society of Criminology, Denver, 1983.

et al. 1979) and American studies. Johnson (1979, 116), for instance, states:

> A stake-in-conformity explanation of delinquency based on parent and school ties seems to suffer as a result of the findings. To be sure, the best explanation incorporated both these control variables and the differential-association (with peers and with values or definitions) variables, but the data point to the latter for greatest influence. . . . it is the school factors that appear to be most relevant. It seems that an adolescent's public life has as much or more to do with his or her deviance or conformity than do "under-the-roof" experiences. Furthermore, the extent of law violation by friends seems to be the key element in the youth's public life. And it is affected only slightly and indirectly by parent-child relationships in the present sample. The primary determinants of delinquent associates are school attachment and school performance, the latter having more direct influence than anticipated.

After considering some of the problems with self-report data and social control theory, we will further explore these findings regarding delinquent associates in chapter 5 and schooling in chapter 6.

CRITICISMS OF SELF-REPORT DATA AND CONTROL THEORY

Problems in Self-Report Data

Self-report questionnaire surveys have attempted to provide a more direct and hence more accurate measure of the distribution of delinquent behavior than the official statistics offer. Nonetheless, such self-report questionnaires have faults as well as merits. Some persons may not recognize themselves as victims (for example, of corporate fraud, or alcohol abuse), or not know that some activities are illegal (for example, gambling). Some individuals may either hide or exaggerate their criminal experiences, though attempts to explore this have not established any systematic patterns of deception (Box 1981). Terms are often not exactly comparable between studies or with legal terminology, and not all respondents tend to define terms similarly. Studies asking for self-reports of offences committed have almost always used high school student populations that probably differ considerably from dropouts or nonattenders, let alone from adults. Elliott and Ageton (1980) point out that many self-report studies use trivial, unrepresentative questions (Vaz 1965). They also argue that theft is overrepresented in the questioning (although, given the predominance of theft in the official statistics, and legislation, it is unclear what would be more representative). They further point out that asking whether a youngster has committed a delinquency "often," "sometimes," and the like, introduces possible ambiguity as to exact meaning, and could lead to unreliable or even invalid responses. Most crucially, they point out that response options tend to limit or discourage responses that would indicate a high number of incidents. And since the samples are not usually probability samples, it may be a mistake to generalize from them.

The time order between variables needs to be more clearly established than at present; many of the factors mentioned here have an unclear sequencing. It is, of course, theoretically plausible that these factors interact in such a way as to be mutually reinforcing, or reciprocally causal, but this is not provided for in the analyses. Some of the most serious criticisms of the prevalent interpretations of self-report research come from the neopositivist camp itself. Elliott and Ageton (1980), and Hindelang, Hirschi, and Weiss (1979) seriously question one of the central claims made on the basis of self-report studies; that is, that there are few differences in delinquent behavior between different social-class and race/ethnic groups.

Both the studies of Elliott and Ageton, and Hindelang et al. make the important basic claim that better self-report techniques indicate that official statistics accurately portray some trends, though greatly exaggerating them (for example, regarding race, class, extent of delinquency, sex, and the like). Fréchette and Leblanc (1979), and Morton, West et al. (1980) similarly found arrested youth to be indeed more serious and more frequent offenders.

One might at this point seriously question the likelihood of obtaining radically improved knowledge from further self-report research. At some point, the basic assumption that each delinquent incident or act of theft is statistically equivalent becomes questionable.

Further, the ambiguities and vagueness of some types of deviance (for example, "sexual immorality or any other vice") make one realize that ultimately, the precise number of delinquent acts is unknown and unknowable. One begins to fear that the fine distinctions teased out of the data by increasingly refined measurement or statistical analysis is beginning to overreach some basic assumptions about the phenomenon being studied.

Even the most sophisticated techniques themselves (for example, path analysis) rely on prior specification of theory. Initial beliefs that such analyses would strictly test hypotheses are being revised, as most experts now see it only as an indication of the fit of the data with a particular model (Gomme 1982). More seriously, we should begin to ask in what ways the methodological techniques employed place limits on the possible theoretical explanations; for self-report research has all the basic old problems of neopositivism.

Criticisms of Control Theory

Success in explaining delinquent behavior does not mean that control theory is without criticism or problems. Compared with anomie or various other theories, it is relatively unelaborated and nonspecific, which may account for its lack of negating empirical evidence: it does not, for instance, define which of the social bonds is more important, or how much nonbonding is needed to cut one loose from social control. In large part it is a theory developed very closely to the available data, and has not been as daring as anomie or other theories in raising new issues. Box's elaboration seems sensible, but has only limited research support. Furthermore, his five facilitators are in many ways reminiscent of anomie considerations: for instance, social support sounds like a gang; symbolic support sounds like subcultural values; skills, secrecy, and supply sound like opportunity. To complicate matters further, the five facilitators seem like the opposite of the bonds: that is, social support is the deviant opposite of attachment; symbolic support is the deviant opposite of beliefs; skills, supply, and secrecy would imply the opposite of commitment. If all this is so, has Box simply reincorporated anomie factors into his version of bond theory, with all their concomitant faults? Or has he encapsulated the same issues as anomie theorists addressed, only more successfully? By elaborating the five facilitators, has Box reduced the scope of will; or more trenchantly stated, is control theory determinist (in an attempt to be more scientific, as Hirschi demands), or is it humanist, incorporating issues of human will and intentionality?

Control theory remains the most satisfactory explanation of delinquent behavior, but it too is incomplete theoretically and empirically. Control theory has a tendency to slide into a situational subjectivism, ignoring cultural and historical background, and the process of making law, and the like. Although both anomie and control theories seem to have hit upon some true correlations (for example, between school failure and delinquency [West 1975a, 1978b, 1979b]), they leave the processes hidden in a "black box", failing to illustrate human dynamics.

More empirically, there are questions about the adequacy of control theory as a general theory of delinquency. Almost all the data supporting it are from self-report studies of typical adolescents, few of whom are officially in trouble. As discussed above, these surveys suffer from their own methodological problems, and serious delinquency, either violent or costly, tends to be buried. Some researchers (for example, Box 1981; Leblanc 1981) are now suggesting that control theory is inadequate to explain serious career delinquents, let alone white collar thieves or corporate criminals who would, for instance, seem to be attached, committed, believing, and involved, yet still commit serious crimes involving huge dollar losses. Leblanc has suggested that subculture and career-labeling theories are more appropriate for such serious delinquents, as we will discuss in chapters 5, 6, and 7.

Most crucially, control theory fails to question its basic problems with the fundamental reasons one might have for asking such questions about delinquency. Of what use is it knowing that delinquents tend to have delinquent friends if nothing can be done about it? Anomie and control theories' discovery that school failure produces delinquency has limited use if society insists that students be ranked, and hence some must finish last (West 1975a, 1978b). In attempting to maintain a value-free and politically neutral stance, too much research has failed to anticipate how its findings might be utilized.

Moral and ethical issues need to be better addressed head on. Anomie and control theories have reasserted traditional positivist claims to be employing a value-free, scientistic approach, just investigating the means possible for the acquisition of various value-laden goals chosen elsewhere. The defining of purposes is thus left to philosophy or the wider society; a (conservative) consensus is assumed regarding school deviance or delinquency and what adolescents should do. Such an abandonement of goals and ethics has left the field open to redefinition by the New Right.

For this research tradition *has* raised some important questions. Self-report studies have indicated that there is far more delinquency than expected, that almost all youngsters are involved in it. Only sexual, ethnic, and class biases in official processing had traditionally prevented the legal system from being overwhelmed: the assumption in liberal jurisprudence that all miscreants should be brought to formal justice proves impossible in practice. Such discoveries demand an as-yet-unexplored reconsideration of our traditional Western belief in, and heritage of, the rule of law.

GENDER

In criminology over the last decade, considerations of gender have begun to be revolutionized. As much as any social science discipline, criminology has been blatantly sexist and blind to patriarchy, as much among liberals and radicals protesting class and racial discrimination as among conservatives quite happy in defending the status quo. This is especially astonishing in studies of delinquency, however, for the juvenile justice system has surely been among the most blatantly sexist of any public institutions.

On the basis of their nonrepresentation in official statistics, women and girls have been generally ignored in theories of delinquency. Almost no mainline criminological theory developed within sociology has explicitly considered the position of women and girls. Taking their initial lead from the official statistics, which indicated that only about 15 percent of juvenile cases involved females, theorists basically wrote them off as an unimportant group. Further examination of the girls in training schools showed almost all of them to be confined for sexual or "incorrigible" kinds of offences, suggesting their offences were really of harm only to themselves; often considered rather pathetic, they were not considered "real delinquents." Thus Cohen discusses girls only briefly in his major book, *Delinquent Boys*. Small in numbers, victimless in terms of offence, girls do not experience the anomie he discusses because they depend upon their accompanying males for status.

Such neglect in the mainline sociological theories has left the topic wide open for what now seems some quite aberrant theorizing. When girls have been considered in the context of legal courts or in theory, their activities have almost always been reduced to their sexuality: when boys stole, it was for profit; when girls stole, it was because of penis envy. The dominant and clear social image of the female offender has been that of the female prostitute or promiscuous girl. Traditionally, of course, male promiscuity has been tolerated, female promiscuity frowned upon.

After reviewing some now quite incredible sounding traditional themes of female delinquency, we will expand upon some of the self-report findings introduced above, which, to their credit, have been partially responsible for initiating this theoretical revolution regarding the sexes. Self-reports not only smashed anomie theory by indicating that middle-class youngsters were as equally likely to be delinquent as working-class ones, but have been, if anything, even more astounding in showing that girls are almost as likely to be delinquent as boys, and in almost exactly the same ways. To their further credit, control theories have been able to account for female delinquency only somewhat less than male, and have suggested reasons why girls might be a little less seriously delinquent than boys. This has led theorists to predict that girls would be less delinquent through being more attached to their parents, but less restrained by the commitment of school success because this is seen as being less important by females than males. Some recent work in this tradition merits further discussion.

But gender is also an exemplary topic for illustrating the weaknesses of control theory, for revealing its limitations. Control theory fails to consider, let alone explain, why girls would be more attached to parents or less committed to school. Its tendency to conservatively and un-questioningly accept dominant ideological beliefs ultimately blinds it. And its fundamental acceptance of the importance of family attachment by adolescents prevents it from questioning this central institution of patriarchy, as well as the social processes throughout society that re-produce patriarchy. For further progress to be made, feminist criticisms must be examined more seriously.

Traditional Malestream Theoretic Blindness: Official Data and Genitalia

Traditional criminology has consistently reduced female deviance to fe-male sexuality. Lombroso and Ferrero (1895) regarded female criminals as both atavistic or "primitive" throwbacks and degenerates, yet also unduly like men, hermaphrodite, lacking in maternal instincts. In their positivistic number-counting studies of imprisoned offenders, they resorted to a biological determinism that confused sex and gender, supporting the double standard and explicitly attempting to enhance the exercise of control.

The Viennese psychiatrist Sigmund Freud ([1925–1931] 1973), also saw women as biologically inferior, though generally less crime-prone than men. Females lack the full development of conscience or superego that men have, as they have not experienced castration anxiety during the Oedipal stage, and had to subordinate their desires to those of the father. This would make them more delinquent, except that they must rely upon men for approval. Delinquent females had unsuccessfully dealt with the penis envy all girls experienced; both their shoplifting and prostitution were attempts to compensate for these "missing parts."

The American, W. I. Thomas, in his study, *The Unadjusted Girl* (1923), saw socialization as the key; he believed women and men had an inherently different balance of instincts or needs, with the former being more desirous of (sexual) response, being duller and more submissive, as indicated by their passive role in sexual intercourse. A leading figure in the Chicago school tradition, Thomas saw moral breakdown and inadequate socialization resulting from culture conflict, urbanization, and the loss of community, especially in inner-city interstitial areas. He represents a more liberal "treatment" viewpoint (indeed, in one of the earliest sociological scandals, he was released from his University of Chicago post for being suspected of some unduly intimate treatment of some of his subjects!) (Faris 1970). Without proper socialization, state control was needed to ensure that women exchanged their sexual favors for domesticity rather than cash payments. Thomas was an active supporter of the early juvenile court movement. He largely ignored class differences that affect the prospects of girls as well as boys; he also ignored the double standard, not only regarding sexuality, but also in training for economic productivity.

This tradition was brought to a climax by Otto Pollak (1950). Pollak believed that women were much more criminal than the official statistics showed, but escaped detection because of their practice and ingenuity at concealment. The latter skill was acquired through females learning sexual wiles and being able to conceal arousal, unlike men, and from their learning how to conceal their menstrual period. These were augmented by underreporting, chivalrous police, and courts who exercised more leniency towards women. Pollak correctly notes that most of the victims of female murder are their intimates or lovers, and it is also becoming apparent in studies of child abuse that much female violence in the home has not been officially reported. But Pollak ignores the possibility (now also becoming a recognized fact) that a probably greater and clearly enormous amount of male domestic violence has also been ignored.

Kingsley Davis (1971) discussed the functional aspects of prostitution, arguing that society needed such "bad" women in order to relieve some men's unsatisfied sexual urges without endangering "good" women. He fails to further investigate the bases of such sex-role relations.

The late sixties produced a generation of criminologists who drew upon this "classical" background that had devoted most of its attention to adult women to turn specific attention to delinquent girls. In *The Adolescent Girl in Conflict* (1966), Konopka saw delinquency springing from poor and broken homes triggering personal maladjustment and loneliness. She feared that girls though less overtly delinquent than boys, instigated much delinquency through controlling their accompanying males. She makes no examination of the social structure that would underly such behavior.

Vedder and Sommerville (1970) saw delinquency as a product of maladjustment to the female role.

Cowie, Cowie, and Slater (1968) identified deprived childhoods and subsequent rebellion against the female sex role as crucial. Using an institutionalized sample, they put much emphasis on physiological factors, finding their subjects to be in impaired physical health, overweight, with an inordinate number of minor physical defects, as well as being more markedly masculine. They then argued that such youngsters have an excess of male chromosomes and hormones. They completely accepted that sex determines gender and regarded stereotyped female behavior as the only behavior appropriate for girls.

One should not assume that the often ludicrous nature of such theories has led to their abandonment in our enlightened era. Leyton's triple theory of delinquency openly sees serious delinquency as evidence of psychological pathology, which he in turn regards as family-derived. The inclusion of an equal number of girls in his case histories is indeed a strength of his research, but his analysis strongly concurs with those of the theorists above, though he makes no direct reference to them. In an Ontario report just a decade ago, Landau (1973) voiced only a few murmurs at the lack of adequate research into the question of the right to intervene with girls harming only themselves, and the like. Her article, "The Adolescent Female Offender," largely accepted that the training school population (with three-quarters of its female wards incarcerated for neglect, "sexual immorality," and the like) adequately represented the population of female offenders. Claiming how different boys were from girls in their delinquencies, it unquestioningly accepts the paternalistic mandate of the juvenile justice system, and centrally bemoans the lack of adequate treatment facilities for such emotionally disturbed and self-destructive girls.

In general, these theories have emphasized the individual and very statistically deviant quality of female delinquency. Women are grouped with children and lunatics as not quite human. Such theories have regarded aberrant behavior as either physiologically or psychologically caused. Individual readjustment to traditional female roles has been regarded as essential to restore social harmony and help delinquents. Women are seen as both evil and malicious, yet also innocent and naïve, gentle and caring. Such classical accounts of female delinquency should, it is hoped, sound somewhat quaint as well as sexist to today's reader. But they retain an active currency among juvenile justice personnel that is truly remarkable.

By now, the astute reader should have begun to raise questions about such theories. Biologically based theories are inadequate to account for the temporal and cultural variation in what is deemed to be delinquent. They share with psychological-abnormality theories a problem in accounting for the episodic character of delinquency: they are too determinist. Psychological accounts assume a stable personality unaffected by situational factors. Gross assumptions are made about temporal relationships: family problems could as easily result from a child being delinquent as being the cause of such behavior. Crucially, psychoanalytic theories have proven for the most part unamenable to scientific testing; both psychoanalytic and biological theories have suffered from an acute lack of research evidence when any careful assessment has been done. But most importantly of all, all these theories make the serious error of assuming that the incarcerated populations that are so readily available to study, represent in an unbiased fashion the total population of girls who commit delinquent acts. Such samples are grossly different even from those appearing in the official court and police statistics. These latter samples were also easily available at the time, and themselves show a radically different pattern, which has itself been even more dramatically challenged with the advent of self-report studies.

The Data

The classical theorists, of course, used the easiest data base available: young women who were incarcerated. Recall that mention was made about how different these girls are from similarly incarcerated boys. They are much fewer in number, and two-thirds to three-quarters of them have been locked up for neglect, for status offences (for example, truancy, running away, unmanageability, and the like), and for "sexual immorality or any other vice." To get to training school, most girls in Ontario, for instance, were routed through (the now repealed) "Section 8" of the Training Schools Act. This was the "neglect" clause, whereby children deemed to have their needs unmet, and without an available alternative community facility, were placed in detention for their own benefit.

Recall also from chapter 3, and in contrast, the available official police and court statistics regarding delinquents. These show boys outnumbering girls by anywhere from five to ten to one, although this ratio has been steadily decreasing throughout this century. Girls are less involved in violent offences (assault, murder, break and entry) than boys, and are much more likely to be charged with sexual offences. But the official police and court statistics clearly show that girls engage in almost exactly the same types of offences as boys: property crime predominating as compared to violent crime, and even their status offences are relatively rare (around 10 percent). Furthermore, recall that even the analysis of official statistics indicates that though less frequently charged, when charged, girls are more likely to be brought to court; when brought before judges, are more likely to be psychiatrically assessed; and when brought to court are more likely to suffer harsh dispositions (Geller 1980). On the grounds of official statistics alone, then, one should begin to question the traditional theories of female delinquency.

When one turns to the self-report data, the traditional theories simply dissolve into absurdity. Self-report research indicates that the official statistic ratio of five or ten to one drops to two or three to one in most studies and seems to be steadily declining. The number of girls seems to be actually increasing in self-reported delinquency. Gomme's (1982) analysis of the 1977 Frontenac data indicates a ratio between males and females of 1.34 to one (see table 4.2). The largest differences appear in the more serious offences (major theft, break and entry, auto theft) and interpersonal violence. Boys still commit more offences per capita than girls. The delinquencies of girls are slightly less specialized than those of boys. Girls however indicate the same offence pattern as boys (theft being the most frequent offence), again with the exception that violence is relatively rarer. Gomme (1983) reports an offence pattern correlation of .923, almost perfect. Regarding sexual offences, however, there is a clear distinction from the official data: boys are *more* active sexually, though far less prosecuted (Cernovich and Giordano 1979). Nye's research (1958) suggests that girls' delinquency is more strongly affected by adverse family relationships. Gomme (1982) and others have found school success to be a less relevant predictor of nondelinquency for girls than for boys; he also found having delinquent friends to be a stronger predictor for girls than for boys.

New Theories: Role Socialization and Structure

The understanding of these kinds of data is enhanced by the role theory developed previous to such research by Hoffman-Bustamonte (1973). In

TABLE 4.2
Sex Differences in Delinquency

Item	Sex	Proportion Reporting	Ratio Reporting	Offence Frequency in Past Year				Mean Frequency	Ratio of Means	Standard Deviation	Correlation with Sex
				Never	Once or Twice	Several Times	Very Often				
1. Truancy	male	54.3	1.34:1	45.7	38.9	12.8	2.6	1.72	1.13:1	.783	.14*
	female	40.3		59.7	30.9	7.3	2.1	1.51		.724	
2. Out over night	male	32.8	1.77:1	67.2	22.4	7.8	2.6	1.45	1.16:1	.749	.16*
	female	18.5		81.5	14.3	2.6	1.6	1.24		.578	
3. Ran away	male	10.7	1.57:1	89.3	9.0	1.7	0.0	1.12	1.05:1	.379	.06
	female	6.8		93.2	6.8	0.0	0.0	1.06		.253	
4. Used alcohol	male	67.2	1.21:1	32.8	31.9	25.0	10.3	2.12	1.11:1	.989	.12*
	female	55.3		44.7	28.4	18.9	7.9	1.90		.973	
5. Used drugs	male	32.6	1.82:1	67.4	17.8	9.1	5.7	1.53	1.17:1	.880	.17*
	female	17.9		82.1	8.9	5.8	3.2	1.30		.720	
6. Minor theft	male	63.1	1.30:1	36.9	48.9	12.9	1.3	1.78	1.11:1	.711	15*
	female	48.4		51.6	38.9	7.9	1.6	1.59		.704	
7. Medium theft	male	20.2	2.26:1	79.8	16.7	2.1	1.3	1.24	1.10:1	.555	.16*
	female	8.9		91.1	6.8	1.0	1.0	1.12		.437	
8. Major theft	male	9.5	5.93:1	90.5	6.1	3.0	0.4	1.13	1.10:1	.451	.17*
	female	1.6		98.4	0.5	1.0	0.0	1.02		.216	
9. Car theft	male	14.5	3.08:1	85.5	11.5	2.6	0.4	1.17	1.11:1	.475	.16*
	female	4.7		95.3	4.2	0.5	0.0	1.05		.246	
10. Break and entry	male	21.8	2.59:1	78.2	18.8	2.1	0.9	1.25	1.13:1	.535	18*
	female	8.4		91.6	6.8	1.6	0.0	1.10		.350	
11. Vandalism	male	39.4	2.11:1	60.9	32.0	5.6	1.7	1.48	1.20:1	.684	.23*
	female	18.6		81.4	14.9	2.7	1.1	1.23		.546	
12. Interpersonal conflict	male	44.0	2.40:1	56.6	33.3	8.1	2.2	1.56	1.31:1	.736	.27*
	female	18.3		81.7	16.8	1.6	0.0	1.19		.438	

*probability < .01

SOURCE: I. M. Gomme et al., "Rates, Types, and Patterns of Male and Female Delinquency in an Ontario County," Canadian Journal of Criminology, table 1, 1984, forthcoming.

focussing upon differential roles for males and females, she argued that five factors must be considered. They are: differential role expectations, sex differences in socialization and social control, structurally determined differential opportunities regarding offences, differential access to criminal subcultures and careers, and finally, sex differences in crime categories. For instance, women are infrequent perpetrators of violent armed robbery because they are not socialized to use physical strength, are not taught to handle guns, are unlikely to be socialized into a delinquent subculture accepting of such behavior, and do not have traditional male role expectations of providing monetary income. However, they are as prominent or more so than males in shoplifting, because shopping fits perfectly with the more usual, female role as consumer. More specifically regarding juveniles, she noted that being out late at night, running away, or engaging in sex are all contrary to the role expectations for the "good girl." Just at puberty when boys begin to increasingly get involved in delinquency, extra restrictions are placed on girls for fear of their getting pregnant. McRobbie and Garber (1976) document how English girls are effectively kept at home while their brothers are allowed to roam the streets; hence their teenage subcultural activities must take place in the parental home.

Using a modified control theory, Hagan et al. (1979) have argued that social restraint mechanisms differ for males and females, and suggest that these differences shape the varying opportunities for males and females to become involved in delinquency.

> In the world of crime and delinquency, as in the world of work, women are denied full access to the public sphere through a socialization sequence that moves from mother to daughter in a cycle that is self-renewing (Hagan et al. 1979, 34).

They provide evidence that females are subject to informal control centering on the family (in contrast to boys being subject to formal controls in the legal, public realm).

Similarly, Gomme (1982, 1983) found belief in the legitimacy of the law to be more predictive of male delinquency. He suggests that peer expectations might have greater impact on females than males because of their being socialized to be more conforming and sensitive to others. The lack of effect of school performance on female delinquency might be attributable to the lesser amount of pressure that society places on them than it does on males to succeed; many girls probably still seek the economic security that school success can provide more through their future husbands' achievements than their own.

In general terms, control theory thus modified has withstood reasonably well the test of data regarding female as well as male delinquency. Box summarizes the situation well in stating:

At the present time, it would not be unreasonable to conclude that amongst strain, cultural diversity and control theory, the last offers the best possibility for explaining both female delinquency and, even more important, why it is less frequent than male delinquency. The answer seems to lie in the extent to which young females are differentially controlled by their parents, which leads to a greater attachment between them, and different gender patterns of socialization which lead to more females being less prepared to take risks or perceive delinquency as fun (Box 1981, 144).

Nonetheless, Leblanc and Gomme found extended control theory variables accounting for 50 percent and 57 percent of the variance in delinquent behavior for boys, but Gomme found that it only accounted for 36 percent of the variance for girls' delinquency. Furthermore, Gomme, and Hagan et al. found that there is a different causal model structure for males and females in contrast to Johnson in his American study (1979). This suggests that theories developed for males are not as entirely adequate for females.

As Smart (1976, 69) points out, it is also true that such role theories attempt to explain different rates of delinquency but fail to place such role prescriptions within a wider context or explain how they come about. By failing to further consider intentionality, they leave open the question as to whether female delinquents are poorly socialized, or to challenge the patriarchal order and its depiction of women. Smart thus calls for various kinds of research on female crime and reactions to it, and placing it within a wider legal, political, economic, and gender perspective.

Campbell (1981) also develops a critical study of theories of female delinquency, charging that they fail to recognize girls as active participants in the construction of their own fates. She argues that it is possible to borrow many ideas from theories of male delinquency, especially social structural, subcultural, and peer group ones. She urges close observational studies of girls that incorporate their own perspectives, and that are to be taken at their face value. There are now beginning to be some studies done in this mode (for example, Player 1979; Keating 1981). These are clearly needed within the Canadian social formation as well as elsewhere. At present the best we have are insightful journalistic accounts (for example, McLaren 1980).

A major theoretical contribution in this direction was made by a Canadian, Marie-Andrée Bertrand (1969). It has long been unrecognized and unutilized. Bertrand draws on David Matza's argument in *Delinquency and Drift* (1964). Matza argues that youth in our society are often likely to feel powerless, their destinies predetermined, and to feel themselves as objects. To break this mood of fatalism, they must assert their humanness as doers. One of the easiest ways to make things happen is to commit a delinquency. Bertrand argues that women are also structurally conditioned into being objects in our society, and hence could be tempted to deviate to reassert their humanity. In her later work (1977), Bertrand attempted to relate female criminality to economic, legal, and political variables in a crosscultural perspective. Her ambitious project did find that where women's consciousness of oppression was low, there was little crime.

Towards a Feminist Theory of Female Delinquency and Patriarchal Justice

The most recent of the theories reviewed above all point in the direction of a more thoroughgoing feminist analysis. For while traditional theories of female crime must be rejected because of their biologism, and anomie theories have simply failed to address female delinquents, control theory has not said enough about differing role structures and role socialization. Furthermore, formalistic conflict theory is of little help.

> . . . we would only need to look at the knots that Turk gets tied in when he tries to explain how a powerless, incompetent and unorganized set of people like women came to have such low crime rates (McIntosh 1978, 396).

Even Marxists, too often retaining a traditional focus on capitalist relations as the fundamental determinant of all human activity, need to further address the questions raised by women and crime.

Patriarchy itself must be directly addressed if one is to comprehend delinquency by girls, not only in its behavioral aspects, but also as it is constituted by the juvenile justice system. Why are girls less likely than boys to engage in the more serious (especially violent) delinquencies, and those that do, less often? Why have these relatively slight behavioral differences been so dramatically transformed by the state response to girls' misbehavior, and especially why has the juvenile justice system so insisted on sexualizing girl delinquencies? Why and how does the state overemphasize the misdemeanors of one subordinate group (working-class youngsters) while grossly underemphasizing those of another (girls)? Why does the law constitute male and female subjects so differently?

McIntosh (1978) and others have identified the family household as central to women's oppression. Seccombe (1974, 1980) and O'Brien (1981) among others have developed fascinating feminist-Marxist analyses of family and reproductive relations. Both have, in different ways, seen women's oppression being akin to exploitation in the factory, whereby fair value is not returned for either domestic service or childbearing and rearing.

Poster (1978) historically contrasts a (somewhat stereotyped) bourgeois family with proletarian ones. The bourgeoisie, he maintains, themselves adopted low fertility to offset their increasingly low mortality rates, seeking to better their economic situation. Before effective birth control, this required a combination of repressed sexuality (for males and females), or resorting to prostitutes (for males). By contrast, the proletarian (often recently peasant) family retained the rural traditions of rearing extra children to contribute to family support; encounters were more casual, and children were "informally" raised with little attention or supervision, surrounded by a wide network of adults. As indicated in chapter 2, Clarke (1975), Platt (1969), and others have argued that the juvenile justice system can be seen as a highly organized state attempt to regulate such proletarian reproduction.

Donzelot (1979) uses Foucault's (1977) idea of the politics of biology being organized through linguistic discourse that locates subjects. For him, the family is an intersection of social practices developed by professions such as medicine, law, social work, and education, all of which are licensed and used by the state. The economy of the physical body becomes a crucial concern with capitalism's explicit recognition of the need for the regulation of labor power; the production and socialization of children must become highly organized. Donzelot's particular argument that the state allied itself with women is, to say the least, controversial, and not accepted by most feminists, yet his analysis does raise interesting problems regarding the role of professionals and ideological discourse.

The neo-Marxist theories of the state outlined in chapter 2 must be extended and revised to account adequately for both female delinquency and the state's response to it. Gramsci (1971) has suggested that one might usefully conceive of a layer of "civil society" between the economic and political, wherein social and cultural institutions such as the family, church, clubs, and media provide grounds for the elaboration of culture. These commonsensical notions are elaborated by intellectuals into semi-coherent ideologies, partly reflecting real-life relations, and partly distorting them, if only through the necessary omission of depicting all of reality. When an ideology is so dominant that it cannot normally be questioned, hegemony is achieved that provides cultural stability. In such a context political actions are able to be taken with assurance. As these civil relations are crucial to maintaining social order, the state is not only concerned with reproducing capitalist relations per se, but also with reproducing gender, ethnic, age, and other relationships. The state is not only capitalist, but also patriarchal, racist, ageist, and so on.

Harrison and Mort (1979), in examining the origins of the nineteenth-century capitalist state, argue that it transformed such previously existing relations in civil society as family, property, marriage, and those of sex. They suggest, then, that patriarchal relations centering on the family must be recognized as both predating capitalism itself, and as retaining some autonomy from capitalist forces. Rather than simplistically seeing the sexual repression required by capitalism as taking place against an essential human sexuality, they too argue that we must recognize that specific practices such as law, literature, and medicine have constructed particular notions of sexuality. The inordinate use of psychiatric facilities for women, compared with men, can be seen as one reflection of this.

One development in the neo-Marxist sociology of law needs to be elaborated with particular reference to females. Pashukanis (1978) introduced the distinction between substantive and formal equality before the law. Pashukanis was inspired to make this distinction following upon Marx's, noting that though employer and employee negotiate in the marketplace as formal equals, substantively they are not, as the latter must sell his or her labor to survive; furthermore, the formal exchange on the labor market of labor for wages conceals an inequality hidden within the private realm of the factory: the capitalist ends the day with a product able to be sold for more than he invested in it (with profit or surplus value). Pashukanis argued that the legal system could similarly be usefully analyzed by distinguishing the formal equality of contractual exchange from the underlying substantive inequality. In liberal democracies operating under the rule of law, formal equality before the law is reverently enshrined; yet we all know that substantive differences in wealth are important in deciding the legal treatment we get, by policemen on the beat or by provincial attorneys general (see the Conrad Black/Norcen affair, MacLean's 1983).

This kind of analysis can be applied to women.

> The formal juridical equality of capitalist society and capitalist rationality [applies] as much to the marital as to the labour contract. In both cases, nominal parity masks real exploitation and inequality. But in both cases the formal equality is itself a certain progress, which can help make possible a further advance (Mitchell 1971, 113).

One must, then, look beyond the criminal law and consider the more general way in which the state relates to women. McIntosh argues that we must not simply ask, "How does the state oppress women?" but also, "What part does the state play in establishing and sustaining systems in which women are oppressed and subordinated to men?" (McIntosh 1978, 259). In traditionally defining families as "private" and beyond direct state interference, for instance, it has left the strongest family members (namely men) with a relatively free hand, ignoring all but the most serious domestic violence. This interestingly fits closely to the analysis of Hagan et al. (1979) regarding the informal control of juvenile females.

Thus McIntosh and others have argued cogently how the family, this seemingly most private of institutions, must be reconceived as being regulated by the state. This occurs not only through marriage contracts and property inheritance legislation, but through the entire administrative apparatus of the welfare system, health care, and schooling. The increasingly obvious state intervention into family affairs formerly left as "private," of course, has all the contradictions of bourgeois law in general: it extends the offering of formal protection for battered women and children, but is very reluctant to alter underlying conditions that precipate such behavior. The working-class men hauled into court for nonpayment of family support are usually among the least able to provide it, and the state's motivation in capturing them is clearly to reduce its own expenses rather than to address the more fundamental question of why women in this society should be so unjustly saddled with child-rearing (witness state reluctance to fund daycare centers: Gibson 1983).

These kinds of recent historical feminist analyses of the evolution of state relations to various family forms shed some light on juvenile justice. The state, for instance, evinces great concern if youngsters who stray are not under direct control of a patriarch (in other words, come from broken homes). It becomes exceedingly concerned if girls flout the legitimate arrangements for reproduction (that is, being married, and under a man's control) by engaging in fornication, and the like. Clearly, the reproductive marketability and health of young women is the central concern of the reactions of the juvenile justice system. Juvenile justice still maintains a commitment to formal equality and fairness, but it also claims a higher commitment to serving substantively unequal needs of the children before it.

> In criminology we must realize that we do not live in a society of individuals who are equal before the law in the sense that the state is equally concerned about their behavior (McIntosh 1978, 396).

When girls and boys commit the same acts (whether they be truancy, precocious sexuality, or shoplifting) the juvenile court moves rapidly from (an often embarrassingly superficial) review of the legal facts to consideration of the children's needs, wherein sexist stereotypes play a dominant role.

Chesney-Lind (1974) argues that any behavior on the part of girls that contravenes the double standard is treated seriously by the juvenile court. She further argues that juvenile justice actively sexualizes other offences by girls: where boys steal for gain, girls steal because of penis envy.

> . . . women apprehended for criminal offences are not released if they refuse to play the traditional female role. In this fashion, the police are not so much responding chivalrously to women as they are patrolling the boundaries of the female sex role (Chesney-Lind 1977, 207).

The contrasting official concern regarding boys' sexuality is revealing. Recall that the self-report studies indicate that more boys than girls are involved in early heterosexual experience, yet they are almost never subjects of juvenile justice attention. In contrast, the boys punished for sexuality have in the majority of cases been involved homosexually, especially with adults (Geller 1980).

Defenders of the traditional approach to girls and sexual delinquency will point out, of course, that an unwanted pregnancy for an underaged, often poor teenage girl is a very serious problem for herself, her child, and society at large. This should not, however, be allowed to excuse the exclusive focus of attention on the female partner in teenage sexual relations, and the ignoring of the male. With modern birth control resources, sexual activity can be technically separated from reproduction; further consideration needs to be devoted, however, to the reluctance among teens to avail themselves of the technology, a reluctance still grounded in partriarchal ideologies regarding sex, and not seriously addressed in educational programs.

Others will cite psychobiological research indicating that males may indeed by more aggressively inclined. Such biological or hormonal predisposition, of course, needs to be further augmented by socialization to produce even the differences in the self-report rates, let alone those in the official statistics. Furthermore, the question needs to be raised as to whether in this area of human behavior we should not consider "feminizing" the socialization of males, in an effort to reduce violence.

We do need more research on the delinquencies of Canadian girls. But there is a danger that simply generating more studies of female delinquents will not move us beyond the terrain of traditional criminology and its individualism (Gavigan 1983). A socially contextualized analysis is required, one that would place females and males in their interrelationships, mediated and complicated by class, ethnicity, and age inequalities. Much of the criticism of juvenile justice in regard to girls can be made on the grounds of the lack of implementation of principles of formal equity. But we must move beyond such fundamentally liberal criticisms, recognizing that responses to them can be easily encapsulated in a retained system of substantive inequality. Analysis is required of the legal statuses that affect women, not only those directly in criminal and juvenile justice, but also those regarding labor relations, welfare, domestic events, and the like. These legal statuses must be related to feminist inspired analyses of the substantive situation of women and girls, and must be seen as grounded in reproduction, childrearing, labor relations, and state policies. Finally, such work needs to thoroughly integrate and extend neo-Marxist conceptions of law and the state.

5

Peers and Subcultural Ethnography: Interaction Theory and Age

He told me that the night before about a dozen or more "rubbing-alcohol fiends" had been taken out of the park. At the corner – a hamburger "joint." This is a hang-out for prostitutes and tough characters. Many teen-age boys also frequent this place. I was in a cigar store where rubbing alcohol could be had at "two-bits a bottle." Small groups of teen-age girls were wandering around trying to be picked up by soldiers. I saw two office girls who were looking for someone with liquor. They had just left an old gentleman who had been duped into sharing with them his precious Scotch. In the park three poker games were going on under a lamp. A man wearing bicycle clips was supplying the players with drinks.

Rogers 1945, 9

NEED FOR OBSERVATIONAL FIELD RESEARCH

We discussed control theory and self-report studies in chapter 4, and through them we identified a number of key variables associated with delinquent behavior. We found that among the strongest predictors were those of having delinquent associates and holding delinquent beliefs or cultural understandings that question the legitimacy of the legal system. But we also found that self-report studies have difficulty telling us what such factors mean in real-life adolescent experience, or how they operate. On its own terms, since not all the variance is explained, other unconsidered factors need to be identified to elaborate control theory.

The claims by feminists of sociology's inattention or misconstruction of female delinquency included the insistence that closer attention be paid to young women's actual experience and exercise of human intentionality. Although such role socialization and role structure theories derived from self-report data and control theory go some way towards explaining both the similarities and differences between female and male delinquency, they assume that rather rigid notions of personality organization and social structure are common for all members of each sex. A number of studies have indicated that some control theory variables such as school failure (a measure of commitment) may not be important in determining girls' delinquent behavior, and other factors such as having delinquent associates may be more important. The fact that an extended control theory explains considerably more of the variance in delinquency of boys than girls (about 50 percent rather than 35 percent) should also encourage us to return to the field and engage in renewed exploratory research to identify possible factors with more exceptional influence on girls, as Campbell (1981) has urged.

Some recent assessments of control theory and self-report measures have suggested that both of these may be appropriate for examining and explaining only the relatively minor, although quite numerous, everyday delinquencies committed by typical adolescents. Leblanc (1981) and others feel that alternative explanations such as career and subcultural approaches are perhaps more useful in explaining really serious delinquency.

Though there have been notable exceptions, most research using either official statistics or self-report data, and either anomie or control theory analyses, has looked at adolescent deviance fundamentally from the viewpoint of official adult society (for example, in assuming the moral value of various acts as deviant). Yet a central thread in sociology holds a view of the human actor as rational and pursuing meaningful actions within constraining limits.

Another research tradition – ethnography – explicitly offers greater hope for the discovery and development of new types of knowledge sensitive to the demands of the situation. In unexplored or moribund areas, participant observational studies (described in detail by: Becker 1970b; Denzin 1970; Lutz and Ramsay 1974; West 1977a; Wilson 1974) are of particular value. Briefly, in this approach, observers go out into the community and begin collecting data before formulating explicit research questions, though they obviously have some topics of concern to direct their inquiry. Topics are refined into research questions through an ongoing and continuously repeated process of observing and interviewing, recording and analysing, reviewing relevant literature, formulating and testing propositions, and the like. Such research (West 1977a) emphasizes onsite observation in the naturally occurring "field" situations (in other words, not in laboratories, or even in interview or questionnaire situations), thereby maximizing "external validity." By this means full attention is given to the situational processes of human interaction, and to subjects' conscious, intended meanings. Observers attempt to understand the culture of the group studied by participating to the extent that they can reconstruct it themselves. Such research attempts to reveal the personal experience of delinquency, showing how activities are carried out in real-life situations. This research has been especially useful in exploring delinquent subcultures and adolescent peer group relations.

The chances of discovering totally unexpected phenomena are thus increased, and the flexibility of research design allows new topics to be incorporated into the project as it evolves. As well, opportunities for developing relevant indicators of concepts are enhanced, and manipulable variables can be incorporated. Such qualitative methods allow one to understand how people's conceptions shape their behavior, and how such conceptions and behavior change over time in an evolving process of interaction. Thus they allow the study of the dialectical process by which people create the very social structures that in turn shape them.

ADOLESCENT SUBCULTURE: STRAIGHTS, GREASERS, AND FREAKS

Unfortunately, to date, almost no such research on delinquent adolescents has been published in Canada. There are some stimulating but rather journalistic accounts (McLaren 1980), some fictional accounts (Garner 1968; Dickson 1973), some work examining educational issues for particular adolescent groups (Seeley et al. 1956; Armogan 1976; Maxwell and Maxwell 1979), some participant observational studies of largely adult criminals (Prus and Irini 1980; West 1979a, 1979–80, 1980a, 1983), and some graduate student work in progress (Visano 1983; Gerin-Lajoie 1983), but there is a lack of observational studies on the delinquent activities of adolescents. I will draw upon such material when possible, but as an example of ethnographic research on delinquent subcultures, I will be forced to draw upon some findings from my own work with Chicago as well as Toronto youngsters, indicating where appropriate their consistency with other participant observational studies. Unlike many similar efforts, at least I had the advantage of comparative analysis of different subcultures with both males and females.

The Subcultures

Though before beginning this field research I had anticipated studying a single adolescent subculture, I immediately noted three subcultures into which the local teenagers divided themselves: "straights," "greasers," and "freaks." Each of these subcultures were readily identified by their apparel.

Straights (also known as dupers, collegians, or "normal kids") wore desert boots, penny loafers, or gym shoes, frequently with white socks. Pants were tight jeans (often wheat-colored), with cuffs above the ankles; in summer, cutoff denim shorts were acceptable. Dress shirts with button-down collars, sweatshirts, and T-shirts were covered by army jackets, squall jackets, ski jackets, or sports-team jackets. In winter, this could be topped off by a knit, woolen toque. In general, the girls were less clearly differentiated by dress, and most easily identified by their accompanying males. Straight girls fell in between the other types in their moderate use of makeup and hairstyling. They wore much the same clothing as their boyfriends, except that for them shorts were even more acceptable in summer. "Getting dressed up" was not as repugnant to straights as it was to freaks.

The greasers appeared as stereotypic lower-class street-corner toughs, though some were lower middle class (by parents' occupations), and class was not directly considered by the teens when classifying people. Greasers wore pointed European shoes ("spick" shoes) or combat boots; loose work pants with rolled cuffs (baggies); tight, black slacks; or tailor-made dress pants (usually with a high, or Spanish waist); plus work shirts or black, cotton shirts. A black leather, hip-length jacket or jean jacket completed the apparel. Hair was short and slicked back with the aid of oil, often in a pompadour. Not infrequently, a knife or chogo sticks (two pieces of wood, one inch in diameter by one foot long, tied together at one end with rope, and used as a blackjack or restraining "vise") were carried.

Greaser "chicks" often had teased or ratted hair, heavy makeup, leather or jean jackets, blue jeans, and not infrequently they wore boots.

Freak costume has been well portrayed in the mass media as "hippy" apparel. These teens went barefoot or in sandals or cowboy boots. Bell-bottom jeans, army shirts, tie-dyed shirts, or other brightly colored clothes were used. Army jackets or jean jackets were worn in cold weather. Most noticeably, hair was worn long, at least ear-length, and frequently to the shoulders, often parted in the middle and supported by a headband. Beads and other unusual items were not uncommon (strange hats, capes, vests, and the like). Army greatcoats (knee length) were popular in winter.

Freak girls cultivated long, straight hair, wore no makeup, and dressed in fringed, suede jackets, sweatshirts, or large-collared shirts, and bell-bottom slacks or jeans. They went barefoot or wore sandals or boots.

It soon became apparent that these clothing styles represented much more. These three social types were common knowledge among the teens of the community, though greasers and freaks comprised a disproportionately small number of the youth. Probably a small percentage of the entire youth population of the neighborhood would fully have fit into any of the three social types or perspectives (Schwendiger 1963); most youth were "impure" representatives of their type. Nonetheless, these types were orienting guideposts for the youth in their self-definition, their affiliations, and their interaction with adults and other youth. They were crucial for communication. The apparent coherence within – and distinction between – perspectives is increased by purposely focussing on the "purest" type individuals. This was justified in that these persons who most thoroughly elaborate the perspectives were utilized by *all* the youth and many adults in categorizing and interacting with teens.

Although the research was done in a particular neighborhood of Chicago from 1969 to 1971, there are good reasons to believe that the types described herein are enduring adaptations to age, sex, and class statuses, and of general significance in contemporary industrialized societies. The straights are "normal," middle-class teenagers, with problems and perspectives similar to those of other Canadian youth (Vaz 1965; Byles 1969; Elkin and Westley 1955; Seeley et al. 1956), American youth (Coleman 1961; Hollingshead 1949; Cusick 1973; Matza 1964a), and British youth (Musgrove 1964). The greasers generally seemed to be the same in their behavior and orientation as those youth described as lower-class delinquents by other authors (Thrasher 1927/1963; Schwendinger 1963; Gillis 1974; Werthman 1969; Matza 1964a; Holtz 1975). "Teds," "rockers," and "skinheads" in Britain over the past two decades have been similarly described (Mungham and Pearson 1976; Willis 1977; Corrigan 1979; Brake 1974, 1980). A few Canadian studies seem corroborative (Rogers 1945; Byles 1969; West 1980). The freaks are a somewhat less well-established type, but nonetheless seem to have been preceded by "romantic rebels" (Gillis 1974), "surfers" (Irwin 1973), beatniks (Polsky 1969; Goodman 1960), and hippies (Roszak 1969; Davis and Munoz 1968; Matza 1964a); for Canada, see Byles (1969). At least two other research efforts in the Chicago area have found the exact same types (Buff 1971; Center for New Schools 1972), which correspond precisely to those the Schwendingers located in Los Angeles (1963); and Toronto informants confirm their existence there, as well as numerous students in my Ontario university classes. Though the straights seem greatly to outnumber the greasers and freaks, the three types do appear to represent socially significant adaptations to adolescent status.

The three perspectives can be seen as both informing and emerging from interactions, which can somewhat arbitrarily be divided into teen-adult and teen-peer categories. To ascertain these perspectives, I asked subjects what problems they and their friends had *as teenagers*. Their responses are best viewed as expressions of particular definitions of their situation worked out over time in the various cultural groups. My data do not systematically address the now obscured question of the origins of the cultures, though the process of individual affiliations is discussed later.

STRAIGHTS

Straights immediately volunteered that parent-youth relations were their most salient problem (as in Elkin and Westley 1955; and Seeley et al. 1956).

> K: Like if a kid skips class, he gets grounded by his parents – now is that sensible? . . . The curfew is stupid. Parents are always getting up tight about that. Most of the kids can't really talk to their parents, the parents are always trying to force something on the kid.
>
> Male straight, 14

There may be domestic arguments and some brave talk of independent action, but all straights' parents exercise a considerable degree of control over them, at least enough for the youth to struggle against. There is no mention of leaving home, of being completely independent; straights thus accept this aspect of their legally defined status.

Related to this, school is also perceived as a major problem in that all straights take for granted that they will continue to be students in the foreseeable future. The relationship between academic success and future economic success is clearly accepted as valid and personally motivating. Experienced difficulty in obtaining part-time or summer employment reinforces this maxim.

> E: . . . I worry about my marks – I only got a C, and I want to go to college. Though I don't know what in yet. The teacher bitches about some things . . .
>
> Female straight, 14

Though straights may have specific criticisms of the educational system, they do not link them into an ideological rejection, or propose radical alternatives. Indeed, they are as likely to complain that teachers lack disciplinary control.

> L: Some can't maintain any order; they just let the kids do anything, and then you don't learn nothing.
>
> Male straight, 14

Five straights who told of disciplinary problems all responded to the threat of greater sanctions by conforming.

Straight youth generally do not perceive adult control agents as causing problems for teenagers.

When police or others attempt to enforce some specific laws, breaking what are taken to be previous tacit agreements to ignore violations, some straights object, but not strenuously.

> G: All the kids are paranoid of [the cops] . . . They sort of come around to pinch us, but you know, I guess they got a job to do, too. They really don't try to be mean, but they do sneak up on you . . . You know [the park manager] isn't there anymore. He got transferred. That's too bad, really.
>
> Male straight, 12

These teens had difficulty finding any employment and felt they had little money.

> D: Well, there is no place to go and nothing to do; of course, it's hard to get money – nobody has any money. That's 'cause there are hardly any jobs around for kids to do.
>
> Female straight, 15

Hence there is little contact with adults in a work situation.

The lack of monetary resources also creates recreational problems, as many entertainments cost money. Proprietors who see teens as small spenders have limited tolerance for their presence.

> L: You can just hang in the parks, or go to a restaurant – in the winter it's cold in the park, unless you're skating there or something. If you go to a restaurant, then you just sit and talk, and they kick you out after awhile, unless you're with an adult. They're going to build a big fieldhouse soon, then that'll be okay – a gym, a pool, places to go. If you go to a pool now, it's two dollars for an hour at the Y, or a hundred and seventy-five dollars for a year's membership; that's too much. You can stay at the health club at the bowl, it's cheaper there, and you can stay all day. But that's where the Whitebacks hang out.
>
> Male straight, 14

For straights (particularly the males), sports are the primary institutionalized "action" (Vaz 1965). Baseball, football, basketball, and hockey provide practices and league schedules around which these teens order their lives.

> At Pitts Park – three baseball games, about two dozen teens watching . . . Back to Tupper Park, a group of ten playing volleyball.
>
> Observation, 110 straights

The girls are much less active in sports, and concentrate on successfully managing interpersonal relations. The lack of sex-related work roles and sociolegal proscriptions on adolescent sexual activity contribute to the feeling that peer relations are a problem.

> G: The boys just want to play sports – so they ignore us. Like B. Or there are so many cliques. They are always evaluating each other and criticizing and cutting each other up. "They do this," or "They do that." It's so picky.

> Or you got to do something to get into this group, or something to get into that one.
>
> GW: What clique do you belong to?
>
> G: None now, we dropped out of one. Anybody who wants to come around with us can if they're nice.
>
> Female straight, 14

Though the girl above opposes cliques, her qualification that anybody is acceptable "if they're nice" indicates that she, too draws limits. Such boundaries (for instance, regarding chastity) seem to serve to develop a personal identity. A straight girl must walk a narrow tightrope between attracting the boys and remaining chaste, at least by reputation (Schwartz and Merten 1967/1969). Such a "balancing act" is not required of the boys, who are publicly encouraged to brag about their sexual exploits, thus vicariously providing the "necessary" element of risk for their female companions.

For excitement, the straights studied tended to rely less than greasers or freaks on behavior deemed illegal. The girls reported few offences; not having sexual intercourse clearly distinguished them from greasers. Other than minor experimentation with alcohol or marijuana (excepting one frequent user whose brother was a freak), and occasional curfew or truancy violations, the most common crime by girls was shoplifting; perhaps once a month they would steal small items (usually jewelry or cosmetics) from stores.

The straight boys report a great deal more illegal behavior; getting drunk and breaking curfew every weekend is common; they have usually tried marijuana a few times, but are not vehemently opposed to the present drug laws.

> Down to Pitts Park, just coming in the north end I see two kids moving to the corner of the park; I hesitate but can't recognize the little cluster through the trees. I go over and find S, K, U, and N . . . – all have big beers.
>
> Observation, 4 straight males, 14

Like the girls, boys admit to shoplifting occasionally. Fights are not uncommon, as straights regard "spontaneous" violence as an acceptable if not desirable demonstration of manly integrity; altercations frequently erupt during sporting events. Gambling (card games and penny tossing) is an almost-daily creator of risk among some straights. In all, only two straights report being apprehended by the police (other than for curfew or gambling) – one for car theft and assault on an old man (which resulted in probation), and one for shoplifting, which was settled out of court (*cf* Vaz 1965).

Straight males and females give considerable evidence of rationally considering possible consequences of illegal acts, and are particularly concerned with parental disapproval. Nor do they feel there is a tremendous pressure to conform to any group illegalities.

> GW: Like could you ever lose prestige if you didn't do something with the group even if it is illegal?

> L: No, not really; you could just back out and not do it.
>
> Male straight, 14

GREASERS

Greasers also mention parent-youth relations as being a problem, but less frequently than straights. An assumption of their own autonomy seems to underly the discussion; family relations are less of a problem since parents have already granted considerable freedom.

> E: Sometimes we have some big arguments – she tells me not to eat stuff; and I take some anyhow. Or she tells me some guy I go with is not too cool, so I should lay off. I just go with him anyway. Or she'll bitch if I steal some of her beer . . . Times I get in late; like if somebody is having a party until four, say for New Years, then I want to stay out. She bitches, so I just go, and catch hell when I come back. That's okay; in one ear and out the other. Then next time I just do the same thing.
>
> Male greaser, 16

Some greasers have had to fend for themselves from an early age, and their assumed autonomy is not surprising.

> U: I was at High School for two years. I lived in [a suburb] for two years when I was fourteen to sixteen. My Mom kicked me out and so I lived with my Dad there until he cut out. He's a salesman. My Mom wouldn't take me back in, so I went to live with my grandmother.
>
> Male greaser, 18

Compared with straights, greasers seem immune to possible sanctions from parents; they appear to have largely worked out a de facto relationship of independence with parents.

School is also troublesome to greasers. But their orientation is different from that of straights – their concern is less with good grades and graduation than with disciplinary rules and lack of autonomy (McLaren 1980).

> GW: Is school a hassle?

> U: I guess so! They make you go – I don't see the point if you're a girl and are going to grow up and get married. You don't need the education for a job – it isn't necessary. That's why I skipped school all the time last year. But I had to go to court . . .
>
> Female greaser, 14

Whereas all teens have some difficulties at school, greasers put less value on a formal education than straights in the sense that they are less likely to stay in school (Gerin-Lajoie 1983). Where straights may try to second-guess teachers in order to comply, greasers stage more open confrontations and are more likely to risk expulsion. Other studies indicate that such refusal to defer to teachers' adult status is crucial in determining "troublemakers" and "terminal students" (Cicourel and Kitsuse 1963; Werthman 1969; Hargreaves 1967; Polk and Schafer 1972; Corrigan 1979; Willis 1977).

Leaving school, however, does not automatically mean employment. While still in school, greasers have difficulty expressing concrete employment plans. Part-time jobs that are available do give highly valued status as a mature person.

> N: It's a good job, I make a lot of money – I couldn't pass it up. I mean these other guys, they'll eventually learn too, only I'll learn a few years ahead of them [what the world is like].
>
> Male greaser, 14

Lack of money, as with straights, curtails recreation.

The police and social workers are irritating problems to greasers, who are similarly defined by these adults for many of their peer group activities. Implicitly, greasers recognize that their adoption of an autonomous life-style bodes trouble. Yet to "back down" would be to relinquish claims to character and adult status.

Although some greasers engage in marginally athletic sports such as bowling or pool, most look elsewhere for excitement and to develop character. They also find life as an adolescent boring (Corrigan 1976).

> U: It's too boring up here . . . There was nothing to do. Those kids would just go to the beach everyday – it got boring. At first when the teen centre opened they had dances and stuff. Then they cut back, and it was dull, the same old thing. I just wanted to get out of here.
>
> GW: How do you mean?
>
> U: Go somewhere else; there's nothing to do. Kids around here have done it all.
>
> Female greaser, 14

If the straights' "moment of action" is on the sports field, the greasers' is in the assertion of individual autonomy, which often includes potentially violent interpersonal confrontations.

> Suddenly, I notice two guys jump up, crouch and circle – [the social worker] spots this after hearing a chair fall, and calls, "H!" [another worker].
>
> He touches the provocateur on the shoulder, and [the social worker] steps between the two boys and tells I to sit down. The other kid leaves on his own – put down.
>
> Observation, 2 greasers, 18

Although physical violence was not unheard of, it did not *actually occur* any more frequently between greasers than straights. But among greasers, it was held to be legitimate to seek and plan fights, and to use weapons. The few group fights that do occur (or, as often, nearly occur) become legendary and are the basis for character assessments (Short and Strodtbeck 1965).

> U: E and I one day at high school we met a bunch of Whitebacks and they wanted to go just the two of us – E took off his belt and was ready to go. And just then some of our guys came around the corner – well, that cooled them. Like that time you met us, we'd challenged them and we were supposed to meet down at the beach. Well, we had some Panthers [as allies] and some Blackstone – maybe five carloads of them – we were ready . . . Only when we got there, there were cops all up and down the beach.
>
> Male greaser, 18

For a few, group fighting can be dangerous, and it is these relatively rare events that shock adults.

> GW: Any kids who give you hassles?
>
> E: Oh, the other guys in gangs do [names some] . . . They give us a lot of trouble, man – just last week they shot one of the boys twice in the head.
>
> GW: Really?
>
> E: Ya. His marbles all over the place . . . We gonna wipe them bastards out.
>
> Male greaser, 16

The various groups exhibited the greatest cohesiveness in times of outside threat (Jansyn 1966). The formal gangs jealously guarded their neighborhoods, honor, and members from each other, though they felt no threat from local nongang youth. Freaks, greasers, and straights could thus coexist in the same neighborhood, though greasers occasionally decided to harass some freaks. The formal gangs thus relied upon each other as a primary source of solidarity and self-esteem (Rogers 1945).

Most of the time, greasers interact with peers in much more conventional ways, listening to rock or soul music, and being involved with "booze, broads, and cars."

> Up the beach, some kids are down by the rocks . . . J stuck his head out from a cave, so did U . . . They smiled sheepishly, retreated back into the cave, threw beer cans out on the lake . . . The other kids were now generally hopping and piling over the rocks . . . Other kids came up to the beer and took swigs, passing the cans on.
>
> Observation, Greasers 14 to 17

The girls concentrate on interpersonal relations, but sex is not proscribed: it is noteworthy that the majority of female juvenile incarcerations involve sexual behavior deemed inappropriate for adolescents.

Use of marijuana and some other drugs is not uncommon. Gambling seems less frequent than among straights. All greasers report running away from home, truancy, or curfew violations, indicative of their particular stance towards school and family (Visano 1983).

Male greasers report a considerable number of property offences. Four greasers reported seven to fifteen car thefts each in the past year; three of them had been apprehended once each and put on probation, and one of them was later incarcerated. A couple have been more than occasionally involved in break and entry and theft.

> N: That's one thing, you know, everybody has their weakness; well stealing stuff is mine – I just want to take something, man. I can't stop myself. Then after, it don't mean nothing, nothing to me . . .
>
> Male greaser, 14

Shoplifting is sometimes indulged in by girls and boys; vandalism sometimes occurs.

A couple of greasers report robbery as a regular source of income.

> E: Last Saturday six of us just sat in the alley and waited, and when one come along we just flashed the knife or the gun, and he gave it over – we don't want to kill nobody. Just the money. We make maybe thirty to forty dollars per week doing that.
>
> Male greaser, 18

Four of the six greaser males interviewed had been to court; three had been placed on probation. These events are taken into consideration in further illegalities.

Felt obligation to defend a friend is frequently cited as a "higher loyalty" (Sykes and Matza 1957), an extenuating circumstance that justifies fighting.

In self-report questions, greasers were indeed somewhat more deviant in behavior than straights, committing perhaps twice as many offences. Nonetheless, the chance of police contact (expressed as a percentage of total laws violated) was three or four times higher for greasers than for straights. Only some of this increase in arrests seemed accounted for by the seriousness of the acts: greasers were inordinately contacted by police for relatively minor offences as well as more serious ones.

FREAKS

Invariably, freaks identify "the pigs" as the most serious problem of teenagers.

> D: There's pigs all over the place man, and you really have to watch out,
> 'cause you never know what somebody will do. Anybody could just come
> up and turn you in. They always stop you when you're walking along –
> I got stopped four times in the last month just for standing around or
> walking down the street. They stop you 'cause they think you're loitering,
> or you got grass, or stuff like that. You just give them a look and then
> they let you go. Or they ask you if you're on something, or where you
> come from.
>
> Female freak, 14

In their attempts to enforce drug laws in particular, police are seen as
political oppressors. Social workers meet with an ambiguous reaction.

Parents, as with other teens, are a problem, but parent-child relations
are not as consistent as with either straights or greasers.

> D: I guess most of the kids here on the beach have some difficulties . . .
> with their parents. They worry over whether the kid uses drugs or if the
> girls are going to be balled down here. Or parents always want to know
> where the kid is; and a lot of them don't want the kid to come down to
> the beach or hang around with us 'cause they think that he'll turn into a
> dope fiend or get into sex or something.
>
> Female freak, 14

Some freaks, then, are as autonomous as greasers, others seem a little
more willing to defer to stricter parental control, and a few have worked
out "liberated" relations with parents who do not share the standard
adult expectations of adolescents.

Like greasers, freaks reject the assumption that a formal education is
valuable; however, like straights, they usually place some value on
"knowledge," especially in an experiential sense (Byles 1969).

> D: Well, last year I left [elementary school] and I was supposed to go to
> [a suburban high school]. But the kids there are such snobs. All they talk
> about is their father's money and stuff, so I just went five days and then
> I couldn't take any more of it so I quit . . . The cops said they'd fine me
> five hundred dollars if I didn't go to school, so last week I went to [another
> high school]. My Mom gave a phony address [in that district]. Only I
> skipped a lot of classes – about twenty so far, and my division teacher
> knows, and he'll get after me tomorrow. Maybe I'll get suspended.
>
> GW: You worry about marks much?
>
> D: No, that's stupid – it's nothing. I mean it could tell your Mom what's
> happening, but it doesn't actually . . .
>
> Female freak, 14

Freaks tend to devalue the rituals of the bureaucratic educational system,
whether it be straights' ritualistic acceptance of subordination, or greasers' ritualistic assertions of autonomy (Westhues 1972).

Freaks reveal the more complicated nature of their life-style in their
comments about jobs and money. Unlike greasers, they do not simply

and immediately aspire to an adult position in the economy; they perceive many jobs as dehumanizing and restrictive of human potentials.

> GW: Any occupation you want to do when you grow up?
>
> D: No, not really.
>
> GW: Any thoughts about that at all?
>
> D: Maybe, I used to want to be a marine biologist, but not now.
>
> Female freak, 14

When freaks do need money, they seek an easy "hustle."
Freaks find excitement in illegal drug use.

> About sixty kids on the beach . . . There were about six clusters of kids who sat and talked, came and left together; a good number of the others knew people in different clusters, and circulated around. About five kids were stoned to the point of locomotive difficulty; they fell down, staggered, etc. . . . Some guitar playing. "Wanna cop some grass?" was a regular cry. Six kids asked me for downers, THC [marijuana derivative] or grass.
>
> Observation

The harder drugs (downers, speed, heroin) are much less frequently used than marijuana, though downers seem to be becoming increasingly popular. Alcohol use is disdained by some freaks, but regularly used by others. Drug use is often considered as essential to personal liberation, and is linked to freaks' involvement with artistic expression (especially music). New Left ideology is embraced to oppose what is seen as sociolegal oppression (Roszak 1969).

> D: Most of the kids disagree with the drug laws. If they made them legal and controlled them, they wouldn't cut them with heroin and strychnine. It'd be safer to use them. They aren't going to stamp out drug use, so they might as well make it safer.
>
> Female freak, 14

Freaks' social structures tend to be comparatively loose, consisting of shifting conglomerations of small groups (often dyads and triads); compared to greaser and straight groups, there is a noticeably more rapid turnover of membership at particular spots, and a lack of stable leadership. There are pervading norms of individual libertarianism ("do your own thing"), and eccentricity is encouraged.

Although freaks are ideologically committed to loving one's neighbor, fights are occasionally reported; a few pitched battles with the police occurred when the latter attempted to clear freak gathering places or enforce drug laws. When police are seen as instruments of social oppression, violence against "the system" is considered legitimate.

Interpersonal relations cause problems especially around the issue of sex, as with the other types of teens. Most of the boys, but fewer girls, have had sexual intercourse.

> D: Sometimes boys come along; they think that just 'cause you're out and a girl, that you'll ball them. So they try to hustle you – you have to put them off. That's the main problem. Most of the guys around here are okay though, they treat you right.
>
> Female freak, 14

Freaks experience a particular problem in finding trustworthy peers, especially if they turn to dealing in drugs with other than close friends.

> C: By the end of the summer, people were getting paranoid, some kids informed on friends, and there were some busts – so that's when I split.
>
> Male freak, 16

Affiliation Patterns

Having looked at these three subcultures, we can now examine affiliation patterns and maintenance processes. Consideration of career sequences allows the linking of the normative aspects of the subcultures with social-psychological identity structure, and the possible acquisition of "delinquent associates" so important in the control theory research (see West, 1984b, forthcoming, for a more extended discussion).

Although socioeconomic status was not initially used in classifying teens according to type, the data indicate that adolescents with middle-class parents tended to be straights, while those with working-class parents tended to be greasers, and the class background of freaks seemed of approximately even distribution. Given the sampling procedure and imperfect correlations, the tentativeness of this finding must be kept in mind, but it is consistent with other research (for example, Hall and Jefferson 1976).

For teens to join a group holding a particular subcultural orientation, a number of conditions were necessary. The location of the family domicile in a particular neighborhood obviously affects affiliation possibilities. The group had to be located somewhere, usually either in adult supervised recreational areas (for straights), or in commercial territories (for greasers), or unsupervised areas (for greasers and freaks) (West 1977b). In such "home territories," teens can most easily elaborate their illegal subcultural activities, in comparison with the restrictions they meet either in compulsory territories (such as parents' residence or school), or in the more closely supervised areas frequented by straights.

Besides such locatable neighborhood sites, many teens met at school. Propinquity, however, was inadequate to explain particular choices. Teens were drawn to particular others to demonstrate their own character and distinguish themselves from undesirables (for example, regarding sexual activity, fighting, having fun, and the like). "Being grease" was considered as much a mark of distinction as "going freak" or straight (West 1984b, forthcoming). Rationalization of beliefs, of course, were also worked out with such peer groupings.

Straight males especially expressed clear adult career goals; straight girls always included marriage with mention of an occupation. Greaser girls named only the latter; by contrast, neither greaser nor freak males had explicit career goals, nor did freak girls (Corrigan 1979; Willis 1977). All, however, identified with some adults, and rejected others.

Although the three perspectives remained fairly stable in the neighborhood studied, and seem generally so in contemporary English-speaking societies, individual teens changed perspectives with surprising frequency, a finding unanticipated from previous research in this area. Most youth of working-class parents were greasers originally, but through the year of study, greasers seem to have become members of other groups. None of those identified at the end of the research as greaser had been straight or freak; no recruits, in other words, moved from the other perspectives into greaser ranks.

SYMBOLIC INTERACTIONIST THEORIES OF DELINQUENCY
Symbolic Interactionism

As we initially suggested in chapter 1, both anomie theory and control theory suffer in some ways from their neopositivist philosophy of social science. In assuming that the meaning of delinquency and of social events is obvious, they eradicate by fiat the ambiguity and subtleties of human intentionality, thus freezing interaction. Their assumption of value consensus is superficial, without serious exploration of either subtle or gross variations in people's belief systems. In sometimes desperately seeking measurable quantities for statistical analysis, they limit their vision of what is real to that which can be measured. They too readily assume that factors meaningful to humans can be counted as fixed units, and also that scientifically, only such factors are important. They further assume that persons are in some sense fundamentally directed, unable to transcend their situations, but rather, reacting to "factors," with little regard for the possibility of human interpretation. Such ethnographic material as presented above throws into question these kinds of assumptions.

The previous section of ethnographic data and analysis of delinquent subcultures and affiliations rests on a major sociological approach different from anomie, control, and conflict theories. Articulated as a sociological theory from a blending of formalism and pragmatism at the

University of Chicago during the 1920s, symbolic interactionist theory is based upon a unique philosophy of social science quite different from other theories (Rock 1979).

In symbolic interactionism, analysis can only start with socially contexted individuals; no others exist! In contrast to anomie theory's assumption that human nature is social, but can be forced towards delinquency by strain, and control theory's assumption that human nature is antisocial and must be controlled, interactionism assumes that human nature is plastic, neither predeterminedly good nor evil. Individuals construct a fluid social order through emergent interaction with others. From birth, they construct a self-image based on the valuation of people around them. These are conveyed in direct response to needs like food and shelter, but also increasingly by symbols. Unlike animals, people are able to communicate complex ideas through symbolization, especially language. Guided by such symbols, people intentionally choose courses of action to reach goals meaningful to them. They as individuals are not fixed immutably through attachment to abstract values or delinquent subcultures, but are constantly emerging through interaction with others in concrete situations. It is through such interaction with others that social life is constituted, including that of the most complex social organizations. Society thus exists only in and through such interactions. One can see how such a strong emphasis on the plasticity of human behavior, on situational interaction as crucial, implies that any interactionist theories must be considered as much more tentative than neopositivist ones. Because of the ever-present possibility of transcendence, human action retains an unpredictable quality for interactionists. What motivates greasers today could easily change tomorrow.

Some Classic Symbolic Interactionist Theories of Delinquency

DIFFERENTIAL ASSOCIATION

This focus on intentionality and belief, coupled with its central regard for interaction, suggests that symbolic interactionism has some particular relevance in understanding two of the major factors isolated by control theory: delinquent beliefs and associates. Indeed, one of the most important criminological theories developed in the symbolic interactionist tradition is that of "differential association," formulated by Edwin Sutherland in 1938. It consists of the following propositions (Sutherland and Cressey 1955, 77–80):

1. Criminal behavior is learned.
2. Criminal behavior is learned in interaction with other persons in a process of communication.

3. The principal part of the learning of criminal behavior occurs within intimate personal groups.
4. When criminal behavior is learned, the learning includes (a) techniques of committing the crime, which are sometimes very complicated, sometimes very simple; (b) the specific direction of motives, drives, rationalizations, and attitudes.
5. The specific direction of motives and drives is learned from definitions of the legal codes as favorable or unfavorable.
6. A person becomes delinquent because of an excess of definitions favorable to violation of law over definitions unfavorable to violation of law.
7. Differential association may vary in frequency, duration, priority, and intensity.
8. The process of learning criminal behavior by association with criminal and anticriminal patterns involves all the mechanisms that are involved in any other learning process.
9. While criminal behavior is an expression of general needs and values, it is not explained by those general needs and values since noncriminal behavior is an expression of the same needs and values.

Such propositions seem quite consistent with the patterns of subcultural affiliation outlined for greasers and freaks.

In some ways differential association is an optimistic theory of delinquency, because it suggests that by changing his or her associates and evaluation of illegality, a youngster can be corrected. Organizations like Synanon for drug addicts (Yablonsky 1968b) and Alcoholics Anonymous seem to work on its principles, as well as some famous delinquency correction programs at Highfields, New Jersey (McCorkle et al. 1958), Provo, Utah (Empey and Erickson 1972), and Silverlake, Los Angeles (Empey and Lubeck 1971).

MATZA'S DRIFT/NEUTRALIZATION THEORY

Later theorists have adapted and extended Sutherland's basic ideas about culture conflict, delinquency as an emergent phenomenon, and symbolic motivation. Sykes and Matza (1957), and Matza and Sykes (1961) have argued that sociological explanations of delinquency must recognize that there are a range of subterranean "deviant" values in mainstream American society, accepted by most people, which delinquents can draw upon for support. Having fun, getting kicks, winning at all costs, not being "square," and the like, are examples of the kinds of rationales that generally conforming adults also subscribe to on occasions (especially during leisure). These may be elaborated by delinquents into "techniques of neutralization," whereby legal values are not fully and explicitly denied, but rather are "bent" or extended, as in the greaser and freak subcultures. Delinquents may (a) deny responsibility for some of their actions, blaming them on others or surrounding circumstances; (b) deny any injury, claiming that no harm was really done; (c) deny claims of their victims, saying that they deserved it anyway (as in wrecking the classroom of an unfair teacher); (d) condemn their condemners, saying that they are just as bad; and (e) appeal to higher loyalties, such as not "squealing" on a friend. Matza (1964a) suggests that these techniques of neutralization may be used in conjunction with the invocation of subterranean values to release youngsters from a constraining mood of "fatalism" into a situation of "drift" (perhaps adolescent boredom?), wherein they may situationally choose to assert their humanity by acting. They are not forced to break the law, but may actively choose to do so as the most situationally available means to restore a "mood of humanism." (Recall that Matza's work provided a basis for Bertrand's theory of female delinquency discussed in chapter 4.) Such a formulation, of course, fits nicely with our legal system's fundamental assumption of free will: if someone was constrained to commit illegalities by being mentally ill, acting in self-defence, or being forced at gunpoint, he or she is not found guilty.

It is clearly the case that many if not most delinquents are much more morally ambivalent than either anomie or control theory would suggest. In conducting some participant observation research on Toronto youngsters between the ages of ten to fourteen, who were identified by the police, courts, and/or social agencies as delinquent, I found most of them to neither be strongly committed to "delinquent values" nor to stable group ("gang") interaction, but rather to be "at loose ends" (West 1968). Short and Strodtbeck (1965) reported the same for older, much more seriously delinquent Chicago youngsters who held middle-class values as well as "deviant" ones. Although they registered some impact of the larger social class structure on their behavior, they found that immediate situational group process was crucial to understanding delinquent episodes.

LABELING OR SOCIAL REACTION THEORY

During the mid-1960s, anti–Vietnam War protests, black riots, and student uprisings swept Western countries, drug subcultures mushroomed, the social order trembled, and it became difficult to sustain anomie or control theories' assumption about moral consensus in society defining delinquency. Self-report data challenged the traditional views of the location of delinquency, and organizational research began to reveal official biases. In such a climate, some relatively tentative statements (mainly) by interactionists about the interplay of social reaction and deviant behavior caught the study of delinquency by storm.

In the famous words of Howard S. Becker (1963,9):

> Deviance is not a quality of the act a person commits but rather a consequence of the application by others of rules and sanctions to an offender. The deviant is one to whom that label has successfully been applied; deviant behaviour is behaviour that people so label.

Some labeling theorists (for example, Tannenbaum 1938) implied that such labeling encouraged subjects to regard themselves as deviant, and hence caused them to assume a deviant status and to commit further deviant acts. One might change from being an ordinary "primary" deviant to a special "secondary" one (Lemert 1951), whose problems are multiplied, whose activities are minutely scrutinized, whose life has been seriously altered. Neopositivist interpretations developed this into a social-psychological hypothesis: labeling people causes them to act accordingly (Gove 1975). In addition, it is claimed that labeling has often been imputed not so much for particular types of deviant behavior as for various subsidiary status characteristics: people have been mislabeled for dressing like greasers (Briar and Piliavin 1965).

In a great burst of enthusiasm, sociologists turned from studying delinquents and what caused their behavior to studying officials who reacted to them. In some wildly overstated and deterministic interpretations (Nettler 1974), it was claimed labeling theory said we need only stop labeling youngsters delinquent, and we would have no more delinquency (see Petrunik 1980, for a thoughtful counteranalysis). More seriously, by indicating how deleterious mislabeling is, more tolerance of diversity would reduce official incidents of deviance and the elaboration of deviant statuses and self-concepts. As Schur articulated it, "Leave the kids alone wherever possible" (1973).

Labeling conceptions of deviance did strengthen the rationale for utilizing self-report instead of official data for studying deviant behavior. They also focussed research attention on how official agencies define, deal with, and classify deviant behavior. Labeling conceptions of deviance have, for instance, clarified how police respond to victim complaints, and so focus on "ordinary" street crime more than "respectable" crime; they have also revealed how police deployment practices "flood" working-class areas near city centers, and hence may be responsible for the disproportionate numbers of working-class arrests. The practices of police and judges of categorizing people as "types" have been studied (Werthman 1969). In addition, there have been further studies of deviant statuses and subcultures, indicating the difficulties involved in abandoning a deviant status once acquired (Hargreaves, Hester, and Mellor 1975). This approach has indicated to what degree official order and deviance are social products (West 1975b).

SYMBOLIC INTERACTIONIST THEORY

Stripped of the excesses shown in some of these interpretations, symbolic interactionism may best be seen as offering a series of principles drawn from a research tradition for studying delinquency, rather than an axiomatic deductive theory (as are anomie and control theories). These principles are based on viewing human behavior as evolving intentionally and transcendently through interaction in concrete situations (Becker 1974).

First, it must be recognized that all behavior must be interpreted, it is not self-evidently meaningful. Meaning can only be assigned by understanding the activity in its situational context, from the viewpoint of the human beings participating. Assuming that isolated incidents from different situations have the same meaning is hazardous at best; consequently, the counting involved in survey research is always of questionable validity.

Secondly, one must study all the relevant participants regarding any delinquent act – the observers or labelers as well as the labeled. Since meaningfulness is achieved through the interaction of people, the social reaction of others (victims, police, parents, and the like) is crucial; because, if neither the "actor" nor the observers consider something delinquent, effectively and socially it is not delinquent.

Discovering how deviance is imputed to certain acts and to certain actors poses key questions. It is also important to analyze how "moral crusaders" have managed to have society adopt their definitions of social problems and deviant behavior (Becker 1963). Why, for instance, is smoking marijuana illegal?

Thirdly, claiming that "deviant behavior is behavior that is so labeled" is not to claim that labeling alone has caused the initial behavior, nor that it will automatically cause it to be repeated, as many neopositivists have misconstrued labeling theory. Some degree of labeling or defining is always essential in characterizing any behavior as humanly meaningful, but this is not the same as claiming that it has caused the event being so labeled to take place. An individual who has been labeled a delinquent remains existentially free as to his future behavior, of course, taking into account others' characterization of him.

Fourthly, attention must be paid to such characterizations of individuals. In many ways, society is more interested in persons deemed to be delinquents, greasers, or freaks than in any particular misdeed that they may commit. Labeling may effectively eliminate most viable options to go "straight," thus encouraging one to accept the imposed label of "delinquent," and to act accordingly.

As with all persons, however, such identities remain plastic and subject to modification; one can change affiliations, though dominant or master statuses are sometimes hard to shake from others' definitions.

Fifthly, one must examine the symbolic significance of delinquency in society. In other words, one must examine the functions of delinquents ("greasers" and "freaks") not only for those so labeled, but for the purposes of other persons, especially as it is used for system maintenance (Erikson 1964b). "Bad kids" are so labeled to distinguish them from "good kids." Like control theory in its use of self-report data, interaction theory carefully distinguishes between those who commit an act and those who are caught for committing it; like anomie theory, in its use of official statistics, interaction theory focuses attention on those caught.

Substantive Example of Interaction Theory: Age Status and Autonomy

The three subcultures described above represent different adaptations by adolescents to their common age status problems and their different socioeconomic status problems. In contemporary Western society, adolescence is a particular age status that imposes certain conditions (differentiated by class, gender, and ethnicity) on its members and thus further differentiates them by age. Chapter 2 indicates how in a social context the law requires adolescents and their families to maintain an ongoing association. Further, we indicated how teenagers are economically handicapped by prohibitive labor laws; even when legally eligible for jobs, adolescents continue to suffer an unemployment rate that is a multiple of that of the general population (Banfield 1970, 93). To the extent that work roles are the primary source of personal identity in our society, adolescents who are denied jobs can be expected to look elsewhere to create worthwhile self-images (Hughes 1958, 42–3). Compulsory school attendance has been required to age sixteen, and social pressure to continue persists beyond this age. Teens under the age of eighteen or sixteen are denied the right to vote and are subject to special courts, the police, and restrictive laws; they cannot enter into legal contracts; they possess less than full citizenship rights. In these ways, adolescents can be seen to constitute an oppressed minority (Kelly 1969). And though only temporary occupants of this status (unlike women, ethnic minorities, and most proletarians), teens have a degree of power and awareness not present in young children. Compared to childhood, and increasingly as the age of physical maturation falls (because of changed diet, and the like) and as social maturity is delayed, adolescence is a status with a questionable physical basis. One of the most salient characteristics of adolescent status, then, can be seen as *denied adulthood*, and this subordinate status is communicated to adolescents whenever they are "put in their place" on any of the above dimensions. Adolescent age status mediates social class, gender, and other relations.

Occupying a legally defined subordinate position, adolescents can be expected to develop routinized responses to their peculiar and recurring problems (Cohen 1955). These responses are elaborated over time in interaction with other teens, thus forming "subcultures" of individuals with common communicative understandings. All of the teens studied complained frequently of boredom, of a lack of interesting things to do and places to go. Other authors (Friedenberg 1959; Goodman 1960; Erikson 1962; Bloch and Niederhoffer 1958) have hypothesized that youth is the time of establishing a stable identity; adolescents need something to be true to, to have commitments that reinforce their self-image, to establish sex roles, and begin mate selection. But identity is most dramatically established in situations involving risk (Goffman 1967), and these are seldom available in our relatively "safe" society. Much peer interaction can be understood as a search for "action," for cheap excitement and kicks (Matza 1964a; Goffman 1967; also Vaz 1965). Adolescent culture defines new situations of such risk, whether in athletic feats, fights, drug use, or interpersonal relations.

Any of the three life-styles described earlier provided a potential latent culture for teens to use when they are in other institutional settings such as schools or family circles (Becker and Geer 1960). The chosen adolescent group may have offered "solutions" to problems felt prior to affiliation; it also offered a common perspective for defining difficulties perceived only after affiliation, and for redefining prior difficulties (*cf.* Cohen 1955; Cloward and Ohlin 1960; Kitsuse and Dietrich 1959; Hirschi 1969).

The data indicated that the subculture adopted by an individual teenager can best be understood as based on his or her core stance towards adolescent status in relation to adult class and gender statuses.

The straights formulated a "make-do" perspective, generally accepting their subordinate status as adolescents. A straight teen must have had some guarantee of continued parental support in the foreseeable future; both parents and teen accepted this arrangement. They both accorded legitimacy to parental control of the adolescent in substantial matters. Although this did not rule out tension over diverging views, it did require that the teen seek at least tacit parental approval for his public acts; straights were unwilling to seriously consider breaking with parents. Similarly, they ruled out leaving school as a realistic possibility; hence, they always eventually deferred to the school's authority, though they occasionally provoked disciplinary measures for minor offences. They also valued academic success. Such prolongation of relations with home and school was directly connected with aspirations to a job of at least middle-class status, coupled with marriage for girls. These aspirations correlated with middle-class origins, replicating other research.

Among peers, straights sought "action" that was legal to relieve boredom; sports prowess and skill in interpersonal relations between the sexes were qualities that all straights accorded a taken-for-granted legitimacy. They had AM radio tastes, and espoused no overtly political ideology (in other words, were status quo conservatives). The minor illegalities regularly committed by the boys were defined as "not serious"; with the exceptions of occasional vandalism, spontaneous violence, and shoplifting, straight misdemeanors were "crimes without victims" (drinking alcohol, gambling, minor experimentation with drugs, curfew violations, sexual experimentation). Straight girls "had to be nice," which prohibited sexual intercourse (or at least any public knowledge of it). The ban on "serious" illegalities for both sexes was directly related to the restraining side bet they all considered first: family disapproval. Straights basically considered the police and teachers as "okay," and "just doing their jobs."

Greasers rejected adolescent status and precociously demanded adulthood. In contrast with straights, their parents did not regularly offer continued economic support in the foreseeable future; these parents seemed to expect their children to be independent at an early age as they themselves had been. Greasers did not automatically defer to parental or school control; they were willing to negotiate as *equals*, not as subordinates, and considered leaving home or school. Their parents generally accepted this egalitarian stance, and worked out a *modus vivendi*. Since continued living at home and completion of a formal education were not taken for granted, threats of expulsion from school carried little weight. Greasers tended to evaluate school in terms of direct relevance to possible jobs, instead of automatically valuing grades; with a job, one could attain status by having money and autonomy from both home and school. Such immediate independence was attractive compared to prolonged subordination in preparation for the tenuous promise of an eventually higher status occupation, though jobs were often unavailable.

Greasers were highly pragmatic, and their seeking of excitement made sense in terms of a "coping" ethic. They mentioned fear of incarceration as a restraint to committing illegal acts rather than parental disapproval or "morality." They had committed the same "crimes without victims" as straights; in addition, all had engaged in sexual intercourse, a crucial prerogative of adulthood (especially for females). All greasers accepted organized gangs; violence could be planned in advance; the cardinal sin was desertion of a friend when he was in danger of attack. Property crimes were considered according to need and chance of success. Spare-time activities revolved around "booze, broads, and cars" (in male chauvinist terms). They listened to AM rock and soul music; any sports engaged in (for example, bowling or pool) were athletically marginal.

Freaks rejected both present adolescent and future adult roles. The preconditions of choosing to be a freak were not clear-cut. Freaks were willing to consider relinquishing economic support of their parents; the parents, in turn, did not guarantee continuation of such support. Though some freaks had come to refuse deference to parental authority, others still attributed some legitimacy to parental wishes; unlike greasers, they were not universally emancipated in their own minds. They did not unquestioningly defer to school authorities, yet they did place some value on education, especially in an experiential sense. Grades were not valued per se, as among straights. Dropping out of school was conceivable, and, as with greasers, this considerably reduced the school's potential for meaningful sanctioning. But freaks did not see employment as automatically conveying a valued adult status. Their somewhat stereotyped view of adults as faceless, miserable, moneygrubbing, puritanical bureaucrats may have been inaccurate, but it was this perceived adulthood that they were reluctant to assume. Jobs were evaluated in terms of self-fulfillment, or strictly as a source of required dollars.

Freaks participated in the drug-pop-leftist culture and ideology that was diffusely spread throughout the larger society. Acid rock was popular. Like greasers, freaks considered incarceration as the primary deterrent to committing illegal acts. They committed all the "crimes without victims" that the other two types did. But one particular illegality, drug use, was revered by all freaks as a necessary experience. The political definition of this behavior as criminal, and police attempts to enforce it, gave freaks an unusually strong political ideology that cast the police as enemies, as enforcers for a repressive establishment. Freaks thus defined violence perpetrated upon the police as justified. Property crimes were justified by a vulgarized conception that "all property is theft." Freak social structures tended to be very loose, consisting of shifting conglomerations of dyads and triads; compared to greasers and straights, there was noticeably more turnover of members at particular places, and a lack of stable leadership.

Although all youth are marginal in our contemporary economy, working-class backgrounds (and futures) exacerbate this marginality (Clarke et al. 1976, 47). Teenagers' frustration with their subordination, which can sometimes take the extreme form of rebellion, can result, not in the correction, but the increase of injustice (Schwendinger and Schwendinger 1976). To the extent that certain behavior is legally required from members of adolescent status, rejection of that status in terms of behavior can easily result in law-violative acts; and to the extent that adult social control agents fail to receive the expected deferential behavior, they frequently assess a particular youth's character as morally defective or antisocial, and define him/her as delinquent.

What is centrally characteristic of the greaser type especially, is a style of orientation repeatedly interpreted as "rebellious" by succeeding commentators. Although their theories differ markedly in psychology, the determining quality of values upon social action, the rationality of delinquents, the nature of social determinism, and the like, Cohen, Matza, and Werthman among others, underline this seemingly unique quality of delinquency that distinguishes it from adult crime. Delinquency is noted as a peculiarly symbolic, age-based confrontation compared with the economic focus of most adult crime. Werthman in particular begins to specify the nature of this defiance when he notes that the obstreperous behavior is evoked only in some classrooms, not in others, and only by some police, not by others.

Some movement between the social types, of course, qualifies the statements of necessary preconditions for holding the particular perspectives given above. The preconditions were developed from analysis of interviews with adolescents at the end of the research. Although by then the youths may have "settled down," it is evident from their claims to have held other perspectives in earlier years that the preconditions were less constraining at that time. Coleman et al. (1974) report similarly that the changes in present self-image apparent between the ages of eight to fourteen years have stabilized in studies of twelve to eighteen year olds, though their future self-images change with age. Schwendinger (1963) found the same pattern of movement with his Los Angeles youths. He explained this by suggesting that the "increased stakes" in rising delinquent behavior among greasers ("essays") caused the more ambivalent youth (and especially those with conventional parents) to adopt a more conventional orientation. By the end of junior high school, the long-term costs of such rebellion would be becoming apparent (see also Noblit 1976; Fréchette, Leblanc, and Biron 1981). It is possible that youth in later years become more selective; they pick and choose aspects of each life-style rather than completely adopting one or another. When the individuals cease to be defined as adolescents, the peculiar (that is, nonadult) aspects of their life-styles usually cease to be relevant and are abandoned. Many of the aspects of these adolescents' life-styles are similar to those of adults; I have focussed upon the more unusual aspects as these attract greater public attention and characterize adolescents as a particular group (Smith 1976), aspects that are crucial in their interaction with adults.

Some Criticisms
ETHNOGRAPHIC RESEARCH
As indicated in chapter one, participant observation research is not immune from criticism (West 1977a, 1984a). Sampling and representative-

ness is always somewhat at issue, because the more intensive such research is, the more microlevel and the less clear is its structural location. Since good access depends so crucially upon the personal characteristics of individual researchers, and as there are so few objective checks upon researchers' recordings, personal bias also remains at issue. Sometimes the analysis is scant as ethnography tends to revere description; at other times it is loosely connected to the data base. Analytic induction has limitations as a mode of analysis (West 1984a). And focussing upon cultural experience, it is easy for researchers to loose sight of material conditions and moral direction (West 1984a).

DIFFERENTIAL ASSOCIATION

Neopositivists argue that Sutherland's theory does not have a clear set of propositions with unambiguous definitions capable of prediction and testing (for example, Empey 1978, 328). And beliefs and attitudes are not always such good predictors of human behavior as differential association implies. It has no explanation for isolated, single law violators.

DRIFT THEORY

Box (1981) offers a sympathetic but very incisive criticism of Matza's drift theory, arguing that if the delinquent is understood to reassert humanism, it is strange that delinquents' techniques of rationalization should be so denying of their own free intentions. Matza's theory of delinquency and drift has similarly eluded testing that would result in a clear verdict either substantiating or refuting it. Again, to some extent, this can be seen as a carping criticism by neopositivists who demand that interactionism give up its own predilections for their own, but everyone would nonetheless enjoy some greater degree of substantiation.

LABELING THEORY

Not all of labeling theory's tenets are borne out by research either. Although police do often seem to have biased attitudes that make them more suspicious of working-class and ethnic minority people as being deviant, they much less often arrest people on these grounds. Instead, legalistic factors such as the victim's wishes, previous record, and seriousness of the offence are more influential (Hagan 1975). "Previous record," of course, may simply indicate accumulated bias. Although labeling may sometimes lead to the assumption of a deviant role, it may also deter (West 1980a). While many ex-inmates are rearrested, many are not. Other research indicates that more subtle biases exist in deployment, supervision, and the like (Nease 1968; Box 1981). The cumulation of a number of small biases at each stage of the certification process results in some groups being unfairly singled out as predominant in the delinquent population (Haldane, Elliott, Whitehead 1972).

Regarding policy application, the main implication from labeling theory has been caution in the exercise of official responses to deviance. Legal decriminalization, police discretion, diversion from official reaction in court, due process, sentencing alternatives, and early decarceration (parole) are some examples. While such considerations seem pertinent for minor, victimless, and especially juvenile status offences, they are hardly relevant to more serious crimes such as murder. Even for the minor offences, one may still wonder what should actually be done about "bothersome" behavior such as youngsters running away from home, and being on the street all night. Canadian governments continue to wrestle with such issues.

SYMBOLIC INTERACTIONIST THEORY

As indicated in our earlier discussion of definitions, although it initially appears straightforwardly simple, interactionist definitions do not "solve" the definitional problem: they do not state who must label, the extent to which the label must stick, or for how long, for a deviant status to be attained. Becker has been criticized (Box 1981) for ambiguity in his use of the term "secret deviant": if deviance depends upon labeling to be so constituted, can there be a secret deviant? Ironically, some of this ambiguity is especially pertinent to the study of delinquency, for it is often quite unclear before a trial as to what will be officially considered delinquent. Status offences (that is, running away, truancy, "sexual immorality or any other vice," and the like) are especially open to negotiated and retrospective interpretations. Some (Kitsuse 1964) have gone so far as to suggest this implies that delinquency can only be identified after an appropriate reaction; the actual amount of delinquency committed must therefore remain fundamentally unknowable.

In referring analysts back to the social world, interactionists tend to ignore the search for causes of deviant behavior, and instead search for causes of labeling behavior; most students of deviance want to know both. There has been an idealistic tendency in interactionism to ignore real behavior and material events that may well be quite independent of the label that controllers impose. In effect, the search for causation has been in danger of being abandoned. Interactionism is not a single neat theory in the axiomatic deductive tradition (like anomie or control theory), and hence retains a context-boundedness that many find disconcerting: if human activity is so unpredictable that general theory is not possible, is sociology of any value?

In part because of its commitment to situational analysis, interactionist theory generally refuses to offer a society-wide analysis that would specify the most crucial structural problems. While studying the inside of the "black box" of deviance, interactionist studies have often strayed in the opposite direction from control and anomie theories by all but ignoring social regularities and their causes in rejoicing over the voluntaristic construction and reconstruction of social reality.

Interactionist or labeling theory has been little more sophisticated about policy adoption processes; it has tended to remain true to its liberal roots. Adoption of policy addressed to structural issues, of course, requires the admission that there are some structural regularities beyond voluntaristic interaction, even if such structures need to be continually, humanly reconstructed.

Interactionist theorists have tended to be more liberal politically than their conservative control theory colleagues, believing in classic social contract negotiation of moral issues within the political forum. Ironically, the right has seen them as amorally accepting the deviants' viewpoint (Yablonsky 1968a), while the left has charged them with accepting the establishment's definitions and subtly committing themselves to the status quo (Thio 1978). As times have gotten more difficult, however, the mere espousal of cultural and moral diversity does not seem enough; a moral ambiguity resides in an "appreciative" stance (Matza 1969).

ADOLESCENT AUTONOMY THEORY

Some of these criticisms apply to the interpretation I developed (West 1984, forthcoming) for the ethnographic material presented above. It remains unclear how generalizable the subcultures described are in both time and space; do they fit all Canadian adolescents (French, English, Native, and the like)? If the analysis has been developed from the "purest" type representatives of each subculture, how does it apply to the majority of teens who are not such "pure" representatives? There remains ambiguity in linking the subcultures to structural factors: if most working-class youth become greaser, how much interactive free choice is involved? Contrarily, if many youngsters switched subcultures, how accurate is the analysis of necessary preconditions?

Although differential association and drift theories are compatible with the ethnographic material and the autonomy theory explanation, it is unclear how carefully they have been tested. The analysis implies police and other adults pick on greasers and freaks; how does this reconcile with survey research disputing such claims (Hagan 1975)? What are the factors actually causing adolescents to change subcultural affiliations? Why do greasers or freaks choose the particular illegalities they do and not others? If the theory was developed from the data presented, where is other independently gathered data to test it? Finally, if adolescent age status is crucial in constituting delinquency, both directly through status offences, and indirectly through encouraging some illegalities as character establishing risk behavior, how and why is this age status developed?

AGE STRUCTURE: ADOLESCENT SUBCULTURES, AFFILIATION, AND AUTONOMY

Early interactionist ethnographic research on delinquent subcultures and affiliation (Shaw 1930; Thrasher 1927/1963) was incorporated in some sense into anomie theory's considerations of delinquent gangs and subcultures arising from particular class dilemmas (Cohen 1955). The resurgence to prominence of interactionist studies during the 1960s raised a number of criticisms of these anomie formulations of subculture. The "subculture" was often unclearly distinguished from the larger culture (Downes 1966; Jahoda and Warren 1965; Arnold 1970); its boundaries remained unclear; its evolution was claimed but not demonstrated (Kitsuse and Dietrich 1959); its content was ambiguous (Matza 1964b; Short and Strodtbeck 1965); and its determinist relation to behavior undemonstrated.

The emphasis on field research from interactionism has more recently been recombined with some needed attention to social structure, especially by researchers working in England at the University of Birmingham (Hall and Jefferson 1976; Willis 1977; Corrigan 1979). Operating from a neo-Marxist framework, they have sought to use ethnography to analyze how macrolevel objective capitalist structures shape microlevel subjectivity, especially as working-class youth respond meaningfully to their situation; such responses are seen as shaping the social structure in turn through class struggle (Young 1983). Drawing especially on Althusser (1971) and Gramsci (1971), the Birmingham School has regarded the accurate description of real-life experience as essential to understanding the possibilities for effective change of oppressive conditions under capitalism (Clarke 1979; Johnston 1979).

> The relationship between consciousness of generation and consciousness of class therefore constitutes an important topic for investigation. It is important not only because it is indispensable to a reconstituted sociology of youth, but also because it is central to an adequate analysis of how class consciousness comes to be formed, and of how this formation may be blocked or forestalled (Murdock and McCron 1976).

The work of Paul Willis (1977) and Paul Corrigan (1979) is exemplary of this approach. Both give detailed ethnographic depictions of English working-class boys having trouble in school. They show how such youth draw upon parental working-class cultures as a resource to help them make sense of their dilemmas and suggest responses; contradictorily, by reason of their racism and sexism, it also ensures their futures as working class by separating them from possible allies. Adolescent working-class, male student subculture is seen as mediating dominant ideologies in ways similar to the description of greaser culture given earlier in this chapter.

As a number of authors have recently been pointing out (Dorn and South 1983; Young 1983; Cohen 1980; West 1982), a number of problems have remained in much of this "second wave" of subcultural studies. There is a certain romanticization of working-class youth, without consideration of middle-class youth, or any detailing of how these would be related. Most delinquency is rather boring and petty, hardly material for building a socialist revolution. Very few studies pay attention to girls (but see Campbell 1981; McRobbie 1976) or ethnic minorities (but see Pryce 1979; Armogan 1976). Many methodological issues remain as to how to link such detailed ethnographies to wider macrolevel structural analysis (West 1984a, 1984b); too often the significance of activities is unquestioningly "read off" without reason. This becomes even more of a problem when the youth studied fail to recognize themselves in the analysis: at some point, they must, if a claim is being made to depict actors' humanistically formulated experience.

Crucially, Young (1983) has raised the possibility that the second wave of subcultural research has slipped back into suffering many of the same old problems as the earlier, anomie subcultural theories: the youth are seen as being superrational, there is lack of a sense of contradiction, a depiction of overcoherence, a failure to show the strong linkage with the dominant order, a failure to note regressive tendencies, or to show historical change. Dorn and South (1983) also point out more substantive problems: there is too often a failure to look at youth within families, and while involved in both formal and informal labor, as well as at play and school; and an ignoring of the political economy of youth. How does youth culture become work and family culture again as youth mature into adulthood?

Despite these criticisms, ethnographic subcultural research, using interactionist approaches, has helped to round out our understanding of delinquency. This research shows how subcultural values are elaborated, in part from dominate or legitimate values, extended in peer interaction, and are ambivalently invoked in particular situations by actors meaningfully constructing their behavior. Some new determinants of delinquency are suggested by exploratory ethnographic research (for example, an attitude of "autonomy," or "risk-excitement") that could be explored in further research (including social surveys of self-report delinquency). The importance of "interpersonal relations" (including family, peer, and anticipated future family considerations) is further revealed as particularly significant for girls, though much more work needs to be done on gender differences. Moreover, the description of various youth subcultures begins to show how age comes into play as a factor in self-report delinquency research. As with class and gender, it is not the simple lack of wealth, different genitalia, or a span of years that causes delinquency, but the highly social organization of these into meaningful dimensions of human existence. Age and its social organization has been a theoretically neglected factor for too long in understanding delinquency (Greenberg 1977) even though it has long been noted in both official statistical and self-report studies.

Interactionist accounts thus can provide a vivid picture of the real-life invocation of subcultural beliefs among affiliated teens. But there is a strong tendency in interactionist ethnographic accounts of delinquent subcultures to ignore recurring regularities, to debase all social patterning into ephemeral encounters. These recurring regularities must instead be related back to the peculiar problems inherent in occupying, for instance, adolescent age status (in combination with social class and gender statuses, already discussed). Furthermore, as with class and gender, it is not sufficient to stop at noting that class, gender, and age make for differences: one must go beyond such considerations to determine not only *how* they make for differences, but also *why*, *when*, and *where*. For as class and gender relations need to be examined as actively constructed through social relations, so do age relations. We will turn in chapters 6 and 7 to explicitly consider two major formal devices of the capitalist state that effect such constructions.

6

Schooling: Discipline and Surveillance in Inculcating Legal Subjectivity

The school system which emerged from the Ryerson era reflected not only the twin goals of consolidation and universality, but also the contradictions involved in promoting at the same time a class society. School reformers did not perhaps intend to create respectable middle class schools for respectable middle class children and tough nasty schools for poor children who needed to be disciplined. Indeed they wanted all children to be respectable and middle class as well as disciplined and orderly. But they clearly felt, nevertheless, that the school system ought to provide different kinds of education for different classes of people.

Prentice 1977, 138–39

One might ask what schooling has to do with delinquency. There is, however, a long history of conceiving of education as having a fundamentally moral purpose in socializing the young to the good society, a purer life, and to a higher calling. More concretely, recall from chapter 2 that the advent of mass, state-funded education occurred during the height of the industrial revolution in Western countries, when rapid urbanization, mass immigration, industrialization, changing labor force participation (specifically the exclusion or at least regulation of child labor), changing family and community structures, and the like, gave rise to grave concerns about moral and civic order, especially regarding the young. In a crude sense, one of the biggest selling points to government and laissez faire businessmen for this new state intervention was that schooling promised to control the unruly children of the restless, urban working classes, and to turn them into disciplined and productive workers and subjects. Such traditional belief that the schools could do more to prevent delinquency finds continued expression in contemporary Ontario public opinion polls that indicate a perceived lack of discipline as the educational issue of greatest concern, outranking discontent with standards, teaching adequacy, and finances (Livingstone and Hart 1980, 1981).

Recall also, from chapters 3 and 4, that both anomie and control theories of delinquency have accorded schooling a central role in causing delinquency. The former saw the school failure of working-class boys (caused by their inability to compete in a middle-class institution for which they were unprepared) as being crucial to their rejection of social values and turning towards a delinquent subculture. Whatever other problems these theories might have, their hypothesis that school failure is related to delinquency has been one of the most recurrent findings in the literature (West 1975a), in self-report as well as official statistics.

In contrast to anomie theory, control theory has seen school success as providing a key commitment that is able to bond individuals to society. The past few decades have witnessed an accumulation of research on the formal organization of the school, its curriculum, social class, and deviance, that has produced overwhelmingly consistent results. This material argues that school failure (intrinsic to strict school standards and compulsory education) intervenes as an intermediate cause between class background and deviant behavior. Much of this research, however, has been done on boys only (Hirschi 1969); what has been done on both boys and girls indicates school failure is either less important (Johnson 1979) or not important at all for girls (Gomme 1982, 1983). There would seem to be an unexplored interaction between schooling and gender that needs to be further examined, especially as schools play such an active part in reproducing gender relations (see for example, Arnot 1981) as well as class ones.

Recall also that the interactionist-derived theory of adolescent age status and autonomy, and the accompanying ethnographic data in the last chapter provided further support for considering the school as an important factor. School student status is an important component of adolescent status in general; interaction with teachers seems important, and peers both interact at school and develop subcultural values. Much of the previous anomie theory inspired literature has often identified "greasers" as lower class; more recent self-report research (Stinchcombe 1964; Polk and Schafer 1972; Schwendinger 1963; West 1975a) indicates that it is more accurate to describe them as having working-class futures through having failed at school. Furthermore, schooling can be seen in more general terms as clearly one of the social institutions that is age specific and hence might be considered to reveal part of the social meaning of the correlation of age and delinquency. It is notable, for instance, that in many jurisdictions the peak age for offences is the last year of compulsory schooling.

Because of its availability to policy changes, schooling may offer some more optimistic insights that suggest that within structurally determined limits, various school approaches can mitigate adverse adolescent reactions. After examining the available research on schooling and delinquency, including an exploration of its possible genesis in classroom interaction, we will discuss commonly proposed policy options. Finally, however, it must be recognized that the issues surrounding schooling and delinquency need to be reconceptualized for these relationships have been poorly conceived in the past. Traditional theoretical paradigms for understanding schooling and deviance (such as anomie, control, labeling, and even early conflict theories) have often been severely flawed: narrowly conceived and sometimes lacking empirical support, too often of limited utility, ignorant of policy processes, failing to address value-biases, and the like.

The intervention of the state in creating schools to deal with youth provides a primary example of governmental attempts to ameliorate contradictions in capitalism, while simultaneously assisting in the accumulation of profit (by teaching children workplace skills and providing the need for educational materials, and the like), the engendering of legitimacy (through civics classes and "the IQ ideology"), and the exercise of coercion (through corporal punishment and compulsory attendance). With its inculcation of particular, differentiated legal subjectivities, a strong argument can be made that the school produces moral inequality as surely as it does other inequalities (West 1975a, 1978b, 1979b). Further examination of schooling as state policy towards the young, then, might produce findings of wider import concerning the nature of order within the contemporary capitalist state.

SCHOOLING AND DELINQUENCY
Failure, Delinquency, and Control Theory Factors

The social sciences have been notoriously weak in producing concrete findings and theories relevant to criminological practice. Few other research traditions in the social sciences, however, have produced more defensible and clear results than those linking school failure to (especially male) student deviance. Dozens of independent studies across cultural and linguistic boundaries have repeatedly found school failure to be among the most persistent and strongest correlates of both out-of-school official juvenile delinquency, in-class misbehavior, and self-reported delinquent behavior (Polk and Shafer 1972; West 1975a).

With official delinquency, it correlates at about .70 (Empey and Lubeck

1971). Even when reading scores, IQ, sex, age, parental socioeconomic status, school neighborhood, and mother's aspirations are controlled, the correlation remains quite high in the .30 to .48 range. And populations with low educational achievement have the highest official crime rates, ranging from 2,200 convictions per 100,000 for those with no schooling, through 289 for those with some elementary or secondary schooling, to 83 for those above high school (Bell-Rowbotham and Boydell 1972). Twenty-five percent of Ontario Training School inmates have been in low streams (levels or tracks); overall they average one year of failure each.

As reviewed in chapter 4, self-reported delinquency is also highly related to accumulated measures of school failure, correlating at .41 in Hirschi's study. Recent analyses of data from Edmonton, Montreal, and Frontenac County, eastern Ontario confirm these findings for Canadian youths. These range from Gomme's relatively low .15 for males (1983), to an astoundingly high .53 in Leblanc's Montreal research, where it was the strongest predictor, accounting by itself for over a quarter of the variance.

Lower origins are associated with educational failure (low streams, nonpromotion, low grades, and dropping out) (Polk and Schafer 1972, 167; Stinchcombe 1964). This first part of Cohen's theory has been borne out by research over the succeeding decades, and has become a major focus of educational concern (Jencks et al. 1972). Initially, then, it would appear that there is a chain of events from lower-class origins, through school failure, to behavioral, and then official delinquency. As discussed in chapter 3, it has also long been known that working-class children are disproportionately arrested and incarcerated for delinquency.

Although school failure (in the middle of this chain) is related both to lower-class origins and to delinquency, the two variables at the ends of the chain are strongly related only when delinquency is "officially" defined, but weakly related when it is defined behaviorally. The accumulated evidence, then, strongly indicates that such school failure intervenes to almost eliminate social class differences; the time ordering seems unusually clear.

Restated, anticipated social class (indicated by school performance) correlates with delinquent behavior much more than social class origins. Those with middle-class origins but who through failing move to low occupational prospects are as delinquent as those with low origins and prospects, and more delinquent than either those with high origins and prospects or low origins but high prospects. School failure can thus be conceived as being crucial in theories of delinquency.

Other research data in this area are highly corroborative. There is considerable evidence both qualitative and quantitative that low-stream and failing pupils are least committed to school with its rules and values, plan to leave as soon as possible, dislike it and its teachers more, spend the least time in extracurricular activities, including athletics, and are more involved in misconduct within the school (Kundratts 1979). Fréchette, Leblanc, and Biron (1981, 58) found that sporadic Montreal male delinquents

> neither appreciate the values on which the school is founded (acquisition of knowledge, preparation for life, future success, etc.) nor find any other justification for it; one out of two even reject the idea that school can be a valid preparation for entry into the labour market.

Regarding serious, persistent delinquents, they found that over three-quarters considered school irrelevant, wanting to drop out immediately (Fréchette, Leblanc, and Biron 1981, 62). Elliott and Voss (1974) concluded that compulsory school attendance exacerbates delinquency by forcing youth to remain in what is sometimes a frustrating situation in which they are stigmatized as failures. For the dropout and the graduate, rates of delinquency decline upon leaving the compulsory school setting.

Delinquents are less "attached" to parents and teachers, Leblanc (1981) citing a negative correlation of $-.32$. But rather than actively rebelling against conventional authorities they seem to find them simply less powerful role models, less attractive to emulate. Personal relations therefore fail effectively to curtail delinquent behavior. Exclusion of troublemakers from school events further weakens possibilities of these attachments. Fréchette, Leblanc, and Biron (1981) found that delinquents who reached the courts much more likely to have been expelled from class.

Research findings such as these are highly consistent with an extended control theory understanding of delinquency. As we argued earlier in criticizing control theory, however, we must go beyond documenting such empirical relationships to understand how such factors themselves are caused, why they are socially important, and how they are understood by human actors.

Schooling and Jobs

To understand these relationships, we must note that learning is as highly organized socially as it is mentally or psychologically. Formal school systems have various, often conflicting, goals. These range from the liberal arts ideal of culturally transmitting the highest social values and truths, to concerns with the social integration of heterogeneous populations into the citizenry of contemporary national states, to moral training, to individualistic personal development.

As suggested in chapter 2, formal schooling has always had as one of its goals preparation for the labor market. Somewhat ironically, the removal of children from participating in society's labor to attend school has been done on the promise of their being better prepared for labor when they do finally enter the adult world of work.

Formal education has a significant role to play in the job market in a "new" country such as Canada. It has promised that competition for employment between individuals from widely different ethnic or cultural groups be put on a universal, "fair" basis. (This is not to say that it has succeeded in actually achieving this state.) Formal school credentials are transportable in a country with great geographic mobility among its population, and where hometown ties have often simply not existed. And it has offered the promise of a "way out" for those growing up on farms or in small, one-industry towns dependent on fishing, mining, logging, and the like (Lucas 1971), where local opportunities for employment training other than for the single employer simply did not exist.

As a result, by 1970, education had become the country's "largest industry," accounting for 8 percent of the gross national product, with 6.5 million students and teachers being involved. It accounted for 20 percent of total government spending, or over six billion dollars.

In large part, of course, this massive investment in education has been triggered by unemployment problems, and a belief that higher levels of education would solve economic difficulties. Youth unemployment over the last few decades has been particularly severe, at a rate some two to three times the national average, among those under twenty-five, who comprise almost half the total unemployed. This seems to be a worldwide problem, certainly one endemic in the Western economies (Walker-Lorrain 1983; Murphy 1983).

Although there has been no recent raising of the official school-leaving age, the educational requirements for most jobs have increased, as have the social and economic pressures to stay in school longer (whether one wants to or not). For those who dislike school, or do poorly in it, and an increasing number of students disillusioned with the shrinking relevance of higher education as it relates to the job market in an underdeveloped hinterland economy (Lockheart 1975, 199), schools are faced with a problem of greater numbers of uncommitted students. The subcultural studies discussed in the previous chapter have situated schooling within neighborhood contexts, and they have shown how youngsters draw on class traditions transmitted by the neighborhood and families, and perpetuate such cultural forms as they deem useful for their anticipated life roles.

Disappointed students adopt precocious claims to adult status, and when they are prohibited from adult perquisites (for instance, jobs) they may turn to serious crime (West 1979a, 1979–80, 1980a, 1983). The argument elaborated by Clarke would seem particularly apt in reinforcing control theory explanations for any deviance.

> I have already argued that the central locus of discipline in capitalism is the workplace, I now want to add two other institutions which are concerned with socialization and discipline – the family and the school – to which are given the functions of preparing the future labour force. My suggestion is that the contemporary concern with adolescence (and the political and social instability which attracts the attention) derives directly from the position on the adolescent in relation to this nexus of institutions – adolescents are *marginal* to all three (Clarke 1975, 5).

With higher formal educational requirements increasingly demanded for access to good jobs, male students who cannot finish high school at least, cannot help but find schooling not only frustrating but irrelevant. In contrast, "commercial," "secretarial" courses offered for girls have been successful at providing access to (admittedly, very low-paying) clerical and office jobs. In addition, of course, if effectively "programmed" through traditional sex-role socialization, girls would be much less likely to see either school success or concomitant jobs as essential. The goal of "getting married and having children" has a currency simply not available to males.

The Social Organization of Schools

The goals of formal school systems are contested and reworked, and in some sense ignored, through organizing modern education as a large state bureaucracy, with administrative authority centralized in offices, formal impersonal rules and standards, and a hierarchical and functional division of labor. School clients are similarly organized into groups by age, academic functioning, and program; and by gender, race, ethnicity, and class (though the latter stratifications are much less publicly justifiable). As a people-processing organization, schools are labor intensive, relying upon large numbers of teachers, who tend to be middle class and prefer middle-class students, and who are trained in individualistic child-psychology approaches to learning, although they themselves are also highly restricted by organizational rules, curricula, and inspectorates. Schooling focuses on individualistic cognitive achievement, demanding relatively passive pupil dependence and giving students little opportunity for responsible action. Any failures are attributed to the child, any success to the school. The focus is on a relatively narrow range of skills, verbal and mathematical in particular.

Canada has had notoriously weak apprenticeship programs, partly as a result of relying on immigration for skilled labor, partly because her resource extraction staples economy has not emphasized skilled labor. Like most Western countries, we have sometimes attempted to combine the best of both apprenticeship and school programs in various vocational and work-study plans. Inevitably, however, the formal characteristics of schooling shape the incorporation of apprenticeship programs, which must fit into a bureaucratically organized system. Vocational education ends up being provided for those academically less able: it couches failure in terms of streaming (placing in various levels). Cicourel and Kitsuse (1963), for instance, report that such "particularistic" factors as display of working-class background characteristics in dress or demeanor greatly influences guidance counselors into directing students into low, noncollege "tracks" or levels, thus reinforcing attitudes accepting of lower status on the part of parents.

In a landmark study of a British low-stream, "secondary modern" school, David Hargreaves (1967) identified the tracking system as a key element not only in the organization of education, but also in the generation of delinquency. The different streams within this school had differential commitments, attachments, involvements, and beliefs (translating his findings into control theory terminology), and this differentiation increased yearly. Increasingly, the lowest streams grew alienated from schooling and teachers, elaborated a delinquent subculture (akin to "greasers' "), and asserted demands for adultlike autonomy in and out of school.

Also following on Hargreaves' work, there have been suggestions that some schools are themselves delinquent, indicated by the high rates of delinquent pupils they produce. Power and his associates (1972) found rates varying from six to seventy-seven delinquents per thousand across different schools, drawing from the same working-class population pool in East London boroughs. A range across schools of 0 to 57 percent of first offenders reappeared a third time, and police practices, economic status, and population movement did not account for this. Some excellent research from a Welsh valley by Reynolds and Sullivan (1979) further developed this line of thought. They found that among nine schools with a similar pupil intake, some consistently produce delinquency rates more than twice as high as others (3.8 percent versus 10.5 percent). The high delinquency schools are larger, with a greater staff turnover, have larger class sizes, are conservative or nonprogressive in their teaching ideology, and do not involve youngsters in helping the school (for instance, by prefect systems). Reynolds has also found that teachers in these schools are less willing to defer to (especially older) adolescents' demands for some autonomy regarding smoking, gum chewing, and behavior outside of school. Although its wider significance is untested, their conclusion that "liberal, progressive, incorporative" schools that included student participation wherever possible produce half as many delinquents as "traditional, authoritarian, coercive" ones is impressively documented. Their research is remarkable in the clarity of the relevant policy implications that schools could follow, since teacher perceptions are identified as crucial and manipulable variables. Rutter et al. (1979), studying nine inner-London schools have reported similar findings. Although, unlike Reynolds, they report that initial intelligence quotient (IQ) scores of pupils on intake do make a difference, internal school and classroom effects are also prominent. They found low delinquency rates associated with teachers who teach more than one subject, discipline being group-based, with low punitiveness, liberal amounts of praise for students' work, closer headmaster (principal) supervision of teachers, joint curriculum planning by staff, and highly stable student peer groups.

There remain many unanswered questions as to how school failure is interpreted by students and "translated" into delinquent behavior and official delinquency. How do different teachers define classroom order and deviance, which most teachers and the population at large perceive as a crucial problem in education?

Classroom Organization: The Social Construction of Order and Deviance

It is within the everyday reality of school classrooms that social class is articulated with failure, and the meaningfulness of the latter somehow becomes a ground for delinquency. Could it simply be that stupidity breeds evil, as Hirschi (1969, 132) has implied: "The causal chain runs from academic incompetence to poor school performance to disliking of school to rejection of the school's authority to the commission of delinquent acts."

Other research has found the same factors to be related (Toby and Toby 1962; Polk and Schafer 1972; Hindelang 1973). Hirschi and Hindelang (1977) have found statistically significant differences in IQ scores between delinquents; these account for more of the variance than social class, but it must be noted that the proportion of the variance explained is nonetheless minuscule – a mere 2 percent. Fortunately, many of the recent ethnographic studies of elementary school classrooms in particular, address the question of classroom order directly, in ways that shed light upon how schools generate delinquency. We are concerned at this point with examining the establishment and maintenance of teacher-defined interactional order, and the imposition of teachers' definitions of order on classroom verbal and nonverbal behavior. Even more pertinent, much of this research is Canadian, having been done at The Ontario Institute for Studies in Education in theses by Baker (1972), Bellamy (1975), Bosence (1974), Hardy (1974), McGeachie and Stone (1972), McIntosh (1976), Schotte (1973), Singer (1975), and Yeung (1975). Across the approximately one-hundred classrooms studied, teachers do seem to have similar definitions of order, centered around behavioral regularities and learning (Dobson, Goldenberg, and Elson 1972; Hoetker and Ahlbrand 1969).

Educators see the establishment and maintenance of order as a very important problem (Hardy 1974; McIntosh 1976; Schotte 1973). There seem to be "structural" reasons for this concern, embedded in formal statuses. Given the legislated mandate for custody and control of their pupils, teachers see themselves, and are seen by supervisors and the public, as responsible for the physical well-being and control of their charges, and the running of the classroom, as well as the production of educational changes as defined in the approved curriculum. Principals are clearly more concerned that new teachers (McIntosh 1976) and supply teachers (Schotte 1973) have custody and control of their pupils, and so avoid any legal problems, than that they educate them. Many teachers and administrators regard such control as a prerequisite to any imparting of knowledge (McIntosh 1976).

> Vice-Principal: "If the children don't do what you want them to do and if you can't make them follow orders or make them behave, you can't run any kind of a program no matter what it is" (Schotte 1973, 51–52).

On an institutional level, schools are funded not according to educational achievement, but according to the number of pupils effectively under their control.

For teachers, order becomes a central problem when they assume their position as leaders of some thirty youngsters, at least a few of whom are usually involuntarily compelled to attend class, and at least a few of whom usually share a reciprocal dislike with the teacher, and thus resist control (Jackson 1968, 47–49). Pupils' being well behaved is more important to teachers than their being intelligent. Unlike adult workers who may have similar problems with supervisors, pupils do not have the easy "safety valves" of changing jobs or bosses; and teachers do not have much control over which pupils are assigned to them. Teachers thus often assume the position of "good people" doing society's "dirty work" (Hughes 1971) in that they are required to perform unpleasant tasks, such as administer corporal punishment, enforce attendance, or inflict the psychological pain of failure on children, some of whom no other adults seem concerned about. In providing this inexpensive "babysitting," teachers are seen by the public as being responsible for the moral safeguarding and uplifting of their charges as much as for their enlightenment. Whether or not moral or educational changes are sought, to the extent that some children resist such transformations, conflict will result (Geer 1968, 560).

McIntosh's (1976) study indicates how new teachers' idealism regarding curricular innovations and egalitarian or democratic pedagogical methods is quickly overwhelmed by discovery of the shocking diversity of ability found among pupils, the failure to quickly demonstrate to themselves and others that "education" is happening, the unexpected workload, the failure of children to co-operate, and so forth. Finding that they have less discretion than they had expected, pressed to accommodate to the provincial departmental curriculum and to prepare their students for next year's teachers, and bearing the responsibility to make students appear in ways that legitimize the teacher, most new teachers revert to standard pedagogy and curriculum as events threaten to get out of control (McIntosh 1976, 66).

If standard methods and subjects are used, the new teacher is sheltered from reproach. With such traditions to hide behind, any failure can be attributed to pupils' shortcomings rather than the new teacher's. "Motivation" and "ability" become key concepts in this grammar of failure. And radical innovators such as McLaren (1980) and Herndon (1965) are likely to be terminated or "burn out."

In attempting to establish an orderly classroom, new teachers encounter a major difficulty in defining for themselves of just what such order would consist. Generally isolated in their own rooms, new teachers find it difficult to learn from older professionals how to define and manage classroom deviance; and even rooms with open floor plans are often socially treated as if the traditional walls remained (Stebbins 1970, 223). For the majority who do not have extensive assistance from more experienced educators, memories of their own student days, hints in teachers' college manuals, and occasional smiles and frowns from colleagues provide the only clues. Interestingly, McIntosh (1976) found that students are often the major conservative influence, as they have already been socialized into traditional expectations of classrooms, and are in most direct contact with new teachers. In establishing order, teachers thus build an etiology of deviance, and develop an appropriate methodology. Despite the haphazardness of this learning process, and the individual idiosyncrasies of teachers, the institutional constraints must be formidable, as most classrooms do operate in similar ways.

> At a certain level of generality, persistently the same kinds of things seem to take place in classrooms all the time [*cf.*, especially Hoetker and Ahlbrand, 1969] . . . One might see the teacher as being the "routine-maker," and the routine as being a special normative one which the teacher is concerned to bring about (Bosence 1974, 21).

Some research (Smith and Geoffrey 1968; Stebbins 1970) gives an understanding of what teachers mean by describing a class as orderly or disorderly – though our knowledge in this area remains inadequate. Bellamy (1975) and Bosence (1974) detail how disruption of established classroom routines and the introduction of inappropriate topics are perceived as disorder. Such routines concern noise levels (Denscombe 1980), individual movement, initiating activities, selecting class groups and leaders, seating, discussion, and drill leadership, and the like (*cf.* Jackson 1968, 104).

These states of order and deviance can be seen as having an indexical quality, in that particular types of activities are taken to be indicative of them or displays of them in a commonsense fashion, yet they attain such meaningfulness only in relation to the teacher's particular normative concepts of deviance and order. The classroom order is never quite "set," in the sense that individuals may precipitate its breakdown at any time, and they may negotiate to change its definition over time. In these senses, it is not possible simply to take the concepts as givens, and therefore the positivist paradigm of social action is misleadingly precise (Wilson 1970). Yet, for practical purposes, teachers' definitions of order and deviance remain constant enough to make generalization and discussion not only possible but useful.

In creating the appearance of order and control, teachers resort to demonstrations of how classroom activities conform to commonsense notions of how a class should appear, and notions of curriculum. This situation seems to occur even in innovative schools, as Novak (1975) showed in his Toronto research. From this viewpoint, the everyday activities of the classroom, including curricular ones, come to be seen as matters of convention.

It is fairly evident that establishing these conventions involves a process whereby the teacher assumes political control of the classroom by becoming the leader of the group and definer of order (Dawe 1970; Roberts 1968). It is normally the teacher who starts lessons, sets requirements, controls activities and interaction, and the like (Hammersley 1974, 1976).

Spady (1974) proposed that obedience is more reliably and effectively assured by establishing authority than by resorting to naked coercion or rational persuasion. Continuous coercion is a drain on resources; persuasion may fail to be convincing.

> The subordinate party in an authority relationship grants legitimacy to the dominant party by virtue of the latter embodying attributes that the former regards as valuable in promoting his general welfare . . . The power to grant authority lies with the students (Spady 1974, 45).

Such authority is not to be confused with authoritarianism. Young children seem generally to grant such authority to almost all adults, and hence present fewer problems to teachers, but such deference is less readily granted in later grades.

Smith and Geoffrey (1968) provide an excellent study of how one teacher carefully established his authority at the beginning of the year by setting clear limits, enforcing sanctions, cajoling compliance, offering rewards, weeding the worst rebels out of class (or at least separating them from other students, both physically and by special individual agreements), and the like. After a few weeks, the routine was clear, the teacher's willfully imposed program attained the legitimacy of being the "way things are done," and dissent was rare. Edwards and Furlong (1978), and Ball (1980) have studied similar "first-day" encounters in England. Sarason (1971, 175–76) reported a similar result in his study of six American classrooms.

> In each classroom there is a constitution, verbalized or unverbalized, consistent or inconsistent, capable or incapable of amendment, that governs behavior. 1) The constitution was invariably determined by the teacher. No teacher ever discussed why a constitution was necessary. 2) The teacher never solicited the opinions and feelings of any pupil about a constitutional question. [3] In three classes, the rules were clear by one week, in two by one month, and in one they were never clear.] 4) Except for the one chaotic classroom, neither children nor teacher evidenced any discomfort with the content of the constitution – it was as if everyone agreed that this is the way things are and should be. 5) In all instances constitutional issues involved what children could or could not, should or should not do. The issue of what a teacher could or could not, should or should not do, never arose.

Corrigan (1979, chapter 3) argues that the imposition of middle-class schooling upon working-class students results in a forced interaction dominated by power dynamics, where any granting of authority is most tentative. Since the pupils see classrooms as a site for some favored "social" activities (for instance, talking) rather than for learning, they experience teachers as invoking rules, sanctions, and discipline. Since pupils often do not give willing compliance, or even follow rules grudgingly, teachers are forced to use punishment and constant surveillance.

Pollard (1979) has extended these ideas into a scheme of possible violations of the implicit contract between teachers and pupils. The teacher is conceded the right to organize and lead the classroom, but he or she cannot exceed school-oriented demands, nor be obviously unfair. Such negotiation may be more tacit than overt. Although pupils may not be consulted, their compliance with the constitution and obedience to teachers' authority implicates them in the joint construction of the social world of the classroom.

Spady (1974) argued that such authority relies not only on (institutional) tradition and legality but also on (personal) expertise and charisma. A survey study by Baker (1972) of 641 suburban Toronto students found that students of high ability valued pedagogic expertise and stimulation, whereas students of low ability and lower-class students valued subject matter expertise and empathic teachers.

Schotte's (1973) study of supply teachers corroborates this other work on the establishment of authority in classrooms by examining its breakdown when occasional teachers take over classes. Although occasional teachers, like teachers at the first of the year, have a knowledge of curriculum and pedagogy, as well as notions of order, they do not know the particular contracts or constitution that regular teachers have established to carry out routine activities, and inadvertently and inevitably do things differently. The spell of legitimacy is broken, and alternative ways of doing things become apparent to pupils. There is little chance that the supply teacher can re-establish order within a day or two when the regular teacher took weeks in its initial construction.

The view that I have been propounding of the classroom as an ordered place is elaborated by some explicit studies of teacher-defined classroom deviance. Hardy (1974) found that all of the twenty-four teachers in whose classrooms he observed, reported that they had some problem students, averaging 3.5 per class. These included students with behavioral difficulties (an average of one per classroom), and those who had learning difficulties. It is interesting that moral fault tends to be attributed to the former but not the latter; only the former are held morally responsible for their actions, although the use of drugs for hyperactive children would imply the illegitimacy of this attribution.

Most of the misbehavers were male, and Hardy found that these teacher-student dyadic relations were highly active. Brophy and Good's (1974, 215) research is consistent with Hardy's, in that they found that "teachers criticized the low-expectation boys in almost a third of their interactions with them, while their criticism rates for the other three groups (low-expectation girls and high expectation boys and girls) were much lower." The generally female teachers in lower grades were especially upset with aggressive (male) behavior. Deosaran (1974) found teachers in his Toronto research more critical of boys, devoting a full third of their interactions with pupils to the lowest-performing boys. Unpopular, nonachieving boys were given a shorter time to answer than usual. The resulting higher failure rate for males cannot fail to have an impact on their commitment.

To the extent that working-class children score less on IQ or aptitude tests, and teachers accept these as valid indicators of ability, the expectation-effects literature suggests that such pupils are given less stimulus, encouragement, and time. These kinds of findings indicate that even microlevel considerations of school success must be seen dynamically as jointly constructed achievements of teacher and pupil. It becomes more understandable that working-class children are more likely to experience school failure. Such findings are theoretically and practically interesting as they suggest that Durkheim's ([1895] 1950) and Erikson's (1964) arguments concerning the social necessity of deviance for defining group rules are borne out in the classroom. It appears, as well, that this function becomes embodied in a few individual students who occupy a particular status as troublemakers.

> The bad student comes to symbolize to others all that a student should not be in terms of the expectations of the school. It is during [the teacher's] major attempts to obtain the conformity of the student that she overtly defines the basic principles of classroom order: indeed, the punishment of the student for his deviance is the most dramatic statement of these principles (Hardy 1974, 337–38).

When deviant individuals are removed from classes, then, we would predict that other individuals would come to occupy the status of troublemaker, and available evidence tends to confirm this. Again, more research would be illuminating, as the implication of this finding is that classroom troublemakers are not individual aberrations, but a regular and normal part of the group. The tragedy is that we tend to psychologistically attribute the difficulties that such children present for teachers to the individual student rather than to group interaction.

This argument reinforces that which was developed in the last chapter regarding the assumed autonomy of subcultural "greasers," and is carried further by Werthman (1969, 1971) in his interview study of the problems that gang boys have in school. Werthman pointed out that since individual youths are not troublemakers in all, but only in some classes, the difficulties lie not with the individual student but in the interaction patterns between the youth and certain teachers. His evidence suggests that the key factor here is the youth's acceptance or rejection of the teacher's claim to authority. Werthman argues that some children (particularly those from lower-class homes) have to fend for themselves and are required by their families to become independent, autonomous individuals from an early age, and hence are less willing to defer automatically to adults. In Spady's terms, they are unwilling to obey unquestioningly, on the basis of institutional authority alone, and require that teacher claims to authority have some personal and explicitly contractual grounds as well. Such an orientation is likely to be seen by teachers as precocity, impudence, and the like – and as a direct challenge to their control of the classroom. Werthman (1971, 47) describes the delightful subtleties of the all pervasive interactional rejection of authority by many rebellious youngsters. It is often not so much overt disobedience that is most annoying to teachers, for this can be clearly forbidden, accurately identified, and legitimately punished. But far more irritating and difficult to deal with is ambiguous, symbolic behavior, such as deliberately walking too slowly, studiously refusing to look directly at the teacher, clothing and grooming oneself in a manner that is technically correct but socially offensive, answering with feigned politeness and using too many repetitions of "yes, sir!" Any direct response by teachers to such ambiguously insolent behavior only risks further escalating the crisis of authority.

Nonetheless, teachers have a distinct advantage in such interaction, as they have the power to retroactively define behavior as deviant. Should a student object, his objections can be transformed into the ground for further sanctioning (Katz 1972; Yeung 1975, 49).

In an important classroom study based partly on interactionist theory, Hargreaves, Hester, and Mellor (1975) outline some further classroom processes regarding deviance that corroborate the school organizational research of Reynolds and Sullivan (1979), Power et al. (1972), and Rutter et al. (1979). They note a hierarchy of rules, running from the school's (institutional), through classroom ones (situational), and teacher-pupil ones (relational), to the teacher's own (personal). They found teachers initially making speculative judgments regarding students' characters, which eventually became stabilized (for instance, as a "troublemaker") through elaboration. They point out that only some teachers are "deviance provocative"; others are "deviance insulative." The former have negative beliefs about pupils, seeing discipline as a contest they must win; distrust pupils, and are not friendly towards them; avoid informal contact, and see some pupils as bad persons. The latter, or deviance insulative teachers, label actions rather than children, are more positive, and actively seek to be fair. Woods (1979) argues that Hargreaves et al. (1975) overemphasize the amount of teacher elaboration of pupil typification. In the larger secondary school he studied, classification was much cruder.

It should be noted in this context that the school and its training are seen as more relevant by those aspiring to middle-class than those aspiring to working-class occupations. Given that most students aspire to equal or better than their parents' status, downwardly mobile students of middle-class parents, and "stationary" working-class students find the school least useful, and are more rebellious (Polk and Schafer 1972; Stinchcombe 1964). Becker's (1970a) study of Chicago public school teachers indicates that they prefer middle-class children on the grounds of teaching ease, acceptance of authority, and morality. Not only working-class pupils, but also their parents are likely to reciprocate this disdain, since such parents usually had unfavorable school experiences themselves, and are more accepting of their children's choosing less school and a working-class future, as this choice would maintain the family and friendship ties (Kahl 1961). The usual middle-class parent-teacher coalition is thus weakened and offset by a parent-child coalition. Keddie (1971, 154) described how such authority relations affect not only discipline but also academic achievement.

It may be that it is remoteness from everyday life that is an important element in legitimating academic knowledge in schools. Pupils who have easy access to this knowledge need an ability to sustain uncertainty about the nature of the learning activity in the belief that some pattern will emerge. This requires a willingness to rely on the teacher's authority in delineating what the salient areas of a problem are to be. This will often mean a pupil putting aside what he "knows" to be the case in an everyday context. Children who demonstrate this facility are likely to be regarded as more educable, and to find their way into high-ability groups or to be defined as of high ability, since these are pupils with whom teachers can feel they are making progress.

Interpersonal authority relations thus become reified into "objective" assessments of pupil ability and knowledge. Rist's (1970) observational study detailed how similarly nonacademic criteria (specifically, lower-class background features) are transformed into ability scores over a two-year period.

The official task of the school – educating pupils – is integrated into its social order in yet other ways described by Bossert (1974) and Singer (1975). A tension is introduced into the regime established by teachers; they are not only responsible for the maintenance of order and the engendering of demonstrable knowledge in their charges, they are also responsible for ranking them (West 1975b). Even when we have eliminated failure in official terms, we have maintained high and low grades and levels, and it is patently obvious to children that being an early "robin" in reading is better than being a late "crow." There is thus introduced an inevitable note of competition, between teacher and pupil and between pupil and pupil. Holt (1965) and others deplore the downplaying of intellectual curiosity, and the striving for knowledge in the scramble for teacher approval in order to gain immediate favors and good marks. The teacher often attempts to avoid teacher-pupil conflict by encouraging competition between the children (Geer 1968; Henry 1974, 174–75; Rist 1970, 174). Bossert's work demonstrates that classrooms that encourage open competition limit group cohesion, and thus heighten an ever-present threat to social order. Ball's study (1980) has shown that mixed ability grouping reduces pupil-teacher friction. Presumably, this is because the sense of failure is lessened by not being organizationally stigmatized; as well, since failing pupils are not grouped together, they are less likely to generate an oppositional culture.

It should now be evident that language plays a key part in the teacher's construction of classroom order (Torode 1976; Titus 1982). Students are treated according to the various labels they are assigned: Yeung (1975) showed how school officials can do different things to the same child depending upon the child's classification as emotionally disturbed, troublesome, or college-bound.

Bosence (1974) clearly showed how different language patterns predominate in different classroom activities. Activities are justified by verbally relating them to the officially prescribed curriculum (Novak 1975). Such curricula are formulated within government bureaucracies, which attempt to mesh the activities taking place in school classrooms with their perceived needs of the wider society. Political decisions are made as to which kinds of knowledge are legitimate and admissible in the classroom. Certain kinds of language are allowed and others not; certain kinds of behavior are symbolically defined as acceptable and others are not.

Generally, the research reviewed is quite consistent with control theory's postulate that people are born free to break the law, and will refrain from so doing only if special circumstances exist. Thus, those students who are less committed to conventional institutions, and for whom the school has the least to offer, at present or in the future, are more likely to be delinquent. Those who are least emotionally attached to parents and teachers are also more likely to commit delinquent acts. Finally, those who least believe in the justness of the moral order are least likely to uphold it. And those least involved in the moral order are more likely to be "troublesome." The research reviewed is thus well explained by control theory.

But a more interactionist perspective is needed to understand such correlations. An image of the individual as consciously and rationally seeking to fulfill desires within his or her own definition of the situation emerges. Self-concept and role are central. Labeling effects and expectancy effects seem to be operative within the school. It is obvious that the interpretive processes of both youths and teachers come into play, not simply as "random errors," but as fundamental elements in the maintenance of the social reality of schooling and delinquency. Using lay theories of misbehavior, opportunity, and the like, people actively construct the statistical correlations by judging, for example, that masculine assertiveness and working-class demeanor are indicative of precocity and a lack of deference to school authority. The usual teacher response to the latter would augment any initial lack of attachment, and probably not enhance learning and its concomitant, school success.

> In general terms, we . . . conceptualize teaching and learning as the intersubjective construction of reality. We . . . argue that teachers have certain core assumptions about their "subjects," about pedagogy, the intellectual status of their pupils, and some idea of what constitutes thinking, including its presence and supposed absence in particular learning situations. They . . . also have an etiology which is activated in the explanation of deviance or school pathology. These constitute an important part of the knowledge content of the occupational ideology of the teacher (Esland 1971, 78).

Such research differs from more traditional studies in revealing the dynamic processes of the classroom, based on the actors' perceptions. It nonetheless remains empirically oriented.

This look inside the hidden world of the classroom has revealed processes akin to Marx's look inside the hidden world of the factory ([1867] 1967). What seemed a fair and objective exchange of "intelligence and work" for "good grades" is revealed as an unfair contract. One becomes more than a bit suspicious when the same old factors of subordinate race and class are as salient as in the official crime statistics. For the central recent work by various Western sociologists of education (for example, Bourdieu and Passeron 1977; Bernstein 1977; Bowles and Gintis 1976) has fundamentally shown how social factors operate in schools to distort educational goals and sustain social inequalities. Most of this work has focussed upon the inequalities of certified knowledge, achievement, social class, gender, and status, but it dovetails almost perfectly with deviance research. Research on classroom order has indicated how well-off children are able to "cash in" on their home-derived "cultural capital" (Bourdieu and Passeron 1977; Bernstein 1977) to achieve not only academic success but also moral certification. Research on the negotiation of student-teacher contracts (Smith and Geoffrey 1968), and the utilization of the hidden curriculum (Apple 1979) has shown how such classroom order is actively constructed in complex interactions between students and teachers. Such typing seems to play a major role in learning that gets reflected in formal testing and achievement scores (Rist 1970; Broadfoot 1979).

This review suggests the potential relevance for criminological theory of studying the classroom as a social microcosm (for example, to better understand how "authority" works). The organizational and moral order of the classroom is as important as that of the educational.

CRITICISMS OF THE SCHOOL FAILURE AND CLASSROOM DYNAMICS ANALYSES

As always, none of this research is flawless. The apparent correlations between school failure and deviance are only that, and even the most neopositivist interpretation would admit that the relationship could in further research be revealed as spurious. This point has even more importance in this substantive area, however, as it should now be apparent that many of the ostensibly independent variables (for example, social class, ethnicity, gender, school failure) used in control theory are quite dialectically intertwined in real life. If teachers view working-class demeanor negatively, for instance, in judging the amenability of their pupils to learning, it should not be so surprising that working-class pupils learn less when they are given less instruction.

The coherence of the moral order research is impressive within contemporary social research criteria for good theory, and it parallels educational achievement research. Nonetheless, much of this research has been done in the United States (especially the self-report surveys upon which control theory is based), and much of it in Britain (especially the school organization research). The Canadian self-report research available is consistent with the American, and the little school organization research done in this country is also confirming of the British findings. Moreover, much of the classroom dynamic research has been done in Canada. Yet, the British subcultural material has not always made fully explicit the linking of class, age, or ethnic minorities. The lack of much comparable material on the United States or Canada leaves us with the difficulty that such real-life, class-based resistances may not be so relevant in "culturally classless" North America.

More crucially, very little of this research (other than the classroom dynamic studies and a few very recent self-report delinquency surveys) has included females. Given the importance of gender difference in both self-report and official delinquency, this is a crucial gap. Unfortunately, the classroom order research has largely focussed on elementary school classrooms, which may be the site of the genesis of delinquency, but are not usually the site of its most serious manifestations, which occur in secondary schools. More direct classroom observation study of Werthman's thesis would be useful in clarifying its universality.

As we shall explore more thoroughly in chapter 8, the policy recommendations flowing from this research have not always been considered useful, nor been easily implemented. Most crucially, school failure cannot be entirely eliminated as long as schools continue ranking and sorting pupils. In large part, this reflects a naïveté about the politics of educational and justice reform, which has remained entrapped within particular value biases and liberal-democratic ideologies.

Even the best of the interactionist research itself remains flawed. Although a number of excellent ethnographies have begun to give us the viewpoint of some pupils, the range and variation of such views remain quite undelineated. The classroom order research has generally operated within the limits of traditional participant observation, and with a lack of connection to a wider context; while not an inherent flaw, this means that the potential of such ethnographies has not yet been fulfilled. More research on indicated topics is needed to clarify findings and ascertain their generalizability. This review can be seen as outlining a program of scholarly activity, in that it explicitly claims links between classroom order and deviance, and (1) family and community background (latent culture) of pupils (Becker and Geer 1960); (2) language use and curriculum; (3) school achievement, pupil ability, and grading; (4) the organization of schooling and teaching careers; and (5) the wider social and political order.

What is most needed is a reconceptualization of the sociology of deviance in education that would transform the traditional research problems. It would demand the examination of the schooling state apparatus as an instrument of control and legitimation, surveillance, and socialization. In effect, the traditional question of why some pupils are deviant would be transformed into asking why any conform (or why more do not revolt).

SCHOOLING: DISCIPLINE, SURVEILLANCE, AND SUBJECTIVITY

Recall from chapter 2 that we criticized crude early versions of conflict theory that saw the bourgeoisie as simply imposing their will on a less powerful proletariat. Instead, we argued, one must recognize the significance of the modern state, not only as a vehicle to legitimize dominant interests (of gender and ethnicity, as well as class) by claiming to act in the general interest of society, but also as an area of class struggle. In that chapter we also introduced the idea that formal, compulsory, universal, and free state education systems were instituted in large part to control and discipline the young. I want to suggest that a conceptual reorientation derived from recent British work on the state, ideology, the subject, and law and discourse will move us in this direction. I will suggestively outline each of these in turn.

The education system, as part of the state, contributes to each of the functions of accumulation, control, and legitimating. Schooling ostensibly contributes to capital accumulation through the teaching of skills; though this process now seems much less central than human capital theory suggests (Karabel and Halsey 1977), at least some pupils learn technical skills necessary for a highly industrialized economy. Certain technical courses, community college programs, and advanced university work in the sciences have fairly immediate payoffs for industry (Apple 1979). Generally speaking, industry controls most scientific research that is performed, either directly in its own laboratories or through contract work with universities (Livingstone and Mason 1978). The costs are thus socialized as much as possible.

Many recent analyses of education have indicated how fundamental an issue is social control by the school (e.g., Sutherland 1976). Compulsory education (as opposed to universal free education) seems to have originated primarily from a concern to control working-class street urchins (Corrigan 1979). The contemporary concern with establishing classroom order is legitimized by the claim that it is essential for learning to occur. The provision of massive, prolonged education has effectively removed large numbers of youngsters from a flooded youth labor force by placing them in community colleges, vocational schools, and polytechnics. The hidden curriculum research (for example, Apple 1979) draws parallels between school authority systems (with relatively autocratic control over large numbers, use of extrinsic rewards, and the like) and adult work relations.

I will focus on educational ideology as an instance in which activities by both super- and subordinates must be examined in order to understand the complex dialectic that maintains moral continuity within the state. In chapter 2, we raised the questions of how the ideological climate is structured and where the key sites of hegemony are. What is specifically bourgeois about bourgeois education, and what is "truly knowledge"? To what extent is education liberating, a great equalizer, the provider of opportunity, and to what extent is its class-neutral appearance merely a facade that serves the interest of domination and inequality? What are the real connections between education and other institutions within and without the state?

The educational system plays a crucial role in maintaining hegemony. Class differences are reconstituted as educational differences, apparently objectively assessed. As Dale puts it, "The basic function of education under capitalism is the reproduction of class structure without the reproduction of class consciousness" (1978, 35). Informal, ongoing assessments occur in processual classroom interaction where biases prevail freely, initial inequalities are confirmed, noncognitive aspects predominate, stereotyping is reflected in self-fulfilling prophecies, and pupil subcultures dialectically amplify effects. Formal assessments "objectively" confirm these informal ones (Broadfoot 1979) in the IQ ideology that Bowles and Gintis (1976) so forcefully argue is used to justify occupational stratification.

> The school may be seen as maintaining the social order through the taken for granted categories of its superordinates who process pupils and knowledge in mutually confirming ways. The ability to maintain these categories as consensual, when there are among the clients in school conflicting definitions of the situation, resides in the unequal distribution of power. There is a need to see how this enters into and shapes the interactional situation in the classroom (Keddie 1971, 156).

It is at this point that Mann (1970) and Freire (1970) offer us some compelling clues as to how school knowledge is ideologically supportive of existing oppressions. Everyday life in classrooms has profound and somewhat ominous implications for our wider society.

For gross material inequalities, injustice, and the like, provide a recurring series of legitimation crises within modern societies (Habermas 1975). Although the present crises of the state may well be seen as determined in the last instance by capitalist crises of accumulation, most recent theories argue that the proffered resolutions are hammered out on the ideological level, a ground of particular relevance to moral issues and education, with a considerable latitude available to activistic setting of agendas and terms for debate. This implies that nothing so immutable as economic or demographic necessity decides policy, just as nothing so rational as criminological research does. Resolution is rather determined by popular democratic discourse (Laclau 1977). The political economy emphasis of the Canadian tradition, then, must be complemented at the more activist and cultural levels to allow understanding of particular outcomes at any historical conjuncture (Hall et al., 1978; Taylor 1980). Ideology functions to protect the overall system by hiding and distorting, revealing partial truths, and reconstituting the perceived contexts and relevancies of events.

It was mentioned in chapter 2 that state theorists (for example, Althusser 1971) have emphasized the importance of this phrasing of political debate, and have argued that the ruling class must amalgamate widespread support within a power bloc in order to control mass democratic struggle. The securing of consent through the unquestioned rule of authority (hegemony) (see Gramsci 1971) is a far cheaper and more effective mode of domination than outright coercion. "Democracy," "citizenship," and "justice" are all seen as key terms that guarantee formal political equality while deflecting attention from substantive inequality (Laclau 1977). Various kinds of centralized negotiations between government, industry, and labor (by means of social democratic contracts, corporatism, or fascism) maintain legitimacy while reconciling crises.

Not only is debate about education dominantly phrased and resolved at the ideological level (although it may be ultimately determined at the mode of production level), but also the resolution has ideological consequences for the educational system. Althusser's (1971) idea that "all ideology hails or interpellates the concrete individuals as concrete subjects" has ramifications at the legal level as well as ramifications (identified by Bowles and Gintis 1976) at the cognitive level. As Pashukanis (1978) asked about law, we might ask about education: What is specifically bourgeois about it? Dale (1978, 35) notes that "the reproduction of class structure without the reproduction of class consciousness" takes place within a bureaucratic structure that constrains activity and rapid change while reinforcing hegemony through its own organization (rule following, punctuality, hierarchy, ranking/sorting, IQ testing, sex-role stereotyping, individualization, and the like).

Attention must be paid to form and content together, these being combined in an apparatus that prevents full popular participation in education, but with some possibility of struggle around points of contradiction. Bourgeois education is characterized by a fetishism wherein formal student equality ignores real substantive differences and where knowledge is regarded rather as a commodity individually possessed than as a relationship. Picciotto (1979) develops Pashukanis' (1978) analysis of the intertwining of legal form and content, with emphasis on either one being prone to the danger of fetishization: formal education or legal equality can mask underlying substantive inequalities; yet the form of education and law must be analyzed in its peculiarities to avoid mesmerization by particular content. Education and the law both embody contradictions. Further work must be done to push Pashukanis' approach beyond the original claim to legal isomorphism with petty commodity exchange (*cf.* also Hirst 1979).

A central question would thus become how legal subjectivity is taught through schooling, requiring attention not only to explicit curricular materials on citizenship, but also ethnographic studies of curriculum in use, and the hidden curriculum (Arnot and Whitty 1982). In the school, young people first experience authority that is social and public. In disciplining to achieve order, informal substantive control taught through subjection to the school bureaucracy is as important as learning (seldom used) abstract, formal legal rights; schooling could thus be seen as good training for further subjection to the private discipline exercised informally in the dull compulsion of market and productive relations. A link would thus be suggested for elaboration with wider subcultural and cultural studies (Johnston 1979).

If the research on school failure and deviance is correct, it would seem that capitalist schools almost inevitably produce deviants. In ranking and sorting, some must fail to measure up; these will likely deviate; they will interact with teachers and others to internalize their failure and adopt deviant roles within the small group of the classroom. Their academic marginality is reflected in their moral marginality. As with the IQ, bourgeois schooling encourages youngsters to identify themselves as subjects, as authors of their own misdeeds, decontextualized into assuming individual responsibility for authoring acts that are repeated with systemic regularity. Where our society has recognized wider responsibility and has mitigated individual responsibility for criminal acts (as in the juvenile court), it has used this widened scope of concern not to assume full collective responsibility but to investigate and regulate individual problem families. The state uses the educational system to shape not only individual careers and life prospects, but also such seemingly private institutions as the family (David 1978). For the differential instruction of students (male and female, working- and middle-class, of dominant and subordinate ethnicity), their streaming into different levels (academic or vocational), and their setting out on different career trajectories, shape and channel possibilities for choosing spouses. And while the child is in school, he or she provides an entrée for constant surveillance of family relations (especially, but not only around child-rearing practices) that is quite unparalleled historically.

CONCLUSION

Other than the law, however, the major institution that defines the lives of adolescents is the school. Indeed, before the advent of the industrial revolution and compulsory schooling, adolescence did not exist as a separate age status (Gillis 1974). Compulsory schooling effectively cuts adolescents off from participating in the social and economic life of the community: it reduces their commitments and attachments, which, I have argued, in turn makes delinquency more likely. The Crowther report (Mays 1972) strongly corroborates this in indicating that the years of school-leaving have the most official delinquents, even when these years are changed, or are different from system to system. Elliott and Voss (1966, 1974) point out that working-class dropouts are markedly less delinquent after leaving school. It must be admitted that contemporary economies seem unable to absorb such an influx into the already overcrowded labor market (Rowntree and Rowntree 1968); a major function of the school, then, has been to delay entry to the labor force, and reduce competition for scarce jobs (Committee on Youth 1971). Relying solely on parents for support, adolescents become a particularly exploited sector of the population (Meyer 1973). Without economic resources of their own, and legally restricted from contracts (including marriage and work), they are unable to form serious attachments that could bind them to conformity. The combination of school functions regarding the control of the young, the inculcation of specific skills and values, and the sorting of students on behalf of the economy, results in contradictions that reflect those in the wider society.

This chapter has examined in some detail one of the key factors identified in self-report surveys as strongly and consistently correlated with delinquent behavior, a factor theoretically accounted for in control theory. The complexity of this factor, when it is more closely examined, is probably not unique to it, but is likely repeatable with the other factors control theorists rather blithely assume to be simple causes. It should now be apparent that deeper examination is required not only to more fully explore the intricacies of the observed relationships revealed in social surveys, but to explore the dialectical interplay of human actions. The classroom interaction literature, for instance, reveals how class, gender, and ethnicity are invoked and used by teachers in informal interactions on a day-to-day basis, but with effects that reinforce traditional inequalities. One cannot make such easy arguments about basic intelligence being primary as Hirschi and Hindelang (1977) do.

Examination of schooling has also been suggestive regarding the reproduction of gender relations. General cultural role expectations encourage male children to be more aggressive and self-assertive, and less deferential to authority. The classroom interaction literature reveals how crucial teachers perceive such deference to be, and how their interaction with boys is skewed towards disciplinary measures rather than "educational," learning ones. The social functioning of the classroom as an ongoing social group requiring the delineation of boundaries of behavior results in the utilization of the "worst pupils" (almost always a few boys) as group scapegoats. Any autonomous orientation derived from family socialization or class and career prospects thus interacts to doubly reinforce the nonbonding that would occur with failure in school.

In addition, of course, to these direct effects, schooling provides a general background structuring of age status for adolescents, and provides a context for differential affiliation and the development of subcultural values (Davies 1981). It does this by its compulsory nature (although not all students are equally interested or benefitted by it), and by its organization as a social institution, classifying students into year-by-year batches and streams.

Revisionist criticisms of the "rise of schooling" have indicated its origins were not due simply to humanitarian concerns, but conjoined with curfew laws to regulate the lives of the young, especially the poor and urban young (Sutherland 1976; Gaffield and West 1978). Basically, upper-middle-class curricula were designed to inculcate moral principles and to sort and weed out students. The later was legitimized through the scientific use of IQ testing – which, as recent ethnomethodological analyses of such testing (for example, MacKay 1978) indicate, constitutes a gross infringement of students' life chances, and it clearly discriminates against racial and ethnic minorities as well as female children. The legal position of children and students can thus be seen as one major determinant of their behavior. These findings regarding the relationship of the school to delinquency thus have relevance to Marxist theories of society. The educational achievement literature has now reached the conclusion that the school functions to perpetuate the class structure of society rather than to change it. In a similar way, the defining of some students as delinquent, both within the classroom and without, can be seen as a means of maintaining the traditional lumpen proletariat at the bottom of the economic and social heap. The school thus perpetuates not only the economic but also the moral order of capitalist Canada.

7

Juveniles in Justice

We now turn to examining how society not only shapes the conditions for juvenile misbehavior, but also reacts to this misbehavior. Although the incoming federal Young Offenders Act may alter the system we will be describing, this system has held sway since the passage of the Juvenile Delinquents Act in 1908.

In chapter 2, after analyzing the historical material on the 1908 Act, using both crude and more sophisticated versions of conflict theory, we noted the need to move beyond theorizing to examine the actual concrete operations of state agencies of juvenile justice: the police, the courts, probation services, and the training schools. We cannot unquestioningly assume that legal statutes and rational procedures deal objectively, similarly, and fairly with different youngsters committing the same offences. Our critical examination of anomie theory and official statistics suggested important biases regarding race, class, gender, and age, which tend to undermine the liberal notion of the impartial rule of law. But we have not directly examined how or why these biases come about. We also cannot unquestioningly assert that the system works in the interests of capital without examining concrete situations and operations (Hussain 1977). And we must also consider Thompson's (1978, 15) challenge that the liberal rule of law offers one of the best hopes for overcoming injustice (Young 1979).

Using some of the same types of official statistics initially encountered in chapter 3 to examine the behavior of officials (not delinquents, as misleadingly done by anomie theory), we shall encounter some old faces, but with a different meaning. It will also be necessary to remember control and interactionist explanations of juvenile misbehavior in order to consider how appropriate the official responses are. For the difficulties encountered by more than a century of research in trying to establish clear differentiations between "real delinquents" and "normal young-sters" become even greater when we examine how the juvenile justice system itself may be partly responsible for the correlations that self-report and observational research have found. In actively considering race, class, gender, age, subcultural values, delinquent associates, and school failure while processing youngsters, justice officials may not only construct official delinquency, but set the conditions for producing further behavioral delinquency. Interactionist theory obviously has further relevance, but needs to be both empirically examined, and extended in more structuralist directions concerning the socialization of persons as legal subjects.

Unfortunately, though official agencies have been collecting statistics on their operations for decades, in Canada we know distressingly little about how we typically deal with delinquents, or even if we do deal with them typically. The various agencies involved in juvenile justice are largely independent bureaucratically and often competitive politically. The police, for instance, are under the official legal control of municipal police commissions or provincial ministers, but often federally commanded by RCMP officers.

Partly in consequence, data are not standardized across subsystems (for instance, between the police and the court), nor have they been consistently collected over time, nor have they been compiled and analyzed in anything but the most crudely superficial, and usually self-serving way by governments, and almost never are they related to self-reported or observational data (Giffen 1979). Consequently, we will be forced to rely heavily upon the few studies done of single Canadian juvenile systems, using data especially collected in connection with the Frontenac Diversion Project (see Morton and West 1980 for the full report). We will however, try to relate this material wherever possible to other research to increase its generalizability.

THE JUVENILE JUSTICE SYSTEM
Self-Report Delinquency

Recall from our criticism of official statistics in chapters 3 and 4 that the juvenile justice system may be depicted as a huge funnel (see figure 7.1). The self-report data from Frontenac are typical in revealing that at the wide end of this funnel, there were large absolute numbers of various offences: the youngsters surveyed committed about 2,500 chargeable acts in 1977, and a majority reported having committed some offence. For instance, 62 percent reported alcohol use, 48 percent truancy, 27 percent staying out all night without parental permission, 27 percent using some drugs other than alcohol, 57 percent minor theft, 15 percent

FIGURE 7.1
Juvenile Justice Funnel

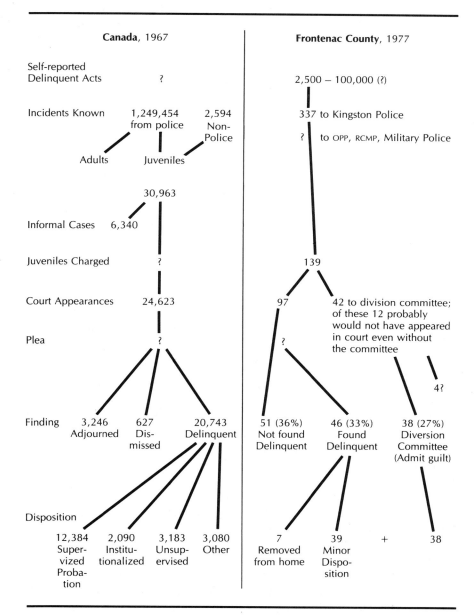

| Canada, 1967 | Frontenac County, 1977 |

Self-reported
Delinquent Acts   ?   2,500 — 100,000 (?)

Incidents Known   1,249,454   2,594   337 to Kingston Police
                from police   Non-
                          Police   ?   to OPP, RCMP, Military Police

      Adults   Juveniles

                30,963

Informal Cases   6,340

Juveniles Charged   ?   139

Court Appearances   24,623   97   42 to division committee;
                                       of these 12 probably
Plea   ?   ?   would not have appeared
                                       in court even without
                                       the committee

                                             4?

Finding   3,246   627   20,743   51 (36%)   46 (33%)   38 (27%)
       Adjourned   Dis-   Delinquent   Not found   Found   Diversion
               missed   Delinquent   Delinquent   Committee
                                                   (Admit guilt)

Disposition

   12,384   2,090   3,183   3,080   7   39   +   38
   Super-   Institu-   Unsup-   Other   Removed   Minor
   vized   tionalized   ervised   from home   Dispo-
   Proba-   sition
   tion

SOURCE: Revised from L. Tepperman, *Crime Control: The Urge to Authority* (Toronto: McGraw-Hill, 1977).

Source: Revised from M. E. Morton and W. G. West et al., *A Research Evaluation of the Frontenac Juvenile Diversion Project* (Ottawa: Solicitor General, 1980) p. 376.

theft of between $5 and $60, 7 percent theft over $50, 16 percent break and entry, 10 percent car theft, 31 percent vandalism, 33 percent assault. Although the first three categories represent relatively minor juvenile ("status") offences, the latter categories indicate behavior generally deemed more serious.

Only some 7 percent of these surveyed youngsters, however, reported being officially charged with delinquency. Many juvenile offences (especially those of "status," such as truancy, sexual activity, running away, and the like) are "victimless," and are hence less likely to be noticed by anyone other than the offender. Of those offences that are noticed, a large number of offenders are initially filtered out because the acts are seen as trivial.

Recall from the data presented in chapter 4 that girls self-report fewer delinquencies than boys (about $1^1/_3$:1 to 2:1 – considerably less than the official ratio of 4:1 to 10:1). The type of delinquencies they commit are very similar, although they are slightly less specialized than are those of the boys (Gomme, Morton, and West 1984).

The Victims

Surveys have indicated that only a small proportion of victimizations are reported to the police; in Toronto, Courtis (1970) established a figure of 20 percent. The more extensive American research yields patterns in many ways similar to official statistics; minor crimes and property crimes are much more frequent than violent ones. In addition, however, such studies have yielded a different perspective on crime. For just as the young seem to figure inordinately in the commission of crime, so are they to an unusual extent likely to be victimized (Empey 1978, 178), with a 24 percent chance of victimization in one year, compared to 10 percent for middle-aged people and 3 percent for the old. Males are more likely to be victimized than females (other than for rape); three out of four murder victims are male; but because age is such a strong factor, young women are more likely to suffer than men in general or middle-aged men in particular. Overall vulnerability to crime is about equal between blacks and whites, but blacks are some two to three times more likely to suffer violence (rape, robbery, and aggravated assault). Young black males are the most vulnerable overall group. Working-class populations are the most vulnerable to violent crimes, though the wealthy experience more theft.

In attempting to get another angle on this initial "filtering," we (Morton and West 1980) interviewed some 113 victims of officially registered juvenile offences about their reactions to various aspects of their experience with juvenile justice. Almost two-thirds of the victims thought that delinquency was a serious problem; most of the rest did not know, or did not provide information. In general, about a quarter thought that delinquency should be handled more leniently, while a fifth thought it should be handled more harshly; similarly, a third were satisfied with the outcome of their particular cases, while a quarter were not.

The victims of youth crime in Frontenac seemed to prefer not to become involved unless they perceived benefits of a concrete material nature (for instance, restitution) for their efforts. (See also Ennis 1967; Evans and Leger 1978.) The victims were seen by the juvenile charged as being the most significant participant in the process only if the juveniles were pleading not guilty (a distinct minority of juvenile cases). Some of these findings become more understandable when it is realized that individual persons comprised only slightly more than half of the total victims; a third were private businesses, and another 10 percent were public corporations (for instance, school boards). Arrested juveniles in the Frontenac sample reported that in only a fifth of their cases did victims or witnesses precipitate the arrest, and victims themselves reported such activity even less frequently.

These findings coincide with other studies of victims conducted over the last fifteen years in the United States, and for the last five years in Canada. As indicated above, though there is increasingly sensationalist media attention to the injuries suffered by a few victims (for instance, *MacLeans*, Sept. 5, 1983, 40 ff) and governmental attention (Solicitor General 1983), most victims do not bother to report incidents to the authorities, for various reasons (for example, thinking the incident was not serious, or a private affair, that the police could do nothing, fearing retaliation, and the like). Those reporting are likely to represent the less alienated or more active members of a community (Teevan 1978, 3; Evans and Leger 1978, 8). Interestingly, there are indications that publicity about crime-prevention programs that stresses public responsibilities may have the effect of (artificially) increasing official rates of crime reportage (Evans and Leger 1978, 9–11, 18) even though the victims themselves are often treated by the authorities as "marks to be cooled out" (Teevan 1978, 11) rather than as full participants in the process of restitution and compensation implied in encouraging their involvement. Interestingly, some research (for example, Waller and Okihiro 1978) has found that most (theft) victims (unless vandalized) are *more* lenient in their attitudes towards sanctions than are the nonvictims; this is probably because the incident has concretized a vague anxiety about crime into the specific (usually minor) incident they themselves experienced. There are some problems with victim studies, in that they do not usually include "corporate" or "white-collar" crime which usually leave victims unaware, and their relevance to studying "victimless" crime is also dubious. Problems such as these, plus the recency of victim studies suggest that we need to turn to points in the funneling system where we have more information in order to assess better how it works.

The Police

The finding from self-report surveys that there is little difference between classes in the proportion of youngsters committing delinquencies (about 1.5:1) contrasted sharply with the official ratio of 5:1 (Box 1981). Some labeling theorists (for example, Piliavin and Briar 1964) have suggested that police officials unduly consider "subsidiary" characteristics (such as lower-class origin or precocious demeanor of greasers) as much as actual commission of an offence, thus becoming the key point of "filtering" youngsters in the juvenile justice funnel.

The passage of juvenile justice legislation has greatly extended the scope of discretionary social control over the young. Police and probation officers are empowered to investigate situations of neglected, dependent, and delinquent youth, and have often "solved" cases without bringing them to trial (Sutherland 1976, 146–9). Although many juveniles are released upon official exercise of discretion, it is obvious that the legislation gives very widespread and relatively unchecked power to the police to control the young.

Over the last two decades, it has been mostly American research that has indicated that the police exercise a great degree of discretion in laying charges in a complex interplay of legally relevant criteria such as prior record and seriousness of offence; attitudes of complainants, suspects, and police; ethnicity and social class of suspects and neighborhoods (all reviewed in Moyer 1977); and legislation, command and deployment of police (Grosman 1975; Morton 1977). Moyer (1975; 1977) reports that the more "legalistic" factors such as prior record and seriousness of offences tend to mitigate social-class differences in many, though not all, studies reviewed. Box (1981), however, points out that prior record is not a wholly objective measure, as police deployment practices tend to concentrate in working-class areas (see also Hagan et al. 1980, for Canadian data on this).

It is generally not clear, however, how the mainly American research on police discretion can easily be generalized to Canada. Even in the United States, the exercise of police discretion seems to vary substantially according to the legislation governing police (Sowle 1962), the organizational style of police command and deployment (Wilson 1968a and 1968b), and the characteristics of the populace being policed (Banton 1964; Bayley and Mendelsohn 1968; Morton 1977). Without a number of careful field studies of the exercise of police discretion in Canada, it is almost impossible to predict the precise effect that variable police practices might have on the charging of juvenile offenders here.

In an early Canadian study using only official statistics, but comparing youngsters contacted by the police and those sent on to court, Nease (1968) has found for Hamilton that the court group were more likely to be older, recidivists, male, have committed more serious offences, and to be from the highest delinquency rate neighborhoods. For Montreal, Fréchette and Leblanc (1979) note in particular that the arrested boys were much more likely to have committed serious interpersonal violence. As does Farrington for England (1977), they state that this indicates that the juvenile justice system has some considerable effectiveness in selecting youngsters appropriately, in order to protect society. There is not, however, any clear line of demarcation, or break, between the two groups, but rather much overlap, or a steady progression, so the question remains of where and how the police do "draw the line."

A suggestive national study by Conly (1977b) has shown how the proportions of apprehended juveniles who are charged by the police varies greatly from community to community: 18 percent of the recorded Ottawa youth contacts were charged, 23 percent from Toronto, 17 percent from Hamilton, 31 percent from London, 20 percent from Windsor, 30 percent from Edmonton, 78 percent from Montreal, 77 percent from Winnipeg, and 96 percent from Calgary. There would thus seem to be a very wide variation.

Relying on the analysis of official statistics and some intensive interviews, Hackler has begun some interesting further exploratory analyses of police processing. He has noted (1981), for instance, that Calgary police charge most juveniles contacted, in contrast to most other police forces. Similarly, some provinces (for example, Manitoba and British Columbia) have police charge rates for petty thefts (1,458 and 1,558 per 100,000) which are more than twice as high as others (from 620 to 352 in Quebec, Newfoundland, PEI, Nova Scotia, and New Brunswick) (Hackler and Paranjape 1981).

Conly's (1977b) and Hackler's and Paranjape's (1983) studies are provocative in raising questions, but what is needed is some detailed comparative case studies of individual police jurisdictions to suggest why and how different forces operate so differently. Our Frontenac research (Morton and West et al. 1980) can provide a further example.

The Frontenac police in 1977 had a charge rate per 1,000 much lower than that of any large Canadian metropolitan area studied by Conly (1977b), and its rate of 0.8 per 1,000 was even noticeably lower than the 1.3 rate in a neighboring, similar county. It would seem that the Frontenac police forces were considerably more discretionary, even though the proportion of charge by type of offence was roughly similar to other Canadian jurisdictions (Morton and West 1980, 69). The youngsters arrested in Frontenac in 1977 were markedly more delinquent in the frequency of serious misbehavior (for example, major theft, car theft, break and entry, and vandalism) that they self-reported than were sampled community youngsters (see also Fréchette and Leblanc 1979). The Frontenac arrestees were overwhelmingly male (some 87 percent), and concentrated in the fourteen- and fifteen-year-old age brackets. The arrested youth also reported more status offences (for example, truancy and staying out without parental permission). It is noteworthy, however, that as many school youngsters as arrested youngsters reported one or two commissions for such serious offences as assault, such less serious Criminal Code offences as minor theft, and status offences such as alcohol use. Consistent with the Elliott and Ageton (1980) research in the States, then, it would seem that major property offences and some status offences are singled out by police for court attention, whereas other status offences, minor theft, and assault are not. The time ordering in such cross-sectional research, however, remains unclear: it is equally plausible that the more serious offences have followed contact with the police.

In trying to understand the significance of both this particular Frontenac research, and the other empirical findings regarding the exercise of discretion by Canadian police, we need to highlight a number of issues. Although we do not yet know exactly the nature of police selectivity, and what effects this has, it is highly probable that some groups of youngsters are more delinquent, or more seriously delinquent, than others. Self-report surveys, for instance, consistently report more violent behavior by working-class youngsters, behavior that is likely to be seen by the police as serious (yet the self-reported differences remain not nearly as large as the official ones). The time order of arrest and delinquency needs more clarification: extra delinquency may occur after arrest rather than before.

There are a number of possible interpretations available to explain the steady increase in official offenders coming to police attention. To argue that such data indicate a growing incidence of juvenile misbehavior, one must assume consistent behavior by the police and courts. The increases would indicate that preventative and curative delinquency programs have failed, and should be eliminated or replaced by alternatives, or one could argue that these programs are working, but are not sufficiently supported and funded to be truly effective. Liberal (for example, Schur 1973) and conservative (for example, Nettler 1974) criminologists have taken these viewpoints. A third interpretation is possible, however, which does not make the assumption that officials operate so consistently that police statistics give us a reliable measure of delinquent behavior. This viewpoint regards the official rise in delinquency rates as the result of increasingly vigilant and restrictive social control (Sutherland 1976, 144). Much of the increase in delinquency rates apparent in police statistics may be attributable to (a) the baby boom disproportionately swelling the 15-to-29-year old, crime-prone age group; (b) increases in the size of police forces, and the justice system (McDonald 1976); (c) increasingly efficient reporting by police and a sensitized public; (d) more goods being available for property crime. There may be some actual increase in delinquency, but police statistics are very poor indicators of whether this is happening or not.

McDonald (1976) has shown that size of police force correlates more strongly with official crime than supposedly causal factors (such as poverty); her earlier work (1969) indicates that most of the total crime increases were traffic offences. The advent of professional youth bureau officers may increase the rate of charge. In our Kingston research again (Morton, West et al. 1980), the reduction of the youth bureau from two to one officer resulted in a similar drop in juvenile delinquents charged.

Some American research reported by Empey (1978, 144–45) shows that as one major city after another improved its record keeping over the last couple of decades, official crime rates soared by 27 to 202 percent within a year. Clearly, such professionalized bookkeeping has contributed enormously to the general perception of rising crime rates.

The police, of course, are as likely as anybody to fear some kinds of youth as harbingers of moral decline, and to fix their attention upon them in particular. With pressures to routinely maintain the public appearance of order, the police are concerned with disruptive displays on the street, exactly where minority and working-class youngsters are often forced to "hang out" as they lack other recreational places (Corrigan 1979). Toronto policemen interviewed by Gandy (1967, 346) claimed that the seriousness of the offence was the major factor in their disposition of juveniles, but also admitted that they were likely to be more lenient in suburban, middle-class districts, and hence likely to "overcharge" in working-class areas. Many types of working-class and ethnic minority behavior have seemed to threaten the bourgeois order (Thompson 1963; Mayhew 1981). Some of these are not simply illegal acts, but the precocious assertion of adulthood, as discussed in chapter 5.

The Court

Recall from chapter 2 the legal situation and rights of young persons charged and brought to juvenile court under the Juvenile Delinquents Act; these obviously greatly affect what goes on in the courts. Yet we cannot easily assume that the letter or spirit of the law is followed behaviorally, and hence we need to look at what actually happens in the courts.

The legal historical research reviewed in chapter 2 documented that juvenile justice proponents and legislation have been as much concerned with morality, neglect, and "predelinquency" as with actual criminal behavior by youngsters (Platt 1969; Leon 1978; Sutherland 1976). The few studies of (mainly American) juvenile courts (Cicourel 1968; Emerson 1969; Matza 1964a; Stoodley 1974) document how organizational priorities shape classificational and dispositional decisions. Researchers generally have remarked on the arbitrariness in decision making, lack of due process, and the derived sense of injustice. Studies on contemporary struggles to redefine the Canadian Juvenile Delinquents Act likewise indicate a continuing concern with morality, neglect, and "predelinquency," particularly by child-treatment organizations (Cousineau and Veevers 1972; Johnston 1977).

Treatment in the juvenile court continues the pattern of police processing. The loose structure of the court, lack of due process, vague definitions of illegalities, and conflicting community pressures to "crack down" or "rehabilitate" force judges to rely on their commonsense (middle-class) notions of delinquency and its causal factors. They assess the "situation" of the child.

Stoodley (1974), for instance, conducted informal interviews with eighteen American and Canadian juvenile judges, and found a wide range in their descriptions of the extent to which they regulated their courts and supportive agencies (for instance, police youth bureaus); wide variations in their theories of delinquency causation and appropriate treatment; and divergences in their beliefs regarding the efficacy of their dispositions.

The court's job is often seen as a predictive classificatory one: which youths are likely to commit further delinquencies, and hence bring public complaints upon the court? There is thus an attempt to determine a child's *character* as much as his past *acts*, and his acts are interpreted in terms of this character assessment. Should he be found delinquent by weighing background factors such as a "bad home" as much as by his deeds, he is defined as of poor moral character.

In examining the role of defence lawyers in juvenile court, Tony Platt has noted the strong organizational and ideological pressures to avoid adversarial confrontations (1969, 165). This is especially true in courts where a "duty counsel" or "public defender" system exists, for in this situation the defence attorney becomes a regular member of the court team, and must balance any strenuous defence of his or her ostensible client against the loss of future co-operation with court officials. The lawyer must thus make judgments as to how worth defending a youngster is. The pervasiveness of this procedural philosophy precludes any radical challenge to the restrictions on the rights of juveniles; alcohol or minor drug use, for instance, can only be discussed in sanctimonious, moral tones, even by officials who are known to indulge themselves.

Pat Erickson (1975) has presented similar findings in the procedures of lawyers in the Toronto courts. She found that more than half the judges interviewed felt that lawyers should act as friends of the court rather than as advocates of the child, and that duty counsel lawyers are less likely to be child advocates than private ones; such a position would be absolutely intolerable in adult cases.

Hackler (1978, and Paranjape 1983) has pursued his examination of various police charge practices in a number of insightful working papers that compare the operations of juvenile courts in Canada, the United States, and Europe. He has offered convincing data that show that some communities filter most juveniles out of the system at the police stage, while others do this at the court stage; Saskatchewan, for instance, sends many children directly into welfare agencies, thus avoiding the court. Obviously such filtering greatly affects how the courts operate. Furthermore, there are marked differences in court dispositions. Hackler has speculated that these variations in system response may not be bad, but represent the best use of unique local resources (for instance, policemen who are effective counselors). He has also speculated that filtering at different levels may be related to the degree of integration or contact between the police and the court, size of a community, age of a community, the physical distance between the courthouse and police station, the disposition of police or social service tasks between different forces or agencies, and the like. But systematic data is not available to either confirm or refute these speculations. Hackler has also become interested in lay knowledge and the role of "minor" officials in the courts (for instance, clerks), who often play a major role in directing court traffic (Hackler 1975).

Research regarding juveniles' perception of their court experiences in the United States reflects the concerns raised in the organizational studies. Matza's (1964a) study of one-hundred male training school youths indicated that they were not committed to an illegal life-style, but rather were "in drift," suspending personal responsibility for their actions and resenting the arbitrariness of their courtroom treatment. Baum and Wheeler (1968) found one-hundred male training school youths to feel shocked, upset, and unhappy regarding the justness of their court hearing. Maher and Stein (1968) found an intense hostility among the same youths towards the courts, who simultaneously held a neutral view of the judge. Snider (1971) found that forty-three male youths predominantly felt fear towards the court, but believed that their hearings were fair. Langley et al. (1978) showed that most of the Ottawa youths studied entered their court hearings without clear expectations regarding the proceedings; another plurality experienced a demonstrable difference between their expectations regarding disposition and the judges' actual disposition. And many feared training school sentencing could result from even minor infractions.

Unfortunately, the other research studies available on the effects of the juvenile court on youngsters provide only sketchy results for baseline comparison. Matza (1964a) argued that the vague proceedings, occasional incompetency, and overriding paternalism of the juvenile court were highly likely to arouse a general sense of injustice. Empirical studies (reviewed in Schur 1973, 161 ff) indicate a lack of favorableness towards the court.

> Processed delinquents expressed extremely negative feelings about the entire court experience, although at the same time they did not claim that they had been unfairly treated. These reactions probably vary a great deal from court to court and from judge to judge. One investigation has indicated that the child's sense of participation in the proceedings (especially the extent to which he is allowed to speak) greatly influences his evaluation of the proceedings (Schur 1973, 162).

Another study suggested that delinquents regarded court and probation as relatively ineffective, but felt positively about the individuals they met; three-quarters agreed with the judge's decision (Giordano 1976). Langley, Thomas, and Parkinson (1978) found that most Ottawa youths who appeared in court had no clear understanding of what to expect, were highly anxious, and at the end of proceedings three-quarters felt positively towards the judge. A great part of the hostility felt by delinquents could easily develop from the disjuncture between the rhetoric and reality of the juvenile courts: the language talks of the child found guilty not being an offender, but "in a condition of delinquency." The court promises to act in the child's best interest, yet terrifies and often punishes him or her. The court finds it difficult to treat and rehabilitate; its provisions are largely ineffective.

Despite the suggestive findings of these exploratory studies, we have been unable to obtain good general reports on the overall operations of Canadian juvenile courts. We are thus left to guess at the extent to which these mainly American studies are relevant in Canada, and how typical is the Frontenanc court that we are about to describe in more detail. Until the present nationwide study of juvenile courts is released, we have few other sources of data on Canadian juvenile courts available. The court has remained particularly unknown because its operations have traditionally been conducted *in camera*, ostensibly to protect the juvenile; but one wonders to what extent this has also allowed the court to avoid public scrutiny. (The new Bill of Rights will change this.)

It is highly likely that the Frontenac court is not entirely typical; it is located in a small university city, with local law students supplying free defence services and the judges seeing the court as a "teaching court." The two local judges who presided during the year of study were legally trained (whereas in 1973 a full third of Ontario judges were *not*) and children's rights oriented; both were young, and very active and prominent in the provincial judges association. In addition, the court was running an experimental "diversion program" (to be discussed in the next chapter), and hence had "direct competition" to "keep it on its toes." As well, court personnel knew they were being researched.

Most juvenile courts tend to be in rather intimidating, austere, institutional buildings. Youngsters and their families are usually kept waiting (often for many hours) on public view in the waiting room; they seldom have much information or knowledge about the operations of the court, or the legal options available to them, even when they retain legal counsel. A number of the Frontenac juveniles commented that the time spent in the waiting room was the worst part of their legal experience, as fantasies reigned unchecked about possible dire consequences.

The youngsters charged in Frontenac in 1977, however, seemed fairly typical. The sample is slightly skewed towards older youth, and there are proportionately more males than females than is the case in the national statistics. Since both older age and male gender typically correlate with higher rates of more serious delinquency, it is particularly interesting that Frontenac youth in general have a relatively low police charge rate, due to increased police filtering of younger, female, and minor offenders.

Two-thirds of the youngsters interviewed indicated that they felt negatively or were afraid of going to court. One-third expected to be "sent up." Two-thirds of the juveniles had to wait for over a month for their first hearing. In most cases, legal niceties were followed in Frontenac: the charges were read, and defence counsel was present. Most youngsters felt that their lawyers did a good job. Seventeen percent of the youngsters pleaded not guilty, a slightly higher percentage than usual, perhaps because of the generous assistance of law students. Juveniles told their own story in only a fifth of the cases, although two-thirds felt that the court was open to hearing their side. Usually in the court setting there were a number of other actors: family, police, social agencies, and sometimes, victims. In the court setting, the police, lawyers, and social workers were most prominent; the police (representing the Crown attorney) were present in almost all cases. A third of the hearings lasted thirty minutes or less, another third lasted up to one hour, and the last third took more time. Court discussion tended to center on the facts regarding the offence, the surrounding circumstance and attitudes, and the juvenile's previous history and character.

Half the juveniles felt that big words were used, and that there were "hard parts," but only 13 percent said they had difficulty understanding the court proceedings and language. Half the subjects did say they found the court hearing formal. Many of them felt some stigma in being brought to court. Whereas Matza (1964a) and others have suggested that the juvenile court process engenders a sense of injustice that causes youngsters to resent their treatment and to further rebel, almost all the Kingston youth felt that they had been treated fairly, yet 77 percent felt negatively about the whole experience or were indifferent. The overwhelming majority felt relief upon hearing the disposition of their case.

As with the police, there are noticeable differences between juvenile courts, some of which seem to balance different police procedures. In comparing Frontenac with a neighboring county, for instance, we found a much higher police charge rate in the latter (some 254 juveniles charged, versus 139 in similar-sized juvenile populations); the neighboring court, however, found 64 percent not guilty, in contrast to only 32 percent being found not guilty in Frontenac (similar to Canadian findings: *Juristat* 1981). This suggests that the court and police are working in tandem, simply varying the stage at which juveniles are being screened out of the system. As further evidence of such "tailored" co-operation between court and police, we found a surprising number of cases treated "exceptionally" in Frontenac: some 10 percent of the youngsters had their cases "rerouted" (for instance, charges were informally dropped in violation of the court's own rules). The active intervention of parents, lawyers, and police affected these cases. For instance, one of these incidents involved a number of youngsters taking the parents' car without permission; when the parents obtained out-of-court satisfaction the charges were dropped. Such "personalized" treatment is probably easier to obtain in small communities such as Frontenac than in larger metropolitan areas.

In addition to such findings of not guilty, the court found many youngsters guilty. Twenty-five percent of the Frontenac youth were given minor dispositions (for instance, adjourned sine die) and 25 percent were given probation (somewhat lower than the Canadian figure of 42 percent: *Juristat* 1981). Overall, in comparison with a neighboring court, the data suggested that Frontenac youngsters were less likely to be charged, and more likely if charged to have their cases dismissed, but if found guilty, they were less likely to receive minor dispositions. A few were ordered to pay restitution, almost all by cash.

Two other particular Canadian research projects have recently been completed that examine the treatment of females in juvenile court, with findings similar to British (Campbell 1981; Smart 1976) and American (Klein 1973) research. Barnhorst (1980) found that at least until 1974–75, girls with short records were more likely to be referred by police to court than boys, and courts were more likely to treat them harshly when they got there. Judges interviewed clearly had a double standard regarding sexual conduct. Geller (1980) similarly found that female juveniles, once charged, were more likely to be incarcerated than any other group, including allegedly dangerous adult males. The fewer girls who did appear in court were seen as more difficult to deal with, and were more often referred to the court psychiatric clinic for assessment. In particular, although truancy constituted only 2.4 percent of all complaints against girls, and 0.7 percent against all boys, it constituted 33 percent of the cases of females referred to the clinic, and 16 percent of the males. For juvenile status offenders, the clinic recommended out-of-home placement for 64 percent of females, but only 22 percent of males. The courts disposed of these clinically assessed cases by placing 54 percent of the girls and 35 percent of the boys out-of-home. Female truants were particularly regarded as being "out of control," that is, sexually self-destructive, and further interviews indicated that these perceived activities were the central reason for the "truancy" charge! In contrast, sexual activity and out-of-control behavior for boys involved a couple of cases of male aggression, and one of possible consorting homosexually with an older man. Geller concluded that the court was very concerned with policing the boundaries of traditional gender stereotypes (see also McIntosh 1978).

As indicated in figure 7.2, overall about three-quarters of all youngsters appearing in Canadian juvenile courts are found delinquent; although the remainder are not formally found delinquent, the guilt of over half of these is established, but the court is adjourned sine die without a formal finding.

FIGURE 7.2
Court Decisions as a Percentage of Total Charges

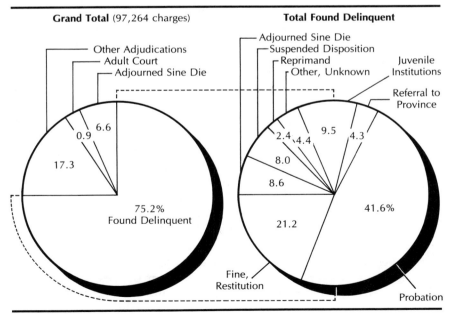

SOURCE: "Juvenile Delinquents," *Juristat* 1, 2: (Ottawa: Statistics Canada) 1981, p. 4. Reproduced by permission of the Minister of Supply and Services Canada.

Dominion Bureau of Statistics pamphlet #85–202 (1969), *Juvenile Delinquents*, indicates that persons adjudged delinquent in Ontario are overwhelmingly from working-class families (p. 56).

Dispositions: Community

Of those found delinquent, about a fifth are "let off" with a "warning" of some sort: they are reprimanded, receive suspended dispositions, or have their cases adjourned sine die without a formal sentence. A further fifth are fined or required to pay restitution; in almost all cases, the monetary value is quite low, usually well under one-hundred dollars. (To an unemployed fifteen year old, this may still be a severe penalty.) These two groups (making up about forty percent of those found delinquent) can be said to receive light sentences, with relatively little disruption to their lives.

Another two-fifths of those found guilty are placed on probation, the juvenile court's favorite disposition, a disposition "pioneered" in recent history through its use in juvenile justice. This may range from informal, occasional meetings with a friendly adult the court deems responsible, to rather formal, required weekly or even daily reporting to an official, professional probation officer, with additional strict terms, such as curfew, disassociation with "troublemakers," nonfrequenting of certain establishments, and the like. In such cases the intervention in a juvenile's life can be quite extensive.

Probation is an interesting social institution, in that it not only aims to provide authoritative control, but also seeks to offer the counseling and guidance of a social work, or even psychiatric, nature. In theory, it would provide an adult "friend" to lead misdirected youths back to social conformity, often bolstering broken-home situations, and offering therapy for those mildly disturbed. Unfortunately, in dozens if not hundreds of studies there is scant evidence that probation has any such positive effect; these studies have been most recently replicated in Canada in the Juvenile Services Project research. Byles and Maurice (1979), in a carefully controlled experiment, found that probationed Hamilton delinquents were no less likely to recidivate than those not counseled, even when an unusually generous provision of resources was available.

In addition to formal dispositions requiring payment of fines or probation supervision, the court often informally "suggests" that youngsters avail themselves of social agency services. These range from suggested consultation with school guidance counselors or social workers, to counsel from children's aid societies, to participation in local recreational and sporting activities offered by YMCAs, settlement houses, and the like. Needless to say, though legally not binding, most youngsters consider such "suggestions" as coercive.

Dispositions: Incarceration in Training Schools and Group Homes

About a tenth of the children before the court who are found guilty are sentenced to training schools or reformatories of one sort or another. Another twentieth are placed in charge of provincial welfare agencies, which often involves removal from home.

Only certain types of juvenile lawbreakers are selected for special treatment and sent to training schools. In Byles' (1969) study, Toronto Ontario Training School youth (one-third of the Ontario Training School [OTS] population) were more deviant than other Toronto youth surveyed (including lower- or working-class youth in the community) in their self-reported behavior for the following activities: truancy, alcohol use, running away, sexual intercourse, fighting, carrying weapons, use of drugs other than alcohol, theft (of cars and other goods), and vandalism (Byles 1969, 39). (The first four of these offences are juvenile-specific – the activities involved are illegal only for juveniles.) His study offers other information, below, on the OTS population from Toronto (which he labels "delinquent").

1. delinquent boys and girls come predominantly from the lower social class . . .;
2. delinquent boys and girls come mainly from the lower status academic streams (ungraded vocational and two-year trade classes for example) [where working class youth predominate];
3. the families of the delinquent group are among the most [geographically] mobile . . .;
4. delinquent boys and girls place significantly less importance on religion than [nonincarcerated] youth;
5. delinquent girls have experienced more conflict with parents than any other group. Delinquent boys . . . have also had more conflict with parents than [nonincarcerated] youth.
6. delinquent boys and girls have experienced considerably more derogatory social typing than community youth . . .;
7. delinquent boys and girls are significantly more tolerant of deviant behaviors than [nonincarcerated] youth . . . (Byles 1969, 79).

Byles' 1965 figures show that three-quarters of the OTS wards' parents earned under $10,000 per year, 78 percent of their fathers had "some high school or less," 91 percent of their fathers were unemployed, unskilled, or skilled workmen, and that only 53 percent of their families still had both parents living together (Byles 1969, 237–40).

The 1972 *Annual Report* of the Ontario Department of Corrections stated that about 90 percent of the OTS admissions were from towns or cities (p. 61); two-thirds of the admissions were from Toronto or other large cities. It is remarkable, then, that most training schools are located in rural areas or small towns, thus making continuing family contact difficult, and providing a retraining environment very different from those to which most juveniles will return on release. One-half of the admissions were fifteen years of age, one-quarter were fourteen, and one-quarter were younger than fourteen.

One Departmental study found that OTS wards used more tobacco, alcohol, marijuana, "speed," psychedelic drugs, and solvents (for inhaling) than Toronto community youth (Surridge and Lambert n.d., 1972?, 11). It also confirmed Byles' findings that just over half of the wards were living with both parents prior to admission, and that one-quarter were from low-status educational streams such as academic-vocational, opportunity, or occupational classes (Surridge and Lambert, question #15). Slightly over half of the wards had working mothers (Surridge and Lambert, table 24).

Conly (1977a) cites figures indicating that some (northern area) training schools have up to 75 percent native children, and he states that training school youngsters come from homes with some serious material deprivation (one-parent families, alcoholism, mental illness, physical disease, unemployment, and the like).

One of the most serious criticisms of training schools is derived from more closely examining their population. In 1973 (the last year Statistics Canada made full reports on training schools) about two-fifths of these youngsters were female (a noticeably higher proportion of females than in juvenile court) and three-fifths male. In that same year, nationally, 54 percent were committed for delinquency, 25 percent for protection, and 10 percent as returns from placement outside of training school upon "graduation." Looking at more detailed Ontario figures, until the late 1970s, between one- and two-fifths of the boys and two-thirds to three-quarters of the girls were incarcerated for being neglected or dependent (for example, in Ontario, under section 8 of the Trainings Schools Act), *not* for having been found delinquent (Weiler 1978). A large minority of males, and a clear majority of females, then, were locked up and treated as young criminals when the courts had found them to be in need of care (*not*, presumably, punishment). Weiler found that the most frequent reasons given by the judges involved were truancy, running away, staying out overnight, swearing, disobedience, tantrums, and the like, and that sexual promiscuity was the main reason for committing girls. Weiler (1978) also found that with the repeal of section 8 in Ontario, judges were increasingly using their prerogative under section 20 of the Juvenile Delinquents Act to commit youngsters to training school, thus bypassing the provisions in section 9 of the Training Schools Act, which requires that a criminal code offence be committed before incarceration is permissible; she speculated that these were similar youngsters to those previously committed under section 8. In examining youngsters confined under similar American legislation, Lerman (1971) has found that such inmates are detained even longer than "criminal" ones. The new Young Offenders Act should end this, but we shall have to wait and see what happens as it is implemented.

Most of the training schools, despite slick promotional literature, are declared by outside observers to be inadequate on their own terms. Forced to deal with a large and diverse population, they have usually been nothing more than custodial institutions (Sinclair 1965, 258). A few of the newer schools have had a higher staff to student ratio, and a more "therapeutic" atmosphere, but at most schools, youth-staff interaction has focussed on discipline and rules, behavior-modification techniques, and solitary confinement. Older youngsters and the group are used to control any rebels in a pecking order based on physical violence. A point system is common; in this system, youths who act appropriately accumulate points each day until a total is reached that permits their release. Segregation, isolation, and loss of privileges are also used to discipline. In sum, "Canadian training schools, as a general rule, have inadequate facilities." (The Committee on Juvenile Delinquency 1965, 180.)

It may be argued that although training schools have been inadequately staffed and equipped, that they have provided a valuable function for society by locking up some violent and desperate youth. While conceding that there may be a few uncontrollable and dangerous young persons needing serious disciplining and control, research indicates that this argument is seriously overblown. Milham, Bullock, and Hosie (1978), for instance, on studying maximum security lockups in the English system, found that those confined to such units were basically similar to "high-risk" youngsters in open community homes. They concluded that such youngsters were seriously failed by the child-care system, in which some institutions had absconding rates five or six times higher than others, widely varying transfer rates (1 to 32 percent and 15 to 65 percent in different studies), and widely varying amounts of violence unaccounted for by admission populations. Markwart (1980) has reported similarly unsettling results in his study of secure treatment in British Columbia training schools, where about half the youngsters were inappropriately placed in locked facilities.

What effect does all this have on the young person committed to a training school? How does a youngster perceive this treatment? There is little research available to tell us; as often happens, we are operating without knowledge. But some things are apparent.

> Should he be removed from his home and committed to a training school, he will view this as punishment. It may be called treatment. It may be in the child's interest. To him, however, it is punishment (Sinclair 1965, 246).

There is usually a sense of injustice as well, partially suggested and supported by our scientific social views that the background environment often "causes" the child's behavior, and by the fact that use of the training schools as a child-welfare instrument is done to counteract a "poor home environment."

It is difficult to reconcile the fact that a youngster is being sent to a place that has (not inaccurately) been presented to him in the past as "bad," or as "to be avoided," with the rationale offered at sentencing that this place is for his own good and rehabilitation. The remembered impressions of ex-inmates are not favorable.

> The first day in training school is strange. It's like walking into a jungle because there are guys there who are just as bad or badder than you are, and they all want to play the part with each other, aggravate each other. They stick together after they've been there awhile, and learn to be friends with each other. And if they don't like your appearance, they'll gang up on you or give you a hard way to go, start beating you up for odd ends, making you do things for them, stealing things off you, like your dessert. They make you do things you don't like, like being a run boy. If you're a real stooge, they make you do homosexual acts on them (Macdougal 1969, 39).

Ironically, when incarcerated by the law, the protection of the law (which normally guarantees one's safety from the predatory acts of others) is withdrawn.

Leyton (1979) of course, in claiming to study delinquents, does not conceive of his study as depicting training school and its inmates, but his ethnographic life histories might be better examined as such. His interviews and observations give some much-needed life and flesh to the bare bones of the above statistics, showing how such youngsters have started from inauspicious circumstances, made some (often minor) mistakes, and been unlucky enough to have families with so few economic and social resources that they are left unprotected before state agency intervention. Without resilience themselves, parents find it less painful to abandon them to programs promising therapy to compensate for their own acknowledged inadequacies, thus assuaging their guilt at such actions of ultimate betrayal. After months of emotional (and sometimes physical) battering in juvenile institutions, tossed from social worker to social worker, it is little wonder that such youngsters feel distrustful of everyone.

The Effects

It is difficult to define exactly how training schools affect these youngsters. They feel unjustly treated, but learn how to survive on their own in a hostile environment, and hence attain a degree of self-directed independence.

It is also difficult to determine how successful training schools are statistically; the Ontario training schools have offered no good data with which to assess their work. There is a self-protective ideology that ex-inmates who falter "aren't recidivists, they just need more training." American data from similar institutions does not encourage optimism.

> Anywhere from 60 to 85 percent of [court adjudged] delinquents [i.e., not just training school wards, but also including lesser offenders who were not committed] do not apparently become adult violators [i.e., 20 to 40 percent do!]. Moreover, this reform seems to occur irrespective of intervention of correctional agencies and irrespective of the quality of correctional service (Matza 1964a, 22).

> . . . upward of 50% of children who are alumni of state training schools become recidivists in the sense of having further court appearances either as children or as adults (Cohen and Short 1966, 131).

The *Annual Report* of the Ontario Department of Corrections for 1972 states that of 1,009 wardships terminated, about 25 percent were for further convictions (responsibility assumed by another agency, probation to adult court, sentenced to an adult institution); these offences must have taken place before age eighteen when wardship is legally terminated. And it must be kept in mind that 75 percent of the children who enter training schools do so at the ages of fourteen or fifteen, which suggests that these further offences took place quite soon after release (*Annual Report*, p. 61). For 1,389 first-time admissions, there were 698 second-time admissions or returns from placement out of training school after "graduation"; thus, about one-third of the total admissions to training schools were recidivists (and these usually return before age sixteen). Assuming that figures per year are relatively constant, about one-third of those released are returned (2,171 released, 698 returns from placement). The aforementioned study of drug use by wards confirms this high recidivism: for one-third of the wards questioned the present incarceration was at least their second; for ten percent it was their fourth or more (Surridge and Lambert, table 14). These figures are very close to the ones cited by Lambert and Birkenmeyer (1972), who found that 34 percent were reconvicted and 48 percent were reinstitutionalized within a year and a half.

The training school experience is disorienting and removes the youth from the community with a resulting detriment to their rehabilitation. Three-quarters of those released go back to their homes (Statistics Canada 1973, 25); according to many popular beliefs, which are often espoused in court, these homes were the initial cause of deviance. Of releasees not in school, fifty percent are unemployed (*Annual Report*, p. 63); so much for the special vocational training! The stigma of incarceration is likely to be a hindrance in the work-world throughout life.

Dunlop's study of English approved school male property offenders found a similar recidivism range of from 46 to 71 percent. After controlling for different selections, she concluded that the boys felt trade training was very important to them, and that those schools emphasizing this training were the most successful, whereas leisure-pursuits emphasis and religious emphasis were the least successful. Other work-training schemes report similar success in community settings. The methodological rigor of such evaluations of community programs is questionable, but it is unclear whether the greater number of delinquent acts committed by training school wards occurred before or after they were adjudged delinquent; the fact that about one-third of the wards are repeat offenders arouses suspicion.

Because of the repeated failure of traditional training schools, various alternatives (usually based on some type of group or talk therapy) have been increasingly tried over the past half century. Many of these innovations and most of the research on them are American, but there is little reason to believe different results would result here. In general, such research overwhelmingly has shown almost all such programs are likewise ineffective (Schur 1973; Tranjanowitz 1978; Hackler 1978, for reviews).

There always seem to be some apparently successful programs, however, that keep hope springing eternal. For example, the Ontario ACTION camp program has been reported (Winterdyk 1980) as successful in changing behavior and attitudes of delinquents through intensive supervision, group dialogue, and challenging wilderness tasks. Leblanc (1977) also has reported considerable success in the intensive group therapy, educational and vocational training program at the Boscoville Training School in Quebec. One apparently important principle underlying these efforts has been differentially treating different youngsters (reviewed in Reitsma-Street, 1984).

Unfortunately, such apparently successful programs are often later found to be much less effective. Sometimes they have relied on unique conditions that cannot be maintained or expanded (for example, charismatic leadership, fortuitous staff combinations, small programs, and the like). Sometimes the initial research results are shown to have been obtained through a faulty design. Initial effectiveness during treatment often fades upon release and the withdrawal of support services.

Despite such discouraging effects from treatment, the majority of even those found delinquent in court do not go on to have adult criminal records. In Frontenac, for instance, within a six-month period, for all youngsters found delinquent in all dispositions, we found a 10 percent official recidivism rate; within a period of a year, the rates in Frontenac and the neighboring county were 18 percent and 23 percent. By contrast, Blomberg (1978) gave rates ranging from 13 to 75 percent in American diversion and treatment programs, with the average being around a quarter or a third.

One major recent development, then, has been to question the very idea of "treating" delinquency, and to consider instead how to minimize its effects in terms of danger and cost to society. We will consider attempts at such reforms in the next chapter.

THEORETIC CONCEPTUALIZATIONS
Careers Through Liberal Bureaucratic Institutions

How might we begin to understand juvenile justice, both as it affects the individual youngsters enmeshed in it, and as it is organized socially? How has this discussion of victims, police, courts, and dispositional institutions affected our understanding of questions raised earlier in chapter 2 regarding the law and the state? What implications has nearly a century of juvenile justice for the theories of delinquency outlined in earlier chapters? We will first outline how juvenile justice has been more traditionally understood, before considering more recent, radical theories.

DELINQUENT CAREERS AND STATUSES

It should immediately be noted that the predominant type of theorizing regarding the youngsters who are contacted by the juvenile justice system tends to get increasingly "psychological" the deeper in the system the juvenile gets. Even at the entry points to the system, many victims and police assume any youngster who commits a real delinquency is "troubled," "out of control," "neglected," "disturbed," and the like, usually because of "inadequate families," although many people are also willing to see some minor delinquencies as "mistakes" or "normal." Developmental personality theories, Freudian interpretations, or conditioned learning theories do not directly concern us here in this sociological text on delinquency, except to note that many juvenile court judges, and most probation officers and training school programs adopt such individualistic "disturbance" theories as the basis for their activities. (Reitsma-Street 1984 overviews some of the best of these.)

Individual delinquents have also been conceptualized sociologically. Merton and Cohen's anomie theories are social versions of frustration-aggression; Leyton argues disturbed nihilistic delinquents originate in oppressed underclass families; Hirschi's control theory sees delinquents as excessively unrestrained egotists; Matza describes them as being in existential drift. Maintaining a sociological level of analysis, they respectively suggest widened social opportunities and job training, family counseling, a better balanced reward-punishment system, and opportunities for humanistic self-expression. Various elements of these sorts have also been incorporated into many programs for adjudicated delinquents. We have noted some of these policy developments that have derived from theories as we went along; unfortunately, whether because of the theoretical inadequacies discussed, or inadequate implementation of suggested programs, or other reasons, few if any programs instituted on these bases have been able to claim much scientifically demonstrated success in "curing" delinquency.

Partially in answer to the nonresponse of delinquents to such conceptualizations, interactionists have advocated seeing delinquency as a master social status adopted in the very process of official reaction. This strand of interactionism has suggested that the cure is worse than the disease; it suggests that most delinquent acts are minor, caused either haphazardly and/or by situationally induced acts of will. Sustained, serious delinquency, however, requires systematic reinforcement, so that the youngster adopts the social status of being a "delinquent," which more or less induces him or her to further "secondary deviant" acts (Lemert 1967). Although such reinforcement in a secondary deviant status may occur in informal groupings, interactionists have suggested that formal adjudication by police or court officials not only carries society's authoritative weight, but also often effectively prevents an easy return to "normalcy." Gaining a reputation as a thief has more serious consequences than simply being caught pilfering does.

As indicated in chapter 5, the more extreme versions of this line of thinking have not gained solid empirical support: official labeling in some circumstances is as likely to cause a rejection of deviance as an embracing of it (West 1978a). The formulation, however, has generated a remarkable interest in studying social reactions to delinquency, and in studying caught delinquents not, as in earlier anomie research, to discover causes of original delinquency, but to assess the effects of societal responses.

A further irony intrudes. If a juvenile court judge decides cases by using legally "extraneous" criteria such as a child's family background, work possibilities, school success, attitudes, and the like, is he not assessing something very close to the child's attachments, commitments, beliefs, and involvements? Could it be that judges actually operate by using control theory to assign delinquent labels? And if they do, could their placing such children under stricter supervision and into a delinquent status be responsible for the predictive success of control theory? The world begins to look very complicated indeed.

ORGANIZATION THEORY

The second major strand of theorizing about juvenile justice focuses on the organizations or institutions involved. It emphasizes the tendency of organizations to assume a life of their own, in a context of negotiating with other bureaucracies, so that their ostensible goals (for example, reforming delinquents) are overlooked in the quest for organizational survival and expansion. The great theorist on this topic, of course, is Max Weber (1947). Weber argued that modern society is increasingly dominated by legal-rational authority: increasingly, people give willing obedience to commands that have a constitutional basis combined with means-ends efficiency. Such domination is more and more frequently exercised within large, formal organizations or bureaucracies. For Weber, bureacracies have the following characteristics: legal-rational authority; impersonal offices; hierarchical structures of command; the separation of personal from professional life embodied in the position of an office; a complex division of labor; rule-governed operations; technical qualifications for employment; and efficiency. All the organizations in juvenile justice, from police, through courts, to training schools and probation services have become increasingly bureaucratized.

Weber believed that this process of increasing bureaucratization was rational and efficient, but he also saw that such organizational forms could subvert their original purposes and encompass people in "iron cages" of bureaucracy. Contemporary organization theorists, in examining juvenile justice, note first the inefficiencies and conflict generated (especially by the legal doctrine of the separation of powers) between organizations such as the police, the juvenile or youth bureau, the Crown attorney's office, the courts, probation services, and residential treatment and custody services. Unlike, for instance, education, the juvenile justice system is not completely rationalized within a single ministry, with a single chain of command.

We earlier noted one small result of this that affects us as researchers: each of these organizations use different bases for developing their statistics (for instance, counting incidents/offences versus persons). Another major problem arises (especially with police) as the persons at the bottom of the hierarchy exercise considerable, independent, and largely uncontrolled discretion, out of sight of commanding superiors. Further, the technical expertise (grounded in the social sciences) is, as we have emphasized throughout this book, often quite shaky. Perhaps most crucially, there is a key contradiction pervading juvenile justice, which espouses a treatment-oriented, caring philosophy, but tries to implement it through impersonal bureaucracies: trust, openness, concern for others, and the like, is unlikely to be generated in youngsters who are forcibly removed from their parents, and then expected to establish intimacy with professional staff that change with each eight-hour shift.

Some Critical Alternatives

LEGAL SUBJECTIVITY

A critical alternative to secondary deviance theory is evolving from theoretical work on "subjectivity": the study of how humans both act and are dominated (Therborn 1979). As we have explored in the last chapter, Foucault also notes (1977) that compulsory, universal schooling provides a disciplinary apparatus for all, an apparatus that records and classifies subjects par excellence, preparing their subjectivity for narrowly classified bureaucratic slots that diffuse social class relationships. The power to classify, discipline, and punish, then, is not simply negative and preventative, but is also a positive broadening of power.

Penal institutions are also constructed to gain complete control through routine spatial and temporal arrangements, in repetitious exercises and recurring examination. Foucault (1977) argues that all of society has become transformed into a field of perception for control, replete with informers, files, and biographies; if this is true anywhere, it is most true of our treatment of juveniles.

Lea (1979) and Cohen (1979), among others, have elaborated this radical notion of broadly dispersed political power. In their conception, varied, dispersed, fragmented, and visually available relations of power are the basis of institutional power, not vice versa. Power is not exercised to repress as much as to discipline and generate more power (Foucault 1977). Wines, an American childsaver, expresses perfectly Foucault's notion of discipline: ". . . the object of reformatory institutions is well stated; it is not punishment for past offences, but training for future usefulness" (Platt 1969, 106).

Foucault's notion of the constitution of persons as legal subjects has been delineated by Fitz (1981a) and Pearce (1981) in ways that rely on formal analysis and suggest that rapid ideological reconstitution is not easy. Drawing on Althusser's (1971) notion of subjectivity and Foucault's (1977) notion of discourse (terminology) as both structuring human experience and existence, Fitz (1981a), in "The child as a Legal Subject," outlines how the courts have formulated a legal category of "childhood" as being especially devoid of the ability to reason, and hence have excluded those in that category from property ownership, entering into contractual agreements, and legal personhood in the juvenile courts. This allows the state to exercise specific moral regulation of the young (for example, regarding status offences such as truancy, sexual immorality, and the like). But childhood must be seen as the point of many determinations (educational, familial, economic, and the like – in addition to legal). Discourse analysis (Donzelot 1979; Fitz 1981a) indicates the ambiguity of the relation between behavior and official classification, and the dominance of the official categories.

First, many types of working-class behavior normal in both the statistical and moral senses (behavior that is frequent and accepted) are defined as illegal. Our laws are made by upper-class people in their own interests and do not reflect working-class mores or "interests." Prohibiting the physical settling of a dispute by mutual consent is an example. Byles remarks:

> Although their Index scores are not significantly different [combining all types of delinquency], the patterns of deviance are different between [middle] and [working class]. Boys in the [middle class] do more smoking [tobacco], drinking, truanting from school, and smoking marijuana than do boys in the [working class]; they engage in less truanting from home, sexual intercourse, fighting, carrying weapons, stealing, and vandalism than do boys in the [working class] (Byles 1969, 38).

In other words, though working-class youths are no more delinquent than middle-class ones, their delinquencies differ in kind, and working-class delinquencies are likely to arouse more severe reactions from (often middle-class) policemen and judges.

Secondly, like other children, working-class children tend to pattern their behavior after their parents (who historically have been forced to join the adult work-world at a young age), and are more likely than middle-class children to engage in "adult" activities before the legal system says these are acceptable for people of juvenile status. Working-class children assume sexual and economic adulthood earlier; they have sexual intercourse earlier, and want or are forced to leave school earlier to work, and usually leave home earlier. They are more assertive of their personal autonomy (for example, in fighting and carrying weapons). Hence, working-class and female juveniles are arrested for immorality, incorrigibility, truancy, running away, and the like. They more frequently resort to alternative income sources (for instance, theft) when work is not available. Middle-class adolescents are more easily "bought off," and hence encouraged to comply with their subordinate status; they can "earn" a big allowance, have use of the family car, and obtain college tuition (with promise of a high-status job) if they are obedient.

Thirdly, law-enforcement agents react differently to these different behavior patterns. In so doing, they reproduce class, gender, and age relations appropriate to the capitalist state.

JUSTICE IN THE CAPITALIST STATE

Similarly, at the level of organizations, state theory (outlined in chapter 2) begins to deal with the functions and interrelations of justice bureaucracies as they relate to the wider social structure. In a patriarchal class society like Canada, the political system generally is effectively dominated by bourgeois interest groups that attempt to insure that the legal system does not undermine their interests. But the state enjoys a measure of autonomy from such dominant economic interests, a measure of autonomy demanded and enhanced by the democratic franchise and enshrined in the necessity of maintaining popular support. Furthermore, the institutionalization of some measure of liberal rights (centered in the notion of the rule of law) provides additional independence of the legal system even from certain forms of state interference.

Earlier versions of conflict theory have tended to adopt earlier state theory's superfunctionalist assumptions that certain policies must be adopted to preserve the capitalist system of production (Clarke 1977). Such crude earlier versions of rationalistic and instrumentalist arguments run aground, of course, at the first policy that contravenes capitalist interests. How, for instance, have credit systems been adopted in secondary schools when so many employers find them difficult to interpret in hiring recruits, and also believe that they have been responsible for lowered standards? It is necessary that structuralist arguments be entertained here, that conflict be recognized as occurring internally to the state apparatus, and that contradictions be explored in studies of concrete historically specific conjectures.

For instance, many lawyers and civil libertarians would challenge the assertion that law is fundamentally an instrument of class control, claiming instead that law is the best – and perhaps the only – means of securing the rights of the individual against the depredations of the powerful. Thompson's criticism of Marxist attacks on the rule of law is relevant here.

> . . . civil rights and democratic practices are discounted as camouflage, or as the relics of "bourgeois liberalism." And to cut short the list, this very often goes along with a wholesale dismissal of *all* law, and *all* police, and sometimes with a soppy notion that *all* crime is some kind of displaced revolutionary activity. . . . these are all half-truths which have a continual tendency to degenerate into rubbish . . . If *all* law and *all* police are utterly abhorrent, then it cannot matter much what *kind* of law, or what *place* the police are held within; and yet the most immediate and consequent struggles to maintain liberty are, exactly, about kinds and places, cases and precedents, and the bringing of power to particular account (Thompson 1978, 15).

Libertarians would be less likely, however, to claim that the law in Canada *does* at this time protect the powerless; the argument is usually phrased in terms of its potential. As of now, the dearth of research on the sociology of law in Canada leaves open the issue of the precise ways in which the courts and the legal profession are related to class interests. But recognizing that the legal system has some independence does not mean that it is completely unbiased.

Moreover, work remains to be done to determine precisely *how* the state and law function in a specific class society such as Canada. Otherwise it becomes difficult to interpret schisms or compromises, and the impact of proposed reforms are either overestimated or denied. One must more carefully specify the limits provided by class structures, while at the same time avoiding simplistically reducing the state or law to the "ruling committee of capitalists." The Canadian economy, for instance, has usually encouraged close co-operation between multinational corporations and governments. But our federal system considerably fragments and complicates such state activities in the justice area as elsewhere, as local provincial elites compete with national ones. We will now further examine the utility of state theory by reviewing some attempts at the reformation of juvenile justice.

8

Juvenile Justice Policies and Politics: Reformism in the Canadian State

With extant social conditions seemingly providing preconditions for delinquency and the problems in schools and juvenile justice systems, there is clearly a need for social change in our handling of delinquency. Governments are specifically charged with eliminating or at least reducing crime and delinquency, with protecting the community, and with providing a proper upbringing for our young. Almost daily, one reads about reform bills, increased police efforts, new school disciplinary measures, and the like. Why are the problems still with us? How are our attempts at reforms so frustrated?

Throughout this text, while discussing research findings on the causes of delinquency, we have made passing suggestions as to policy implication. There is some evidence that adolescents' age combines with social class, gender, and school failure so that the young really are more frequently deviant than the rest of us (Greenberg 1977). How could these relations be changed? Adolescents are relatively marginal to the major institutions of the family, school, and workplace, which exercise direct disciplinary control over most members of society (Clark 1975), but this deviant-behavior-generating marginality would also seem to vary, for example, according to economic conditions and admissibility to the labor market, the role set for the school, support given to families, and the like. As it seems a particularly manipulable variable, we will first examine efforts to lessen delinquency through the alleviation of school failure.

Secondly, internal contradictions in Canadian law have caused recent outspoken discontent over the juvenile delinquency legislation. Lawyers and treatment professionals decry the lack of realization of their ideals, the middle class has been disturbed at the punishment of some of their youth for petty misdemeanors, and the police and courts have been overwhelmed. We will thus examine proposed reforms in our legal responses to delinquency.

Thirdly, there have been attempts to change the treatment of juveniles deemed to be delinquent. Among the most touted changes of the last decade are police discretion, court diversion, and decarceration from training schools. Some such innovations have been established in experimental programs, one of which we will examine in some detail.

These attempted reforms of juvenile justice offer us a further opportunity to examine the liberal and neo-Marxist state theories introduced in chapter 1 for understanding juvenile justice. One cannot ignore the central role of the contemporary state in influencing both material conditions and ideological climate. For the state clearly acts as a regulatory mechanism in adjusting economic, educational, and family policies, and responding to popular opinion, which it not infrequently has a large hand in manipulating. Recent European depictions of the state as functioning to maintain business prosperity, ensure social integrity through coercion, and maintain order through engendering legitimacy, become relevant in examining juvenile justice policy.

I will argue that such recent state theories offer one major explanation addressing the discrepancy between research findings and policy initiatives. Nonetheless, they need certain extensions if we are to adequately understand the state construction of delinquency.

SOCIAL POLICY EXPERIMENTS

Many of these attempted changes in the juvenile justice system are actually social experiments, pilot projects that are regarded as tentative models showing directions for social change. Because they are initiated by governments they are often reasonably well funded, clearly articulated, well staffed, and open to public scrutiny and evaluation. If they are successful they are made part of general policy and imitated elsewhere. If not successful, the programs should be terminated, and others should be tried.

Such conscious efforts at social change have become a hallmark of modern policy and administration in contemporary societies. Such efforts provide opportunities for activities that are not only experiments in a social sense, but that are also scientific experiments (Campbell 1969). They thus offer us a glimpse at yet another major methodological approach to understanding delinquency, comparable to the use of official statistics, social surveys, and participant observation which we discussed in chapters 3, 4, and 5.

The experimental tradition is strongest in social psychology. Basically this tradition relies upon a very powerful and logically clear design. A group of subjects is randomly divided into two groups; the randomization should, over repeated trials, eliminate any biasing differences between the two groups. An experimental treatment is then administered to one group, and not to the other, which serves as a control group. Comparison of the measurements taken on both groups both before and after the experimental treatment is administered allows the determination of any effects of the treatment upon the experimental group. There are further elaborations on this basic experimental design (see, for example, Campbell and Stanley 1963), and some of the most interesting have been suggested as ways to assess social programs introduced on an experimental basis (Campbell 1969). Many of these now demand a research evaluation component.

There are a number of obvious advantages to using such experimental designs. The logic of experiments allows us to control potential extraneous factors (through randomization), thus enabling us to isolate the effects of the experimental variable alone. Such testing provides the strongest proof and verification for any of our theories. It allows precision, replication, objectivity, and prediction.

On the other hand, experiments are often unclear as to how representative their populations are; to what extent can results obtained be generalized? This is often referred to as the problem of "external validity" as opposed to the problem of "internal validity" – did the hypothesized effect really take place because of the experimental treatment? Interactionists and other humanist sociologists raise the same questions they do of quantitative survey researchers: To what extent does it make sense to strive for exceptional precision in measuring self-transcendent, interpretable human behavior? But most importantly, there are very few occasions in everyday life when experimental designs are applicable in juvenile delinquency research: society does not believe the merits of the knowledge gained warrants such gross interference in natural processes as experiments demand. For instance, few of us would approve of the random assignment of babies to working-class and middle-class households to test the effects of class cultural socialization upon delinquent behavior. Such ethical considerations thus limit the utilization of experimental designs to some administrations of experimental treatments (for example, group therapy programs for delinquents, or the diversion program referred to below), or some changes in administrative procedures (for example, introduction of new legislation).

SOME REFORMS

Policy to Eliminate the Causes of Delinquency

Of the many apparent correlates of delinquent behavior that we have cited in earlier chapters, some would seem more amenable to policy change than others. Gender differences, for instance, would seem very deeply rooted and pervasive, though pursuing some issues might be worthwhile, such as changing the socialization of inordinate male aggressiveness. It would also seem to be difficult to make effective policy decisions concerning youngsters' friendship patterns, in response to the finding that delinquent associates are more frequent among deviant youth. Similarly, attitudes towards police or authority figures may be exclusively difficult to change.

Although gender, subculture, affiliations, age, and unemployment are important factors associated with delinquency, school failure is perhaps a much more policy-manipulable variable (West 1978b) as it involves public issues open to political change. A number of policy recommendations based on these data and explanations have been offered (see Polk and Schafer 1972, for an extensive list). Interestingly, many have been implemented in some way in educational reforms of the last decade, and so some evaluation is possible.

Most directly, school failure has been reduced. Expanded preschool programs (for instance, Operation Head Start) should ensure better prepared working-class children; teachers' beliefs in limited potential of some children has been changed to avoid self-fulfilling prophecies (Rosenthal and Jacobson 1968). Tracking based on IQ has been modified or eliminated; credit systems were adopted to reduce the impact of single-subject failures (Ryan 1974). New instructional methods were developed for divergent groups of students; curricula were made more relevant (Pomfret 1974). In-service teacher training and community/school cooperation were encouraged; bussing to achieve better mixes of students should have improved student performances (Coleman, Campbell, Hobson, McPartland, Mood, Weinfeld, and York 1966).

Commitment of students to schools should have been improved by better relating present school activities with future job prospects. New careers, work/study programs, and community colleges of applied arts and technology have attempted to achieve this goal (but see Harvey 1974). Doors were kept open for stream transfers. Schools have been made more responsible for student welfare until graduates are placed in jobs (Taylor 1971). While students remain at school their participation in planning and decision making, exercise of authority, and activities have been increased.

Rather than reacting to exclude or degrade misbehaving students, schools have avoided labeling and alienating students by eliminating corporal punishment and discontinuing secret files that carry reputations from year to year. Philosophically, student-centered education entails a respect for the autonomy and self-direction of pupils. Positive reinforcement and wide course options should enhance students' self-concepts, and allow all students to succeed in some areas. As far as possible, excluding students by placement in special classes has been avoided; grades should not be used as disciplinary measures.

More community co-ordination of special services would be possible if the school offered to house additional welfare services, such as probation, Children's Aid, and the like (Taylor 1971). Opening the school to the community was seen as strengthening such ties, and instituting school/community councils would allow parents as well as students to participate in the running of such services. The growth of "students' rights" has filtered down from the universities to the elementary schools. These measures seek to increase student attachments to law-abiding adults.

In general, delinquency should be seen as an interaction between youths and institutional authorities, rather than as action attributable simply to the children or their parents. Such an orientation would keep open the examination of within-school factors. Various enticements, such as trips and projects, and the most advanced technology encourage students' efforts.

Such participatory decision making, and more open honesty on the part of educators, should have a positive effect on pupils' beliefs. Attempts at moral education should have had a similarly positive effect on pupils' beliefs, substituting for doctrinal orthodoxies in a postreligious age. Quality assessments of programs and changes have been encouraged to aid in establishing institutions that regularly and consciously innovate. The overall consistency of the moral reproduction research reviewed in chapter 6 for supporting the progressive educational policies of the late sixties and early seventies is quite clear.

Assessing the impact upon delinquency of such policy recommendations, however, is more difficult. Few policy recommendations have been introduced specifically to reduce delinquency, nor have experimental designs been widely used. Furthermore, many of the reforms (the "treatment variables") mentioned have not been seriously implemented. Often they have been "top-down" proposals that have failed to retrain implementers for new roles, and hence have been subverted at the user level (Fullan 1972). Programs have often been proposed in ignorance of political realities; vested interests have been naïvely overlooked, but have demonstrated their power in resistance and inertia (Pomfret 1974). Budget restrictions have curtailed some implementations and encouraged piecemeal adoption. Funds that could have been used to fundamentally alter the teacher-pupil ratio have instead been used to buy expensive hardware from the education technology industries (Martell 1974). Thus, any chance of altering the teacher-pupil distance from one demanding authority-submission to one of honest encounter is precluded (Ryan and Greenfield 1975).

Administrative discretion still remains unclarified and unsystematized within schools (Manley-Casimir 1978). Magsino (1978) demonstrates in great detail how weak the legislative support for students' rights is. And compulsory attendance remains. Cosmetic declarations of students' rights may little affect classroom authority relations, showcase school community councils are rarities in real life (Martell 1974), as are truly "open" classrooms (Dale 1977, 12–14). Departmental endorsement of new courses has not ensured their development. Some significant research suggests that schools may have negligible effects on achievement in any case, and so reforms cannot be seriously expected to accomplish all that we had originally hoped (Coleman et al. 1966; Jencks et al. 1972).

In many ways, however, these measures only obliquely address the key factors that research identifies as participating in delinquency. While the reforms just suggested may go some distance to help students progress at their own pace, implement guided learning programs and the like, they do not fundamentally attack the ranking system of schools. Even if all pupils are passed, some are still passed conditionally, and some are passed into low streams or "levels." Moreover, the schools overwhelmingly classify students along a fairly narrow dimension. Individual, cognitive, and verbal skills are constantly emphasized; being humane, artistic, or athletic is desirable, but is not sufficient if one cannot read and write well. It may be that individual work-study programs (Dunlop 1974) are successful in giving students some sense of accomplishment, self-worth, and the like, hence resulting in fewer delinquent acts. But they are certainly open to the question of whether such success merely indicates successful brainwashing of the oppressed to accept their lowly fate.

Evaluation of these school changes in scientific experimental terms, then, is difficult. If the effective causal variable of delinquency is ranking, rather than failure as narrowly defined, continuation of ranking could not be expected to reduce delinquency. This kind of vagueness regarding definitions and goals is frequent in large-scale policy changes, and makes assessment difficult if not impossible.

Moreover, while some reforms were tried in the sixties and early seventies, the last half of the seventies has seen a resurgence of traditional pedagogy and curricula, and a retreat from the new. Compulsory subjects have been reinstated, "back to the basics" of reading, 'riting, and 'rithmetic are emphasized, job training is sought, streaming and honors programs reinstated, the power of students, parents, and teachers curtailed, and the medieval conceptions of the centrality of pure knowledge reasserted. Business, universities, newspaper editors, and many parents have supported these "returns to standards." Although the progressive reforms were probably not implemented as much as they were touted, and the present conservative backlash is probably less real at the classroom level than in official policy, the swing of the policy pendulum is fairly clear.

Law Reforms

The seemingly endless parade of government commissions on education (Hall-Dennis et al. 1968), youth (Committee on Youth 1971), drugs (LeDain et al. 1970), and the like, attest to the recurring desire to seek remedies to our perceived problems with young people through legislative changes. As elsewhere (Muncie 1981a, 24, regarding the 1969 British Children and Young Persons Act), Canadian governments have also specifically studied delinquency (Committee on Juvenile Delinquency 1965) and proposed changes.

Many of the provinces have introduced some changes without the federal government explicitly changing the law pertaining to delinquency itself. Ontario, for instance, has introduced legal aid and duty counsel lawyers to juvenile courts, so that due process is informally more encouraged. Subject to casual agreements between individual judges and lawyers, however, rather than being grounded in statutes, such arrangements mean duty counsel lawyers often see themselves as representing the community, parents, or court as much as representing the child. They are perhaps subject to informal pressures to co-operate with court officials with whom they regularly interact, rather than truly seeking the best interests of the juveniles they represent. Paid by the state, directed by adult parents, yet morally representing the youngster, it is quite unclear who is their "real" client (Platt 1969; Erickson 1975). The increasing trend towards legally trained judges may have thus been as effective in enhancing the legal rights of juveniles as legal aid has been.

In revoking section 8 of the Training Schools Act, Ontario has attempted to end the practice of allowing dependent children (who may have committed no crime) to be incarcerated, "if no suitable community facility were available." Unfortunately, however, Weiler (1978) has made it clear that the revocation of section 8 still allows such dependency cases to be incarcerated under a formerly seldom-used clause in the federal Juvenile Delinquents Act.

Similarly, the Quebec Youth Protection Act (loi 19) passed in 1977 and put into effect in 1979, institutionalized diversion of young offenders as well as neglected children. Such youngsters are now referred to social workers for assessment rather than simply being charged and sent to court. Official charge rates have soared as (often disgruntled) police send more of the youngsters they contact for assessment; it is unclear how effective the social service provisions are for such referrals (Trépanier 1983).

Our attention, however, must be focussed on federal attempts to revise the Juvenile Delinquents Act itself. Since the 1965 Committee on Juvenile Delinquency reported, three bills had to be introduced before enough support was gained to finally pass the new Young Offenders Act in 1982 (proclaimed April 1, 1984). This new legislation eliminates all status offences (for example, truancy and sexual morality), thus confining delinquency to federal crimes. Maximum three-year sentences replace the present indefinite terms.

The new Act also provides for administrative review of any special treatment, and the addition of some safeguards at the trial stage, such as the right to legal counsel, stricter rules of evidence and proof, press access, and appeals (Leon 1978, 167). These are combined, however, with the encouragement of screening or diversion procedures, ostensibly to involve minor offenders as little as possible in the justice process. There is, however, the danger in such procedures of a greatly expanded net, as seems to have occurred in Quebec, with previously released minor offenders being "treated" with wide discretion and without being found guilty of an offence. Some very serious unresolved problems thus remain in the conjoining of legal and welfare approaches (Grimes 1978).

The juvenile age is raised from sixteen to eighteen across the country. Consequently, sixteen- to eighteen-year-olds are protected from any harshness to which adults are subjected in contrast to juveniles, but they also lose any adult rights that are not extended to juveniles. In some sense, then, the oppressed age group is expanded. Below age twelve children lose all vestiges of responsible personhood in being basically deprived of the opportunity for a court trial: they are relegated to the administration of the same types of welfare bureaucracies that have so obviously failed to uplift the old, the native peoples, the poor, and previous delinquents (Schur 1973).

These legally oriented reforms have generally originated from within government bureaucracies staffed by lawyers; they may be seen as attempts to re-establish some liberal civil rights taken away from children by the traditional state response to youthful deviance. Coinciding with their increased entry into juvenile court and government policy units, their concerns with stricter definitions and due process have found support among civil libertarians in general and children's rights activists in particular. The increased firsthand knowledge of juvenile justice by middle-class parents whose children have been increasingly arrested has perhaps widened this constituency. Provincial governments have been increasingly tempted during the seventies by the opportunity to reduce budgets (O'Connor 1973) and have been quick to seek to slash programs, or have been attracted to the possibility of transferring the excess reformatory population to empty training schools by raising the age limit of delinquency from sixteen to eighteen. It is hard to avoid considering the pressing organizational advantages of the new legislation: under the guise of state humanitarianism, the administered population will be redistributed so that the staff and facilities will be least disrupted.

Yet, as indicated above, strong opposition to these legislative changes has existed both provincially and federally. From a "law and order perspective," police have been concerned about legalistic restrictions, and have wanted to keep the lower juvenile age limit down to retain the legal accountability of younger children. From a treatment perspective, the Canadian Mental Health Association and the Canadian Corrections Association (mainly comprising social workers, psychiatrists, and criminologists) have lobbied strongly against the legislative trend, claiming that the treatment needs of the young should take precedence over formal legality (Cousineau and Veevers 1972; Johnston 1977). Local child welfare organizations (for example, Children's Aid Societies) that would be held responsible for providing alternative services to children no longer admissible to training schools, succeeded in delaying the implementation of the Ontario Training Schools legislation for over a year while seeking adequate government financing for the new programs. Although almost two decades have passed since the federal commission reported in 1965, at the time of writing, not one province has reached agreement with the federal government regarding implementation of the new federal Young Offenders Act.

Provincial and private opposition to such changes may best be viewed as resulting from more immediate organizational conflicts and needs. Abolishing the juvenile court, with its lack of due process, nonadversary system, and high rate of guilty pleas, may reduce the official crime rate markedly (Schur 1973). Such changes in official rates, of course, would not indicate any changes in adolescent behavior. But seriously assessing the effects of reforms in the empirical situation, however, will be much more difficult than drawing such logical implications. Again, variables tend to become confused and ambiguous in the real world where changes take place over many years.

Reforms in Responses

With the ambiguities in support of potential delinquency reduction programs, and the morass of delays in legislative changes, perhaps it is fair to say that most reforms over the last decades have been administrative, in response to delinquency. The federal government and the provinces have often found it easiest to alter their own behavior, rather than that of youngsters or each other. Diversion, police discretion, and community treatment are examples.

In the last decade the federal government in particular has espoused the exercise of diversion wherever feasible. This refers to the turning away of offenders from formal court processing at the postcharge, pretrial stage, in order to minimize penetration into the justice system. The most favored model for implementing this idea consists of a small, citizens' committee that would meet with the offender, victim, and police to work out some suitable reconciliation (often involving monetary restitution), after which charges would be withdrawn. Following labeling theory (Schur 1973), the diversion committee attempts to be as noninterventionist as possible, averting official findings of delinquency, encouraging active participation by the child, and seeking to generate in offenders and victims a sense of having been treated fairly. By involving the community, a sense of collective responsibility should be developed. Legal guidelines seek to avoid abusive discretionary powers; the victim, the crown, and the offender retain the option of returning to court if not satisfied; double jeopardy is avoided by the judge's agreement not to receive testimony given in committee. If the youngster or his family wish to have additional social services provided, they may voluntarily request them; the committee's basic "coercive" response, however, must be directed at the offence only.

Diversion obviously draws upon a number of intellectual traditions (Schur 1973). Labeling theory has suggested that sanctioning deviance may amplify it. Self-report studies indicate that those who are caught for delinquency are a small and relatively undifferentiated minority of behavioral offenders. Organizational research has concluded that the available bed-space has as much to do with disposition as the therapeutic need. Evaluation of therapeutic programs has pessimistically concluded that few if any have positive effects. And lawyers in particular have been increasingly concerned regarding children's legal rights.

Unfortunately, from a correctionalist point of view, even when such a model diversion program has been successfully implemented, there seem to have been few intended effects (Morton and West 1980). The Frontenac program we experimentally examined in Kingston seemed to enhance youngsters' respect for the justice system, made them feel there was more interest in their being heard, involved more citizen participation, and reduced the number of youngsters with official findings of delinquency. On most measures (including recidivism), however, there were no effects, and such programs seem to quickly become absorbed into the traditional juvenile justice system. Such experience replicates American findings, which indicate that most diversion attempts have resulted in greatly extended social control of double the number of youngsters that were handled previously (Blomberg 1978).

Although diversion has been adopted as federal government policy and is being implemented in literally dozens of experimental pilot projects across Canada, such lack of intended effects probably results from a number of fundamentally unquestioned assumptions. The noninterventionist, nonlabeling ideal of diversion seems rather a fundamental contradiction, as outright release is ideologically unacceptable to most community members, and treatment professionals in particular are often anxious to assist youngsters and families.

In the Frontenac research, it became apparent that most victims were generally much less distressed than is often assumed in images of irate citizens suing for their losses. Although invited, only a minority of victims in cases involving restitution for property losses participated in court hearings. Many of them seemed to appreciate the special arrangements for repayment more for their material worth than for any abstract considerations of justice, confronting youngsters with their misdeeds, or reforming them, though a few were such "model" victims. They were more often equivocal in terms of satisfaction than data in official records would indicate. Victims were less likely to admit in interviews that they had been responsible for bringing about a charge against offending juveniles, perhaps indicating their reluctance to be the "bad guy," in turning in a delinquent.

The voluntariness of diversion is questionable. A youngster before a diversion committee knows that the alternative to accepting its plan is a return to court, and more than half the arrested youngsters fear that juvenile court appearance will result in their being removed from their home (Langley et al. 1978). The personal dynamics in diversion programs are such that few youngsters or families dare challenge treatment professionals. It is thus highly questionable whether diversion as it is implemented is more liberating than repressive.

Finally, the desirability of diversion as a community response, as community participation in the justice system, seems questionable. Diversion programs are overwhelmingly staffed by justice system and child welfare system personnel, not average citizens, and almost never by working-class people. These diversion program personnel tend to represent the wealthier parts of town, the very parts most juveniles have offended against, and they have vested interests in "treating" the typically working-class youngsters who appear before them. Diversion, then, seems to perform a similar function to that of the justice system in general: class divisions are reconstituted as legal conflicts and welfare problems. Although the juvenile justice system has justified itself as a general advocate to effect positive social change on behalf of troubled youth, it has almost never moved beyond the traditional liberal attribution of individual guilt and punishment.

Changed police discretion offers a second type of administrative reform. The postcharge, pretrial stage of juvenile justice emphasized in diversion may not be the most effective one, especially given that police discretion varies widely by jurisdiction, being based more on administrative policy than on the constraints of "real crime" (recalling from chapter 7 that some communities have charge rates eight times higher than others).

Why was the charge rate in Frontenac so low but the pattern of charges similar? It is possible that there really was that much more delinquency in the neighboring jurisdiction, but our brief inquiries (Morton and West 1980) turned up no qualitative support for this possibility. (Comparative self-report surveys would be necessary to ascertain any differences in real behavior.) Assuming no difference in behavior, what could account for the arrest patterns? Various officials we asked, including a judge who had sat in both counties, suggested that the neighboring police were more likely to bring in minor cases and status offences (for example, vandalism, between-juvenile assaults, runaways), and additional quantitative analysis of the charges tended to confirm this. Furthermore, although the percentage of first arrestees who recidivated was similar in both counties, the neighboring jurisdiction had many more recidivists in actual numbers, since the base was larger.

What could account for such different policies in implementing the same legal code? Although not a central question in our research, our exploratory interviews with nine police officers and observations of court hearings suggest some answers. Almost all the officers claimed that they routinely warned juveniles in three-quarters or more of their cases, rather than charging them. They felt the main reason for laying a charge was to obtain help or treatment for youths' problems. They all disliked taking juvenile cases to court, not wanting to appear to be the "bad guy."

The Frontenac court had the benefit of two young, children's-rights-oriented liberal judges who were well-educated, legally trained, and willing to experiment. The Frontenac judges were publicly known to espouse diversion, and we believe a number of police officers were convinced of the appropriateness of such a policy, at least to the point of using it to justify not charging as many youngsters as they had previously done. Secondly, because they took children's rights and the rule of law seriously, the Frontenac judges were willing to "throw cases out of court" on "technicalities." Combined with this, the local Crown attorney did not usually send a Crown lawyer to juvenile court, therefore leaving the police youth bureau officers to contend with regular lawyers and eager university law students acting as defence counsel. The officers, needless to say, were probably somewhat intimidated and therefore less inclined to charge youngsters under doubtful circumstances. Thirdly, some officers indicated considerable disagreement with such a courtroom situation, and also with the diversion committee, where most first offenders were sent, especially regarding the legalistic focus on the offence, as opposed to the "whole child" and saw charging as a "useless exercise" that failed to get at underlying family problems. These findings strongly suggest that the orientation of the sitting juvenile court judge may have a considerable influence on police practices.

Furthermore, Kingston police force figures indicated that there was a steady decline from 1974 to 1977 in the numbers of juveniles dealt with, charges laid, warnings issued, and referrals made to agencies. However, the ratio of police charges to warnings increased, as did the ratio of charges to persons contacted formally. Therefore this suggests that the police were contacting fewer juveniles officially, but charging more of those contacted.

Even with a rarely executed "perfect" experimental design to assess diversion, then, so many changes occurred around the experiment itself as to make interpretation of the results difficult (Morton and West 1980, 1983). Indeed, the experiment in diversion from court seems likely to have had more impact upon police behavior regarding the exercise of discretion than upon either youngsters or the court.

A third example of changes in the administrative response to delinquency is the increasing substitution of training school placement by community group home placement for those youngsters who the court believes must be removed from home. These latter placements are self-evidently more humane in allowing youngsters to remain in or near their communities, in small, family-like settings, usually with more personalized attention, and sometimes with explicit programs of therapy. Ontario and British Columbia have led the provinces in reducing their bed capacities in secure training school settings: Ontario, for instance, planned to reduce its training school capacity from about one thousand to about two hundred (Toronto Star, Feb. 3, 1978). It is noteworthy that in addition to the presumed therapeutic benefit, groups homes have offered the promise of greater economy than training schools.

A potential danger exists, however, of more children actually being removed from home coercively, albeit to a pleasanter environment (Muncie 1981a, 24). It has been the typical finding in Canada and elsewhere that community treatment programs expand the net by including supervision of offenders who would previously have been released, rather than lessening the number of persons incarcerated (Hylton, 1981). Carol Smart (1976, chap. 6) has appropriately criticized patriarchal criminology for ignoring women incarcerated in mental hospitals, whose number more than offsets the excess of men in prisons. But it is still too early to judge the success of decarceration efforts for juveniles.

Understanding Policy Research

As we noted in the discussion at the beginning of this chapter, it is usually very difficult to organize even planned social reforms so that they meet the rigorous criteria of formal experiments. The attempts at school reform that one could have predicted that might have lessened delinquency were introduced in too piecemeal a fashion over a decade, during which time many other potential causal variables were also changed: police forces increased in size, youth unemployment grew, gender relations changed to some extent, and the like. The logic of scientific experiment and the techniques of social analysis simply cannot adequately deal with such complexity.

Similarly, even such apparently discrete measures as changes in juvenile delinquency legislation are seldom as neat in administrative compliance as they initially appear. Often the legislation is better described as following changed practices, as in the Ontario revocation of section 8 in its Training Schools Act. Likewise, the length of the debate about changing the federal legislation indicates not only varying pre-existing practices, and piecemeal administrative changes during the debate, but provincial reluctance also indicates the likelihood of variable and delayed implementation.

Even relatively small and discrete programs such as the Frontenac Diversion Program almost always have flaws in the actual execution of the experimental design: subjects self-selected themselves into and out of the experimental and control groups, thus violating the requirement of randomness; some measures were inadequate; other crucial factors such as the important exercise of police discretion only became apparent during the research, and hence were uncontrolled.

Consequently, none of these reforms have told us as much about delinquency's causes or the effectiveness of suggested "cures" as we initially had hoped they might. Furthermore, we often seem thrown back upon less rigorous approaches such as historical analysis and case study to best understand some of the most important questions about delinquency (Touraine 1981). Even when we do get generally consistent results, the rational model of research and policy development assumed by liberal social theorists (for example, Solomon 1981) is revealed as inadequate: public problem definition, ingenious research designs, massive funding, careful and sophisticated analyses, and well-expressed policy implications are all too often ignored. The traditional policy makers' excuse that "other political and economic factors have to be considered too," increasingly begs the question: How can such other factors be rationally understood and addressed, rather than left to the whim of politicians? Just what processes are involved that encourage and enable governments to formulate policies that are contrary to our best knowledge? Such questioning of the liberal model of policy development is consistent with our earlier questioning of the liberal model of Canadian society in chapter 1.

TOWARDS A POLITICAL ECONOMY OF CANADIAN DELINQUENCY

The Young in the Contemporary Canadian Social Formation

In the remainder of this chapter we will thus use these attempted reforms to try to better understand the wider context of delinquency, to understand what such phenomena tell us about the Canadian state, and hence how we collectively construct delinquency. It should be apparent that single studies are unlikely to clearly and explicitly suggest particular policy directions for government (Lindblom and Cohen 1979). But, given the huge government commitment to sponsor policy research, it is also often unclear why, in the case of the school reforms, for instance, the pendulum should swing back to regressive policies in the face of so much counterevidence. While the effects of the liberal reforms on delinquency have been unclear, there is little research to encourage such a "return to standards" and failure (see West 1981). We thus need to place such policy decisions in a wider material context.

Recall from chapters 1 and 2 how various ruling-class fractions have organized and utilized the Canadian federal state to maximize resource extraction on behalf of succeeding French, British, and now American interests. Existing on the staples trade of furs, lumber, minerals, wheat, and now energy, government policies have attempted to maintain legitimacy, control, and especially profitability, in governing a hundred-mile wide, three-thousand-mile-long strip of twenty-five million ethnically, religiously, racially, and linguistically divided Canadians. Although the system as a whole requires a continuous supply of new citizens and workers, it is economically now personally disadvantageous for any particular adults to bear and rear children. Western societies have thus struggled for a century to entice people into reproducing, but at a steady and controlled rate. Modern free-market societies require steady consumer demands and a steady supply of trained labor. Rapid fluctuations in birth rates present problems. Wartimes have needed more people for cannon fodder and work; recessions have needed fewer, and thus assigned the young as well as women, the old, and racial minorities to the "surplus army of labor" (namely, unemployment).

Canada in particular experienced the largest post–World War II baby boom of all the Western countries, a boom responsible for much of our economic growth. It constituted a market opportunity for the provision of new physical facilities (homes, schools, recreation centers), jobs for caretakers (teachers, youth workers, and professors), and general consumer demand, especially in the new teenage market. In 1971, children and youth comprised almost half of the Canadian population: some 10.4 million of 21.5 million Canadians were under twenty-four years of age

(Committee on Youth, 1971). In terms of percentage increase, the zero to twenty-five-year-old segment of the population increased from 1951 to 1971 by 54 percent, with the fifteen to nineteen year olds increasing by 100 percent, and the twenty to twenty-four year olds by 75 percent.

As a result, a tidal wave of young persons has swamped the labor market, creating massive structural unemployment. Our private industry has simply been unable to absorb this increase in the labor supply. In an American study, of the increase in the laboring population from 1951 to 1966, teachers and students (above age eighteen, considered as job holders) accounted for 45 percent of the new jobs, defence for a further 21 percent, and private industry for only the remaining 33 percent (Rowntree and Rowntree 1968). Although our Canadian defence industry is negligible compared to that of the United States, the relation between educational positions and the labor force is probably similar here. Whereas the overall 1970 Canadian unemployment rates for males and females were 6.6 percent and 4.5 percent, for fourteen to nineteen year olds they were 15 percent and 11.4 percent, and for twenty- to twenty-four year olds they were 10.5 percent and 5.1 percent. Youth has continued to be unemployed at two to three times the national average, and constitutes about 45 percent of the total unemployed (Committee on Youth, 1971; *Toronto Star*, 1975). Temporary job creation programs (such as Opportunities for Youth, and Local Initiatives programs) have been unable to absorb the unemployed young.

Labor laws effectively prohibit employment of the very young. In terms of training and experience, then, youth stand at a disadvantage to other workers; even when legally eligible for jobs, their pay is differentially lower. They consequently must rely to an unusual extent on alternative sources of income (for example, parents or theft). To the extent that work roles are the primary source of personal identity in our society, juveniles who are denied jobs can be expected to look elsewhere to create worthwhile identities (Hughes 1958, 42–43), for example, in the various "youth cultures."

Partly as a result of this need to do something with the young, education systems in Canada have expanded enormously, to become one of the largest Canadian "industries." Recall from chapter 6 that by 1970, they consumed 8 percent of the GNP, occupied 6.5 million students and teachers, and consumed 20 percent of total government spending (over $6 billion). From 1960 to 1970 postsecondary education expanded to three times its former size. One could argue that this all amounted to unpaid student "labor" (especially in the expanded higher education sector), the cutting of real production in an overproducing economy, and the subsidization of industry by attempting to provide sophisticated training at public rather than private expense. It would seem that most of the progressive educational reforms sought to attract students. In any case, it is clear that purveyors of educational physical plant and equipment profited handsomely. The end of the long boom, however, and the present fiscal crises of the state, have resulted in real cuts in spending as world capital attempts to restructure itself.

The failure of private enterprise to create the required number of new jobs encouraged government growth, especially in education and other service sectors that cared for and controlled the newcomers; Armstrong's data (1977) shows a five-fold increase in educational workers from 1946 to 1974, when the population only doubled. The end of the baby boom, however, has exacerbated the purely economic crisis, with absolute student levels falling, especially east of Manitoba. Further widespread teacher layoffs and school closings have been averted only by strong teacher unions and militant communities. The unusually high foreign domination of the economy has recently meant centralization elsewhere of top-level managerial and scientific jobs, low research funding, and no guarantee of work at the end of extended schooling (Lockheart 1975, 199). Expanding the higher education system, seen as a partial solution to labor market problems a decade ago, has thus now become the source of further contradictions.

The legal structure has created a special group of second-class persons called children, who are denied citizenship rights and responsibilities (Ariès 1962; Lee 1982). Socially, the law requires juveniles and their families to maintain ongoing association. And in addition to economic dependence on parents, minors require parental permission for contracts (for example, marriage, purchases, club memberships, and the like). The family is also charged with the responsibility of controlling the juvenile's behavior.

Moral issues in child care are complicated. Most children's caretakers (parents, teachers, training school attendants, and the like) have good intentions, but some are given nigh impossible tasks and are then blamed for any failures. Delegated the responsibility of controlling juvenile behavior in ways that may be personally disagreeable or abhorrent, many parents (especially working-class ones), teachers and staff (isolated in understaffed, inadequately equipped schools) find standing guard a nasty, thankless, and impossible task. With custody functions delegated to parents and teachers, the responsibility for creating the conditions that may engender ensuing rebellions is avoided by the schools, the state, and the corporations, which maintain their hegemony by such bureaucratic division of people. This mystification can become complete when the truants, the delinquents, and the unemployed assume blame for their situation and actions, believing their troubles result from their own stupidity, emotional disturbance, and shiftlessness.

The law requires adolescents to attend school until they are sixteen years of age. In schools, the young are defined as students, and are subjugated to the administrative authority of teachers and principals. There they are still subject to relatively arbitrary rules and hindered by the expense and time-consuming nature of any attempted rectification of violations of their rights through the courts. Since job opportunities are increasingly tied to years and stream of educational experience, and subjection to mystifying and questionable testing (MacKay 1978), social pressures persist to remain in school far beyond the legal minimum age of leaving. And in addition to the schools, voluntary youth agencies offer recreational programs that maintain control over young lives.

The Canadian welfare state has been as severely shaken as any Western society by the ending of the long economic boom that began with World War II. The peculiarities of Canadian dependency on multinationals, our ethnicity, and our federalism, however, have diffused these shock waves. Our fortune in possessing rich energy resources has to this point enabled us to survive this crisis relatively well, though with obviously unresolved outcomes. As Gough (1979) so brilliantly argues, it may be now impossible, however, for the capitalist states to resolve the tensions between strong, demanding labor movements and ever greater profit-seeking.

During the last couple of decades, criminal justice system costs have risen remarkably (Solicitor General 1979). Official crime rates have soared as children of the postwar baby boom reached adolescence; high unemployment rates have probably increased the temptation of property crime (the most common Criminal Code offence).

Within this Canadian political economy framework, we can now reconsider whether the liberal-pluralist model of the contemporary state, or the neo-Marxist conflict model better accounts for recent delinquency policies. Basically, it seems that Canadian governments have been less concerned with justice and the prevention of delinquency than with maintaining their control and legitimacy by managing youth. In reversing the progressive educational policies of the sixties and early seventies, for instance, governments have responded to parents', universities', and industry's call to restore ranking and the teaching of skills. The extension of the delinquency legislation to include all sixteen and seventeen year olds extends the state's control over this age group, and raises the age of total noncitizens from seven to twelve. The cutting of costs in responses to delinquency, while increasing the net through cheaper measures such as diversion and community corrections, helps to meet the fiscal crisis of the state. In all these ways, for instance, it would seem that the recent policy decisions would be basically in the interests of the Canadian corporate sector.

In contrast, the measures would not generally seem to be in the interests of either working-class populations, or more generally, the young. The reassertion of the old mode of education would serve to maintain the subordinate position of working-class youth, and perpetuate class relations. Certainly neither working-class populations nor the young were involved in formulating these reforms.

It must be acknowledged, however, that such arguments that recent reforms favor the capitalist class are not at all beyond question. If one argues that the progressive sixties reforms favored the working class, then how could they have been instituted in the first place? If the new delinquency legislation is simply to control youngsters more easily, then why would it extend some considerable civil liberties to them? Even if the responses to delinquency might extend the numbers of persons controlled, why would it lessen the control for most?

Extending State Theory

To understand these policy initiatives better, we must examine the contradictory demands on the modern state. Although we need to have regard for the material (especially, but not only economic) condition of Canadian society, we must also examine class relations in more precise detail. It has often, for instance, been middle-class professionals, not the bourgeoisie themselves, who have initiated reforms. We must examine in more detail the crucial role of ideology. And finally, we need to be aware of the contradictory nature of the law.

STATE AND CLASS

It is immediately apparent that the Canadian federal system considerably complicates analyses based on the recent European state theory tradition. Constitutional delegation of powers and responsibilities have been to a large extent distorted by economic realities, so that purely legalistic analyses are insufficient. Federal wealth and provincial poverty have exacerbated tensions. This would seem to recommend a number of more specific studies of provincial state subsystems and provincial class relations in order to achieve more concrete analyses.

For in a constitutional sense, there is no Canadian criminal justice system but rather ten provincial ones, with possible conflicts between them, as in the case of the Young Offenders Act. These constitutional differences can be overplayed in the sense that the populations of the two central provinces of Ontario and Quebec comprise about three-quarters of the total Canadian population, and that the federal government provided much of the total justice revenues by 1970 through various earmarked transfer schemes especially focussing on technology. But these schemes have been as actively debated politically as have most other federal-provincial schemes; although their shape has been actively constructed, the eventual Canadian structure shows marked similarities to other industrial countries.

The new strength of public sector unionization of criminal justice personnel has clearly shifted the balance in this area, as labor militancy has increasingly replaced professionalism. The role of the new middle class, the professionals, as well as the new blue-collar workers must be examined (Taylor 1981; Livingstone 1983; Wright 1978). Much more detailed work is required to ascertain how these relations work within a federal system. For it is precisely the intricacies of class and professional relations within government bureaucracies that suggest some open pluralism. Nonetheless, "the system" maintains continuity by perpetuating the necessary conditions for capital.

IDEOLOGY

The bare bones of the economic and class aspects of the Canadian situation would allow a number of possible solutions for delinquency, even within the framework of advanced international industrial capitalism. Following the school reforms, certification could have been relegated to the universities and industries that were interested in it. Seed money could have been offered to unemployed students and other young people to start new businesses. Stringent budgets could be managed without cuts in needed social services or in training school accommodation. Economic necessity alone does not finally decide policy: political decisions do.

As indicated in chapter 6, Gramsci (1971) emphasized the importance of the phrasing in political and moral debate, arguing that the bourgeoisie and the state must consolidate widespread support within a power bloc in order to control mass democratic struggle and continue their rule. The securing of consent is done through key terms that promise formal political and legal equality while deflecting attention from substantive (real or economic) inequality. Various kinds of centralized negotiations between government, industry, and labor (by means of social democratic contracts, corporatism, or fascism) maintain legitimacy while reconciling crises within contemporary societies.

The mass media are a key site for ideology (Ng 1981). The media attraction for spectacular crime news, the demands of their deadlines, the reliance on authoritative sources, and so forth, all set up distinct media cultures separate from the state, and reflect the interaction of classes rather than simply upper-class domination through ownership (*cf.* Clement 1975). Nonetheless, bourgeois ownership of the key media doubtlessly has a strong influence in setting agendas.

Consciousness, ideology, and knowledge about such issues as delinquency are thus central to the state debate, especially regarding the necessity of guaranteeing legitimacy in liberal democracies (Laclau 1977). This Gramscian tradition concerning legitimacy is drawn upon by Hall et al. (1978) in their analysis of criminal justice and the state, which Taylor (1980) in turn propounds as being particularly apt for analyzing delinquency politics and policies in Canada.

There are further substantive questions. How is it that ideological climates change? Given Anderson's (1977) critical appraisal of Gramsci's ambiguities in his discussion of ideological hegemony, are not Hall et al. (1978) subject to the same criticism? Where is the locus of hegemony and ideological discourse – in civil society or the state? Where is the locus of coercion? When do ideologies change? Why is one content used rather than another? What are the theoretical limits of agency in the construction of ideologies? How does the state balance off fiscal crisis and the need for extended control? How do levels of crises (for example, economic, political, state, legitimacy) interact or relate? Do these levels of crises entail the same old problems of Althusser's economic, political, and cultural levels, with an extra level thrown in for good measure (Clarke 1977)?

Most importantly, somehow the courts and legality seem to shrivel in *Policing the Crisis* to a tiny corner wherein English justice, with all its faults and shortcomings, cannot be distinguished in its impact from Stalinist or Hitlerite show trials, as E. P. Thompson has complained (1978).

LAW

More profound radical structuralist criticisms of law, however, arise from the work of the German capital logic school (Holloway and Picciotto 1978). They point out that arguing that there is a shift from consensual to coercive modalities (Hall et al. 1978) does not get us far. It explains neither the form of coercion involved, nor how consent is obtained. Instead, Picciotto (1979) invokes Pashukanis' (1978) analysis of the intertwining of legal form and content, with emphasis on either of the latter being prone to the danger of fetishization: formal legal equality can mask underlying substantive inequalities; yet the form of law must be analyzed in its peculiarities to avoid mesmerization by particular content. Thus the law is contradictory.

Picciotto's stimulating essay (1979) raises more questions than it answers, however, and he clearly admits that an enormous amount of work must yet be done to push Pashukanis' approach beyond the original claim to legal isomorphism with petty commodity exchange (*cf.* also Hirst 1979). Otherwise, the law can be understood through simple economic reductionism, and it would have no effectiveness itself (Fitz 1981). Furthermore, Hirst (1979) points out that there are many kinds of law, and not all center on commodity exchange. He points out that persons cannot act as legal subjects prior to legal definitions, that contemporary commercial relations can only be maintained in a context of legality. Unfortunately, Pashukanis is perhaps weakest precisely in regard to criminal law, our subject of interest here.

Liberal ideology regards the law as impartial, but a disproportionate number of the best lawyers work in larger firms, serving not the interests of society at large, but the interests of their corporate clients. Although the rule of law does provide some guarantee of individual liberties (lacking in communist and fascist societies), formal equality often obscures substantive inequality in access to the law. For instance, while legal equality between men and women has been a formal gain for women, in many ways it has served to make more apparent women's substantive subordination in regard to child care, domestic tasks, education, occupations, and the like. Contradicting such gains in formal equality, much of the legal system supports and maintains a political economy that continually generates such further substantive inequality. Pashukanis (1978), Foucault (1977), and Picciotto (1979) bring us full circle in the sense that they base not only criminal activity, but also the legal framing of the response to it, in political economy.

Such contradictions need to be analyzed for specific instances of delinquency and the law. For example, moral crises over juvenile delinquency, coupled with legal concerns for children's rights, and the further displacement of the young from the mainstream of Canadian life have led to renewed attempts to reform juvenile justice during the past two decades. Such policies as diversion can be seen as the Canadian state's response to the contemporary revelation of a fundamental contradiction in the traditional liberal rule of law. Self-report studies have conclusively indicated that there is far too much delinquency for the legal apparatus to deal with. The state and society simply cannot afford to respond formally to every violation. This problem was previously hidden by class-biased selective enforcement, but the continuation of such policy affronts liberal claims to guarantee equality before the law. Diversion upon more rational grounds attempts to provide a possible solution to this problem of legitimacy. It thus represents an attempt to "save" the legal ideology of liberalism (Morton and West 1980; West 1980c).

The contemporary concern with children's rights seems to have taken the same turn from issues of children's freedom to issues of children's (adult defined) needs for protection, with, of course, accompanying adult supervisors to regulate erring families.

Most school-produced delinquents only engage in minor nuisance behavior which provides the neighbors' gossip along the street and youth bureau officers' time at the local juvenile court. But these delinquents generally develop such sour relations with school personnel by the time that they reach the minimum leaving age that they choose to leave quietly to join the ranks of the unemployed or to take the worst manual labor jobs (Willis 1977). Some, however, rebel further against their lot and become involved in serious, though nonprofessional, low-paying crime (West 1979a, 1978a). Stealing as often from their working-class neighbors as from petit bourgeois merchants, they generate demands from their working-class victims for police protection by the state (Matza 1969; Hall et al. 1978). In gross terms, there results a split between the deserving and undeserving poor, the respectable and unrespectable working class, a split that serves to reduce class solidarity and to maintain bourgeois hegemony.

Whether all social systems produce some basic human anxieties or the rapid change and economic insecurity of capitalism in particular generates them, current victimology research indicates widespread public unease. This seems to focus especially upon strangers, immigrants, outsiders, and in particular, I would suggest, the young, perhaps the quintessential strangers in our midst. Inordinately concentrated in the ever-threatening working class, the young are seen as unappreciative of our past, unsocialized, menacingly strong and healthy, and seductively sexy. With crime and delinquency as the third-ranking issue of concern to Canadians after inflation and unemployment, moral reproduction becomes fertile material for the reconstruction of domination.

Youth are thus further pressed to serve our society in some peculiar ways. They have been used as a vanguard to test ideas and add some ideological dynamism to the existing order. Although most youth are as conservative as their parents, the few rebels and delinquents serve as scapegoats upon whom sexual fantasies and dreams that the "golden age has passed" (Jahoda and Warren 1965) and decadent fears can be projected. Girls are seen as precocious and boys as shiftless and undisciplined (Musgrove 1964, 102–5).

One of the most salient characteristics of juvenile status, then, is *denied adulthood* (see also Lee 1982). As with blacks and women, this institutionalized (often legalized) oppression is mystifyingly justified by *claiming to be in the interests of the oppressed*. Children are deemed to be of a fundamentally different nature from adults (for example, immature, dependent, ignorant, frivolous, happy, and the like). In our society, they often *are* such little outcasts; but we fail to recognize the self-fulfilling, vicious-circle nature of this oppression until we learn that children of other societies and times act much as adults do when they are allowed and expected to (Ariès 1962). In our society, it is *illegal* for a person under sixteen to act maturely (that is, as an adult).

CONCLUSION

Space has not permitted more than a cursory exploration of how policy initiatives and decisions might be used to analyze how the Canadian state constructs delinquency. It would seem that neo-Marxist theories of the Canadian social formation are more consistent with the facts than liberal theories, though the latter do retain some merit, especially in microlevel analyses. There is clearly a need to extend neo-Marxist theories to incorporate finer class analyses, consideration of ideology, and examination of the law. Such extensions encourage the empirical examination of concrete political activity, and promise to show the historical construction of delinquency through active conflicts and struggles.

9

Summing Up

There is an absence of value, not a distortion. When life becomes not just a cheap or exchangeable commodity, but worthless, and plunder is seemingly neither for consumption, wealth nor power, it is as petty as it is fearful, as oppressive as it is mundane. The violence, the destruction and the youth of its perpetrators combine to produce a barbarity without splendour or honour; something tatty, haphazard and sordid, as trivial as baby talk in a world where we are increasingly sport for wanton little boys.

Morgan 1978, 13; in Box 1981, 29

Criminal law . . . includes . . . the man or woman who steals the goose from off the common, but leaves the greater villain loose who steals the common from the goose.

Box 1981, 48

Recurrent moral panics have projected the young onto center stage in the public perception of deviance and disorder. There is some substantive reason in this, and with the media's thirst for new copy, each new variant of youthful misbehavior quickly becomes projected into overdrawn new roles and cultural artifacts. The young, dissatisfied with the subordinate status provided by the officially approved roles, are quite receptive to proffered new scripts through which their alienation can be expressed (Hall et al. 1976). The tragic irony, of course, is that such subcultural scripts usually have limited potential, and they increasingly attract the attention of the moral authorities, justifying closer social control of the young.

Many popular beliefs about crime, delinquency, and deviance are misconceptions or only partial truths. Most of us have tended to take for granted that deviants and delinquents come from the "wrong side of the tracks," are poor youth from deprived families, or are undeserving, depraved predators, lying in wait for unsuspecting, innocent victims. We also have believed that delinquency is an unusual, antisocial event, though growing at an alarmingly increasing rate. Many of us have believed that it is caused by a lack of care for children, a lack of discipline and virtue, irresponsibility, and perhaps poverty. These beliefs are convenient myths. For it is clearly incorrect to assume that a youngster who commits a delinquent act is atypical or unusual; on the contrary, some delinquency would seem to be quite normal (Leblanc 1983), and the totally nondelinquent youth is the one who is statistically unusual. Furthermore, there is no obvious "break" in the juvenile population, a clear dividing line between those "real delinquents" and others who are "just kids." Perhaps surprisingly, these facts are more consistent with most people's personal knowledge of delinquency than they are with media/public knowledge or with official statistics.

One might ask, then, why the young are so inordinately singled out for official law enforcement attention and sociological research. In some senses, they are easier targets for policing activity: they are less experienced, have fewer resources to call upon in bargaining with the police and other officials, and have less privacy (and hence anonymity, for instance, for using illicit drugs).

In some other ways, however, the legal status of the young would seem to reflect their wider social status. For over a century in the industrialized Western countries, the young have been something of a social problem. They are a problem population – either too many, or too few, overwhelming social institutions established to deal with them, and revealing structural problems within Western societies. Their being singled out for special attention by justice agencies is a barometer of their general social situation, and acts to divert our discussion from what are perhaps more serious underlying problems in our lives (Sayer 1975, 1979).

We have seen how most delinquents are quite normal psychologically, and that almost all teenagers in contemporary society commit some delinquencies. Although the economic system is best seen as the creator of this problem population, the intervention of the state to create institutions (schools, courts, and reformatories) to deal with it provides a primary example of governmental attempts to ameliorate contradictions. It is ironic that by isolating young people in such institutions, in schools, courts, and reformatories, loosens precisely those bonds that control theory argues prevent delinquency. By legally preventing youngsters from working, while at the same time insisting on failing and publicly degrading academic nonconformists, cutting them loose from affective ties to both parents and mates, and by encouraging in them, yet denying them the realization of idealistic values, we further increase the marginalization of the young, allowing them to commit further deviant behavior.

The passage of education and juvenile justice legislation has greatly extended the scope of social control over the young. With more laws to break and their being more easily convicted in juvenile courts, young people are more predominant in crime rates. Although many juveniles are released upon official exercise of discretion, it is obvious that the legislation gives very widespread and relatively unchecked power to control the young.

NEEDED RESEARCH

Although the material reviewed throughout this text should have indicated that we now possess much knowledge about delinquency in Canada, it should also have indicated gaps and suggested the need for further research. More detailed historical studies are needed to better inform us about how delinquency has been constituted, especially in law. And although we have begun to suggest how the peculiarities of the Canadian social formation and laws might inform criminological analyses by taking account, for instance, of youthful labor markets, much more needs to be done. What effects, for example, do world market price fluctuations in Canadian staples (wheat, oil, minerals, pulpwood) have? If Canadian–United States comparisons are reconceived as hinterland-metropolis differences, can higher American arrest rates be seen as resulting from more surplus value (profits amassed in the metropolis on the basis of extraction from the hinterland) being spent on control efforts (McDonald 1976)? It remains to be explored, of course, how social control is maintained in poorer hinterland areas, which presumably experience more material pressures towards crime as a consequence of economic exploitation, but have fewer resources for law enforcement.

Gomme (1983) concludes that the rates, types, and patterns of both male and female delinquency in Canada appear quite similar to those reported in American research. He takes this to imply that the need to develop unique Canadian explanations of delinquency may be overstated. It may turn out to be true that there is little difference as seems to be indicated in the few Canadian studies to date; nonetheless such a sweeping conclusion would seem a bit premature. A radically different ethnic composition means that Canadian minorities (for example, natives, francophones, West Indian immigrants, and the like) cannot simply be "read off" from American studies of blacks, Puerto Ricans, and the like. This suggests that different variables may indeed be pertinent; research seeking to explore any such differences largely remains undone.

Furthermore, some delinquent phenomena, such as highly organized street gangs in working-class areas of large American cities, higher murder rates, and so on, also suggest that there are some real behavioral differences between American and Canadian delinquents, at least for some serious delinquencies.

We desperately need more detailed ethnographies of varieties of youth cultures, not only to reveal our differences from the Americans, but also to contrast us with the British (Hall and Jefferson 1976). We could gain from examining more closely British Marxist discussions of race and delinquency (Scraton 1982; Lea and Young 1984; Hall et al. 1978, chap. 10; Pryce 1979; Sumner 1981a), which raise a number of thorny theoretical and political issues: If oppression does in some way cause delinquency, would not the most oppressed racial groups actually be more delinquent (as well as being singled out inordinately by the police, and the like)? What revisions are needed in the traditional Marxist stereotype of the "lumpenproletariat"? How do different segments of minority racial groups view delinquency, and which views should be supported by progressives? Similarly, we need to follow up some other "uncomfortable" research findings, such as that working-class youth are more violent, and incorporate these into our theories.

Careful self-report research could assist us in better understanding age distributions, and trends over time. The most lively debate within the criminology of women has centered around the impact of the women's liberation movement upon female delinquency. Given the apparent increase in crime and delinquency by both women and girls, coinciding with the apparent growth in women's liberation and changing roles, might not the former be attributed to the latter? Using official statistics to indicate a much greater percentage increase in female crime, Adler (1975) makes this charge. Few adolescents, and even fewer delinquents, however, appear to be liberationists (Widom 1977). Furthermore, there is little indication of any rapid increase in female delinquency. As Gomme points out (1983, 17), suggesting that masculinization or women's liberation has caused female delinquency is a monocausal claim, grossly unwarranted given the complexity of the factors involved.

We need to know more about how our society reacts to, and processes delinquency. This area might be expected to reveal clear Canadian differences, as our social institutions and legal framework are uniquely ours. More attention as objects of study in their own right to the official statistics produced by justice agencies would be informative.

Criminal justice researchers have been slow to recognize the importance of ideology. How do different groups (police, politicians, classes, local authorities, and the like) interrelate within the juvenile justice subsystem? Asking what exactly is bourgeois about bourgeois delinquency legislation implies the parallel question of what is by implication "truly just?" To what extent is law liberating, a great equalizer, the provider of opportunity, and to what extent is its class-neutral appearance merely a fetishization of form that serves the interest of domination and inequality? Which working-class gains for children (for example, legal aid, health care, and the like) must be retained, are progressive and should be defended, and how can they be extended? How can state delinquency personnel as workers be allied with the wider labor movement? What are the important crises points around which future struggles must be organized? What are the real connections between justice and other institutions within and without the state? Why in modern societies is delinquency control exercised by the state? Why is progressive or liberal policy presently in retreat at this historic conjuncture?

THEORETIC INTEGRATION

In this text, we have examined a number of theories of delinquency. Robert Merton (1968) argued that in egalitarian societies, citizens were socialized to aspire to common goals, such as economic success, even though different means were required for different class and ethnic groups to succeed. Hence, he argued, working-class people are more likely to be anomie and hence deviant. Cohen (1955), Cloward and Ohlin (1960), and others specified this theory for delinquency. Besides the theoretical problems involved, such as whether there are common goals in contemporary complex societies, the advent of self-report statistics to replace official police ones have indicated that being working class is at best only weakly connected to the possibility of committing more deviant acts. Age and sex are equally important factors that are relatively ignored by anomie theory.

In explaining delinquent behavior, control theory is now much more widely accepted than anomie theory (see chapter 4). Durkheim (1951), Hirschi (1969), and Nye (1958) have argued that it is more sensible to assume people are free to break the law unless restrained by social ties or bonds consisting of commitments (rational calculations of means/ends considerations), attachments (emotional connections to others), beliefs (moral evaluations of right and wrong), and involvements (time allocations to conventional activities). Although unable to account for many other types of crime (for example, white-collar), control theory is much better supported by research on delinquency and ordinary property crime than is anomie theory. There is, however, little attention paid in control theory to how delinquency is constructed socially.

Concerns with who gets labeled were elaborated in chapters 5 and 6 by symbolic interactionists or labeling theorists (Becker 1963). Like control theory in its use of self-report data, labeling theory carefully distinguishes between those who commit an act and those who get caught;

and like anomie theory in its use of official statistics, labeling theory focuses on those who get caught. It also insists on studying those doing the labeling as well as those being labeled. But labeling theory does not state who must label, the extent to which the label must stick, or for how long, how labeling power is established, and so forth. It tends to ignore the search for causes of delinquent behavior, and instead searches for causes of labeling behavior; most students of delinquency now want to know both.

Conflict theory is hence elaborated on in chapters 2, 6, 7, and 8 to explore the divergences in society concerning goals and standards, crimes of the powerful versus crimes of the powerless, and conflicts between labelers and labelees. Power is here seen as a key element in understanding deviance (Thio 1978). Earlier conflict theorists (for example, Quinney 1969; Turk 1969) were relatively positivistic and unsophisticated, lacking an explanation as to the basis of dominant groups' power over subordinate groups. Nor did they pay explicit attention to the evolution of criminal law and activities through history relating them to changing dominant modes of production within specific historical formations. Quinney (1977) suggests that capitalism itself generates crimes of exploitation and oppression by the powerful, and crimes of resistance and accommodation by the proletariat. The former refers to such activities as corporate crime (both property and violent), the latter to ordinary street crime, employee theft, or delinquency.

But the relations of production underlying deviance neither exist naturally, nor are they maintained without considerable effort (Hall et al. 1978). Power does not simply reside in the economic elite alone, but in other institutional sectors, including the political and legal (the government, administration and civil service bureaucracy, the military and police, the judiciary, and subcentral governments). Management of the means of production, and the crime it engenders, falls to the state in capitalist society, in close alliance with the dominant economic classes. Furthermore, the capitalist state must fulfill three specific functions: accumulation, legitimation, and coercion (Panitch 1977, 8; *cf.* O'Connor 1973).

One cannot ignore the central role of the contemporary state in influencing both material conditions and ideological climate. For the state clearly acts as a regulatory mechanism, adjusting economic, educational, and family policies, and responding to popular opinion, which it not infrequently has a large hand in manipulating.

Although application of contemporary theories of the state to juvenile justice offers a fruitful line for further enquiry, much remains to be done in specifying how such abstract formulations apply to concrete situations. A more careful delineation of the dialectic between coercion and consensus is required, one that recognizes that order is maintained through real struggles, and is always in doubt. Such a delineation must attempt to join more microlevel analyses of specific institutions with a more macrolevel framework. Only within such an extended analysis will the possibilities for practical action on the part of criminologists become clearer.

Thus Taylor, Walton, and Young (1973, 270–77) have advocated that attention be given to the wider origins of the illegal act (the political economy of crime); the immediate origins of the act (the social psychology of crime); the act itself (the social dynamics); the immediate origins of social reaction (the social psychology of control); the wider origins of reaction (the political economy of legitimation and coercion); the outcome of the social reaction on the "deviant's" further action (career); and the nature of the process of social control as a whole.

Each theory asks a limited range of questions, whereas a more holistic approach is required which tries to integrate various fields into a general theory of deviance. Anomie and control theories ask what social situations, subcultures, or attitudes cause individuals to commit deviant acts. Interactionist or "labeling" theory examines how such acts are reacted to, defined, and classified, and what consequences such reactions have for deterrence or amplification into a deviant status and further deviant acts. Conflict theory has centrally been concerned with what macrolevel background factors create the situations that anomie and control theory examine, and how these background macrolevel factors shape the political and legal system that directs officials to do the labeling. To the extent that all these questions are important and properly framed, a good theory should incorporate all of them. The integration herein proposed appears in figure 9.1. It should be noted that it is being proposed that control theory basically supplant anomie theory, but is complementary to both labeling and conflict theory.

In examining traditional explanatory paradigms, this book has attempted to articulate a superior theoretical synthesis, drawing heavily on recent neo-Marxist developments. It suggests that "delinquency" and its sanctioning must be theoretically reformulated around the constitution of the young as legal subjects (Fine et al. 1979; Pashukanis 1978; Fitz 1981a; Foucault 1977) within agencies of the capitalist state (Education Group, Centre for Contemporary Cultural Studies 1981; Dale et al. 1982; West 1981), involving the political socialization of hegemony (Mann 1970; Gramsci 1971; Laclau 1977; Althusser 1971) through and against working-class consciousness (Willis 1977; Hall and Jefferson 1976; Education Group, Centre for Contemporary Cultural Studies 1981; Clarke 1975, 1979; Johnston 1979). Methodologically, this will involve not only doing critical ethnography (West 1984a), but developing means of reading ideological discourses (Sumner 1979; Repo 1982) and identifying social forms (Apple 1979; Hargreaves, Hester, Mellor 1975), and linking intimate family justice (Donzelot 1979; Foucault 1977; Poster 1978; Morton 1981; Gavigan 1981) with civil and criminal law (Pashukanis 1978; Hirst 1979; Thompson 1978; Hall et al. 1978; Fine et al. 1979). These elaborations are indicated by the titles identified as *b* in figure 9.1.

SOME KEY THEORETIC PROBLEMS

Although the above summary, chapter by chapter, may suggest some theoretic coherence, there are serious underlying problems that such an analysis entails, and with which this book has implicitly wrestled throughout.

These theories, while only addressing a limited number of questions, or basing themselves on limited data (for example, delinquency) obtained by limited methods (for example, self-report surveys), attempt an explanation of delinquency in general. One must seriously question, however, whether this is possible, given the wide variety of types of delinquent behavior possible; there is no obvious reason to assume that murder, sexual precociousness, theft, and vandalism have common causes.

To further complicate matters, there is no unanimity among sociologists as to what constitutes a proper theoretical understanding. Most sociologists continue to lean towards a positivistic philosophy of social research. This argues that all science is fundamentally unified in its method, and hence social research can and should adopt natural science procedures (scientific method) to find the truth and explain the facts. Objectively observed data should be formulated into a hypothesis or theory by means of deductive reasoning; the theory is then confirmed or tested to find behavioral causes. Truth or falsity of a theory is ascertained according to how well it fits the facts; quantification assists in the precise establishment of the latter. Generally speaking, anomie and control theories hold to this scientific approach. But simple reliance on accurate fact-gathering is ultimately unsatisfactory.

An alternative methodology known as pragmatism has been criminologically important, being especially associated with the symbolic interactionist or "labeling" theory discussed here. Such interactionists argue that social science differs from natural science in that it must pay attention to human conceptions and intentions, as people act on the basis of these thoughts, values, and the like. Because the latter always exist in some specific context, and meanings change across cultural and subcultural groups, and because there is no assumption that the social world is either logical or integrated, theoretical analysis is always tentative and can make no claim to universality. Theory is only validated by its utility in accomplishing specific practical ends. On the other hand, pragmatism is criticized for failing to provide an overview of society.

Finally, although most American conflict criminologists revert to a positivistic philosophy (for example, Turk 1969), we have developed here a dialectical materialist version of conflict theory. As stated above, a large part of the reason why reliance on data collection methods alone is ultimately unsatisfactory is that it basically relies upon an empiricist (positivistic) concept of social research. Fundamentally, this assumes that the social world can be understood by relating frequently recurring superficially similar events to each other. What is needed instead is a realist (historical materialist, political economy) approach that demands analysis that goes beyond the inadequate relating of surface appearances, to understand deeper, underlying connections (West 1984a; Keat and Urry 1976; Sayer 1975). A more satisfactory explanation would result by unearthing the conditions that make delinquency (a social form) possible within a structured totality. Attention must be paid centrally to the material means of subsistence that interact dialectically with conceptions that reflect reality. Like pragmatism, such Marxist types of social science believe that science cannot be value-free, but is always shaped by the context, issues, and politics of the societies in which it occurs.

To the extent that the various theories reviewed in this text have strongly relied upon their respective scientific philosophies, and these are in conflict, it is probable that there are unresolved problems and conflicts within the theoretical synthesis that we have proposed. Integration would require abandoning, or at least modifying, some major presuppositions. It should be apparent that we have been unsympathetic towards neopositivism in this text, qualifying its findings within a dialectical materialist framework that seeks to combine the best of pragmatism with neo-Marxism. But doubtlessly, problems remain (West 1984a).

Partly as a result of these theoretical and empirical gaps, the theories themselves have had limited utility. This problem has been intensified because these theories have not been sufficiently self-reflective (with the possible exception of interactionism), and hence have not clearly recognized how they fit into the policy process. They have also failed to explicitly address the issues of morality that are intrinsically involved in the study of deviance and law. This has been as much a fault of liberal or leftist theorizing as of conservative.

Young (1975) has criticized earlier conflict theory for providing few practical alternatives; having no organized constituency; remaining idealist; focussing on the nonutilitarian, expressive, and romantic forms of deviance; ignoring the context of deviance; being morally relativistic in accepting the taken-for-granted social definitions; and ignoring some basic consensuses (for example, against murder).

Critical criminology must also address a different constituency, articulating the concerns of the oppressed, the working class, and even the criminalized. It must emphasize the need for praxis, the unity of theory

234 □ Summing Up

and practice to bring about socialist change. Since the existing order reflects capitalist interests, it is not adequate to simply provide a thorough empirical test of critical theory against existing reality, for critical theory seeks to institutionalize new relationships; the test of critical conflict theory is in its success in bringing about socialist change. Only under conditions of socialist diversity can the free potential of people be realized.

With regard to anomie and control theories' policy advocacy of measures to alleviate school failure, it at least seemed in the progressive era of the late sixties and early seventies that within the confines of a ranking school system, appropriate policies were being adopted, even if they often were not implemented (Fullan 1972). Since then, however, the "back to the basics movement," and the like, have championed policies that seem contrary to research findings (West 1978b). It has become apparent, then, that a simple rationalistic model of research being translated into policy is inadequate; policy is much more dependent on ideological climate and politics than the mainline positivistic evaluation research tradition acknowledges (Lindblom and Cohen 1979). Therefore, just doing more and better research is insufficient (see West 1981).

On a practical political level, perhaps our greatest failure as students of justice through all of this has been our amazing lack of preparedness and ineffectiveness in challenging the emerging dominant definitions of problems by the Right. Theories must be related to the daily practice and experience of our potential allies. Our concerns must be expressed in understandable language, and concrete, viable alternative strategies must be developed and implemented that make sense in the North American context of "cultural classlessness." Furthermore, only through active political engagement with teachers, social workers, youngsters, and parents could one organize to deal with such issues in progressive political ways. In such a reconceptualization, then, research could renew its quest not only for truth, but also for justice. We must attend to education and justice as they are practised – in classrooms, in government policy committees, and in the mass media.

It is clearly a mistake to see the state, or parts of it, as either monolithically representing solely capitalist interests, or to regard it as captured by socialists since the advent of "welfarism" (and hence open to "New Right" demands for cuts); the state is itself an arena of contradiction and class struggle. There have been working-class gains in bourgeois law that are not negligible and should be fought for in order to retain them. Progressives thus are caught in a contradictory position of working both for and against the state.

> The abolition of bourgeois law cannot precede the abolition of the objective social relation which is its content and from which the legal form derives.

FIGURE 9.1
Deviance Flowchart

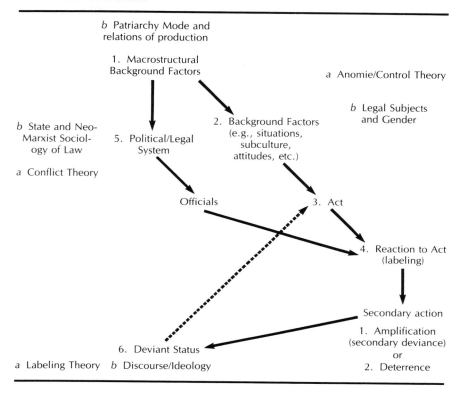

Law is not just a mask; it has an objective social basis . . . The real "content" or "substance" of the form of law consists in particular relations of *production* and not the exchange relations of the sphere of circulation itself. . . (Fine 1979, 39, 44).

In general, this brief analysis of Canadian justice using recent European theories of the state perhaps raises as many questions as it answers. The complexities of such an analytic approach reveal the task to be rather awesome, but that is not unique to this approach to state theory: the object of study is itself complex. The methodology certainly helps to organize the material, and raises a number of interesting research questions. Methodological alternatives to axiomatic/deductive/empiricist/positivist theorizing must be clearly articulated and exemplified. Most crucially, the approach can only be established as viable by the production of concrete studies of the justice policy process such as those proposed here.

Bibliography

Adler, F. (1975). *Sisters in Crime*. New York: McGraw-Hill.

Althusser, L. (1971). "Ideology and Ideological State Apparatuses," in his *Lenin and Philosophy and Other Essays*. London: New Left Books.

Anderson, P. (1977). "The Antinomies of Antonio Gramsci." *New Left Review* 100: 5–80.

Apple, M. (1979). *Ideology and Curriculum*. London: Routledge and Kegan Paul.

Ariès, P. (1962). *Centuries of Childhood*. New York: Random House.

Armogan, G. (1976). "An Inquiry into the Lives of Black Students in Toronto Schools." M.A. thesis, The Ontario Institute for Studies in Education/University of Toronto.

Armstrong, H. (1977). "The Labour Force and State Workers in Canada," in Leo Panitch (ed.), *The Canadian State: Political Economy and Political Power*. Toronto: University of Toronto Press.

Arnold, D. O. (1970). *The Sociology of Subcultures*. Berkeley: Glendessary Press.

Arnot, M. (formerly MacDonald) (1981). *Class, Gender and Education* (Block 4, Course E-353). Milton Keynes: Open University Press.

Arnot, M., and Whitty, G. (1982). "From Reproduction to Transformation: Recent Radical Perspectives on the Curriculum from the USA." *British Journal of Sociology of Education* 3, 1: 93–106.

Bagnell, K. (1980). *The Little Immigrants*. Toronto: Macmillan.

Baker, C. (1972). "A Study of Student Perception of Teacher Effectiveness." M.A. thesis, The Ontario Institute for Studies in Education/University of Toronto.

Ball, S. (1980). "Initial Encounters and the Process of Establishment." P. E. Woods (ed.). *Pupil Strategies*. London: Croom Helm.

Banfield, R. (1970). *The Unheavenly City*. Boston: Little Brown.

Bankowski, L.; Mungham, O.; and Young, P. (1977). "Radical Criminology or Radical Criminologists." *Contemporary Crises* 1, 1: 37–52.

Banton, M. (1964). *The Policeman in the Community*. New York: Basic.

Barnhorst, S. (1980). "Female Delinquency and Sex-Role Stereotype." LL.M. thesis, Queen's University, Kingston, Ontario.

Barrett, L. (1980) "Adolescent Deviance: An Examination of the Phenomenon Among West Indians in Toronto." M.A. thesis, The Ontario Institute for Studies in Education/University of Toronto.

Barrett, M., and McIntosh, M. (1982). *The Anti-Social Family*. London: Verso/New Left.

Baum, M., and Wheeler, S. (1968). "Becoming an Inmate," in S. Wheeler (ed.), 77*Controlling Delinquents*. New York: Wiley.

Bayley, D. H., and Mendelsohn, H. (1968). *Minorities and the Police: Confrontation in America*. New York: Free Press.

Beattie, J. (1977). *Attitudes toward Crime and Punishment in Upper Canada, 1830–1850: A Documentary Study*. Toronto: Centre of Criminology, University of Toronto.

Becker, H. S. (1963). *Outsiders*. Glencoe, Ill.: Free Press.

—— (1970a). "The Chicago Public School Teacher," in his *Sociological Work*. Chicago: Aldine.

—— (1970b). *Sociological Work*. Chicago: Aldine.

—— (1974). "Labelling Theory Revisited," in his *Outsiders*, 2nd edition. New York: Free Press/Macmillan.

Becker, H. S., and Geer, B. (1960). "A Note on Latent Culture." *Administrative Science Quarterly* 5: 304–13.

Bell, D. (1960). "The Myth of Crime Waves," in his *The End of Ideology*. New York: Free Press.

Bellamy, B. (1975). "Classroom Order and Deviance." M.A. thesis, The Ontario Institute for Studies in Education/University of Toronto.

Bell-Rowbotham, B., and Boydell, C. (1972). "Crime in Canada," in C. Boydell, P. Whitehead, and C. Grindstaff (eds.), *Deviant Behaviour and Societal Reaction*. Toronto: Holt, Rinehart and Winston.

Bennett, E. J., and West, W. G. (1983). "Criminal and Deviant Acts," in J. P. Grayson (ed.) *Introduction to Sociology: An Alternate Approach*. Toronto: Gage.

Bernstein, B. (1977). *Class, Codes, and Control*, Vol. III. London: Routledge and Kegan Paul.

Bertrand, F. (1982). "Public Opinions About Criminal Justice Issues: Some Cautions About Poll Data," in *Impact 1, Crime and the Community*. Ottawa: Solicitor General.

Bertrand, M. A. (1969). "Self Image and Delinquency." *Acta Criminologica*, Jan.: 73–144.

—— (1977). "Le caractère discriminatoire et inique de la justice pour mineurs: les filles dites 'délinquantes' au Canada." *Déviance et Societé* 1/2: 187–202.

Birkenmeyer, A., and Lambert, L. (1972). "An Assessment of the Classification System for Placement of Wards in Training Schools," Vol. 2. Toronto: Ministry of Correctional Services.

Blanch, M. (1979). "Imperialism, Nationalism and Organized Youth," in J. Clarke, C. Critcher, and R. Johnson (eds.), *Working Class Culture: History and Theory*. London: Hutchinson.

Bliss, M. (1974). *A Living Profit: Studies in the Social History of Canadian Business, 1883–1911*. Toronto: McClelland and Stewart.

Bloch, H. A., and Niederhoffer, A. (1958). *The Gang*. New York: Philosophical Library.

Blomberg, D. (1978). "Diversion from Court: A Review of the Evidence," in F. Faust, and P. Brantingham (eds.), *Juvenile Justice Philosophy*, 2nd ed. Minneapolis: West Publishing Co.

Bosence, O. (1974). "Classroom Contexts and Classroom Talk." M.A. thesis, The Ontario Institude for Studies in Education/University of Toronto.

Bossert, S. (1974). "The Organization of Work and the Social Organization of a Classroom." PH.D. thesis, University of Chicago.

Bourdieu, P., and Passeron, J. C. (1977). *Reproduction in Education, Culture and Society*. Beverly-Hills: Sage.

Bowles, S., and Gintis, H. (1976). *Schooling in Capitalist America*. New York: Basic.

Box, S. (1981). *Deviance, Reality and Society* (2nd ed.). Toronto: Holt, Rinehart and Winston.

Brake, M. (1974). "The Skinheads." *Youth and Society* 6, 2 (Dec.): 179–200.

———— (1980). *The Sociology of Youth and Youth Subcultures.* London: Routledge and Kegan Paul.

Briar, S., and Piliavin, I. (1965). "Delinquency, Situational Inducements and Commitments to Conformity." *Social Problems* 13: 35–45.

Broadfoot, P. (1979). *Assessment, Schools and Society.* London: Methuen.

Brookes, A. A. (1982). "Family, Youth and Leaving Home in Late–Nineteenth Century Rural Nova Scotia," in J. Parr (ed.), *Childhood and Family in Canadian History.* Toronto: McClelland and Stewart.

Brophy, J., and Good, T. (1974). *Teacher-Student Relationships.* New York: Holt, Rinehart and Winston.

Buff, S. (1971). "Greasers, Dupers and Hippies," in L. Kapp (ed.), *The White Majority Between Poverty and Affluence.* New York: Doubleday-Anchor.

Byles, J. (1969). *Alienation, Deviance and Social Control.* Toronto: Ministry of Education, Interim Research Project on Unreached Youth.

Byles, J., and Maurice, A. (1979). "The Juvenile Services Project: An Experiment in Delinquency Control." *Canadian Journal of Criminology* 21: 155–65.

Calliste, A. (1980). "Ethnicity, Sex, Social Class, Occupational and Educational Aspirations and Expectations of High School Students: A Multivariate Analysis." PH.D. thesis, The Ontario Institute for Studies in Education/ University of Toronto.

Campbell, A. (1981). *Girl Delinquents.* Oxford: Basil Blackwell.

Campbell, D. T. (1969). "Reforms as Experiments." *American Psychologist* 24: 409–29.

Campbell, D. T., and Stanley, J. (1963). *Experimental and Quasi-Experimental Design.* Chicago: Rand-McNally.

Canada (1893). *Sessional Papers,* No. 18.

Canadian Centre for Justice Statistics (1980). *Juvenile Delinquents.* Ottawa: Supply and Services.

Canadian Federal–Provincial Task Force on Justice for Victims of Crime (1983). *Report.* Ottawa: Solicitor General.

Centre for New Schools (1972). "Strengthening Alternative High Schools." *Harvard Educational Review* 42, 3: 313–50.

Cernovich, S. A., and Giordano, P. C. (1979). "A Comparative Analysis of Male and Female Delinquency." *The Sociological Quarterly* 20: 131–45.

Chambliss, W. J. (1976). "Functional and Conflict Theories of Crime," in W. Chambliss, and M. Mankoff (eds.), *Whose Law? What Order?* New York: Wiley.

Chesney-Lind, M. (1974). "Juvenile Delinquency: The Sexualization of Female Crime." *Psychology Today,* July: 43–46.

———— (1977). "Judicial Paternalism and the Female Statue Offender: Training Women to Know their Place." *Crime and Delinquency* 23, 2: 121–30.

———— (1978). "Women Re-examined: Women and the Criminal Justice System," in L. H. Bowker (ed.), *Women, Crime and the Criminal Justice System.* Lexington: D. C. Heath.

Chimbos, P. D. (1973). "A Study of Break and Enter Offences in Northern City, Ontario." *Canadian Journal of Criminology and Corrections* 15, 3: 316–25.

Christie, N. (1965). "A Study of Self-Reported Crime." *Scandinavian Studies in Criminology* I.

Chunn, D. (1983). "Social Control Through the Family Courts: The Reorganization of Summary Justice in Ontario, 1888–1938." Paper presented to

Annual Meetings of Canadian Sociology and Anthropology Association, Vancouver.

Cicourel, A. V. (1968). *The Social Organization of Juvenile Justice.* New York: Wiley.

Cicourel A.V., and Kitsuse, J. I. (1963). *The Educational Decision-Makers.* Chicago: Rand-McNally.

Clark, S. D. (1976). *Canadian Society in Historical Perspective.* Toronto: McGraw-Hill.

Clark, J. P., and Wenninger, E. P. (1962). "Socio-Economic Class and Area as Correlates of Illegal Behaviour Among Juveniles." *American Sociological Review* 27: 826–34.

Clarke, J. (1975). "Learning the Three R's: Repression, Rescue and Rehabilitation." Birmingham: Centre for Contemporary Cultural Studies. Stenciled paper.

—— (1979). "Capital and Culture," in J. Clarke, C. Critcher, and R. Johnson (eds.), *Working Class Culture: History and Theory.* London: Hutchinson.

Clarke, J.; Hall, S.; Jefferson, T.; and Roberts, B. (1976). "Subcultures, Cultures and Class: A Theoretical Overview," in S. Hall and T. Jefferson (eds.), *Resistane Through Ritual.* London: Hutchinson.

Clarke, S. (1977). "Marxism, Sociology and Poulantzas' Theory of the State." *Capital and Class* 2: 1–23.

Clement, W. (1975). *The Canadian Corporate Elite.* Toronto: McClelland and Stewart.

Cloward, R., and Ohlin, L. (1960). *Delinquency and Opportunity.* New York: Free Press.

Cockerill, R. M. (1975). "Probation Effectiveness in Alberta." *Canadian Journal of Criminology and Corrections* 17, 4: 284–91.

Cohen, A. K. (1955). *Delinquent Boys.* New York: Free Press/Macmillan.

Cohen, A. K., and Short, J. F. (1966). "Juvenile Delinquency," in R. Merton, and R. Nisbet (eds.), *Contemporary Social Problems.* New York: Harcourt Brace Jovanovich.

Cohen, S. (1979a). "Guilt, Justice and Tolerance," in D. Downes, and P. Rock (eds.), *Deviant Interpretations.* London: Martin Robertson.

—— (1979b). "The Punitive City: Notes on the Dispersal of Social Control." *Contemporary Crises* 3: 339–63.

—— (1980). "Symbols of Trouble," in his *Folk Devils and Moral Panics* (2nd ed.). London: Martin Robertson.

Coleman, J. (1961). *The Adolescent Society.* Glencoe, Ill.: Free Press/Macmillan.

Coleman, J.; Campbell, E.; Hobson, C. F.; McPartland, J.; Mood, A.; Weinfeld, F. D.; and York, R. L. (1966). *Equality of Educational Opportunity.* Washington: United States Government Printing Office.

Coleman, J., et al. (1974). Panel on Youth of the President's Science Advisory Committee. *Youth: Transition to Adulthood.* Chicago: University of Chicago Press.

Committee on Youth (1971). *It's Your Turn . . . .* Ottawa: Queen's Printer.

Committee on Juvenile Delinquency (1965). *Juvenile Delinquency in Canada.* Ottawa: Queen's Printer.

Comte, A. (1912). *Système de Politique Positive* (4th ed.). Paris: Au Siège de la Société Positiviste.

Conly, D. (1977a). "A Critique of the Institutional Response to Juvenile Delinquency in Ontario." *Interchange* 8, 1–2: 194–202.

—— (1977b). "A Descriptive Analysis of Delinquency Patterns and Police Action in Twelve Major Metropolitan Canadian Cities During the Month of December 1976." Ottawa: Solicitor General.

Corrigan, P. (1976). "Doing Nothing," in S. Hall, and T. Jefferson (eds.), *Resistance Through Ritual: Youth Subcultures in Post-War Britain*. London: Hutchinson.

―――― (1979). *Schooling the Smash Street Kids*. London. Macmillan.

Courtis, M. C. (1970). "The Police and the Public," Sec. 7 of *Attitudes to Crime and the Police in Toronto*. Toronto: Centre of Criminology. Reprinted in C. Boydell, P. Whitehead, and C. Grindstaff (eds.), *The Administration of Criminal Justice in Canada*. Toronto: Holt, Rinehart and Winston, 1974.

Cousineau, D., and Veevers, J. (1972). "Juvenile Justice: An Analysis of the Canadian Young Offenders Act," in C. Boydell, C. Grindstaff, and P. Whitehead (eds.), *Deviant Behaviour and Social Reaction*. Toronto: Holt, Rinehart and Winston.

Cowie, J.; Cowie, V.; and Slater, E. (1968). *Delinquency in Girls*. London: Heinemann.

Cusick, P. A. (1973). *Inside High School*. New York: Holt, Rinehart and Winston.

Dale, R. (1977a). *Liberal and Radical Alternatives* (Unit 31, Block VI, Course E-202). Milton Keynes, England: Open University Press.

―――― (1977b). "Implications of the Discovery of the Hidden Curriculum," in D. Gleeson, (ed.), *Identity and Social Structure*. Driffield, England: Nafferton.

―――― (1978). "Education in the Crisis and the Crisis in Education." Unpublished paper. Milton Keynes, England: Open University.

―――― (1982). "Education and the Capitalist State: Contributions and Contradictions," in M. Apple (ed.), *Cultural and Economic Reproduction in Education*. London: Routledge and Kegan Paul.

Dale, R.; Esland, G.; Fergusson, R.; and MacDonald, M. (eds.) (1980). *Education and the State*: Vol. I, *Schooling and the National Interest*; Vol. II, *Politics, Patriarchy, and Practice*. England: Falmer Press.

David, M. (1978). "The Family – Education Couple," in G. Littlejohn, et al. (eds.). *Power and the State*. London: Croom Helm.

Davies, D. (1981). "Popular Culture, Class, and Schooling," *The Politics of Cultural Production* (Block 3, Unit 9, of Open University Course E-353). Milton Keynes, England: Open University Press.

Davin, A. (1978). "Imperialism and Motherhood." *History Workshop* 5: 9–65.

Davis, A. (1971). "Canadian Society and History as Hinterland versus Metropolis," in R. J. Ossenberg (ed.). *Canadian Society: Pluralism, Change, and Conflict*. Toronto: Prentice-Hall.

Davis, F., and Munoz, L. (1968). "Heads and Freaks: Patterns of Drug Use Among Hippies." *Journal of Health and Social Behavior*, 9, 2: 156–63.

Davis, K. (1971). "Sexual Behavior," in R. Merton and R. Nisbet (eds.), *Contemporary Social Problems* (3rd ed.). New York: Harcourt Brace Jovanovich.

Dawe, A. (1970). "The Two Sociologies," *British Journal of Sociology* 21: 207–18.

de Mause, L. (1974). *The History of Childhood*. New York: Harper Row.

Denscombe, M. (1980), "Keeping 'em Quiet: The Significance of Noise for the Practical Activity of Teaching," in P. Woods (ed.), *Teacher Strategies*. London: Croom Helm.

Denzin, N. K. (1970). *The Research Act*. Chicago: Aldine.

Deosaran, R. (1974). "Sexual Socialization in a Grade Six Class: A Participant Observation Study." M.A. thesis, The Ontario Institute for Studies in Education/University of Toronto.

Dickson, B. (1973). *Home Safely to Me*. Toronto: Anansi.

Dobson, R.; Goldenberg, R.; and Elson, B. (1972). "Pupil Control, Ideology, and

Teacher Influence in the Class." *Journal of Educational Research* 66, 2: 76–80.

Dominion Bureau of Statistics (1969). "Juvenile Delinquents" #85–202. Ottawa: Information Canada.

Donzelot, J. (1979). *The Policing of Families*. New York: Random House.

Dorn, N., and South, N. (1983). *Of Males and Markets: A Critical Review of Youth Culture Theory*. Research paper #1. London: Middlesex Polytechnic, Centre for Occupational and Community Research.

Downes, D. (1966). *The Delinquent Solution*. London: Routledge and Kegan Paul.

Dunlop, A. (1974), *The Approved School Experience*. London: H.M. Stationery Office.

Durkheim, E. ([1895] 1950). *The Rules of Sociological Method*. Glen, Ill.: Free Press.

——— ([1897] 1951). *Suicide*. Glencoe, Ill.: Free Press.

——— ([1893] 1933). *The Division of Labour in Society*. New York: Free Press.

Economic Council of Canada (1970). *Patterns of Growth: Seventh Annual Review*. Ottawa: Queen's Printer.

Education Group (S. Baron, D. Finn, N. Grant, M. Green, and R. Johnson), Centre for Contemporary Cultural Studies (1981). *Unpopular Education*. London: Hutchinson.

Edwards, A., and Furlong, V. (1978). *The Language of Teaching*. London: Heinemann.

Elkin, F., and Westley, W. (1955). "The Myth of Adolescent Culture." *American Sociological Review* 20: 680–84.

Elliott, D. S. (1966). "Delinquency, School Attendance and Dropout." *Social Problems* 13, 3: 307–14.

Elliott, D. S., and Voss, H. L. (1974). *Delinquency and Dropout*. Lexington, Mass.: Heath-Lexington.

Elliott, D. S., and Ageton, S. (1980). "Reconciling Race and Class Differences in Self-Reported and Official Estimates of Delinquency." *American Sociological Review* 45: 95–110.

Emerson, R. (1969). *Judging Delinquents*. Chicago: Aldine.

Empey, L. T. and Lubeck, G. (1971). *Explaining Delinquency*. Lexington: Heath-Lexington.

Empey, L. T., and Erickson, M. L. (1972). *The Provo Experiment*. Lexington: Heath-Lexington.

Empey, L. T. (1978). *American Delinquency: Its Meaning and Construction*. Homewood, Ill.: Dorsey Press.

Engels, Friedrich ([1892] 1969). *The Condition of the Working Class in England in 1844*. London: Granada.

Ennis, P. (1967). *Criminal Victimization*. Washington, D.C.: President's Commission on Law Enforcement and the Administration of Justice.

Erickson, P. (1975). "Legalistic and Traditional Role Expectations for Defence Counsel in Juvenile Court." *Canadian Journal of Criminology and Corrections*. 17: 78–93.

Erikson, E. (1962). "Fidelity and Diversity." *Daedalus* 91, 1: 5–25.

Erikson, K. T. (1964a). *Wayward Puritans*. New York: Wiley.

——— (1964b). "Notes on the Sociology of Deviance," in H. S. Becker, (ed.), *The Other Side*. New York: Free Press.

Esland, G. (1971). "Teaching and Learning as the Organization of Knowledge," in M. F. D. Young (ed.), *Knowledge and Control*. London: Collier-Macmillan.

Evans, J., and Leger, J. (1978). "Canadian Victimization Surveys: A Discussion

Paper." Ottawa: Solicitor General, Research Branch. Revised in *Canadian Journal of Criminology* 1979, 21, 2: 166–83.

Faris, R. E. L. (1970). *Chicago Sociology 1920–1930*. Chicago: University of Chicago Press.

Farrington, D. (1977). "The Effects of Public Labelling." *British Journal of Criminology* 17, 2: 112–25.

Fine, B. (1979). "Law and Class." B. Fine, R. Kinsey, J. Lea, S. Picciotto, and J. Young (eds.), *Capitalism and the Rule of Law: From Deviancy Theory to Marxism*. London: Hutchinson.

Fischer, D. G. and Martin, R. D. (1979). "Family Relationship Variables, Diversion and Delinquency." Ottawa: Solicitor General.

Fitz, J. (1979). "The Child as a Legal Subject." Paper presented to the British Sociological Association; revised as

——— (1981a). "The Child as a Legal Subject." R. Dale, G. Esland, R. Fergusson, and M. MacDonald (eds.), *Education and the State*. Vol. II, *Politics, Patriarchy and Practice*. Milton Keynes, England: Open University Press.

——— (1981b). "Welfare, the Family and the Child" (Unit 12, Block 5 of Course E-353), in J. Fitz, and J. Shaw, *Education, Welfare and Social Order*. Milton Keynes, England: Open University Press.

Foucault, M. (1977). *Discipline and Punish*. Harmondsworth, England: Penguin, and New York: Random House.

Frank, A. G. (1972). "The Development of Underdevelopment." J. Cockcroft, A. G. Frank, and D. L. Johnston (eds.), *Dependence and Underdevelopment*. New York: Doubleday-Anchor.

Frease, D. (1972). "The Schools, Self Concept and Juvenile Delinquency." *British Journal of Criminology* 12: 133–53.

——— (1973). "Delinquency, Social Class and the Schools." *Sociology and Social Research*. 57, 4: 443–59.

Fréchette, M., and Leblanc, M. (1978–79). *La Délinquance Cachée à l'Adolescente*, Montreal: Le Groupe de Recherche sur l'Inadaptation Juvénile, Université de Montréal (Vol. I du Rapport Final).

Fréchette, M.; Leblanc, M.; and Biron, L. (1981). "A Continuum of Social Adaptability." Chap. II of Social Sciences and Humanities Research Council of Canada, *Report*, School of Criminology, Le Groupe de Recherche sur l'Inadaptation Juvénile, University of Montreal, May.

Freire, P. (1970). *The Pedagogy of the Oppressed*. New York: Herder and Herder.

Friedenberg, E. Z. (1959). *The Vanishing Adolescent*. New York: Dell.

Freud, Sigmund ([1925–31] 1973). "Feminity." *New Introductory Lectures on Psychoanalysis*. J. Strachey and A. Richards (eds.). Harmondsworth, England: Penguin.

Fullan, M. (1972). "The Innovative Process and the User: An Overview." *Interchange* 3, 2–3: 1–46.

Gaffield, C., and West, W. G. (1978). "Children's Rights in the Canadian Context." H. Berkeley, C. Gaffield, and W. G. West, (eds.), *Children's Rights: Legal and Educational Issues*. Toronto: Ontario Institute for Studies in Education Press, pp. 1–14.

Gagnon, R., and Biron, L. (1979). *Les Filles Marginalisées: Perspective Statistique*. Rapport No. 1. Montreal: Le Groupe de Recherche sur l'Inadaptation Juvénile, Université de Montréal.

Gandy, J. (1967). "The Exercise of Discretion by the Police in the Handling of Juveniles." D.S.W. thesis, School of Social Work, University of Toronto.

Garner, H. (1968). *Cabbagetown*. Toronto: Simon and Schuster.

Gavigan, S. (1983). "Women's Crime and Feminist Critiques." *Canadian Criminology Forum* 6, 1: 75–90.

—— (1981). "Marxist Theories of Law: A Survey, with some Thoughts on Women and Law." *Canadian Criminology Forum* 4, 1: 1–12.

Gaucher, R. (1982). "Class and State in Lower and Upper Canada 1760 to 1873." PH.D. thesis, University of Sheffield.

Geer, B. (1968). "Teaching." *International Encyclopedia of the Social Sciences*. D. Sills (ed.). New York: Free Press, vol. 15: 560–65.

Geller, G. (1980). "The Streaming of Males and Females in the Juvenile Court Clinic." PH.D. thesis, Ontario Institute for Studies in Education/University of Toronto.

Gerin-Lajoie, D. (1983). "Micro-Analysis and Neo-Marxist Perspective: Comparative Analysis of Two Work-Experience Programs." PH.D. thesis proposal, The Ontario Institute for Studies in Education.

Gibson, L. (1983). "The Day Care Center as Women's Work." M.A. thesis, Ontario Institute for Studies in Education/University of Toronto.

Giffen, P. J. (1979). "Official Rates of Crime and Delinquency," in E. W. Vaz, and A. Lodhi (eds.), *Crime and Delinquency in Canada*. Scarborough, Ont.: Prentice-Hall.

Gillis, J. R. (1974). *Youth and History*. New York: Academic.

Giordano, P. (1976). "The Sense of Injustice? An Analysis of Juveniles' Reactions to the Justice System." *Criminology* 14, 1: 93–112.

Giordano, P., and Cernovich, G. (1979). "A Comparative Analysis of Male and Female Delinquency." *Sociological Quarterly* 20: 131–45.

Glenday, D.; Guindon, H.; and Turowetz, A. (eds.) (1978). *Modernization and the Canadian State*. Toronto: Macmillan.

Godfrey, D., and Watkins, M. (1970). *Gordon to Watkins to You*. Toronto: New Press.

Goff, C., and Reasons, C. E. (1978). *Corporate Crime in Canada: A Critical Analysis of Anti-Combines Legislation*. Scarborough, Ont.: Prentice-Hall.

Goffman, E. (1967). "Where the Action is," in his *Interaction Ritual*. Garden City, N.Y.: Doubleday-Anchor.

Gold, M. (1963). *Status Forces in Delinquent Boys*. Ann Arbor: University of Mich. Press.

Gomme, I. M. (1982). "A Multivariate Analysis of Self-Report Delinquency Among Students." ED.D. thesis, Ontario Institute for Studies in Education/University of Toronto.

—— (1983), "Predictors of Status and Criminal Offences Among Male and Female Adolescents in an Ontario Community." Paper presented at the annual meeting of American Society of Criminology, Denver.

Gomme, I. M.; Morton, M.; and West, W. G. (1984). "Rates, Types, and Patterns of Male and Female Delinquency in an Ontario County." *Canadian Journal of Criminology*, forthcoming.

Goodman, P. (1960). *Growing Up Absurd*. New York: Random House.

Gordon, D. M. (1971). "Class and the Economics of Crime." *Review of Radical Political Economics* 3, 3: 51–72. Reprinted in W. Chambliss and M. Mankoff (eds.), *Whose Law? What Order?* New York: Wiley, 1976.

Gough, I. (1979). *The Political Economy of the Welfare State*. London: Macmillan.

Gove, W. (1975). *The Labelling of Deviance: Evaluating a Perspective*. New York: Sage.

Gramsci, A. (1971). *Selections from the Prison Notebooks*. Q. Hoare (ed.). London: Lawrence and Wishart.

Grayson, J. P. (ed.) (1983). *Introduction to Sociology: An Alternate Approach*. Toronto: Gage.

Greenberg, D. (1977). "Delinquency and the Age-Structure of Society." *Contemporary Crises* 1: 189–223.

Grimes, R. E. (1978). "A Theoretical Overview of the Canadian Juvenile Justice Legislation." Paper presented at the annual meeting of the Canadian Sociology and Anthropology Association, London, Ontario.

Grosman, B. A. (1975). *Police Command: Decisions and Discretion*. Toronto: Macmillan.

Habermas, J. (1975). *Legitimation Crisis*. Boston: Beacon.

Hackler, J. (1975). "The Flow of Information in Court." *Canadian Journal of Criminology* 17: 57–68.

—— (1978). *The Prevention of Delinquency: The Great Stumble Forward*. Toronto: Methuen.

—— (1981). "Comparing Delinquency Statistics in Two Cities." *Canadian Police College Journal* 5, 3: 117–28.

Hackler, J., and Paranjape, W. (1981). "Official Reactions to Juvenile Theft: Comparisons Across Provinces." Paper presented to American Society of Criminology Meetings, Washington.

—— (1983). "Analyzing Juvenile Justice Statistics in Metropolitan Press." *Canadian Journal of Criminology* 25, 4: 447–62.

Hagan, J. (1974a). "Extra Legal Attributes and Criminal Sentencing." *Law and Society Review* 8, 3: 357–83.

—— (1974b). "Criminal Justice and Native People: A Study of Incarceration in a Canadian Province." *Canadian Review of Sociology and Anthropology* Special Issue: 220–36.

—— (1974c). "Criminal Justice in a Canadian Province." PH.D. thesis, University of Alberta.

—— (1975). "Policing Delinquency," in Robert S. Silverman, and James J. Teevan (eds.), *Crime in Canadian Society*. Toronto: Butterworths.

—— (1977). *Disreputable Pleasures*. Toronto: McGraw-Hill.

Hagan, J., and Leon, J. (1977). "Rediscovering Delinquency: Social History, Political Ideology, and the Sociology of Law." *American Sociological Review* 42: 587–98.

Hagan, J.; Simpson, J.; and Gillis, A. R. (1979). "The Sexual Stratification of Social Control: A Gender Based Perspective on Crime and Delinquency." *British Journal of Sociology* 30: 25–37.

Hagan, J.; Gillis, A. R.; and Chan, J. (1980). "Explaining Official Delinquency: A Spacial Study of Class, Conflict and Control," in R. S. Silverman and J. J. Teevan (eds.), *Crime in Canadian Society* (2nd ed.). Toronto: Butterworths.

Haldane, L.; Elliott, D.; and Whitehead, P. (1972). "Particularism in the Sentencing of Juvenile Delinquents," in C. Boydell, et al. (eds.), *Deviant Behaviour and Societal Reaction*. Toronto: Holt, Rinehart and Winston.

Hall, E., and Dennis, L., et al. (1968). The Provincial Committee on Aims and Objectives of Education in the Schools of Ontario. *Living and Learning*. Toronto: Ontario Department of Education.

Hall, S. (1971). "Deviancy, Politics, and the Media." Birmingham: Centre for Contemporary Cultural Studies, stenciled paper No. 11.

Hall, S., and Jefferson, T. (eds.) (1976). *Resistance Through Ritual: Youth Subcultures in Post-War Britain*. London: Hutchinson.

Hall, S.; Clarke, J.; Critcher, C.; Jefferson, T.; and Roberts, B. (1978). *Policing the Crisis: Mugging, The State, and Law and Order*. London: Macmillan.

Hamilton, R., and Pinard, M. (1977). "Poverty in Canada: Illusion and Reality."*Canadian Review of Sociology and Anthropology* 14, 2: 247–52.

Hammersley, M. (1974). "The Organization of Pupil Participation." *Sociological Review* (August) 22, 3: 355–68.

——— (1976). "The Mobilisation of Pupil Attention," in M. Hammersley, and P. Woods, (eds.), *The Process of Schooling*. London: Routledge and Kegan Paul.

Hardy, T. (1974). "Teacher Student Dyadic Relationships in the Elementary School Classroom." PH.D. thesis, Ontario Institute for Studies in Education/University of Toronto.

Hargreaves, D. (1967). *Social Relations in a Secondary School*. London: Routledge.

Hargreaves, D.; Hester, S.; and Mellor, F. (1975). *Deviance in Classrooms*. London: Routledge and Kegan Paul.

Harrison, R., and Mort, F. (1979). "Patriarchal Aspects of Nineteenth Century State Formation: Property Relations, Marriage and Divorce, and Sexuality," in P. R. D. Corrigan (ed.), *Capitalism, State Formation and Marxist Theory*. London: Quartet.

Harvey, Edward B. (1974). *Educational Systems and the Labour Market*, Toronto: Longmans.

Havemann, P. (1981). "Prairie Justice: The Law, The State, and Indigenous Peoples: Some Dilemmas." Paper presented to American Society of Criminology, Washington, D.C.

Henry, J. (1974). "Docility, or Giving the Teacher What She Wants," in S. Fishman, A. Kazamias, and H. Kliebard (eds.), *Teacher, Student and Society: Perspectives in Education*. Boston: Little, Brown.

Herndon, J. (1965). *The Way It 'Spozed to Be*. New York: Simon and Schuster.

Hindelang, M. J. (1973). "Causes of Delinquency: A Partial Replication and Extension." *Social Problems* 20, 4: 471–87.

Hindelang, M. J.; Hirschi, T.; and Weiss, J. (1979). "Correlates of Delinquency." *American Sociological Review* 44: 995–1014.

——— (1981) *Measuring Delinquency*. Beverley Hills: Sage.

Hirschi, T. (1969). *Causes of Delinquency*. Berkeley: University of California Press.

Hirschi, T., and Hindelang, M. (1977). "Intelligence and Delinquency." *American Sociological Review* 42: 571–87. Reprinted in S. Messinger and E. Bittner (eds.), *Criminology Review Yearbook*. Beverley Hills, Sage, 1979.

Hirst, P. Q. (1975). "Marx and Engels on Law, Crime and Morality," in I. Taylor, P. Walton, and J. Young (eds.), *Critical Criminology*. London: Routledge and Kegan Paul.

——— (1979). *Law and Ideology*. London: Macmillan.

Hoetker, J., and Ahlbrand, N. P. (1969). "The Persistence of the Recitation." *American Educational Research Journal* 6: 145–68.

Hoffman-Bustamonte, D. (1973). "The Nature of Female Criminality." *Issues in Criminology (Crime and Social Justice)* 8: 117–37.

Hogarth, J. (1974). *Studies in Diversion. The East York Community Law Reform Project*. Ottawa: Law Reform Commission of Canada.

Hollingshead, A. deB. (1949). *Elmtown's Youth*. New York: John Wiley.

Holloway, J., and Picciotto, S. (1978). "Introduction," in their edited *State and Capital: A Marxist Debate*. London: Edward Arnold.

Holt, J. (1965). *How Children Fail*. London: Pitman.

Holtz, J. A. (1975). "The Low-Riders: Portrait of an Urban Youth Subculture." *Youth and Society* 6, 4: 495–508.

Horton, J. (1966). "Order and Conflict Theories of Social Problems." *American Journal of Sociology* 71, 6: 701–13.

Houston, S. (1972). "The Victorian Origins of Juvenile Delinquency." *History of Education Quarterly* 12: 254–80.

—— (1982). "The Waifs and Strays of a Late Victorian City: Juvenile Delinquents in Toronto," in J. Parr (ed.), *Childhood and Family in Canadian History*. Toronto: McClelland and Stewart.

Hughes, E. C. (1958). *Men and Their Work*. Glencoe, Ill.: Free Press.

—— (1971). *The Sociological Eye*. Chicago: Aldine.

Hussain, A. (1976). "The Economy of Education." *Economy and Society* 5, 4.

Hylton, J. (1981). "Community Corrections and Social Control: The Case of Saskatchewan." *Contemporary Crises* 5: 193–215.

Ignatieff, M. (1978). *A Just Measure of Pain*. New York: Columbia University Press.

Innis, H. (1950). *Empire and Communications*. London: Routledge and Kegan Paul.

—— (1956). *The Fur Trade in Canada*. Toronto: University of Toronto Press.

Irwin, J. (1973). "Surfing: The Natural History of an Urban Scene." *Urban Life and Culture* 2, 2: 131–60.

Jackson, P. (1968). *Life in Classrooms*. New York: Holt, Rinehart and Winston.

Jahoda, M., and Warren, N. (1965). "The Myths of Youth." *Sociology of Education* 38, 2: 138–47.

Janowitz, M. (1966). "Introduction" to W. I. Thomas, *W. I. Thomas on Social Organization and Social Personality*, ed. by M. Janowitz. Chicago: University of Chicago Press.

Jansyn, L. (1966). "Solidarity and Delinquency in a Streetcorner Group." *American Sociological Review* 31: 600–14.

Jencks, C.; Smith, M.; Acland, H.; Bane, M.; Cohen, D.; Gintis, H.; Heyns, B.; Michelson, S. (1972). *Inequality*. New York: Harper and Row.

Jensen, G. F. (1969). "Crime Doesn't Pay: Correlates of a Shared Misunderstanding." *Social Problems* 17: 189–201.

Johnson, L. (1972). "The Development of Class in Canada in the Twentieth Century," in G. Teeple (ed.), *Capitalism and the National Question in Canada*. Toronto: University of Toronto Press.

Johnson, R. E. (1979). *Juvenile Delinquency and Its Origins*. Cambridge: Cambridge University Press.

Johnston, A. (1977). "Legal Change in the Canadian Juvenile Court System." B.A. thesis, Queen's University, Kingston, Ont.

Johnston, R. (1976). "Notes on the Schooling of the English Working Class, 1780–1850," in R. Dale, G. Esland, and M. MacDonald (eds.), *Schooling and Capitalism*. London: Routledge and Kegan Paul, and Open University Press.

—— (1979). "Three Problematics: Elements of a Theory of Working Class Culture," in J. Clarke, C. Critcher, and R. Johnston (eds.), *Working Class Culture: History and Theory*. London: Hutchinson.

Juristat (1981), "Juvenile Delinquents." *Juristat* 1, 2. Ottawa: Statistics Canada.

Justice Assistance News, 2, 4. (May 1981). "30% of U.S. Households Hit by Crime."

Kahl, J. (1961). "Common Man Boys," in A. H. Halsey et al. (eds.), *Education, Economy and Society*. Glencoe, Ill.: Free Press.

Karabel, J., and Halsey, A. H. (eds.) (1977). *Power and Ideology in Education*. New York: Oxford University Press.

Katz, J. (1972). "Deviance, Charisma, and Rule-Defined Behavior." *Social Problems* 20: 156–201.

Keat, R. and Urry, J. (1976). *Social Theory as Science*. London: Routledge and Kegan Paul.

Keating, C. (1981). "Female Delinquency." M.A. thesis proposal, Centre of Criminology, University of Toronto.

Keddie, N. (1971). "Classroom Knowledge," in M. F. D. Young (ed.), *Knowledge and Control*. London: Collier-Macmillan.

Kelly, D. H. (1971). "Academic Self-Evaluation, School Avoidance and Deviant Behavior." *Youth and Society* 2, 4: 489–502.

Kelly, H. (1969). "Adolescents: A Suppressed Minority Group." *The Personnel and Guidance Journal* 47 (March): 634–40.

Kitsuse, J. I. (1964). "Societal Reaction to Deviant Behavior: Problems of Theory and Method," in H. S. Becker (ed.), *The Other Side*. Glencoe, Ill.: Free Press.

Kitsuse, J. I., and Dietrick D. (1959). "Delinquent Boys: A Critique." *American Sociological Review* 24: 208–15. Reprinted in H. Voss (ed.), *Society Delinquency and Delinquent Behavior*. Boston: Little, Brown, 1970.

Kitsuse, J. I., and Cicourel, A. V. (1963). "A Note on the Use of Official Statistics." *Social Problems* 11: 131–39.

Klein, D. (1973). "The Etiology of Female Crime: A Review of the Literature." *Issues in Criminology (Crime and Social Justice)* 8: 3–30.

Konopka, G. (1966). *Adolescent Girls in Conflict*. Englewood Cliffs, N.J.: Prentice-Hall.

Krisberg, B., and Austin, J. (1978). *The Children of Ishmael: Critical Perspectives in Juvenile Justice*. Palo Alto, Cal.: Mayfield Publishing.

Kundratts, U. (1979). "Role Commitment and Delinquency," in E. Vaz and A. Lodhi (eds.), *Crime and Delinquency in Canada*. Toronto: Prentice-Hall.

Laclau, E. (1977). *Politics and Ideology in Marxist Theory*. London: New Left Books.

Lambert, L., and Birkenmeyer, A. (1972). *An Assessment of the Classification System for Placement of Wards in Training Schools*. Toronto: Ministry of Correctional Services.

Land, H. (1978). "Who Cares for the Family." *Journal of Social Policy* 7: 257–84.

———— (1980). "The Family Wage," *Feminist Review* 6: 55–77.

Landau, B. (1973). "The Adolescent Female Offender." *Ontario Psychology* 5: 56–62.

Langley, M.; Thomas, B.; and Parkinson, R. (1978). "Youths' Expectations and Perceptions of Their Initial Juvenile Court Experience." *Canadian Journal of Criminology* 20, 1: 43–53.

Laprairie, C. P. (1983). "Native Juveniles in Court," in T. Fleming, and L. A. Visano (eds.), *Deviant Designations*. Toronto: Butterworths.

Lautt, M. (1979). "Natives and Justice: A Topic Requiring Research Priority?" in D. Hepworth (ed.), *Explorations in Prairie Justice Research*. Regina: Canadian Plains Research Centre, University of Regina.

Law Reform Commission (1974). *The Native Offender and The Law*. Ottawa: Information Canada.

Laxer, J. (1970). *The Energy Poker Game*. Toronto: James Lewis and Samuel.

———— (1973). "Introduction," in R. Laxer (ed.), *Canada (Ltd.)*. Toronto: McClelland and Stewart.

Lea, J., and Young, J. (1984 forthcoming). *What is to be Done About Law and Order?* Harmondsworth, England: Penguin.

Lea, J. (1979). "Discipline and Capitalist Development," in Bob Fine, et al. (eds.), *Capitalism and the Rule of Law*. London: Hutchinson.

Leblanc, M. (1975). "Upper Class Versus Working Class Delinquency," in R. Silverman and J. J. Teevan (eds.), *Crime in Canadian Society*. Toronto: Butterworths.

—— (1977). *Structure et Dynamique du Comportment Délinquent*, Rapport d'Étape. Montréal: Le Groupe de Recherche sur l'Inadaptation Juvénile, Université de Montréal.

—— (1981). "An Integrative Control Theory of Delinquent Behaviour." Paper presented to American Society of Criminology, Washington, D.C.

—— (1983). "Delinquency as an Epiphenomenon of Adolescence," in R. Corrado, M. Leblanc, and J. Trépanier (eds.), *Current Issues in Juvenile Justice*. Toronto: Butterworths.

Leblanc, M.; Biron, L.; Fréchette, M. (1981). "The Structure and Dynamics of Delinquent Behaviour." Montreal: University of Montreal.

LeDain, G., et al. (1970). *Interim Report of the Commission of Inquiry Into the Non-Medical Use of Drugs*. Ottawa: Health and Welfare.

Lee, J. A. (1982). "Three Paradigms of Childhood." *Canadian Review of Sociology and Anthropology* 19, 4: 591–608.

Lemert, E. (1951). *Social Pathology*. New York: McGraw-Hill.

—— (1967). *Human Deviance, Social Problems and Social Control*. Englewood Cliffs, N.J.: Prentice-Hall.

Leon, J. S. (1978). "Children's Rights Revisited," in H. Berkeley, C. Gaffield, and W. G. West (eds.), *Children's Rights: Legal and Educational Issues*. Toronto: Ontario Institute for Studies in Education Press.

Lerman, P. (1967). "Gangs, Networks, and Subcultural Delinquency." *American Journal of Sociology* 73: 63–72.

—— (1971). "Delinquents Without Crime." *Transaction* 8. Reprinted in *Children's Liberation*. Edited by D. Gottlieb, Englewood Cliffs, N.J.: Prentice-Hall, 1973.

Levitt, K. (1970). *Silent Surrender*. Toronto: James Lewis and Samuel.

Leyton, E. (1979). *The Myth of Delinquency: An Anatomy of Juvenile Nihilism*. Toronto: McClelland and Stewart.

Liazos, A. (1974). "Class Oppression: The Function of Juvenile Justice." *Insurgent Sociologist* (Fall) 1: 2–24.

Lindblom, C. E., and Cohen, D. K. (1979). *Useable Knowledge*. New Haven: Yale University Press.

Linden, R., and Filmore, C. (1980). "A Comparative Study of Delinquency Involvement," in R. Silverman and J. J. Teevan (eds.), *Crime in Canadian Society*. Toronto: Butterworths.

Livingstone, D. W. (1978). *Public Attitudes Towards Education in Ontario, 1978*. Toronto: Ontario Institute for Studies in Education Press.

—— (1983). *Class Ideologies and Educational Futures*. Brighton, England: Falmer.

Livingstone, D. W., and Mason, R. V. (1978). "Ecological Crisis and the Autonomy of Science in Capitalist Society: A Canadian Case Study." *Alternatives* 8, 1: 3–11.

Livingstone, D. W., and Hart, D. (1980). *Public Attitudes Toward Education in Ontario, 1979*. Toronto: Ontario Institute for Studies in Education Press.

—— (1981). *Public Attitudes Toward Education in Ontario, 1980*. Third Ontario Institute for Studies in Education Survey. Toronto: Ontario Institute for Studies in Education Press.

Lockheart, A. (1975). "Future Failure: The Unanticipated Consequences of Educational Planning," in R. M. Pike, and E. Zureik (eds.), *Socialization and Values in Canadian Society*, Vol. II. Toronto: McClelland and Stewart.

Lombroso, G., and Ferrero, W. ([1895] 1959). *The Female Offender*. New York: Peter Owen.

Lower, A. R. M. (1946). *Colony to Nation*. Toronto: University of Toronto Press.

Lucas, R. (1971). *Minetown, Milltown, Railtown*. Toronto: University of Toronto Press.

Lutz, F., and Ramsay, M. (1974). "The Use of Anthropological Field Methods in Education." *Educational Researcher* 3, 11: 5–9.

Macdougal, C. (1969). "You Need Imagination in the Hole." *This Magazine is About Schools* 3, 3: 36–56.

MacKay, R. (1978). "Children's Intellectual Rights," in H. Berkeley, C. Gaffield, and W. G. West (eds.), *Children's Rights: Legal and Educational Issues*. Toronto: Ontario Institute for Studies in Education Press.

MacLean's (May 9, 1983). "Explaining the Black Decision."

———— (Sept. 5, 1983). "Fighting for Victims of Crime."

Magsino, R. (1978). "Student Rights: Nonsense Upon Stilts," in H. Berkeley, C. Gaffield, and W. G. West (eds.), *Children's Rights: Legal and Educational Issues*. Toronto: Ontario Institute for Studies in Education Press.

Maher, B., and Stein, E. (1968). "The Delinquent's Perception of the Law and The Community," in S. Wheeler (ed.), *Controlling Delinquents*. New York: Wiley.

Manley-Casimir, M. (1978). "Discretion in School Discipline," in H. Berkeley, C. Gaffield, and W. G. West (eds.), *Children's Rights: Legal and Educational Issues*. Toronto: Ontario Institute for Studies in Education Press.

Mann, M. (1970). "The Social Cohesion of Liberal Democracies." *American Sociological Review* 35, 3: 423–39.

Mann, W. E. (1968). "The Social Order of the Slum." *Deviant Behaviour in Canada*. Toronto: Social Science.

Marchak, P. (1975). *Ideological Perspectives in Canada*. Toronto: McGraw-Hill Ryerson.

Maris, P., and Rein, M. (1972). *Dilemmas of Social Reform*. Harmondsworth: Penguin.

Martell, G. (1974). *The Politics of the Canadian Public School*. Toronto: McClelland and Stewart.

Markwart, A. (1980). "Containment/Remand Study." Vancouver: Ministry of Attorney General of British Columbia. Reported in (1981) "Youth Containment in British Columbia." Paper presented to Canadian Sociology and Anthropology Association, Halifax.

Marx, K. ([1867] 1967). *Capital*. New York: Progress International.

Marx, K., and Engels, F. (1848). *Manifesto of the Communist Party*, in *Marx-Engels Selected Works*, Vol. I. London: Lawrence and Wishart, 1950.

Matza, D. (1964a). *Delinquency and Drift*. New York: John Wiley.

———— (1964b). "Positions and Behavior Patterns of Youth," in R. E. L. Faris (ed.), *Handbook of Modern Sociology*. Chicago: Rand-McNally.

———— (1969). *Becoming Deviant*. Englewood Cliffs, N.J.: Prentice-Hall.

Matza, D., and Sykes, G. (1961). "Juvenile Delinquency and Subterranean Values." *American Sociological Review* 26: 712–19.

Maxwell, M., and Maxwell, J. (1979). "Private Schools: The Culture, Structure, and Processes of Elite Socialization in English Canada," in K. Ishwaren (ed.), *Childhood and Adolescence in Canada*. Toronto: McGraw-Hill Ryerson.

Mayhew, H. ([1861] 1981). "A Visit to the Rookery of St. Giles and Its Neighbourhood," and "On the Number of Costermongers and Other Street Folk," in M. Fitzgerald, G. MacLennan, and J. Pawson (eds.), *Crime and*

Society: Readings in History and Theory. London/Milton Keynes, England: Routledge and Kegan Paul, and Open University Press.

Mays, J. B. (1972). "Delinquency and the Transition from School to Work," in J. B. Mays (ed.), *Juvenile Delinquency, The Family and The Social Group.* London: Longman.

McCaghy, C. (1976). *Deviant Behavior.* New York: Macmillan.

McCorkle, L. W.; Elias, A.; and Bixby, F. L. (1958). *The Highfields Story.* New York: Holt, Rinehart and Winston.

McDaniel, S. A., and Agger, B. (1982). *Social Problems Through Conflict and Order.* Don Mills: Addison-Wesley.

McDonald, L. (1969). "Crime and Punishment in Canada: A Statistical Test of the Conventional Wisdom." *Canadian Review of Sociology and Anthropology* 6, 4: 212–36.

——— (1976). *The Sociology of Law and Order.* Montreal: Book Centre (1979, Toronto: Methuen).

McGeachie, P., and Stone, P. (1972). "A Phenomenological Approach to the Sociology of Education." M.A. thesis, The Ontario Institute for Studies in Education/University of Toronto.

McIntosh, J. (1976). "The First Year of Experience: Influences on Beginning Teachers." PH.D. thesis, The Ontario Institute for Studies in Education/University of Toronto.

McIntosh, M. (1978). "The State and the Oppression of Women," in A. Kuhn, and A. M. Wolpe (eds.), *Feminism and Materialism: Women and the Modes of Production.* London: Routledge and Kegan Paul.

McKie, C. (1976). "Some Views on Canadian Corporations." Paper delivered at annual meeting, Canadian Sociology and Anthropology Association, Quebec City.

McLaren, P. (1980). *Cries from the Corridor.* Toronto: Methuen.

McRobbie, A., and Garber, J. (1976). "Girls and Subcultures: An Exploration," in S. Hall, and T. Jefferson (eds.), *Resistance Through Rituals: Youth Subcultures in Post-War Britain.* London: Hutchinson.

Merton, R. K. (1968). *Social Theory and Social Structure.* New York: Free Press/Macmillan.

Miller, W. B. (1958). "Lower Class Culture as a Generating Milieu of Gang Delinquency." *Journal of Social Issues* 14, 3: 5–19.

Meyer, P. B. (1973). "The Exploitation of the American Growing Class," in D. Gottlieb (ed.), *Children's Liberation.* Englewood Cliffs, N.J.: Prentice-Hall.

Millham, S.; Bullock, R.; and Hosie, K. (1978). *Locking Up Children.* Westmead, England: Saxon House.

Miliband, R. (1969). *The State in Capitalist Society.* London: Quartet.

Mills, C. W. (1959). *The Power Elite.* New York: Oxford.

Mitchell, J. (1971). *Women's Estate.* Harmondsworth, England: Penguin.

Mohr, H. (1975). "Facts, Figures, Perspectives and Myths – Ways of Describing and Understanding Crime," in R. A. Silverman, and J. J. Teevan (eds.), *Crime in Canadian Society.* Toronto: Butterworths.

Moogk, P. N. (1982). "Les Petits Sauvages: The Children of Eighteenth Century New France," in J. Parr (ed.), *Childhood and Family in Canadian History.* Toronto: McClelland and Stewart.

Morgan, P. (1978). *Delinquent Fantasies.* London: Temple Smith.

Morton, M. E. (1977). "Society, Police and Citizen Sanctions: Dimensions of Conflict and Consensus in England as Compared with the United States." PH.D. thesis, Cambridge, Mass.: Harvard University.

―――― (1981). "Out of the Mouths of Babes: Sociological Implications of the Criminal/Civil Distinction in Family Law: The Analog of the Fact/Value Distinction." Paper presented at annual meeting of the Canadian Sociology and Anthropology Association, Halifax.

Morton, M. E., and West, W. G., with assistance of B. Ward, J. Clifford, J. McCulligh, G. Burrill, G. Vaz, D. Card, and L. Pender. (1980). *A Research Evaluation of the Frontenac Juvenile Diversion Project.* Ottawa: Solicitor General, pp. 376.

Morton, M. E., and West, W. G. (1983). "An Experiment in Diversion by a Citizen Committee: The Frontenac Diversion Programme," in R. Corrado, M. Leblanc, J. Trépanier (eds.), *Current Issues in Juvenile Justice.* Toronto: Butterworths.

Moyer, S. (1977). *The Pre-judicial Exercise of Discretion and Impact on Children: A Review of the Literature.* Ottawa: Solicitor General.

Moynihan, D. P. (1970). *Maximum Feasible Misunderstanding.* New York: Free Press/Macmillan.

Muncie, J. (1981a). "Youth and the Reforming Zeal" (Part 4, Block 2) in *Law and Disorder: Histories of Crime and Criminal Justice.* Milton Keynes, England: Open University Press.

―――― (1981b). *Talking About Crime* (Block I, Course on Issues in Crime and Society). Milton Keynes, England: Open University Press.

Mungham, G. (1980). "The Career of a Confusion: Radical Criminology in Britain," in J. Inciardi (ed.), *Radical Criminology.* Beverley Hills: Sage.

Mungham, G., and Pearson, G. (eds.) (1976). *Working Class Youth Subcultures.* London: Routledge and Kegan Paul.

Murdock, G., and McCron, R. (1976). "Consciousness of Generation and Consciousness of Class," in S. Hall, and T. Jefferson (eds.), *Resistance Through Ritual: Youth Subcultures in Post-War Britain.* London: Hutchinson.

Murphy, E. (1983). "An Approach to Vocational Training of Disadvantaged Adolescents." PH.D. thesis proposal, The Ontario Institute for Studies in Education, Toronto.

Musgrove, F. (1964). *Youth and the Social Order.* London: Routledge and Kegan Paul.

Nagler, M. (1975). *Natives Without a Home.* Toronto: Longman.

Nease, B. (1968). "Measuring Juvenile Delinquency in Hamilton," in W. E. Mann, *Deviant Behaviour in Canada.* Toronto: Social Science Publications.

Nettler, G. (1974). *Explaining Crime.* New York: McGraw-Hill.

Ng, Y. (1981). "Ideology, Media and Moral Panics: An Analysis of the Jaques Murder." M.A. thesis, Centre of Criminology, University of Toronto.

Noblit, G. W. (1976). "The Adolescent Experience and Delinquency: School Versus Subcultural Effects." *Youth and Society* 8, 1: 27–44.

Novak, M. (1975). *Living and Learning in the Free School.* Toronto: McClelland and Stewart.

Nye, F. I. (1958). *Family Relationships and Delinquent Behaviour.* New York: Wiley.

O'Brien, M. (1981). *The Politics of Reproduction.* London: Routledge and Kegan Paul.

O'Connor, J. (1973). *The Fiscal Crisis of the State.* New York: St. Martins.

Offe, C., and Ronge, V. (1975). "Theses on the Theory of the State." *New German Critique* 6 (Fall).

Ontario, n.d. (1980?). *Crime in Ontario: Questions and Answers.* Toronto: Provincial Secretariat for Justice.

Ontario Department of Corrections (1972). *Annual Report*. Toronto: Department of Corrections.

Ossenberg, R. J. (ed.) (1980). *Power and Change in Canada*. Toronto: McClelland and Stewart.

Panitch, L. (1977). "The Role and Nature of the Canadian State," in L. Panitch (ed.), *The Canadian State: Political Economy and Political Power*. Toronto: University of Toronto Press, pp. 3–27.

Parr, J. (ed.) (1982). *Childhood and Family in Canadian History*. Toronto: McClelland and Stewart.

Parsons, T. (1951). *The Social System*. Glencoe, Ill.: Free Press.

Pashukanis, E. (1978). *Law and Marxism*. London: Ink Links.

Pearce, F. (1981). "Putting Foucault and Althusser to Work: The Legal Subject." Paper presented at the annual meeting of the Canadian Sociology and Anthropology Association, Halifax.

Petrunik, M. (1980). "The Rise and Fall of 'Labelling Theory': The Construction and Destruction of a Sociological Straw Man." *Canadian Journal of Sociology* 5, 3: 213–34.

Picciotto, S. (1979). "The Theory of the State, Class-Struggle and the Rule of Law," in B. Fine et al. (eds.), *Capitalism and the Role of Law*. London: Hutchinson.

Piliavin, J., and Briar, S. (1964). "Police Encounters with Juveniles." *American Journal of Sociology* 70, 2: 206–47.

Platt, A. (1969, rev. 1974). *The Child-Savers*. Chicago: University of Chicago.

Player, C. (1979). "Female Thieves." Paper presented to Doctoral Seminar, Sociology, London School of Economics.

Polk, K., and Schafer, W. (eds.) (1972). *Schools and Delinquency*. Scarborough, Ont.: Prentice-Hall.

Pollak, O. (1950). *The Criminality of Women*. Philadelphia: University of Pennsylvania Press.

Pollard, A. (1979). "Negotiating Deviance," in L. Barton, and R. Meighan (eds.), *Schools, Pupils, and Deviance*. Driffield, England: Nafferton.

Polsky, N. (1969). *Hustlers, Beats and Others*. New York: Doubleday-Anchor.

Pomfret, A. (1974). "Parental Intervention in the Process of Planned Social Change in an Inner City School." Toronto: The Ontario Institute for Studies in Education. Mimeo.

Porter, J. (1965). *The Vertical Mosaic*. Toronto: University of Toronto Press.

Poster, M. (1978). *Critical Theory of the Family*. New York: Seabury.

Poulantzas, N. (1973). *Political Power and Social Classes*. London: Verso.

Power, M.; Benn, R. J.; and Morris, J. N. (1972). "Neighbourhood, School, and Juveniles Before the Court." *British Journal of Criminology* 12: 111–32.

Prentice, A. (1977). *The School Promoters*. Toronto: McClelland and Stewart.

President's Commission on Law Enforcement and the Administration of Justice (1967). *The Challenge of Crime in a Free Society*, esp.: *Task Force Report: Juvenile Delinquency and Youth Crime*. Washington, D.C.: U.S. Government Printing Office.

Prus, R., and Irini, S. (1980). *Hookers, Rounders, and Desk Clerks*. Toronto: Gage.

Pryce, K. (1979). *Endless Pressure*. Harmondsworth, England: Penguin.

Quinney, R. (1969). *The Social Reality of Crime*. Boston: Little, Brown.

———— (1974). *Critique of Legal Order*. Boston: Little, Brown.

———— (1977). *Class, State, and Crime*. New York: David MacKay.

Reasons, C.; Ross, L.; and Patterson, C. (1981). *Assault on the Worker*. Toronto: Butterworths.

Reitsma-Street, M. (1984). "Differential Treatment of Young Offenders: A Review of the Conceptual Level Matching Model." *Canadian Journal of Criminology.* In press.

Repo, S. (1982). "The Problem of Working Class Consciousness in Marxist Cultural Theory." M.A. thesis, The Ontario Institute for Studies in Education/University of Toronto.

Report of the Commissioners Appointed to Enquire into the Prison and Reformatory System of Ontario (1891). Toronto: Queen's Printer.

Reynolds, D., and Sullivan, M. (1979). "Bringing Schools Back In," in L. Barton, and R. Meighan (eds.), *Schools, Pupils and Deviance.* Driffield, England: Nafferton.

Rhodes, A., and Reiss, A. (1969). "Apathy, Truancy, and Delinquency as Adaptations to School Failure." *Social Forces* 8: 12–23.

Ribordy, F. (1975). "Culture, Conflict and Crime Among Italian Immigrants." R. A. Silverman, and J. J. Teevan, (eds.), *Crime in Canadian Society.* Toronto: Butterworths.

——— (1977). "Conscience et Connaissance du Droit dans les Écoles." *Droit et Justice: Revue de l'Université Laurentiènne.* F. Ribordy (ed.) 11, 1: 63–87.

Rist, R. (1970). "Student Social Class and Teacher Expectations: The Self-fulfilling Prophecy in Ghetto Education." *Harvard Educational Review* 40: 411–51.

Roberts, J. I. (1968). *Scene of the Battle: Group Behavior in the Urban Classroom.* Garden City, N.Y.: Doubleday Anchor.

Rock, P. (1979). *The Making of Symbolic Interactionism.* London: Macmillan.

Rogers, K. (1945). *Streetgangs of Toronto.* Toronto: Ryerson.

Rosenthal, R., and Jacobson, L. (1968). *Pygmalion in the Classroom.* New York: Holt, Rinehart and Winston.

Ross, M. (1973). "Economic Conditions and Crime: Metropolitan Toronto." M.A. thesis, Centre of Criminology, University of Toronto.

Ross, R., and Gendreau, P. (1979). *Effective Correctional Treatment.* Toronto: Butterworths.

Roszak, T. (1969). *The Making of the Counterculture.* New York: Vintage.

Rothman, D. (1971). *The Discovery of the Asylum.* Boston: Little, Brown.

Rothman, J. (1968). "Three Models of Community Organization Practice." *Social Work Practice* 13. New York: Columbia University Press, 20–36.

Rowntree, J., and Rowntree, M. (1968). "The Political Economy of Youth." *Our Generation* 6, 1–2: 155–90.

Rutter, M.; Maugham, B.; Mortimore, P.; and Ousten, J. (1979). *Fifteen Thousand Hours.* London: Open Books.

Ryan, D. (1974). *The Individualized System: Administration and Leadership.* Toronto: Ontario Institute for Studies in Education.

Ryan, D., and Greenfield, T. B. (1975). *The Class Size Question.* Toronto: Ministry of Education.

Sarason, S. B. (1971). *The Culture of the School and the Problem of Change.* Boston: Allyn and Bacon.

Sayer, D. (1975). "Method and Dogma in Historical Materialism." *Sociological Review* 23, 4: 779–810.

——— (1979). *Marx's Method: Ideology, Science and Critique in Capital.* England: Harvestor.

Scanlon, R. L. (1982). "Canadian Crime Rates: Sources and Trends," in *Impact #1: Crime and the Community.* Ottawa: Solicitor General.

Schecter, S. (1977). "Capitalism, Class, and Educational Reform in Canada," in L. Panitch (ed.), *The Canadian State.* Toronto: University of Toronto Press.

Schotte, F. (1973). "The Occupation of Substitute Teaching." M.A. thesis, The Ontario Institute for Studies in Education/University of Toronto.

Schur, E. (1973). *Radical Non-intervention: Rethinking the Delinquency Problem*. Englewood Cliffs, N.J.: Prentice-Hall.

Schwartz, G., and Merten, D. (1967). "The Language of Adolescence: An Anthropological Approach to Youth Culture." *American Journal of Sociology* 72: 453–68. Reprinted in R. Grinder (ed.), *Studies in Adolescence*. New York: Macmillan, 1969.

Schwendinger, H. (1963). *The Instrumental Theory of Delinquency: A Tentative Formulation*. Doctoral diss., University of California, Los Angeles.

Schwendinger, H., and Schwendinger, J. (1976). "Delinquency and the Collective Varieties of Youth." *Crime and Social Justice* 5: 7–25.

———— (1975). "Defenders of Order or Guardians of Human Rights," in I. Taylor; P. Walton; and J. Young (eds.), *Critical Criminology*. London: Routledge.

Scraton, P. (1982). "Policing Society, Policing Crime," in *Law and Disorder: Histories of Crime and Justice*. (Block 2, Part 5 of course on Issues in Crime and Society). Milton Keynes, England: Open University Press.

Seccombe, W. (1974). "The Housewife and Her Labour Under Capitalism." *New Left Review* 83: 3–24.

———— (1980). "Domestic Labour and the Working Class Household," and "The Expanded Reproduction Cycle of Labour Power in Twentieth Century Capitalism," in B. Fox (ed.), *Hidden in the Household*. Toronto: Women's Press.

Seeley, J.; Sim, A.; and Looseley, E. (1956). *Crestwood Heights*. Toronto: University of Toronto Press.

Sellin, T. (1938). *Culture, Conflict, and Crime*. New York: Social Science Research Council.

Shaw, C. R. (1930). *The Jackroller: A Delinquent Boy's Story*. Chicago: University of Chicago Press.

Shaw, C. R., and McKay, H. D. (1942). *Juvenile Delinquency and Urban Areas*. Chicago: University of Chicago Press.

Shaw, J. (1981). "Family, State, and Compulsory Education," in *Education, Welfare, and Social Order* (Block 5, Unit 13 of Course E-353). Milton Keynes: Open University Press.

Short, J. F., and Strodtbeck, F. L. (1965). *Group Process and Gang Delinquency*. Chicago: University of Chicago Press.

Sinclair, D. (1965). "Training Schools in Canada," in W. T. McGrath (ed.), *Crime and Its Treatment in Canada*. Toronto: Macmillan.

Singer, B. (1975). "Cooperative and Competitive Behaviour Among Students." M.A. thesis, The Ontario Institute for Studies in Education/University of Toronto.

Skogan, W. (1975). "Measurement Problems in Official and Survey Crime Rates." *Journal of Criminal Justice* 3: 17–32.

Smart, C. (1976). *Women, Crime and Criminology: A Feminist Critique*. London: Routledge and Kegan Paul.

Smith, D. M. (1976). "The Concept of a Youth Culture: A Reevaluation." *Youth and Society* 7, 4: 347–66.

Smith, L. B., and Geoffrey, M. (1968). *The Complexities of the Urban Classroom*. New York: John Wiley.

Snider, D. L. (1977). "Does the Legal Order Reflect the Power Structure: A Test of Conflict Theory." PH.D. thesis, University of Toronto.

———— (1978). "Corporate Crime in Canada: A Preliminary Report." *Canadian Journal of Criminology* 20: 142–68.

Snider, D. L., and West, W. G. (1980). "A Critical Perspective on Law in the Canadian State: Delinquency and Corporate Crime," in R. J. Ossenberg (ed.), *Power and Change in Canada*. Toronto: McClelland and Stewart.

Snider, E. C. (1971). "The Impact of the Juvenile Court Hearing on the Child." *Crime and Delinquency* 17: 180–90.

Solicitor General (1979). *Selected Trends in Canadian Criminal Justice*. Ottawa: Ministry of Solicitor General.

Solicitor General (1981). *The Young Offenders Act: Highlights*. Ottawa: Solicitor General.

Solicitor General (1983). *Canadian Urban Victimization Survey, Bulletin 1*. Ottawa: Solicitor General.

Solomon, P. (1981). "The Policy Process in Canadian Criminal Justice: A Perspective and Research Agenda." *Canadian Journal of Criminology* 23, 1: 5–25.

Sowle, C. R. (ed.) (1962). *Police Power and Individual Freedom*. Chicago: Aldine.

Spady, W. G. (1974). "The Authority System of the School and Student Unrest: A Theoretical Explanation," in National Society for the Study of Education, *1974 Yearbook on Education*. Chicago: University of Chicago Press, pp. 36–77.

Spitzer, S. (1975). "Toward a Marxian Theory of Deviance." *Social Problems* 22 (June): 638–51.

Stanbury, W. P. (1977). *Business Interests and the Reform of Canadian Competition Policy, 1971–75*. Toronto: Carswell-Methuen.

Statistics Canada (1969a). *Training Schools*. Ottawa: Statistics Canada.

———— (1969b). *Juvenile Delinquents*. Ottawa: Statistics Canada.

———— (1973). *Training Schools* (#85–208). Ottawa: Supply and Services.

———— Juvenile Statistics Division (1977). *Juvenile Statistics, 1977*. Ottawa: Statistics Canada.

———— (1980a). *Juvenile Delinquents*. Ottawa: Statistics Canada, Canadian Centre for Justice Statistics.

———— (1980b). *Crime and Traffic Enforcement Statistics*. Ottawa: Statistics Canada.

Stebbins, R. (1970). "The Meaning of Disorderly Behavior." *Sociology of Education* 44: 217–36.

Stinchcombe, A. (1964). *Rebellion in a High School*. Chicago: Quadrangle.

Stoodley, B. (1974). "The Juvenile Court – Today and Tomorrow." Unpublished Paper, Queen's University, Kingston, Ont.

Sumner, C. (1979). *Reading Ideologies*. London: Academic.

———— (ed.) (1981a). *Crime, Justice and Underdevelopment*. London: Heinemann.

———— (1981b). "Abandoning Deviancy Theory in Marxist Criminology in Britain Since 1975." Paper delivered to American Society of Criminology, Washington, D.C.

Surridge, R. T., and Lambert, I. R. n.d. (1972?). "Survey of Drug Use Among Wards Prior to Admission to Training School." Toronto: Research Branch, Department of Correctional Services, p. 328–35.

Sutherland, E. (1950). "The Diffusion of the Sexual Psychopath Laws." *American Journal of Sociology* 56: 142–48.

Sutherland, E., and Cressey, D. (1955). *Principles of Criminology*. Philadelphia: Lippincott.

Sutherland, N. (1976). *Children in English-Canadian Society: Framing the Twentieth-Century Consensus*. Toronto: University of Toronto Press.

Sykes, G., and Matza, D. (1957). "Techniques of Neutralization: A Theory of Delinquency." *American Sociological Review* 22: 664–70.

Tannenbaum, F. (1938). *Crime and the Community*. Boston: Ginn.

Tappan, P. (1947). "Who Is the Criminal?" *American Sociological Review* 12: 96–102.

Task Force on the Structure of Canadian Industry (1968). *Report* (The Watkins Report). Ottawa: Queen's Printer.

Taylor, E. M. (1971). "Delinquents and Students." *Youth and Society* 2, 4: 387–420.

Taylor, I. (1978). Review Essay: L. McDonald, *The Sociology of Law and Order*. *Canadian Journal of Sociology* 3, 2: 263–69.

—— (1980). "The Law and Order Issue in the British General Election and the Canadian Federal Election of 1979: Crime and Populism and the State." *Canadian Journal of Sociology* 5, 3: 285–311.

—— (1981). *Law and Order: Arguments for Socialism*. London: Macmillan.

Taylor, I.; Walton, P.; and Young J. (1973). *The New Criminology: For a Social Theory of Deviance*. London: Routledge and Kegan Paul.

—— (eds.) (1975). *Critical Criminology*. London: Routledge and Kegan Paul.

Teeple, G. (1972). *Capitalism and the National Question in Canada*. Toronto: University of Toronto Press.

Teevan, J. J. (1978). "An Often Neglected Consideration in Criminological Research: The Victim." Paper presented at the annual meeting of the Canadian Sociology and Anthropology Association, London, Ontario.

Tepperman, L. (1977). *Crime Control: The Urge to Authority*. Toronto: McGraw-Hill.

Therborn, G. (1976). *Science, Class and Society*. London: New Left/Verso.

—— (1979). *The Ideology of Power/The Power of Ideology*. London: New Left/Verso.

Thio, A. (1978). *Deviant Behavior*. Boston: Houghton-Mifflin.

Thomas, C. W., Gage, R. J., and Foster, S. C. (1976). "Public Opinion on Criminal Law and Legal Sanctions: An Examination of Two Conceptual Models." *Journal of Criminal Law and Criminology* 67, 1: 110–16.

Thomas, W. I. (1923). *The Unadjusted Girl*. Boston:

Thompson, E. P. (1963). *The Making of the English Working Class*. London: Victor Gollancz (London: Penguin, 1968).

—— (1978). *The Poverty of Theory*. London: Merlin.

—— (1979). *The Secret State Within The State*. London: State Research, Pamphlet #1.

Thrasher, F. M., ([1927] 1963). *The Gang*. Chicago: University of Chicago Press.

Titus, W. (1982). "Discursively Accomplishing Classroom Knowledge." M.A. thesis, The Ontario Institute for Studies in Education/University of Toronto.

Toby, J., and Toby, M. (1962). "Low School Status as a Predisposing Factor in Subcultural Delinquency." Rutgers University, New Brunswick, N.J. Mimeo.

Torode, B. (1976). "Teacher's Talk and Classroom Discipline," in M. Stubbs and S. Delamont (eds.), *Explorations in Classroom Observation*. London: John Wiley.

Toronto Star (1975). "Employment Singles Out a Victim: Youth." July 19: B1.

—— (1978). "Ontario Starts Closing Its Jails for Children." Feb. 3.

—— (1982). "600,000 Would Die in A-Bomb Blast Over Toronto." May 4.

Touraine, A. (1981). *The Voice and the Eye*. Cambridge: Cambridge University Press.

Trépanier, J. (1983). "The Quebec Youth Protection Act: Institutionalized Diversion," in R. Corrado, M. Leblanc, and J. Trépanier (eds.), *Issues in Juvenile Justice*. Toronto: Butterworths.

Trojanowitz, R. (1978). *Juvenile Delinquency: Concepts and Control*. Englewood Cliffs, N.J.: Prentice-Hall.

Turk, A. (1969). *Criminality and the Legal Order*. Chicago: Rand McNally.

——— (1976). "Law, Conflict, and Order." *Canadian Review of Sociology and Anthropology* 13, 3: 282–94.

Vaz, E. (1965). "Middle Class Adolescents: Self-Reported Delinquency and Youth Culture Activities." *Canadian Review of Sociology and Anthropology* 2: 52–70.

——— (1967). *Middle-Class Juvenile Delinquency*. New York: Harper and Row.

Vedder, C. B., and Sommerville, D. B. (1970; 1975, 2nd ed.). *The Delinquent Girl*. Springfield, Ill.: Charles C. Thomas.

Visano, L. (1983). "Tramps, Tricks and Troubles: Street Transients and Their Controls," in T. Fleming and L. Visano (eds.), *Deviant Designations*. Toronto: Butterworths.

Walker-Lorrain, H. (1983). "Marginal Youth in Chile: Deviance Within a Context of Social Reproduction," in *Canadian Criminology Forum* 6, 1: 19–34.

Waller, I. (Solicitor General) (1979). *Selected Trends in Canadian Criminal Justice*. Ottawa: Solicitor General.

Waller, I., and Okihiro, N. (1978). *Burglary: The Victim and The Public*. Toronto: University of Toronto.

Wallerstein, J. S. and Wyle, C. J. (1947). "Our Law-Abiding Law-Breakers." *Probation* 25: 107–12.

Weber, M. (1947). *The Theory of Social and Economic Organizations*. Glencoe, Ill.: Free Press.

Weiler, K. (1978). "Unmanageable Children and Section 8," in H. Berkeley, C. Gaffield, and W. G. West (eds.), *Children's Rights: Educational and Legal Issues*. Toronto: Ontario Institute for Studies in Education Press.

Werthman, C. (1969). "Delinquency and Moral Character," in D. Cressey, and D. Ward (eds.), *Crime, Delinquency and Social Process*. Evanston, Ill.: Harper and Row.

——— (1971). "Delinquents and School, in B. Cosin, et al. (eds.), *School and Society*. London: Routledge and Kegan Paul, and Milton Keynes: Open University Press.

West, W. G. (1968). "Drifting Clusters: A Study of Non-Gang Delinquency." B.A. thesis, York University, Toronto.

——— (1975a). "Adolescent Deviance and The School." *Interchange* 6, 2: 49–55.

——— (1975b). "Participant Observation Research on The Social Construction of Everyday Classroom Order." *Interchange* 6, 4: 35–43.

——— (1977a). "Participant Observation in Canadian Classrooms." *Canadian Journal of Education* 2, 3: 55–74.

——— (1977b). "Adolescent Territoriality," unpublished MS

——— (1978a). "The Short Term Careers of Serious Thieves." *Canadian Journal of Criminology* 20, 2: 169–90; reprinted in R. Silverman, and J. Teevan (eds.), *Crime in Canadian Society*. Toronto: Butterworths, 1980, pp. 317–34.

——— (1978b). "Educational Reforms and Delinquency." *Crime et/and Justice* 6, 1: 41–52.

——— (1979a). "Serious Thieves: Lower Class Adolescent Males in a Short-term Deviant Occupation," in E. Vaz, and A. Lodhi (eds.), *Crime and Delinquency in Canada*. Toronto: Prentice Hall, pp. 247–69; reprinted in K. Ishmaran (ed.), *Childhood and Adolescence in Canada*. Toronto: McGraw-Hill, 1979, pp. 322–44.

———— (1979b). "Adolescent Autonomy, Education, and Pupil Deviance," in L. Barton, and R. Meighan (eds.), *Schools, Pupils and Deviance*. Driffield, England: Nafferton.

———— (1979/80). "Trust Among Serious Thieves." *Crime et/and Justice*. 7/8, 3/4: 239–48.

———— (1980a). "The Short Term Careers of Serious Thieves," in R. A. Silverman, and J. J. Teevan (eds.), *Crime in Canadian Society*. Toronto: Butterworths.

———— (1980b). "Access to Adolescent Deviants and Deviance," in W. Shaffir, R. Stebbins, and A. Turowetz (eds.), *Fieldwork Experience*. New York: St. Martins, pp. 31–44.

———— (1980c). "Juveniles in Justice," in J. Laplante (ed.), *Social Control in State of Crisis: Proceedings of the 4th Canadian Conference of Applied Criminology*. Ottawa: Department of Criminology, pp. 144–59.

———— (1981). "Education, Moral Reproduction and the State." *Interchange* 12, 2-3: 86–101.

———— (1982). Review of P. McLaren, *Cries From the Corridor*; P. Willis, *Learning to Labour*; and P. Corrigan, *Schooling the Smash St. Kids*. *Canadian Journal of Criminology* 24, 4: 469–76.

———— (1983). "Serious Theft as an Occupation," in T. Fleming, and L. A. Visano (eds.), *Deviant Designations*: Toronto: Butterworths.

———— (1984a). "Phenomenon and Form in Interactionist and Neo-Marxist Qualitative Educational Research." in L. Barton, and S. Walker (eds.), *Educational Research and Social Crisis*. London: Croom Helm.

———— (1984b, forthcoming). "Adolescent Perspectives and Identity Changes." *Adolescence*: 31.

Westhues, K. (1972). *Society's Shadow: Counter Culture*. Toronto: McGraw-Hill Ryerson.

Widom, C. S. (1977). "Perspectives on Female Criminality: A Critical Examination of Assumptions," in Allison Morris, and L. Gelsthorpe (eds.), *Women and Crime* (Cropwood Conference Series #13). Cambridge: Institute of Criminology, pp. 33–49.

Williams, R. (1976). "Base and Superstructure in Marxist Culture Theory." *New Left Review* 82 (1973); reprinted in R. Dale, G. Esland, and M. Macdonald (eds.), *Schooling and Capitalism*. London: Routledge and Kegan Paul.

Willis, P. (1977). *Learning to Labour*. Westmead, England: Saxon House/Teakfield.

Wilson, J. Q. (1968a). "The Police and the Delinquent in Two Cities," in S. Wheeler (ed.), *Controlling Delinquents*. New York: Wiley.

———— (1968b). *Varieties of Police Behavior: The Management of Law and Order in Eight Communities*. Cambridge, Mass.: Harvard University Press.

Wilson, T. P. (1970). "Normative and Interpretive Paradigms in Sociology," in J. D. Douglas (ed.), *Understanding Everyday Life*. Chicago: Aldine.

Wilson, S. (1974). "A Review of the Use of Ethnographic Methods in Educational Research." Revised paper in *Review of Educational Research*, 1977 (47): 245–66.

Winterdyk, F. A. (1980). "A Wilderness Adventure Program as an Alternative For Probation: An Evaluation." M.A. thesis, Burnaby, B.C., Department of Criminology, Simon Fraser University.

Wolfgang, M. E., Figlio, R. M., and Sellin, T. (1972). *Delinquency in a Birth Cohort*. Chicago: University of Chicago Press.

Woods, P. (1979). *The Divided School*. London: Routledge.

Wright, E. O. (1977). "Class Boundaries in Advanced Capitalist Societies." *New Left Review* 98.

—— (1978). *Class, Crisis and the State*. London: New Left Books.

Wynne, D., and Hartnagel, T. (1975). "Plea Negotiation in Canada." *Canadian Journal of Criminology and Corrections* 17, 1: 45–56.

Yablonsky, L. (1962). *The Violent Gang*. Baltimore, Penguin.

—— (1968a). "On Crime, Violence, LSD, and Legal Immunity for Social Scientists." *American Sociologist* 3: 148–49.

—— (1968b). *The Hippie Trip*. New York: Pergamon.

Yeung, A. K-C. (1975). "Deviance in the School: The Interactionist Perspective." M.A. thesis, The Ontario Institute for Studies in Education/University of Toronto.

Young, J. (1975). "Working Class Criminology," in I. Taylor, P. Walton, and J. Young (eds.), *Critical Criminology*. London: Routledge and Kegan Paul, pp. 63–94.

—— (1979). "Left Idealism," in B. Fine et al. (eds.), *Capitalism and the Rule of Law*. London: Hutchinson.

—— (1983). "Subcultural Theories." Paper presented at The Ontario Institute for Studies in Education, Critical Pedagogy and Cultural Studies Summer Institute.

Index

A

Adler, F., 228
Age, Age Status, 24, 32–33, 42, 46, 53, 57, 58–59, 60, 61, 62–64, 86–87, 93, 115–18, 134–38, 141–44, 146, 150, 169–70, 196–99, 201, 208, 211–19, 223, 226
Althusser, L., 50–51, 142, 167, 196, 231
Anderson, P., 221
Anomie Theory, 10, 15, 71–83, 146, 229
Apple, M., 163, 165, 166, 232
Apprenticeship, 151
Ariés, P., 25, 217, 223
Armogan, G., 67, 116, 143
Armstrong, H. 217
Arnold, D. O., 142
Arnot, M., 146
Arnot, M., and Whitty, G., 168
Autonomy, adolescent autonomy, 72, 74, 134–38, 141–44, 155–63, 176–79
Authority, 153–63, 195

B

Bagnell, K., 35
Baker C., 153, 157
Ball, S., 157, 161
Banfield, R., 134
Bankowski, L.; Mungham, G.; and Young, P., 41
Banton, M., 176
Barnhorst, S., 184
Barrett, M., and McIntosh, M., 28, 42
Baum, M., and Wheeler, S., 181
Bayley, D. H., and Mendelsohn, H., 176

Beattie, J., 31
Becker, H. S., 12, 32, 114, 132–33, 160, 229
Becker, H. S., and Geer, Blanche, 135, 164
Bell, D., 6
Bellamy, B., 153, 155
Bell-Rowbotham, B., and Boydell, C., 68, 70, 73, 148
Bernstein, B., 163
Bertrand, F., 4
Bertrand, M-A., 107–8, 131
Birmingham School, 142–44
Blanch, M., 28
Bliss, M., 19
Block, H. A., and Niederhoffer, A., 135
Blomberg, D., 193, 210
Bosence, O., 153, 155, 161
Bossert, S., 161
Bourdieu, P., and Passeron, J. C., 163
Bowles, S., and Gintis, H., 163, 166, 167
Box, S., 79, 90, 92, 94–95, 98, 106–7, 139–40, 176, 225
Brake, M., 117
Briar S., and Pilliavin, I., 132
Broadfoot, P., 163, 166
Brookes, A. A., 26
Brophy, J., and Good, T., 158
Buff, S., 117
Byles, J., 70, 87–90, 117, 125, 187, 197
Byles, J., and Maurice, A., 68, 79, 186

C

Calliste, A., 67
Campbell, A., 66, 107, 114, 143, 184
Campbell, D. T., 202–3

Campbell, D. T., and Stanley, J., 203
Canada, 24
Canadian Centre for Justice Statistics 1980, 58–59
Canadian Political Economy, 18–20, 74–75, 215–19
Canadian Social Formation, 18–20, 26–29, 36, 43, 215–19, 227
Capitalism, 16, 17, 36–40, 43, 46–53, 74–75, 108–13, 165–70, 196–99, 215–24, 228–30. *See also* Canadian Political Economy
Careers and Statuses of Delinquents, 193–95
Center for New Schools, 117
Cernovich, S. A., and Giordano, P. C., 104
Chambliss, W. J., 38–40
Chesney-Lind, M., 111
Chimbos, P. D., 70
Christie, N., 87
Chunn, D., 34, 93
Cicourel, A. V., 180
Cicourel A. V., and Kitsuse, J. I., 122, 152
Cities and Urbanization, 26, 68, 78, 89, 177
City Neighborhoods, 55, 68–69, 89, 127, 176, 179
Civil Society, 109
Clark, S. D., 19
Clark, J. P., and Wenninger, E. P., 87
Clarke, John, 29, 46, 109, 137, 142, 157, 181, 231
Clarke, S., 49, 198, 221
Class (Social Class), 16–20, 28, 30, 37–40, 41, 45, 47–53, 68, 73, 74–75, 80, 88, 94, 108–9, 117, 127, 145, 146, 148, 159, 171–79, 187, 197, 219–20
Classrooms, 153–63, 165
Clement W., 17, 19, 20, 45, 48, 220
Cloward, E., and Ohlin, L., 73–74, 76, 80, 135, 228
Cockerill, R. M., 67
Cohen, A. K., 71–76, 79–81, 92, 100, 135, 138, 142–48, 193, 228
Cohen, A. K., and Short, J. F., 33, 191
Cohen, S., 42, 143, 196

Coleman, J., 117, 138
Coleman, J. C.; Campbell, E.; Hobsom, C. F.; McPartland, J.; Mood, A.; Weinfeld, F. D.; and York, R. L., 204–6
Committee on Youth, 94, 169, 207, 215–6
Committee on Juvenile Delinquency, 189, 207
Comte, A., 15
Conflict Theory, 13–14, 15, 17–18, 35–53, 40–43, 108–13, 139, 140–42, 163–70, 195–99, 213–24, 226, 230–31, 233–35
Conly, D., 68, 78, 177, 188
Consensus, 73, 75–76. *See also* Functionalism
Control Theory, 92–96, 98–99, 100–1, 106–7, 114, 146, 148–49, 162, 194, 229
Corporations, 16, 61, 65
Corrigan, P., 117, 122, 128, 142, 157, 165, 179
Courtis, M. C., 174
Courts, Juvenile, 78, 179–86
Cousineau, D., and Veevers, J., 180, 209
Cowie, J.; Cowie, V.; and Slater, E., 102
Criminology in Canada, 20, 52, 229–35

D

Dale, R., 50, 106, 117, 166, 167, 231
David, M., 168
Davies, D., 170
Davin, A., 28
Davis, A., 18
Davis, F., with Munoz, L., 117
Davis, K., 102
Dawe, A., 156
Definitions of Delinquency, 8–14, 75–79, 97, 232
   in Juvenile Delinquents Act, 23, 33–34
Delinquent Schools, 152–53
DeMause, L., 25
Demography, 28, 216
Denscombe, M., 155

Denzin, N. K., 114
Deosaran, R., 158
Dickson, B., 116
Differential Association, 94, 129–30, 139
Discipline, 27, 46, 57, 146, 151, 165–70
Discretion (police), 176–79, 207, 210–13
Dispositions, 185–86, 187–90
Diversion, 172, 209–13, 226
Diversity of Delinquency, 2, 58–59, 87, 173, 232
Dobson, R.; Goldenberg, R.; and Elson, B., 154
Dominion Bureau of Statistics, 186
Donzelot, J., 28, 53, 109, 196, 232
Dorn, N., and South, N., 143
Downes, D., 142
Drift Theory, 130–31, 139
Drugs and Alcohol, 1, 2, 5, 55, 65, 87, 114, 120, 125, 126, 188
Dunlop, A., 192, 206
Durkheim, E., 15, 71, 92, 158, 229

E

Economism, 42, 49, 208. *See also* Neo-Marxism
Education Group (S. Baron, D. Finn, N. Grant, M. Green, R. Johnson), 31, 232
Edwards A., and Furlong, V., 156
Effects of Treatment, 181, 185, 190–94, 210–13
Elite (upper class, bourgeois), 19, 37, 109. *See also* Class, Lumpenproletariat
Elkin, F., and Wesley, W., 117, 118
Elliott, D. S., and Ageton, S., 82, 97, 178
Elliott, D. S., and Voss, H. L., 90, 149, 169
Emerson, R., 180
Empey, L. T., 25, 32, 57, 65, 78, 87, 88, 139, 174, 179
Empey, L. T., and Erickson, M. L., 130
Empey, L. T., and Lubeck, G., 70, 87, 89, 93, 130, 147–48

Employment, Jobs, 119, 122–26, 134–38, 149–51, 169, 215
Engels, F., 42
England, 25, 32, 55
Ennis, P., 175
Erickson, Pat, 180, 207
Erikson, E., 135
Erikson, K. T., 134, 158
Esland, G., 162
Ethnicity, 66, 68, 88, 188. *See also* Race
Ethnography (*See* Participant Observation)
Evans, J., and Leger, J., 78, 175
Experiments, 202–3, 213–14

F

Facts, Data, 1, 8, 14, 43, 79
Family, 14, 28, 32, 46, 70, 73–75, 81–82, 89, 108–12, 118, 121, 125, 135–37, 143, 157, 159, 169, 190. *See also* Parents
Family Court, 34
Faris, R. E. L., 101
Farrington, D., 177
Feminist Theory, 13, 28, 42, 99–112, 114, 143–44, 151, 158, 164, 174, 184–85, 228, 232, 235. *See also* Gender
Fine, B., 231–32, 234–45
Fischer, D. G., and Martin, R. D., 70
Fitz, J., 28, 42, 45, 53, 196, 221, 231
Foucault, M., 31, 81, 109, 196, 222, 231, 232
France, Childhood in, 25
Frank, A. G., 18
"Freaks," 115–18, 124–27, 134–38, 141–42
Frease, D., 90
Fréchette, M., and Leblanc, M., 87, 88, 90, 97, 177–78
Fréchette, M.; Leblanc, M.; and Biron, L., 138, 148
Freire, P., 166
Friedenberg, E., 135
Freud, S., 101
Frontenac Diversion Project. *See* Diversion
Fullan, M., 234
Functionalism, 10, 15, 38–40, 47–53

G

Gaffield, C., and West, W. G., 42, 170
Gagnon, R., and Biron, L., 66
Gandy, J., 179
Gang, 55, 64, 71, 73, 80, 90, 122–23, 141–42. *See also* Peers
Garner, H., 116
Gaucher, R., 18, 27, 38
Gavigan, S., 53, 122, 232
Geer, B., 154, 161
Geller, G., 66, 104, 112, 184–85
Gender, 13, 23, 41, 45, 58–59, 60, 66, 99–113, 87–88, 113–15, 116, 143, 146, 151, 158, 164, 170, 184–85, 188, 204, 227–28. *See also* Feminist Theory, "Freaks," "Greasers," "Straights"
Gerin-Lajoie, D., 115, 122
Gibson, L., 111
Giffen, P. J., 7, 57, 66, 68, 77, 172
Gillis, J. R., 25, 117, 169
Giordano, P., 182
Glenday, D.; Guindon, H.; and Turowetz, A., 18
Godfrey, D., and Watkins, M., 20
Goff, C., and Reasons, C. E., 19, 64
Goffman, E., 135
Gomme, I. M., 87–90, 94–95, 104, 106–7, 146, 148, 227–28
Gomme, I. M.; Morton, M. E.; and West, W. G., 7, 88, 105, 174
Goodman, P., 117, 135
Gordon, D. M., 94
Gough, I., 218
Gove, W., 132
Gramsci, A., 109, 142, 220, 231
Grayson, J. P., 18, 20
"Greasers," 115–17, 121–24, 127–28, 134–38, 141–42, 159, 176
Greenberg, D., 57, 82, 86, 144, 201
Grimes, R. E., 208
Grosman, B. A., 176

H

Habermas, J., 51, 166
Hackler, J., 177, 181, 192
Hackler, J., and Paranjape, W., 7, 68, 78, 177, 181
Hagan, J., 9, 10, 15, 41, 67, 94, 106, 139, 141, 176

Hagan, J.; Gillis, A. R.; and Chan, J., 69
Hagan, J., and Leon, J., 44–46, 52–53
Hagan, J.; Simpson, J.; and Gillis, R., 107, 110
Haldane, L.; Elliott, D.; and Whitehead, P., 140
Hall, E.; Dennis, L.; et al., 207
Hall, S., 4
Hall, S., and Jefferson, T., 81, 127, 142, 228, 232
Hall, S.; Critcher, C.; Jefferson, T.; and Roberts, B., 5–6, 51, 167, 221, 223, 225, 228, 230, 232
Hamilton, R., and Pinard, M., 48
Hammersley, M., 156
Hardy, T., 66, 153, 154, 158–59
Hargreaves, D., 89, 122, 152, 160
Hargreaves, D.; Hester, S.; and Mellor, F., 132, 232
Harrison, R., and Mort, F., 109
Harvey, E. B., 204
Havermann, P., 67
Herndon, J., 155
Hindelang, M. J., 89, 90, 93, 153
Hindelang, M.; Hirschi, T.; and Weiss, J., 82, 97
Hirschi, T., 80, 89, 90, 92, 98, 135, 146, 148, 153, 229
Hirschi, T., and Hindelang, M., 153, 169
Hirst, P. Q., 41, 168, 221, 232
History of Childhood, 24–35
Hoetker, J., and Ahlbrand, N. P., 154
Hoffman-Bustamonte, D., 88, 104
Hogarth, J., 65, 69
Hollingshead, A. deB., 117
Holloway, J., and Picciotto, S., 49, 221
Holt, J., 161
Holtz, J. A., 117
Horton, J., 15
Houston, S., 26, 29, 30, 32, 45
Hughes, E. C., 134, 154, 216
Hussain, A., 171
Hilton, J., 213

I

Ideology, 14, 51, 76, 109, 165–68, 220–23, 228–29, 239
Ignatieff, M., 31
Indians (native Canadians), 67, 88

Innis, H., 18
IQ (Intelligence Quotient), 153, 166
Irwin, J., 117

J

Jackson, P., 154, 156
Jahoda, M., and Warren, N., 142, 223
Jansyn, L., 123
Jencks, C.; Smith, M.; Acland, H.;
    Bane, M.; Cohen, D.; Gintis, H.;
    Heyns, B.; and Michelson, S.,
    148, 206
Jensen, G. F., 89, 93
Johnson, L., 48
Johnson, R. E., 96, 107, 146
Johnston, A., 180, 209
Johnston, R., 26, 142, 231
Juristat, 184–85
Justice Assistance News, 87
Juvenile Delinquents Act, 11–12,
    29–35, 171
Juvenile Justice System, 78, 172–99

K

Kahl, J., 160
Karabel, J., and Halsey, A. H., 165
Katz, J., 160
Keat, R., and Urry, J., 233
Keating, C., 107
Keddie, N., 160, 161, 166
Kelly, D. H., 89
Kelly, H., 134
Kitsuse, J. I., 140
Kitsuse, J. I., and Dietrick, D., 80,
    135, 142
Konopka, G., 102
Krisberg, B., and Austin, J., 65
Kundratts, U., 149

L

Labeling Theory, 12, 131–32, 139–40.
    See also Symbolic Interactionism
Laclau, E., 51, 167, 220, 231
Lambert, L., and Birkenmeyer, A.,
    191
Land, H., 53
Landau, B., 102

Langley, M.; Thomas, B.; and
    Parkinson, R., 181–82, 211
Lautt, M., 67
Law, 10, 13, 16, 18, 19, 23, 29–35,
    37–40, 41, 44, 47–53, 110–11, 134,
    154, 168, 171, 196–99, 207–9,
    221–23, 229, 234–35. *See also*
    Court, Juvenile; Juvenile Justice
    System; Juvenile Delinquents
    Act; State
Law Reform Commission, 67
Lawyers, 51, 180–1, 183, 207–8
Laxer, J., 20
Lea, J., 196
Lea, J., and Young, J., 228
Leblanc, M., 65, 70, 87, 94, 98, 107,
    114, 149, 192, 226
Leblanc, M.; Biron, L.; and
    Fréchette, M., 61, 87, 88
LeDain, G., et al., 7, 207
Lee, J. A., 23, 217, 223
Lemert, E., 132, 194
Leon, J. S., 28, 29, 31, 35, 44, 52, 180,
    208
Lerman, P., 80, 188
Levitt, K., 19, 20
Leyton, E., 74–75, 81–82, 102, 190,
    193
Liazos, A., 13
Liberal, 15–16, 215–19. *See also*
    Functionalism
Lindblom, R. E., and Cohen, D. K.,
    215, 234
Linden, R., and Filmore, C., 87, 94
Livingstone, D. W., 4, 42
Livingstone, D. W., and Hart, D.,
    4, 146
Livingstone, D. W., and Mason, R. V.,
    165, 220
Lockheart, A., 48, 150, 217
Lombroso, T., and Ferrero, W., 100
Lower, A. R. M., 19
Lucas, R., 150
Lumpenproletariat, 41–42, 74–75,
    81–82
Lutz, F., and Ramsay, M., 114

M

Macdougal, C., 190
Mackay, R., 170, 218
MacLean's, 110, 175

Magsino, R., 206
Maher, B., and Stein, E., 181
Manley-Casimir, M., 206
Mann, M., 4, 166, 231
Mann, W. E., 69
Marchak, P., 15, 16, 19
Maris, P., and Rein, M., 74
Martell, G., 205–6
Markwart, A., 189
Marx, K., 17, 42, 110, 163
Matza, D., 76, 80, 107, 117, 135, 138,
    139–40, 142, 180–83, 191, 194, 223
Matza, E., and Sykes, G., 130, 131
Maxwell, M., and Maxwell, J., 116
Mayhew, H., 14–15, 23, 179
Mays, J. B., 169
McCaghy, C., 64
McCorkle, L. W.; Elias, A.; and
    Bixby, F. L., 130
McDaniel, S. A., and Agger, B., 15
McDonald, L., 7, 41, 179, 227
McGeachie, P., and Stone, P., 153
McIntosh, J., 153, 154–55
McIntosh, M., 108, 110, 111, 185
McKie, C., 19
McLaren, P., 1, 69, 107, 115, 121, 155
McRobbie, A., and Garber, J., 106,
    143
Meaningful Behavior, 1, 114–15,
    128–29, 130–31, 133–34, 155, 162
Media, 3–6, 220, 225
Merton, R. K., 15, 71–73, 193
Methodology, 1, 2–8, 20, 24, 43, 56,
    77–79, 85–86, 96–97, 113–15, 138,
    142–43, 163–65, 171–72, 202–3,
    213–14. *See also* Survey Research;
    Experiments; Participant
    Observation; Self-Report;
    Delinquency, Official Statistics
Meyer, P. B., 169
Miliband, R., 47, 52
Millham, S.; Bullock, R.; and
    Hosie, K., 189
Miller, W. B., 36
Mills, C. W., 17
Mitchell, J., 110
Mohr, H., 5
Moogk, P. N., 26
Moral Entrepreneurs, 32, 35, 44, 133,
    222–23. *See also* Ideology, State
Morality, 42, 51

Moral Panic, 5–6, 26, 41, 225
Morgan, P., 227
Morton, M. E., 176, 232
Morton, M. E.; West, W. G.; et al.,
    87, 91, 97, 174, 177–79, 182–84,
    192–93, 210–13
Morton, M. E., and West, W. G.,
    172–74, 177–78, 210, 222
Moyer, S., 176
Moynihan, D. P., 74
Muncie, J., 4, 32, 57, 207, 213
Mungham, G., 42
Mungham, G., and Pearson, G., 117
Murdock, G., and McCron, R., 142
Murphy, E., 150
Musgrove, F., 25, 46, 117, 223

N

Nagler, M., 67
Nease, B., 70, 139, 177
Neo-Marxism, 14, 17–20, 35–43,
    46–53, 83, 108–12, 141–44,
    145–47, 165–70, 196–99, 215–24,
    230–35. *See also* Conflict Theory,
    Canadian Political Economy
Neo-positivism, 20, 36, 86, 92, 232
Nettler, G., 10, 132, 178
Ng, Y., 5–6, 64, 220
Noblit, G. W., 90, 138
Non-reporting of Offences, 174–76
Novak, M., 156, 162
Nye, F. I., 89, 92, 104, 229

O

O'Brien, M., 108
O'Connor, J., 208, 230
Offe, C., and Ronge, V., 49
Official Knowledge, 4, 6, 30
Official (delinquency) Statistics, 6–7,
    9, 40, 56–71, 75–79, 82, 85,
    171–72, 173, 176–93
Ontario Department of Corrections,
    68, 187, 191
Order, 153–63, 166. *See also*
    Functionalism
Organization Theory, 195
Organized Crime, 61

P

Panitch, L. 20, 48, 230
Parents, 28, 56. *See also* Families
Parr, J., 26
Parsons, T., 15
Participant Observation, 74, 113–15, 115–28, 138, 141–44, 164, 228. *See also* Methods
Pashukanis, E., 110, 167–68, 221–22, 231–32
Patriarchy, 108–13
Pearce, F., 196
Peers, 71, 90, 115–28, 129-30. *See also* Gangs
Penitentiary, Kingston Penitentiary, 31
Personal Knowledge, 2–3
Perspectives. *See* Subculture
Petrunik, M., 132
Picciotto, S., 168, 221–22
Piliavin, J., and Briar, S., 176
Platt, A., 29, 30, 32, 43–46, 109, 180, 196, 207
Player, C., 107
Police, 7, 35, 69, 77–79, 118, 122, 124–25, 176–79, 209, 211–12
Policy, 6, 7, 20, 25–35, 74, 75, 81, 99, 130, 132, 140, 147, 153, 164, 201–24, 234. *See also* Juvenile Delinquents Act, Young Offenders Act
Politics, 15–20, 28, 201–24
Polk, K., and Schafer, W., 70, 79–80, 89, 90, 94, 122, 146–48, 153, 160, 204
Pollak, O., 101
Pollard, A., 157
Polsky, N., 117
Pomfret, A., 204–5
Popular Knowledge, 2–7, 174, 225
Porter, J., 16, 19, 45, 48
Poster, M., 108, 232
Poulantzas, N., 47–49
Poverty, 26, 55–56
Power, M.; Benn, R. J.; and Morris, J. N., 152, 160
Prentice, A., 25, 27, 28, 29, 31, 52, 145
President's Commission on Law Enforcement and the

Administration of Justice, 61
Primary Deviance, 132
Property Crime, Theft, 57, 60, 61, 62–64, 94, 120, 124
Prus, R., and Irini, S., 116
Pryce, K., 143, 228
Psychology, 73, 101–2, 112, 192, 193–94, 202, 226
Public Opinion, 4

Q

Quebec Youth Protection Act, 207
Quinney, R., 36–38, 47, 230

R

Race, 66, 88, 188. *See also* Indians, Ethnicity
Reasons, C.; Ross, L.; and Patterson, C., 65
Recidivism, 190–93, 210
Reforms, 203–13. *See also* Policy
Reitsma-Street, M., 192–93
Repo, S., 231
Report of the Commissioners Appointed to Enquire into the Prison and Reformatory System of Ontario (1981), 24
Reynolds, D., and Sullivan, M., 152–53, 160
Rhodes, A., and Reiss, A., 71, 89, 93
Ribordy, F., 66
Rist, R., 161, 163
Roberts, J. I., 156
Rock, P., 129
Rogers, K., 55–56, 85, 113, 117, 123
Role Socialization Theory, 106–7
Rosenthal, R., and Jacobson, L., 204
Ross, M., 94
Roszak, T., 117, 126
Rothman, J., 31
Rowntree, J., and Rowntree, M., 169, 216
Rutter, M.; Maugham, B.; Mortimore, P.; and Ousten, J., 95–96, 153, 160
Ryan, D., 204
Ryan, D., and Greenfield, T. B., 205

S

Sarason, S. B., 157
Sayer, D., 226, 233
Scanlon, R. L., 7
School, schooling, 26–29, 93–94, 118, 121, 125, 127, 134–38, 145–70, 216
School Failure, 70, 76, 80, 89, 96, 147–49, 153–65, 202, 206. *See also* "Greasers," "Freaks"
Schotte, F., 153, 154, 157
Schur, E., 132, 178, 182, 192, 208–10
Schwartz, G., 120
Schwendinger, H., 117, 138, 146
Schwendinger, H., and Schwendinger, J., 40, 42, 137
Scraton, P., 228
Seccombe, W., 108
Secondary Deviance, 132, 194. *See also* Recidivism
Seeley, J.; Sim, A.; and Looseley, E., 116, 117, 118
Self-report Delinquency, 7, 8, 79–80, 82, 85–92, 95, 96–98, 100, 103–6, 132, 148, 164, 172–74, 228
Sellin, T., 36
Serious Versus Non-serious Delinquency, 3, 4, 11, 12, 34, 61, 65, 72, 78, 82, 90, 120, 131, 172, 174–75, 176, 226
Sexual Behaviour, 120, 125, 126. *See also* Gender, Feminist Theory
Sex Offences, 5, 11, 13, 23, 45, 85, 102, 104, 112. *See also* Gender
Shaw, C. R., 142
Shaw, C. R., and Mackay, H. D., 66, 68, 71
Shaw, J., 28
Short, James, F., and Strodtbeck, F. L., 80, 90, 123, 131, 142
Sinclair, D., 189
Singer, B., 153, 161
Skogan, W., 78
Smart, C., 66, 107, 184, 213
Smith D. M., 138
Smith, L. B., and Geoffrey, M., 155–56, 163
Snider, D. L., 19
Snider, D. L., and West, W. G., 20
Snyder, E. C., 181
Social Formation (society), 15–20, 215–19
Solicitor General, 60, 78, 175, 218

Solomon, P., 214
Sowle, C. R., 176
Spady, W. G., 156, 157
Spitzer, S., 40
Sports, 119, 122
Stanbury, W. P., 19
State, 10, 13, 14, 15–20, 28, 37–40, 45, 47–51, 56, 65, 81–82, 108–12, 145–70, 171–99, 201–2, 208, 215, 218, 219–24, 228, 230, 235. *See also* Police, School, Law, Canadian Social Formation, Government
Statistics Canada, 61, 62–64, 71, 73, 188, 191
Status Offences, 11, 32–34, 65, 75, 104, 111–13, 165–70, 173, 179, 188, 207–8. *See also* Peers, Subculture
Stebbins, R., 155
Stinchcombe, A., 79, 80, 146, 148, 160
Stoodley, B., 180
"Straights," 115–21, 127–28, 134–38, 141
Streaming (tracking, school levels), 152
Subculture, 73, 107, 115–28, 134–38, 142–44, 190
Subjectivity, 165–70, 196–99
Sumner, C., 14, 228, 231
Surridge, R. T., and Lambert, I. R., 188, 191
Surveillance, 157, 165–70
Survey Questionnaires, 86. *See also* Self-report Delinquency
Sutherland, E., 6
Sutherland, E., and Cressey, D., 129
Sutherland, Neil, 24–25, 26, 27, 28, 32, 35, 44–46, 165, 170, 176, 178, 180
Sykes, G., 124, 130
Symbolic Interactionism, 12, 101, 114–15, 128–38, 139–41, 153–65, 193–94, 229–30, 232

T

Tannenbaum, F., 132
Tappan, P., 11
Task Force on the Structure of Canadian Industry 1968, 20
Taylor, E. M., 204–5
Taylor, I., 6–7, 51, 167, 220, 221

Taylor, I.; Walton, P.; and Young, J., 36, 321
Teachers, 153–63. *See also* School
Techniques of Neutralization, 130–31
Teeple, G., 19
Teevan, J. J., 78, 175
Tepperman, L., 57, 66, 173
Therborn, G., 7, 196
Thio, A., 37, 141, 230
Thomas, C. W.; Gage, R. J.; and Foster, S. C., 43
Thomas, W. I., 101
Thompson, E. P., 171, 179, 198, 221, 232
Thrasher, F. M., 117, 142
Titus, W., 161
Toby, J., and Toby, M., 153
Torode, B., 161
Toronto Star, 65, 94, 213, 216
Touraine, A., 214
Training Schools, 11, 33–43, 44, 65, 74–75, 81–82, 102, 104, 187–93, 213. *See also* Penitentiary
Trépanier, J., 207
Trends, 57, 87
"Triple Delinquency" Theory, 74–75, 81–82, 102, 190
Trojanowitz, R., 192
Turk, A., 36, 41, 230, 233

V

Vaz, E., 87, 96, 117, 119, 120
Vedder, C. B., and Sommerville, D. B., 102
Victims, 2, 77–78, 86, 174–75, 223
Violence, 57, 60, 61, 62–64, 65, 88, 120, 122, 126, 189, 211
Visano, L., 115, 124
Volume of Delinquency, 90, 173

W

Walker-Lorrain, H., 150
Waller, I., and Okihiro, N., 175
Wallerstein, J. S., and Wyle, C. J., 93
"War on Poverty," 74
Weber, M., 1, 36, 195
Weiler, K., 11, 66, 188, 207
Werthman, C., 81, 89, 117, 122, 159, 164
West, W. G., 24, 42, 61, 69, 70, 86, 98–99, 114, 116, 117, 127, 128, 131–32, 138–39, 141, 143, 145, 146, 147, 150, 161, 194, 204, 215, 222–23, 231, 232, 233–34
Westhues, K., 125
Widom, C. S., 228
Will, Free Will, 3, 92, 98, 107–8, 130–31, 133, 162, 211
Williams, R., 50
Willis, P., 50, 81, 117, 122, 128, 142, 223, 232
Wilson, J. Q., 176
Wilson, T. P., 155
Wilson, S., 114
Winterdyk, F. A., 192
Wolfgang, M. E.; Figlio, R. M.; and Sellin, T., 82
Woods, P., 180
Wright, E. O., 220

Y

Yablonsky, L., 130, 141
Yeung, A. K-C., 153, 160, 161
Young, J., 142, 143, 171, 233
Young Offenders Act, 77, 171, 189, 207–9, 219
Youth, 31, 40, 43, 145, 219, 223, 225–26. *See also* Age, Autonomy
Youth Clubs, 28–29